THE
ANCIENT HISTORY
OF
WILTSHIRE
BY
SIR RICHARD COLT HOARE

VOLUME I

Introduction by Jack Simmons and D. D. A. Simpson

This edition originally published by William Miller,
London 1812 and Lackington, Hughes, Harding,
Maver and Lepard, 1821.
Republished 1975 by EP Publishing Limited in collaboration
with Wiltshire County Library.

PUBLISHER'S NOTES

This work was published in five parts for binding in two volumes between 1810 and 1821; Volume I was completed in 1812 and Volume II in 1821. The title-page *The Ancient History of Wiltshire*, issued with Parts I and II, was replaced by the new title-page *The Ancient History of South Wiltshire* when the publication of Part III completed this volume. The maps and plates in this volume are arranged according to the *Order of the Plates*: and an extended list of plates has been included with the new introductory material. A Map of the Antiquities of the District of South Wiltshire issued with Volume II, Part I; has been bound in this volume; it has been reprinted in black and white and no attempt has been made to reproduce the red and green colouring of the Roman roads and sites of the original map. The leaflets circulated with the individual parts as published have been reprinted as an appendix at the end of Volume 1

The text, maps and plates for this reprint have been reproduced from the Wiltshire Library and Museum Service's copies Nos. B120A and 2/378817. Full details of these are deposited with the Wiltshire Library and Museum Service. The leaflets found in a copy of the work at Stourhead are reproduced with the permission of the National Trust for Places of Historic Interest and Natural Beauty.

On publication of Part II in 1811, further information was added to page 95 of Part I; the original page was cancelled and the new page 95, sometimes signed BB*, was issued for insertion in the work. A copy (Accession No. 2/23982) of the original page 95 is in the possession of Avon County Library and may be consulted in the local collection at Bath Reference Library.

The text and plates, where necessary, have been reduced to 93% of original size.

~~ISBN 0 85409 947 6 (Volume I)~~
ISBN 0 85409 619 1 (Complete Set) ✔

Reprinted in Great Britain by Scolar Press, Ilkley, Yorkshire.

LIST OF PLATES

**Inscription missing on the plate

INTRODUCTION

SIR RICHARD COLT HOARE

Colt Hoare's *Ancient Wiltshire* enjoys a double distinction : as the first instalment of one of the most sumptuous, and at the same time one of the last, of the classical county histories; and as the first of them all to show any sophisticated attempt at archaeological investigation, based on examining and excavating the sites of ancient settlement.[1] This introduction begins by considering the author and the making of his book, and then turns to assess the work in the light of modern archaeology.

Richard Colt Hoare was born in 1758 : to abundant wealth, as a member of a distinguished family of bankers.[2] He was educated at private schools, and went to no university. His adult career began in a conventional way. He entered the family business very early and married Hester Lyttelton, a politician's daughter, in 1783. His grandfather Henry Hoare, whose only son had died young, made him his immediate heir, during his own life-time. Saddened by private grief and the public disasters of the War of American Independence, the old man decided to abandon Stourhead, his estate in Wiltshire, and retire to live at his villa on Clapham Common. Shortly after Richard's marriage, Henry Hoare made over to him all his extensive property in Wiltshire, Somerset, and Dorset.

It was a splendid gift. The Hoares had purchased the Stourhead estate in 1717. They promptly built a new house. Then Richard's grandfather settled down to the creation of a new landscape, and in the forty years of his life there (1741–83) he fashioned the spectacle that we see now : a transcendent example of the special affinities between Italy and England.

All this came to Richard Colt Hoare at the age of twenty-five. His grandfather had appraised the young man's qualities exactly. He steered him away from banking, for which he seems to have shown no special aptitude, and by making over the Stourhead property he could enjoy, in his sad old age, the consolation of knowing that the estate he loved was in the hands of a worthy heir. Richard lived there with his wife two years. She bore him two sons, one of whom quickly died, and then she was dead herself. Next month the old man died too.

To assuage his grief the young heir took a quick decision to travel abroad. He set off at once for Italy, accompanied by a family friend. His run of misfortune was not concluded : the friend died too, from malaria caught in the undrained Pontine Marshes. He must have felt alone even more completely than before. But he pursued his travelling steadily, through Italy up into Switzerland, across by Avignon to Montserrat and Barcelona, then back into Italy again, returning to England by way of Paris after an absence of nearly two years. His father died in 1788, and he succeeded to the baronetcy. His mind now possessed with Italy, after less than a year at home he set off to travel there again : at a fateful moment, with the outbreak of the revolution in France, in the very month of the fall of the Bastille. This time he made his way by Germany and Austria, passing into Italy through Trieste. There he stayed, moving round the whole Italian world from Sicily and Malta to Florence. Again he was away two years, returning in August 1791 with a pile of journals and notes, and a library of books concerned with the history and topography of Italy, ancient and modern.

He planned to travel next to Spain and Portugal. But for the moment he was preoccupied with private business. By the time he might have considered going abroad again, war had broken out with France. Some of his countrymen paid no attention to that disturbance and continued their travels, at

---

[1] In his *Antiquities of Cornwall*, however, first published in 1754, Borlase had displayed an interest in some other aspects of archaeology : cf. Professor Charles Thomas's introduction to the reprint in this series.

[2] Until very recently, the best account of him was the straightforward summary in the *Dictionary of National Biography*, based partly on the autobiographical memoranda he gave to John Bowyer Nichols, which are printed in Nichols's *Catalogue of the Hoare Library at Stourhead* (1840). However, Mr. Kenneth Woodbridge's *Landscape and Antiquity* (1970) is largely devoted to Hoare and to his work at Stourhead. The account given here owes much to it.

increasing risk—one thinks of the Earl of Bristol (who was also Bishop of Derry), caught by the French, imprisoned in Milan, and dying eventually at Albano. Richard Colt Hoare was not a man of that kind. He realised that the Continent was now closed to him, as long as the war might last; and that turned out to be for over twenty years. Though he was a child of good fortune, he had been schooled severely by suffering and his calm good temper now showed at its best. Prevented from pursuing his travels and studies in the Mediterranean world, he set himself to tasks nearer home.

The first was to continue and extend his grandfather's shaping of the landscape at Stourhead. He was an accomplished amateur botanist, and already on his return from Italy in 1791 he had begun to turn the banks of the lake into an arboretum, with a variety of trees most carefully selected and disposed. At the same time he put in the first of the rhododendrons that have become one of the spectacular elements in that landscape as we see it today. Everything he planted was recorded meticulously in his "Stourhead Annals", which have happily been preserved. He was a careful man of business—not a Hoare for nothing—and he kept all his nurserymen's bills, so that we have an exceptionally detailed knowledge of the whole course of his work at Stourhead, which continued for the rest of his life.

At the same time he extended the house, adding wings to it in 1793 and building himself the library that forms one of its chief distinctions now. The furniture was made for it by the younger Thomas Chippendale in 1805; it has been well said that it "almost aspires to the state of architecture".[1] Into this noble room he moved his great and growing collection of books, together with his notes and drawings. He was himself a well-trained and competent draughtsman. If he made no claim to be an artist, he knew something of what art was. He had made extensive purchases of pictures in Italy, and he commissioned work from the young Turner. All this would be clearer today in the house if it had not been hit by a disgraceful disaster in the Victorian age.

Meanwhile, Colt Hoare had turned his inquiring mind in a new direction. He had begun to make friends with some of the most active students of the antiquities and history of Britain. Among them was William Coxe, who had come into Wiltshire as rector of Bemerton in 1788. With him, and with another friend, Richard Fenton, Hoare travelled extensively in Wales, making four journeys there in 1793–8, an annual pilgrimage in 1801–4, and at least one more journey, in 1810. He became interested, as a consequence, in the twelfth-century traveller Giraldus Cambrensis, publishing an edition of his *Itinerary of Wales* in 1804 and a translation of the work two years later. In 1807 he crossed the sea once more, to make a journey through Ireland.

All this brought him face to face with the ancient world of Britain, its Celtic past. In Wiltshire he lived surrounded with the monuments of a past still older: the great stone circles of Stonehenge and Avebury, the numberless tumuli and barrows on the chalk downs—all alike mysterious, a matter of fierce controversy, and just beginning to be investigated for the first time in an ordered way by William Cunnington.[2] Hoare met him first in 1803 and soon began to appreciate something of the significance of the work to which he was dedicated. In his own words, "from a neighbouring antiquary, Mr William Cunnington of Heytesbury, who, during his rides over the open downs had made many new and important discoveries, especially as to the history of the ancient British inhabitants, he became infected with the mania of antiquarianism",[3] and that led him to conceive the idea of recording all these discoveries at large in a book.

The way was wide open. Nobody had ever attempted to write the history of Wiltshire: a strange omission, for in its history, ancient and modern, it is one of the richest counties in England. The seventeenth-century antiquary, John Aubrey, a Wiltshire man himself, had compiled notes on the subject—scrappy, ill organised, and then suddenly perceptive, like everything else he wrote; but they were not printed until 1821. For the rest, there were books on Salisbury and one or two of the other towns of the county; Stukeley's observations on Avebury and Stonehenge, plainly at variance with many of Cunnington's observations; and little more.

The work was first projected about 1801, to be written jointly with Coxe, and in consultation with Thomas Leman, whose special interest lay in the antiquities of Roman Britain. But Coxe married in 1803 and turned away for a long time from the study of antiquities, to the political history of modern Europe. His *History of the House of Austria*, published in 1807, remained the standard work in English on that subject throughout the nineteenth century. Hoare recognised therefore that if the history was to be recorded, he must undertake the task himself.

[1] K. Woodbridge, *Stourhead* (National Trust, 1971), 26. This, and Mr. Woodbridge's companion guide *The Stourhead Landscape*, form a most admirable introduction to the house and estate as they are today.

[2] For him see R. H. Cunnington, *From Antiquary to Archaeologist* (1975).

[3] See the dedication of the second volume of *Ancient Wiltshire* to Coxe.

He seems to have reached this conclusion before the end of 1803. He could not act on it very quickly. He had still his work on Giraldus to complete, and he had a public duty in front of him, as High Sheriff of Wiltshire in 1805–6. But his mind all the time was playing over the subject, stimulated by correspondence with Cunnington and visits to the sites he was investigating. He arranged with Cunnington to supply him with reports, digesting his observations and conclusions on each of them, and these formed the basis of much of the published book.[1] He also engaged a surveyor, Philip Crocker, to draw maps and plans of the sites for him.

So everything was set to enable him to give his full attention to the work as soon as he was free from his other commitments. One fresh impediment, however, now appeared, which we first hear of early in 1805. Writing to Cunnington, he speaks of "a violent rheumatism in my right hand and symptoms of gout in both my feet".[2] The symptoms were presently confirmed, and those two diseases remained his enemies for the rest of his life, often interrupting his work and occasioning visits to Cheltenham and Bath. He also came to suffer intermittently from disabling headaches (perhaps a form of migraine), treated once very violently with arsenic.[3] On top of all this, he began to grow deaf in 1807.[4] He battled with these troubles courageously until his death.

He showed indeed great tenacity. "I cannot bear to be *beaten* by a tumulus", he exclaims at one moment.[5] He was a highly intelligent man, and he recognised the magnitude of the task he had undertaken: not with any silly desire to inflate it, and the achievement that resulted, but because he knew he was entering an almost entirely uncharted world. His earlier experience in Wales had taught him that Wiltshire could not be understood in isolation. The very first letter we have from him to Cunnington, written in January 1804, shows it: "There seems *so much* variety and so little uniformity in the construction and contents of all our barrows that I almost despair of forming any regular system respecting them. . . . I wish we could find any *French* antiquarian who would make some researches in Normandy or Brittany". (This calmly, in the midst of the war against Napoleon.) Whatever his faults and limitations, the view he took of his subject was never myopic or merely provincial.

He started to write the book in January 1808, working very methodically.[6] By November 1809 he could report—writing, under the arsenic treatment, from Bath—that the whole of the introduction was printed.[7] On his return home he sprang back into activity: "I am again *all alive*, and think of nothing but Ancient Wiltshire".[8] In the following summer he practically completed his account of Stonehenge, and that autumn found him busy on the second part of the work.

He had decided to issue it in parts, for reasons he explains in the preface. The first of them appeared in 1812, followed by the others in 1819 and 1821. Each bears a separate dedication. The first part, with a very proper feeling, he inscribed to Cunnington, to whom the book owed so much; but the compliment came, in a sense, too late, for Cunnington had died in December 1810. The second part had what might be called a public dedication, to Sir Joseph Banks, President of the Royal Society; but the third was again personal, and highly appropriate, to Coxe, recalling the origins of the work, back at the beginning of the century.

The publisher of the first part in 1812 was William Miller, but he went out of business in that year, making over his rights to John Murray. The other two parts were issued by a consortium of publishers headed by Lackington's, one of the best-known London firms of the time. The same printers, Bulmer's, were employed throughout. The accounts for the engraving of the plates and the making of the maps are extant.[9] Basire, the engraver of the plates, received £863; Cary, who engraved the maps, £189; and Philip Crocker £140.

The reception of the work was mixed. A number of people complained of its unnecessarily ponderous size and weight: with good reason, one may feel, especially in handling the large-paper copies. Some of the praise accorded to the book was toadying, to the rich man of rank who had produced it; some of its detractors were moved, as one would expect, by the spite that arises from envy. The enduring

---

[1] For these reports see p. 13 below. Nearly 100 of Hoare's letters to Cunnington are preserved in the Museum of the Wiltshire Archaeological and Natural History Society at Devizes. They are incompletely dated. In the quotations from them that follow, they are referred to simply by their present numbers in the series.

[2] Letter 7.

[3] Cf. Letters 28, 36, 38, 77–8.

[4] Letter 48.

[5] Letter 11.

[6] Letter 51.

[7] Letter 77.

[8] Letter 78.

[9] Devizes Museum.

value of the book, and its defects, are discussed in the second part of this introduction. Here one thing may be added, which belongs properly to an account of Hoare himself.

It is natural that some people, then and later, should have supposed the book was not really his work. Especially since the importance of Cunnington's contribution to it has come to be recognised, it can easily be suggested that Hoare merely put a veneer on what had been done by his coadjutor and complacently took the credit for the result. That is wrong. Hoare goes out of his way, both in the dedication and elsewhere, to make clear how much of the information contained in the book came from Cunnington. He did not steal credit from him, or from anybody else. It is true that in their correspondence, friendly and pleasant as it is, there is often a touch of the peremptory on Hoare's side (unhappily Cunnington's replies have not survived, so that we can only infer what was in them); for Hoare was rich, knew what he wanted, and expected to get it. Beyond doubt he put too great a pressure on his patient collaborator at times.[1] But at least it can be said that he drove himself hard too.

All in all, we can sum up: the book is genuinely and legitimately Hoare's. He was not just a man of wealth, who commissioned a history; he was the author of it in his own right.

As the work drew to a close he came to feel that it ought not to stand on its own: that the history of Wiltshire must be continued beyond the departure of the Romans. But to record its whole modern history was a no less formidable task. Hoare was now sixty, and his health was poor. He could hardly hope to complete a second work, with all the inquiry into documents that would be involved, in his life-time. Nevertheless, he thought the attempt should be made; and about 1818 he drew up a series of questions, directed to parishes, in a manner sometimes used by county historians before.[2] He had already begun work himself on the Hundred of Mere, in which Stourhead was situated; and he hoped to forward the undertaking by pressing a number of his friends and neighbours into service—not in order to feed him with information, as Cunnington had done, but to write self-contained accounts of Hundreds themselves. Lord Arundell of Wardour agreed to contribute two; Hoare was in hopes that Coxe would return to his earlier antiquarian studies and join in. Eventually, the fourteen parts of *Modern Wiltshire* that were published (1822–44) were written by eight authors, and the work was never completed.[3] Still, the greater part of the whole task was accomplished, and the county could at length point with pride to a history worthy of itself. It could do more than look neighbouring counties in the face: for of the six that lay closest to it only two, Gloucestershire and Dorset, could show works comparable in merit. And for none of them—for no English county whatever in 1821—was there any survey like that presented in *Ancient Wiltshire*.

So Hoare could justly feel satisfied. In later life his work continued steadily, without interruption except through illness. When the long war with France ended, his mind went back for a little while to his past life. In 1815 he produced a small volume of *Hints to Travellers in Italy*, making it clear in the preface that he had no hope of ever returning there himself. In 1815–18 he published four volumes of notes on his journeys there. His library grew relentlessly, and in 1815 he printed twenty-five copies of his catalogue of it.[4] Perhaps it became uncomfortably large, even in the amplitude of Stourhead. At all events, in 1825 he presented the whole of his Italian library to the British Museum.[5]

One more personal misfortunate had still to befall him. His son Henry died in 1836. He took all the precautions he could to safeguard the inheritance he had cherished and prized so highly, and he died—after long ill health, nevertheless at the age of eighty—on 19 May 1838.

Alas, those precautions were insufficient, through no fault of his own.[6] His son having died before him, the estate passed to a half-brother and that half-brother's son, both of them conscientious heirs; but it descended next to Sir Henry Ainslie Hoare, who became a Liberal M.P. and squandered money to such purpose that in 1883 he was reduced to selling many of the pictures and the whole of Sir Richard's library.[7] No greater insult can ever have been thrown by a contemptible heir at one of his forebears. It is an infamy beyond any redemption. His successor Sir Henry Hugh Hoare grappled with the problems of a depleted inheritance. On top of that the house was seriously damaged by fire

---

[1] They are printed in his *Hints on the Topography of Wiltshire* [1818].

[2] Cf., for example, letters 71, 77, 90.

[3] The printers' bills for eight of the parts are in Devizes Museum. They show a total expenditure by Hoare of £2,580.

[4] *Catalogue of Books relating to the History and Topography of England, Wales, Scotland, and Ireland* (1815).

[5] He had printed twelve copies of a catalogue of it in 1812. See the note in his own hand on the flyleaf of the British Museum's copy (C61 b 12).

[6] His elaborate will is at the Public Record Office: PROB 11/1898. See particularly ff. 33–4.

[7] A priced copy of the catalogue of the sale of the pictures is at the British Museum.

in 1902—although, through a touching dispensation, the splendid room that Colt Hoare had built for his library, and all its furniture, was spared. Sir Henry Hoare and his wife battled valiantly on. Their only son was killed in the First World War, and at length in 1946 they determined to give the estate to the National Trust. The Trust has no more priceless possession.

Sir Richard Colt Hoare has left lasting memorials behind him. In the tradition of his class and age, they are not wholly individual. He would be content to know that his contribution to the landscape at Stourhead is remembered, taking its place with those of his grandfather and his successors: for no landscape can be finite, it must change with the succession of the years. The same is true of the historical studies he pursued. He made no pretence that they were all his own, acknowledging candidly the contributions made by his collaborators. But in the work he undertook he was—like Carnot in the field of war—the organiser of victory. The *History of Wiltshire*, taking it all together, remains incomplete, and it has its shortcomings. But nobody else—neither Coxe nor Cunnington—could have turned it into a reality as he did. Men of inherited wealth have often been attacked, and they are not much beloved today. Many of them were drones, frivolous and irresponsible. The family we are concerned with here displays one outstanding example of that type. In Sir Richard Colt Hoare it also displays another in strong opposition, who used his wealth generously and wisely, to the public advantage quite as much as to his own.

JACK SIMMONS

ANCIENT WILTSHIRE

Although *Ancient Wiltshire* was published under a single author's name the work is, as has been seen, the product of collaboration between Sir Richard Colt Hoare and William Cunnington, one of the most significant figures in the history of British Archaeology.

William Cunnington was born, in humble circumstances, near the village of Gretton, Northamptonshire, in 1754. In 1768 he was sent to Wiltshire as an apprentice in the woollen trade and by 1772 had established himself as a woollen merchant at Heytesbury, where he was to remain for the rest of his life. It is not known when, precisely, he began to take an active interest in local antiquities although in his early years at Heytesbury was probably more involved in business affairs. Throughout his life he suffered from severe headaches, and poor health may have driven him out on to the Downs where he came in contact with the many surviving earthworks and barrows, for he wrote that his doctors "told me I must ride out or die—I preferred the former, and thank God, though poorly, I am yet alive".[1] Modern medical opinion, based on the physical characteristics displayed in the portrait painted by Samuel Woodforde in 1808, is that Cunnington suffered from acromegaly, a disease produced by an overactive pituitary gland.

He was visited by John Britton, the Wiltshire topographer, in 1798. At that time the latter was collecting material for his *Beauties of Wiltshire* and obviously considered Cunnington as a potential source of information. In the same year Cunnington wrote to Britton describing pottery which he had discovered "digging with a large stick" beneath two fallen sarsen stones at Stonehenge. By 1800 he was in correspondence with H. P. Wyndham, M.P. for Wiltshire, who was contemplating the writing of a history of Wiltshire antiquities. The latter appears to have been particularly interested in long barrows, which he considered to cover the bodies of those slain in battle, and to confirm this hypothesis Cunnington undertook the excavation of several of these monuments in the succeeding two years: the work in part being undertaken at Wyndham's expense. The results confirmed, at least to Wyndham's satisfaction, that these were "battle barrows", although Cunnington was more cautious. He found only a small number of skeletons beneath the Old Ditch barrow at Tilshead, and the black earth beneath it, which Wyndham considered as evidence of slaughter, proved, on chemical analysis, not to be of animal origin. At this site one sees Cunnington adopting for the first time the now standard archaeological practice of submitting samples of material from an excavation for scientific examination. In later years he consulted other experts, notably William Smith, the most celebrated geologist of the day, and even presented animal remains to his local butcher for comment.

Another antiquarian, and associate of Wyndham, with whom Cunnington was in correspondence at this time was William Coxe, rector of Bemerton, near Salisbury. Like his learned contemporaries he was steeped in the classical tradition and embarked initially on a study of the Roman antiquities

---

[1] The quotations in this section are all from letters published in R. H. Cunnington's biography or preserved in the Museum at Devizes.

of the county with which he was more familiar and whose elucidation would be less costly, being based on literary sources, than the excavation of British barrows and other barbarian monuments. With Roman sites and roads in mind Coxe wrote to Cunnington with a view to employing Cunnington's young friend, Philip Crocker, then a surveyor employed by the Ordnance Survey, to survey all the Roman roads and stations in the county. Here was a further member of the group which was ultimately to be responsible for the preparation of Hoare's *Ancient Wiltshire*. Coxe, like Wyndham, contributed towards the cost of Cunnington's barrow digging to gain material for his projected history although pressing Cunnington to "confine ourselves to low barrows" in order to reduce the cost.

In these same first two years of the nineteenth century Coxe introduced Cunnington to the Rev. Thomas Leman of Bath, a distinguished classical scholar, and to Sir Richard Colt Hoare. Leman too was to play an important part in the shaping of *Ancient Wiltshire*. To him must be given credit for at least some of the techniques and ideas which Hoare and Cunnington adopted, although in Hoare's case not always wisely. Cunnington, as a self-educated man without classical training, was greatly impressed by Leman's formidable reputation and knowledge of ancient authors, and all his early reports written for Coxe were submitted to Leman for his comments.

In 1801 Leman wrote to Cunnington: "You will excuse me I am sure when I take the liberty of pointing out to you the necessity of *immediately pasting a small piece of paper on every piece of pottery or coin* that you may hereafter find, describing with accuracy the very spot in which you found them. The people who succeed us may possibly know more about these things than we do (or else I am confident they will know very little), but we ought to mark the steps we have advanced and afford *them* all the information we can with clearness. We are too apt to suppose that even we ourselves shall know *tomorrow*, what we have learn'd *today*, and yet every day's experience has told me that I do not, and as it may possibly be so with others, I would wish you to be on your guard against this fatal error. To collect either coins or any other pieces of antiquity without it is done with the honest zeal of being of use to others in explaining the obscure history of antiquities of our country is little better than collecting rubbish which may impede but cannot add to our improvement". It is to be regretted that this sound advice, which was followed by Hoare, was to be ignored by a great many other nineteenth-century excavators whose collections now have little archaeological value. In another letter the same year he urges caution in the use of single finds such as coins or pottery to date the construction of a site. Although he had no practical experience of excavation, in common with other contemporary antiquaries, he was not unappreciative of Cunnington's practical work and of his early barrow reports wrote: "a few such papers would throw more light on this very obscure part of our antiquities (for to own the truth we know little about them) than the many theoretical volumes which have been given to the world". In later years, with increasing experience Cunnington was less inclined to accept many of Leman's conclusions and interpretations, based as they largely were on literary evidence, and in 1807 he wrote: "The information to be gathered from Caesar and Tacitus relate (*sic*) to the Britons in their times: thereafter all theories drawn from such sources are ever at war with the facts".

The critical year for the making of *Ancient Wiltshire* was 1803. On 24 March, Colt Hoare, Coxe and Crocker visited Cunnington at Heytesbury and it was then agreed that Hoare should finance all future operations. Shortly after the visit Coxe married unexpectedly, an event which led Crocker to write to Cunnington that he was "fearful that it will affect the *whole county* of Wiltshire". Coxe lost interest in the project and embarked on his *History of the House of Austria*. It was left to Hoare to continue and complete the work, a task which he prosecuted with a vigour and thoroughness which contrasts sharply with Coxe's earlier disorganised approach to the subject.

Although Colt Hoare and Cunnington were intially drawn together by a mutual interest in antiquities it is clear from the letters they exchanged that a warm and deep friendship grew up between the two men which was to endure until Cunnington's death in 1810. It says much for the personalities of the two that such a relationship could be established between a wealthy baronet and "an ingenious tradesman", as Coxe described Cunnington, in an era governed by strict rules of social etiquette.

In their meeting in March 1803 the division of responsibility for the preparation of a history of Wiltshire antiquities appears to have been worked out. Cunnington was to undertake the excavations and Hoare would carry out surface fieldwork and the description of earthworks. Hoare sent Cunnington detailed instructions on each season's programme, what he referred to as his "campaigns" following the initial explorations he had often made of a region on horseback, frequently in the company of Philip Crocker. In the early part of the work Crocker was still employed by the Ordnance Survey: but he appeared to have little difficulty in obtaining leave to work for Hoare, owing no doubt to the latter's influence. Later Crocker became Hoare's steward. All the maps, plans and meticulous drawings of the excavated material which were to appear in *Ancient Wiltshire* were prepared by him. Of particular value to archaeology were the numbered plans of barrow cemeteries which make it possible still to locate the majority of barrows opened by Cunnington and Hoare. This example was regrettably not followed by other contemporary barrow diggers, and some who came later.

The details of Cunnington's excavations are set out in a long series of letters sent to Hoare at regular intervals. The majority are in the hand of one or other of his daughters to whom he dictated them. All the archaeological papers were written in duplicate, Cunnington retaining one copy. The material for Hoare's use was written in five specially bound manuscript volumes (the Stourhead MSS.) with one side left blank for comments (largely by Leman). These are now in the library of the Society of Antiquaries in Burlington House. The copies retained by Cunnington, in thirteen books bound in three volumes, are now in the library of the Wiltshire Archaeological and Natural History Society in Devizes Museum. This collection also contains letters written to Cunnington.

These reports form the basis for the information set out in *Ancient Wiltshire*, and in particular in Vol. I. Cunnington's rather ponderous and verbose style was altered by Hoare but his basic information and conclusions were seldom changed. There are, however, two notable exceptions. The first concerns the Sarsen stones at Stonehenge. William Stukeley, the eighteenth-century antiquary, believed that the sarsens were "spewed out" as the body of chalk hardened at Creation. Cunnington, following the views of the geologist William Smith, advised Hoare that they were a sedimentary deposit (the modern view). In *Ancient Wiltshire*, Volume I, Hoare follows Cunnington and accepts Smith's view. In Volume II he quotes only Stukeley's theory although in a further account of Stonehenge in *Modern Wiltshire* he reverts to the sedimentary concept.

More important is the account of the great Late Neolithic earthwork at Marden given in Volume II. The enormous bank of this irregularly shaped henge had already been considerably damaged when first visited by Hoare and Cunnington in 1807, and a gap occurred in the south-east adjacent to the river Avon. It was the view of John Mayo, vicar of Beechingstoke, that the bank originally extended across the stream. Cunnington examined the area carefully but could find no evidence to support this contention, but having visited the site Hoare wrote in his diary: "Though no traces whatever of its complete continuation remain at present, I have no doubt of such a continuance, and that, in forming the water meadows, where only the vallum is interrupted, these vestiges were removed. This work, though certainly laborious and expensive, was much facilitated by the light sandy nature of the soil, and the value of water meadows to a Wiltshire farmer is such as to render my supposition of that part of the vallum which stood in their way having been removed, highly probable". This was the opinion printed in *Ancient Wiltshire*, where an area of fifty-one acres is given for the site as opposed to Cunnington's estimate of twenty-eight to thirty acres. Inside the henge was a gigantic mound, the Hatfield Barrow, all surface traces of which have since vanished. Crocker's survey of the site showed that in 1807 it had a diameter of 483 ft and a height of 22½ ft. Eight men were employed over the unusually long period of ten days to open an area 23 ft by 24 ft in the centre of the structure. Not surprisingly beneath a barrow which covered an acre in area no burial was found, although Cunnington remained convinced that it was a funerary monument. Leman, on hearing of the excavation and the negative results, wrote to Cunnington evincing no surprise at the absence of burials, stating flatly that the mound was a hill altar and at most only the bones of one High Priest might be expected to be found beneath it. In *Ancient Wiltshire*, Volume II, Hoare writes: "Mr. Cunnington was of the opinion that the mound was sepulchral, but from the discoveries we made when digging down from the summit to the floor, I do not think he found a sufficient basis to support his hypothesis. . . . Although I have so frequently agreed in opinion with Mr. Cunnington on British topics, I cannot justify myself in coalescing with him respecting the sepulchral origin of this tumulus. . . . It may probably have been either a Hill Altar or *Locus Consecratus*, at which the Druids attended to decide various causes and issue their decrees".

It must be significant that both these cases where Hoare sets aside Cunnington's judgement appear in Volume II, written after the latter's death. Cunnington was ever fearful, and justifiably so, of using classical sources and literary evidence in the interpretation of prehistoric sites. Shortly before his death Cunnington began a letter which although unaddressed must have been intended for Hoare although never seen by him: "In your rides over the county with Crocker (after he has finished his survey) I am persuaded you will see these things as I have done, but you will be so hard beset with old systems from the Book-men that I very much doubt whether you would have the hardyhood to withstand them".

It is clear that Hoare seldom attended the excavations conducted on his behalf by Cunnington, and then only briefly, and yet he normally uses the plural "we" as though he had been present when the discoveries he describes were made. He wrote, for example, regarding the Normanton barrow cemetery: "Circumstances prevented my being present at the opening of them. The superintendence of our research was therefore committed to the penetrating eye and experienced judgement of Mr.

Cunnington". Throughout the succeeding account however he continually refers to "we" and "our". This may to some extent have been editorial licence, although Hoare may have felt that as he was paying for the work he deserved a fair share of the credit for it, and it is interesting to note that in his accounts of material excavated before 1803, when he assumed financial responsibility, Cunnington alone is referred to as the excavator. Cunnington did not, of course, involve himself in the physical side of digging, which was accomplished by labourers. Several were employed on long barrows and the great Hatfield Barrow at Marden, but the standard digging "team" who remained with Cunnington throughout his excavating period were Stephen Parker and his son John, of Heytesbury. John appears to have been temperamental. "Tell John", wrote Hoare, "that I will have no *sulking fits*, not even when he *begins again* upon the large barrow which *failed us*". But both took an informed and enthusiastic interest in their work and after a particularly successful excavation Cunnington wrote to Hoare: "Had John found a purse of guineas he could not have been better pleased". The Parkers appear to have acquired a considerable reputation as excavators, for Hoare's friend, Iremonger, contemplating the opening of some Hampshire barrows wrote to Cunnington requesting the help of "your Wiltshire labourers on this occasion, for my Hampshire men have disgraced themselves by their exorbitant demands: and I am confident that the expenses of their journey will be amply repaid by their superior skill and alacrity". Both were also capable of forming their own judgment of the sites they were digging as on the occasion of the excavation of the Sherrington long barrow in 1804: "Mr. Wyndham paid us a visit at the barrow; he was of opinion that this must have been a Saxon barrow. Against this opinion Stephen, John and myself entered our protest". On a number of occasions the Parkers worked on their own, and when Cunnington was too ill to take part he directed them to cut a section across the junction of a Roman road and the Wansdyke to try and determine their relationship. The Parkers pronounced the road to be the earlier structure although final confirmation of this, correct, assumption had to await the excavations of General Pitt-Rivers over seventy years later. John Parker also presents an interesting link with a later generation of archaeologists in that he provided Pitt-Rivers with information concerning a barrow which he had dug for Cunnington.

In all Hoare and Cunnington opened some 465 barrows, using techniques which by modern standards must be considered execrable; the normal method being to sink a vertical shaft from the centre of the mound to its base or to cut a trench running from the barrow's perimeter to its centre. Such techniques continued to be employed throughout the nineteenth century and even beyond, with the notable exception of the meticulous work of Pitt-Rivers in the last two decades of that century. Labourers were frequently allowed to dig for long periods without supervision and as a result much evidence was lost and many finds, in particular pottery, broken, although such disasters are reported calmly in the pages of *Ancient Wiltshire*. Broken pots were in some instances left in the grave and there is frequent mention of flints and bone articles which were not preserved. A notable example of the loss of such finds occurred in the excavation of Bush Barrow in the Normanton group, one of the most important of the Early Bronze Age Wessex Culture graves discovered by Cunnington. One of the three daggers in the grave group had the pommel decorated with thousands of minute lengths of gold wire. Of these Cunnington wrote to Hoare: "There are now a number of these minute gold rivets in the remainder of the wood which still adheres to the brass. When we first discovered these shining points of gold, we had no conception of their nature, otherwise we might perhaps have preserved thousands of them; but unfortunately John with his trowel had scattered them in every direction before I had examined them with a glass". The opening of a barrow appears to have been something of a social occasion, being in many cases attended by the local gentry and their ladies who picnicked by the side and had the various trinkets recovered from the barrow brought to them for their examination. Quite often finds, particularly beads, appear to have been given to the ladies as keepsakes. Another major failing, for which Hoare and Cunnington were criticised by later excavators, was their habit of re-interring the human remains in the barrows, thus depriving later scholars of much valuable anthropological data.

In spite of the limitations of their excavation technique the work of Cunnington and Colt Hoare and the publication of their findings in *Ancient Wiltshire* are of cardinal importance in the history and development of British archaeology, representing a major step forward from antiquarianism. It was the first and most magnificent of the county archaeologies in which an account of the prehistory and early history of a region was built up as the result of a systematic programme of fieldwork and excavation. Inherent in the work is the now universally accepted concept of the importance of archaeological objects, not simply as objects but as sources of information; and they adhered to the principle that excavations should be undertaken not merely to recover such objects but to answer specific archaeological problems. "We speak from facts not theory" begins the introduction to Volume I, but although the bulk of the volume is concerned with a straightforward account of barrow excavations and descriptions of earthworks, Hoare in his introduction, could not resist including lengthy quotations from classical sources, most of them irrelevant. He also includes Johnson's remark "All that is really known of the ancient state of Britain is contained in a few pages. We can know no more than what old writers have told us". The evidence set out in *Ancient Wiltshire* clearly disproves this statement, but again one can see here the influence of Hoare's classical and literary background and also, one suspects, the ever-present influence of Leman. Hoare's love of the Gothick is also seen in the archaic lettering of the title page "Auncient Wiltescire" with its border of beads and flint arrowheads or in his description of a skeleton from a barrow on Whitesheet Hill: "It's mouth was open and it grinn'd horribly a ghastly smile". However, in so far as possible they abandoned references to Druids. Their descriptive terms for the various barrow types, long, bowl, bell, pond and saucer, are those still employed today although, following Stukeley, they referred to disc barrows as Druid barrows. Within these barrows they were able to distinguish between primary and secondary burials. They failed, however, to recognise that some were Anglo-Saxon, although parallels for a number had already been illustrated and described by the Rev. James Douglas in his *Nenia Britannica*, the first part of which appeared in 1786. Hoare and Cunnington were also the first antiquaries to consider hillforts and other non-funerary earthworks, and rightly interpreted henge monuments as ceremonial rather than domestic sites. They believed, however, that all the earthworks represented the domestic sites of those interred in the barrows although in fact the former belong, on the whole, to a considerably later period.

Their major stumbling block was their inability to break down the apparent contemporaneity of the material from the barrows which had all to be lumped together as "British" or "Ancient British", and Hoare confesses in his introduction to "our total ignorance of the authors of these sepulchral memorials". Cunnington believed most round barrows to have been erected between 500 and 100 B.C. and that the Early Bronze Age burial beneath the Golden Barrow at Upton Lovell was that of a chief buried "near the time of Caesar's invasion". Leman wrote to Cunnington "I think we distinguish three great eras by the arms of offence found in our barrows. 1st those of bone and stone, certainly belonging to the primeval inhabitants in their savage state, and which may be safely attributed to the Celts. 2nd those of brass, probably imported into this island from the more polished nations of Africa in exchange for our tin, and which may be given to the Belgae. 3rd those of iron, introduced but a little while before the invasion of the Romans". No mention of this nascent concept of a Three-Age system is made in *Ancient Wiltshire* although Cunnington appears to have cautiously accepted the scheme while drawing attention to the fact that objects of bone, stone and bronze in some cases occurred in the same grave; and it was a further thirty years before the basic chronological division of Stone, Bronze and Iron Ages was published by Thomsen in Denmark. A severe limitation on Hoare and Cunnington's speculations on the antiquity of the material they were finding in the barrows was the contemporary theological view of the recent date of Creation, and many accepted Archbishop Ussher's date of 4004 B.C. which was printed in the margin of the Authorised Version of the Bible. Within this short span had to be fitted the rise and development of the great Near Eastern and Mediterranean civilisations, which left little time for the evolution of "Ancient British" Society. It required the publication and acceptance of the views of Lyell in his *Principles of Geology* (1830–3) and Darwin's *Origin of the Species* (1859) for the high antiquity of man and his environment to be appreciated.

Hoare began his draft in 1808 and the first of the three folio parts for South Wiltshire appeared in 1810 shortly before Cunnington's death. The work was completed in 1812. North Wiltshire appeared in 1819 under a new publisher and the final part, "The Roman Aera", with separate pagination, in 1821. The model for the format appears to have been Douglas's *Nenia Britannica* which, like *Ancient Wiltshire*, was first issued in folio parts. Colt Hoare had close associations with Douglas and on the latter's death in 1819 his widow presented the Jutish material from his barrow excavations to Hoare, who finally gave the material to the Ashmolean Museum in 1829.

During Cunnington's lifetime the material they had amassed from their excavations was kept in a summer house or moss house, together with his considerable geological and palaeontological collections, in the garden at Heytesbury. Eight years after his death Hoare bought the material from the Cunnington daughters for £200, although they had originally asked for more. It was preserved at Stourhead for some time after Hoare's death in 1838, where it lay neglected in the cellars until deposited on loan with the Wiltshire Archaeological Society in their museum at Devizes in 1878; an occasion which prompted the columnist in the *Devizes and Wiltshire Gazette* to write: "To rescue a 'collection' of what—as it lies in the cellars at Stourhead—appears to unarchaeological eyes more like the refuse of a marine store than anything else, augurs a degree of antiquarian eccentricity which few persons will be able to appreciate". The collection was finally purchased for the museum in 1883 for £250. It can now be appreciated that the objects recovered from Cunnington and Hoare's excavations constitute one of the most important assemblages of material of the Early Bronze Age in north-western

Europe. As valuable to scholars as the finds themselves are the detailed accounts of their discovery contained in the pages of *Ancient Wiltshire*, which remains a primary and seminal source for one of the most interesting phases of British Prehistory.

D. D. A. SIMPSON

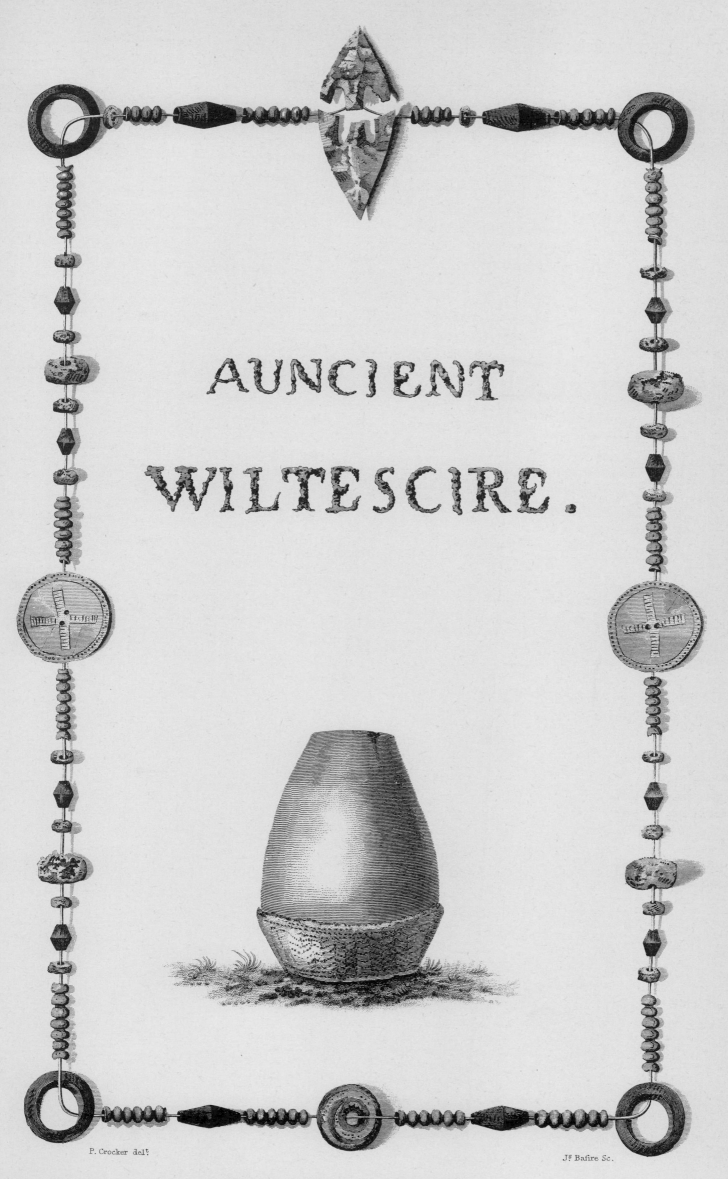

AUNCIENT

WILTESCIRE.

P. Crocker delt.

Jsᵉ Basire Sc.

Published for W. Miller, Albemarle Street, London, Janᵞ 1. 1810.

Samuel Woodforde R.A. pinx.t   James Basire sculp.t

Mr WILLIAM CUNNINGTON, F.S.A.

OF HEYTESBURY, WILTS.

Publifhed for W. Miller, Albemarle Street, London, Jany 1. 1810.

THE

ANCIENT HISTORY

OF

SOUTH WILTSHIRE,

BY

SIR RICHARD COLT HOARE, BART.

─────────────

SED QUONIAM NOBILES ALIARUM REGIONUM HISTORIÆ EGREGIIS OLIM EDITÆ SCRIPTORIBUS, IN
LUCEM PRODIERE; NOS OB PATRIÆ FAVOREM, ET POSTERITATIS, FINIUM NOSTRORUM ABDITA
QUIDEM EVOLVERE, ET INCLYTE GESTA, NECDUM TAMEN IN MEMORIAM LUCULENTO LABORE
DIGESTA, TENEBRIS EXUERE, HUMILEMQUE STILO MATERIAM EFFERRE, NEC INUTILE QUIDEM NEC
ILLAUDABILE REPUTAVIMUS.   Ex GIRALDO CAMBRENSE.

─────────────

LONDON.
──────

PUBLISHED BY WILLIAM MILLER, ALBEMARLE-STREET.
PRINTED BY W. BULMER AND CO. CLEVELAND-ROW, ST. JAMES'S.
1812.

TO

MR. WILLIAM CUNNINGTON,

F. S. A.

———

MEN, ILLUSTRIOUS EITHER FOR THEIR NOBLE BIRTH, CONSPICUOUS CHARACTER, OR DISTINGUISHED LITERARY ABILITIES, HAVE IN GENERAL ENGROSSED THE HOMAGE OF DEDICATIONS; BUT ON THE PRESENT OCCASION I SHALL DEVIATE FROM THIS LONG ESTABLISHED CUSTOM, AND GRATIFY MY PRIVATE FEELINGS, BY PAYING A TRIBUTE THAT IS DUE TO JUSTICE AND FRIENDSHIP.

TO YOU, THEREFORE, SIR, WHO FIRST PROJECTED THE PLAN OF THIS HISTORY, AND BY YOUR INTERESTING COLLECTIONS, AND IMPORTANT DISCOVERIES, ENCOURAGED ME TO PURSUE IT, THIS WORK IS MOST GRATEFULLY AND APPROPRIATELY DEDICATED

BY

YOUR SINCERE FRIEND, &c.

RICHARD COLT HOARE.

Stourhead,
1 *January*, 1810.

PREFACE.

I‍T is somewhat singular, that amongst our numerous writers on the subject of English Topography, no one should have employed his pen in the description of Wiltshire; and that a county so abundant in British and Roman Antiquities, and so interesting in a more modern point of view, should have been so very imperfectly illustrated; for, if I except the writings of Dr. Stukeley and others on our celebrated temples at Abury and Stonehenge, nothing important has been added to the ample store of county history which our topographical libraries have collected.

The ancient stone temples at Abury and Stonehenge stand unrivalled, not only in our own dominions, but even in Europe: traces of British population are every where apparent upon our extensive downs; and numerous Roman roads, towns, villas, &c. mark the power and residence of that conquering and civilizing nation. And if we descend to the antiquities of the succeeding æra, our county is equally fertile and interesting; for the Abbey of Malmsbury presents the richest specimen of Saxon architecture; and the Cathedral Church of Salisbury the purest example of the Pointed architecture existing in England.

My present researches will commence with the most early period of British history, and will terminate with the Roman æra. I can neither flatter my readers or myself with the hopes of ascertaining the origin of those stupendous temples at Abury and Stonehenge, which for ages past have attracted the curiosity of every passenger; but I

B

hope to throw some new light on the history of those Britons who formerly resided on our hills; to point out the sites they selected for habitation, and to mark their gradual progress from the bleak hill to the fertile valley, and from barbarism to civilization.

When I cast my eye over the widely extended plains of Wiltshire that must furnish materials for this history; when I consider that each hill and valley must be explored with accuracy and caution; and when I reflect that I am to treat of a people unaided by science, and unenlightened by letters, my pen almost shrinks from the undertaking. But when, on the contrary, I consider that the important and valuable information, which, for several years past we have been collecting, must lie buried in my library, and be lost to the community; when I consider that few people may have the same zeal, or the same means to prosecute so expensive an undertaking; the duty I owe my countrymen and the public urges me to proceed, and not abandon a task, however difficult and laborious.

In my proposed arrangement of this Work, I shall divide our county into different stations, from which, as from head-quarters, I shall make as many digressions as distance and time will allow of for one day; and in naming them, I shall take the liberty of anglicizing a Latin word, and call them Iters.

The first station will be STOURTON, the village in which I reside. Its southern boundary will be the road leading from thence through Mere to Willoughby-hedge turnpike gate; from whence I shall continue the road to Longbridge Deverill. On the west, my line will be extended a short way into Somersetshire; and on the north, I shall follow the road from Maiden Bradley to Longbridge Deverill.

The second station will be WARMINSTER. On the south, the road will be continued from Longbridge Deverill to Heytesbury, from whence I shall pursue a direct line from south to north across the downs to Tinhead. My northern boundary will be formed by the range of chalk hills overlooking the rich vale of Eddington, Westbury, &c. and on the west I shall follow the division line of the counties of Wilts and Somerset.

The third station, HEYTESBURY, will comprehend a very extensive tract of hill and vale. It will be bounded on the south by the great road leading from Heytesbury to Salisbury as far as the village of Stapleford; from whence the boundary line will take a direct northerly course along the thickly peopled vales of Winterbourn Stoke, Maddenton, Shrewton, Elston, and Orcheston, to a very conspicuous *tumulus*, called Ell Barrow, and from thence to Red Horn turnpike, on the road leading from Sarum to Devizes. On the north I shall follow the ridge of chalk hills; and on the west this station will be united with the preceding one of Warminster by a straight trackway leading from Tinhead to Heytesbury.

The fourth station, WILY, will be bounded on the north by the turnpike road leading from Heytesbury to Stapleford; and on the south, by the road from Wilton to Hendon. On the east it will follow the course of the river Wily; and on the west its limits will be formed by the road leading from Willoughby-hedge turnpike to Longbridge Deverill.

The fifth station will be AMESBURY; and the portion allotted to it will be so extensive, that I must divide it into two districts. The one will be united to the Heytesbury station on the west, and will be separated from the Wily station on the south by the road leading from Winterbourn Stoke to Amesbury. On the north it will be bounded by the chalk hills, and on the east by the river Avon. In this station will be comprehended the celebrated antiquities of Stonehenge. The second district, extending to Salisbury, will be bounded on the north by the turnpike leading from Amesbury to Andover; on the east by the limits of the county; on the south, by the great road from Salisbury to London; and on the west by the river Wily.

The sixth station, Everley, will be separated from the preceding one on the west by the vale of the river Avon, and on the east by the county boundary. Its northern limits will be confined by the ridge of chalk hills, and those on the south by the road leading from Amesbury to Andover.

The seventh station, of Salisbury, will be separated from that of Amesbury by the London road. On the east and south it will follow the boundary lines of the county; and its western limits will be formed by the Roman road leading from Old Sarum to Dorchester.

The eighth station, Fovant, will be bounded on the east by the aforesaid Roman road; on the south by the county line; and on the north and west by the river Nadder.

The ninth station, Hendon, will complete the southern division of our county, which Nature seems to have separated in a most decided manner from the northern district, by a rich and extensive valley that disunites the *stratum* of chalk hills. My researches have not yet been extended so sufficiently into the northern district of Wiltshire, as to enable me to ascertain the precise number of stations, and their respective limits. The same plan, however, of arrangement, will be observed in the northern, as in the southern district. The southern district will form the first part of this Work; the northern district, the second; and the third part will be allotted to the Roman æra, and contain an accurate survey of the numerous Roman roads within our county, and a description of the cities, stations, and villas ascribed to that people.

Though I cannot flatter myself that many of my countrymen will have sufficient zeal in the investigation of our British antiquities to follow my steps through the intricate mazes, and apparently desolate regions of our chalk hills; yet as an historian and topographer, I think it a duty incumbent on me, so to lay down each track, and so to note each individual *tumulus* and earthen work, that have occurred during my progress through the county, that the follower of my steps shall experience no difficulty in tracing out any particular object which may excite his curiosity. To effect this purpose, I must have recourse to maps, one or more of which will be affixed to each station, according to its respective extent; and when the work is completed, a large map will be added, in which the several stations will be united, and one general view given of all the British and Roman antiquities within them.

Two strong reasons have induced me to bring out this work in parts. First, my anxiety to fulfil the promise I have long made to my friends, and the literary community. Secondly, to alleviate, as much as possible, the expense attending a work, where so many maps, and other engravings are absolutely necessary towards its proper illustration. I wish to present my countrymen with an exact account of a county little known, and hitherto undescribed, though superior to all others in early British antiquities.

Should however any unforeseen event arrest the progress of my own pen, this work need not be deemed totally incomplete, though not advanced to its proposed extent. Each station will be complete; and by the assistance of the materials we have collected, any future historian may have the means of continuing the work, according to the same arrangement under which it is now commenced.

Stourhead, January 1, 1810.   RICHARD COLT HOARE.

INTRODUCTION.

WE SPEAK FROM FACTS, NOT THEORY.

Such is the motto I adopt, and to this text I shall most strictly adhere. I shall not seek amongst the fanciful regions of romance, an origin for our Wiltshire Britons, nor, by endeavouring to prove by whom, and at what period our island was first peopled, involve myself in a Celtic or Belgic controversy ; * neither shall I place too much reliance on the very imperfect traditions handed down to us by former antiquaries on this subject. I shall describe to you what we have found ; what we have seen ; in short, I shall tell you a plain unvarnished tale, and draw from it such conclusions as shall appear not only reasonable, but even uncontradictable.

The general population of the western parts of Europe has been attributed to a nation bordering on the Frozen Ocean, called in ancient times Scythia, and now forming a part of the kingdom of Russia in Asia, and Independent Tartary. They were at first known by the name of Scythæ, and from their rambling mode of life gained the appellation of *Nomades* by *Homer* and other Greek writers.+ They were afterwards called Celtæ and Iberi, and by a conjunction

---

* Much has been written by learned writers on this abstruse subject which still remains unsettled. Those who wish to gain further information, may consult the writings of Whitaker, Pinkerton, Pelloutier, Pezron, and a numerous list of Welsh writers on the subject of ancient British genealogy.

+ *Nomades* from νεμω, *pascor*. The Scythians and Tartars gained that appellation from their rambling mode of life in feeding their cattle from place to place, and never having any fixed habitation :

> Campestres melius Scythæ,
> Quorum plaustra vagas rite trahunt domos,
> Vivunt, et rigidi Getæ,
> Immetata quibus jugera liberas
> Fruges et Cererem ferunt,
> Nec cultura placet longior annuâ.
>
> Horatius, Carm. III. 24.

Pomponius Mela, in speaking of these people, says, " *Vagi Nomades pecorum pabula sequuntur, atque ut illa durant, ità diù statam sedem agunt.*"

A modern traveller, *Reinbeck*, in his description of Mount Caucasus, says, " that a remnant of the most ancient *Nomades* still dwell in the Kuban, who are true *tecto-vagi ;* for they have no settled habitation, but

of these two titles, Celtiberi and Celto-Scythæ.* *Nam de priscorum Græcorum sententiâ hoc dico, quòd sicut notæ versus septentrionem gentes, uno prius nomine, omnes vel Scythæ, vel Nomades (ut ab Homero) appellabantur, ac postea temporis, cognitis regionibus occiduis, Celtæ, Iberi, aut mixto nomine Celtiberi+ ac Celto-Scythæ dici cœperunt, cum prius ob ignorantiam singulæ gentes uno omnes nomine afficerentur.* Strabo, Tom. I. p. 48.

These Scythians, or Celts, commenced their emigrations at a very early period, and continued them probably to a very late one: for the Gauls, leading the vagabond life of *Nomades*, did not begin to construct regular towns, or apply themselves to agriculture, till after the foundation of Marseilles, by the Phoceens, in the reign of Tarquin the Elder at Rome, about six hundred years before the Christian æra.‡ And we are informed by a celebrated French author (Pelloutier), that even in the time of the first emperors, the greater part of the Germans were *Nomades*.

Much difference of opinion has arisen amongst modern authors respecting the countries formerly occupied by the Celts ; but the ancient writers (from whom alone we can expect any authentic information) have assigned to them all the western part of Europe : " *Celtarum vocabulo veteres Græci Romanique, Gallos, Germanos, Britannos, gentesque omnes quæ τα εσχατα Ευρωπης incolunt, complecti amant:*" I can have little doubt but that the whole district of Gaul was origin-

---

change their pasturage every day, and carry their felt-tents with their goods and chattels in covered two-wheel carts. *Herodotus* and *Strabo* would still find amongst these people, their ancient and so well described Scythians, who have as little renounced their old rude manners, as the coarse sensibility of their hearing, for the grating of their never-greased cart wheels and axletrees is still the most insupportable noise that can offend the human ear."

Sir William Jones, in his Asiatic Researches, says that " Tartary, which contained, according to *Pliny*, an innumerable quantity of nations, by whom the rest of Asia, and all Europe, has in different ages been over-run, is denominated, as various images have presented themselves to various fancies, the great hive of the northern swarms, the nursery of irresistible legions, and, by a stronger metaphor, the *foundery of the human race.*"

* *Plutarch* in his life of Marius, speaking of this nation, says, " Some assert that the country of the Celtæ is of such vast extent, that it stretches from the Western Ocean, and most northern climes, to the Lake Mæotis eastward, and to that part of Scythia which borders upon Pontus : that these two nations mingle, and thence issue ; not all at once, nor at all seasons, but in the spring of every year ; that by means of these annual supplies, they had gradually opened themselves a way over the greatest part of the European continent: and that, though they are distinguished by different names according to their tribes, yet their whole body is comprehended under the general name of Celto-Scythæ."

+ The Celtiberi inhabited that district of Spain now called Biscay, and are mentioned by the poet *Lucan* as runaways from the more ancient nation of Gauls :

———*Profugique à gente vetustâ*
Gallorum, Celtæ miscentes nomen Iberis.

‡ *Justin*, speaking of this colony, says, " *Ab his Galli et usum vitæ cultioris, deposita et mansuefacta barbaria, et agrorum cultus, et urbes mœnibus cingere didicerunt. Tunc et regibus non armis vivere, tunc et vitem putare, tunc olivam serere consueverunt.*"

ally peopled and inhabited by them, and that the nation bore the sole title of
Celts, though in later times we find it divided into three districts, one of which
only preserved the appellation of Celtic. *Pausanias* says, that their general
name was in ancient times *Celtæ*, and that the tribe of *Galli* was of a later origin.
" *Verum ut Galli appellarentur, non nisi serò usus obtinuit. Celtas enim quum ipsi se
antiquitùs, tum alii eos nominarunt. Strabo* also is of the same opinion." *Arbitror
universos Gallos ab Græcis Celtas fuisse dictos ; arbitror, à Græcis nomen Celtarum
universis Galatis seu Gallis inditum esse.*

At the period when *Julius Cæsar* wrote his Commentaries, Gaul was divided
into three parts, of which the *Belgæ* inhabited one, the *Aquitani* another, and a
people called in their own language *Celtæ*, and in ours, *Galli*, the third. The
Celtæ were separated from the *Aquitani* by the river Garonne, and from the
Belgæ by the Marne and Seine. These all differed from each other in their
language, customs, and laws. But in the time of the Greek historian *Polybius*,
who was born a century before *Cæsar*, the country near Narbonne, which was
afterwards included within the limits of Aquitania, was inhabited by *Celtæ*,
" *Narboni vicina Celtæ habitant, et inde ad montes quos dicunt Pyrenæos.*"

Thus we see the province of Aquitania inhabited by Celtic tribes, scarcely
more than a century before the time when *Cæsar* allots it to the Aquitani.

POPULATION OF BRITAIN.

THAT our island is indebted to the neighbouring continent of Gaul for its
population, there can, I think, be little doubt ; though some writers, zealous
for the antiquity of their country, have bestowed the honours of primogeniture
on the English Britons. The inhabitants of Gaul and Britain were originally
the same people ; they had the same customs, the same arms, the same language,
and the same names of towns and persons : " *Britannos quoque cum Gallis, atque
Germanis, Hispanisque ejusdem fuisse generis, ejusdemque originis, deducetur ex lin-
guâ, tum ex hominum, oppidorumque nominibus propriis, quæ dictis nationibus fuere com-
munia [Cluverii Germania, p. 20.]**

The early state of Britain is involved in great obscurity, and "all that is really

---

* The Cornish historian, *Borlase*, is of opinion that Britain received its first inhabitants from Gaul, and
says, " Some may think that it derogates from the dignity of our country to allow of a Gaulish original ;
but, be the consequences what they will, whenever we are in search of truth, although we discover her in
ruins and rubbish, we must acknowledge and revere her."

known, is contained in a few pages. We can know no more than what the old
writers have told us." To them therefore we must apply for the scanty information respecting our island. They point out to us the western shores of Britain as enjoying the first commercial intercourse with the Phœnicians, Romans
and Gauls; and we are informed by various Greek and Roman authors, that
the coast of Cornwall was resorted to at a very early period by foreign merchants in search of the tin ore with which that county abounds, and which
bore the epithet of Celtic: *Stannum ferunt Celticum, multò quam plumbum citius
liquefieri (Aristotle de Mirabilibus.)* This metal was so abundant on the coast of
Cornwall, that it gave the title of *Cassiterides* (from the Greek word ΚΑΣΣΙΤΕΡΟΣ,
tin) to a cluster of islands, now called Scilly, from whence the tin ore was dug
and exported. *Pliny*, says, " *Ex adverso Celtiberiæ complures sunt insulæ, Cassiterides dictæ Græcis, à fertilitate plumbi.*" To the geographer *Strabo* we are
highly indebted for a very interesting and satisfactory account of these islands
and their inhabitants. He tells us that the islands of Cassiterides are ten in
number, situated near each other in the open sea, and bearing a northerly direction from the port of the Artabri (Cape Finisterre.) One of them is desert;
the others are inhabited by a people wearing black garments or cloaks reaching down to their heels, and bound round their breasts. They walk with
sticks, and have beards like goats. They live upon the produce of their herds,
and have no fixed places of abode. They have the metals of lead and tin, which,
together with skins, they exchange for pottery, salt, and works of brass. In
early times the Phœnicians were the only traders who resorted hither from
Cadiz, and they carefully kept other nations in ignorance of this navigation.
The Romans, however, at length, after repeated trials, made themselves masters
of it. So great was the caution used on this occasion by the Phœnicians, that
the master of one of their vessels, being pursued by a Roman for the purpose
of discovering the place of trade, ran his own vessel on shore: that of the
Romans followed, and both were lost; but the Phœnician was indemnified
out of the public treasury. The Romans, however, after repeated attempts,
made themselves acquainted with the navigation.

*Cassiterides insulæ decem sunt numero, vicinæ invicem, ab Artabrorum portu, versùs
septentrionem in alto sitæ mari. Una earum deserta est: reliquæ ab hominibus inco-
luntur atras vestes gerentibus, tunicas indutis ad talos usque demissas, cinctis circum
pectus, cum baculis ambulantibus, barbas hircorum in morem alentibus. Vivunt ii ex
pecore, vagantes ferè incertis sedibus. Metalla habent stanni et plumbi, quorum et
pellium loco, fictilia, sales, et ærea opera à mercatoribus recipiunt.*

Primis temporibus soli Phœnices a Gadibus eò negociatum iverunt, celantes alios istam navigationem. Quum autem Romani quendam navis magistrum sequerentur, ut et. ipsi emporia ista addiscerent, is invidiâ ductus, deditâ operâ, navem suam in vadum compulit, in eandem que perniciem iis qui insequebantur conjectis, ipse a naufragio servatus, ex ærario publico pretium amissarum mercium accepit. Tamen Romani, re sæpius tentatâ, navigationem addidicerunt.*

Pliny tells us, that the first person who brought tin from the *Cassiterides*, was a person named Midacritus; but authors who have commented on this name, say it ought to have been *Midas Phrygius.* *Hyginus* says, " *Midas rex, Cybeles filius, Phryx, plumbum album et nigrum primus attulit.*" And *Cassiodorus* adds, " *Æs enim Ionos Thessaliæ rex; plumbum Midas regnator Phrygiæ, repererunt.* *Pliny* also says, that this metal was in such high request, that it was exchanged for the most precious gems: " *India neque æs neque plumbum habet, gemmisque suis ac margaritis hæc permutat.*" *Strabo*, on the same subject, says, " *Stannum nasci in Cassiteridibus insulis, ex Britannicis quoque Massiliam deferri.*" We learn also from *Diodorus Siculus*, that it was conveyed from Cornwall to a certain island adjacent to Britain, called *Ictis*, (probably *Vectis*, or the Isle of Wight,) and from thence transported by the foreign merchants into Gaul, and carried over land by a journey of thirty days, to the mouth of the Rhone.+

The same author informs us, that this metal was also conveyed from Cornwall by horses through the Celtic province of Gaul to Marseilles and Narbonne.‡

No further proofs are necessary to convince us, that a very extensive commerce was carried on, first, by the Phœnicians; secondly, by the Romans; and lastly, by the inhabitants of Gaul with the Scilly Islands, whose natives have been represented to us as living like *Nomades*, in a very uncivilized state, on

---

* Various other names have been given to these islands. According to *Solinus*, they were called *Hesperides* by the Greeks, and were first discovered by Hamilco, a Carthaginian. They are also styled *Ostrymnides* by *Festus Avienus;* and by the Romans *Sillinæ Insulæ*, from which the modern English title of Scilly, has probably been derived. *Instantius*, a factious heretic, was banished thither by the Emperor Maximus. " *Ad Sillinam insulam ultra Britanniam deportatus*" *(Sulp. Severus).* Richard of Cirencester also gives them the name of *Sygdiles.*

+ *Qui Belerium Britanniæ promontorium accolunt, hospitales sunt apprimè, et propter mercatorum illic commercia mansuetiore vitæ cultu. Hi stannum, terrâ, quæ illud parturit, solerti opere subactâ, conficiunt. Quæ cum petricosa sit, venas quasdem habet terrestres, e quibus erutum metalli proventum liquefaciunt et expurgant. Talorum deinde modo conformatum in quandam Britanniæ adjectam insulam cui nomen Ictis, deportant. Inde stannum ab incolis emtum in Galliam mercatores transferunt, et xxx dierum itinere per Galliam pedestri sarcinas equis impositas, ad Rhodani tandem ostia deportant.* Lib. 5, p. 347.

‡ *Supra Lusitanorum provinciam multum stannei est metalli, in insulis videlicet in Oceano Hiberiæ objacentibus, quas idcirco Cassiterides nuncupant. Multum quoque ejus, in oppositam Galliæ continentem ex insulâ Britannicâ transportatur, quod per Celticæ mediterranea equis mercatores ad Massylienses et Narbonensium urbem deferunt.*

the produce of their flocks and herds, and receiving salt, pottery, and articles of brass in exchange for their metals.

The progress of population may still be traced from this remote corner along the western shores of our island. Numerous remains of stone circles, crom- lechs, rocking stones, and *tumuli* still exist in the Scilly islands, and are con- tinued along the coasts of Cornwall and Dorset to the widely extended plains of Wiltshire; all, from their rudeness, bespeaking a very ancient, and I may pronounce, a Celtic origin, and corresponding in a very striking degree with those on the opposite shores of our mother-country, Gaul.

But with respect to the precise æra of the first colonization of Britain, we have no certain *data*. Richard of Cirencester, to whom we are indebted for many interesting particulars respecting the early history of our island, places it at a thousand years before Christ. " *A. M. 3000. Circà hæc tempora cultam et habitatam primùm Britanniam arbitrantur nonnulli, cum illam salutarent Græci Phænicesque mercatores.*" And the same author introduces the Belgæ into our island, A. M. 3650. This nation (according to *Cæsar)* was situated next to the Germans, who inhabit beyond the Rhine, and with whom they differed very materially in civil and religious matters ; " *neque Druides habent qui rebus divinis præsint, neque sacrificiis student.*" Their population was so great, that they could enumerate 300,000 men capable of bearing arms : " *Quam numerosa horum mortalium frequentia sit, eo patet indicio, quòd ex Belgis qui ferre arma pote- rant, 300,000 millia censeri dicebantur. Strabo,* Lib. 4.

The invasion of Britain by *Julius Cæsar,* which has been fixed by Dr. Halley in the year LV. before Christ, opens to us a new epocha in history. Tradition, often fabulous, now ceases, and History begins to rest upon a more solid foundation; yet the mass of information collected from the writings of this cele- brated Roman will be found to be very scanty, and by no means so satisfactory as we might reasonably expect from the *stylus* of one, who, in the same per- sonage, united the talent both of Conqueror and Historian.

He informs us, that the inland parts of Britain are inhabited by those, whom he reports to be natives of the soil. The sea coast is peopled with Belgæ, drawn thither by the love of war and plunder. These last, passing over from different parts, and settling in the country, still retain the names of the states from whence they are descended. The island is well peopled, full of houses built after the manner of the Gauls, and abounds in cattle. They use brass money, and iron rings of a certain weight. The provinces remote from the sea pro- duce tin, and those upon the coast, iron ; but the latter in no great quantity.

Their brass is all imported. All kinds of wood grow here the same as in Gaul, except the fir and beech tree. They think it unlawful to feed upon hares, pullets, or geese; yet they breed them up for their diversion and pleasure. The climate is more temperate than Gaul, and the colds less intense.

The inhabitants of Kent, which lies wholly on the sea coast, are the most civilized of all the Britons, and differ but little in their manner, from the Gauls. The greater part of those within the country never sow their lands, but live on flesh and milk, and go clad in skins. All the Britons in general paint themselves with woad, which gives a bluish cast to the skin, and makes them look dreadful in battle. They are long haired, and shave every part of the body except the head and upper lip. Ten or twelve of them live together, having their wives in common, especially brothers, or parents and children amongst themselves; but the issue is always ascribed to him who first espoused the mother.

" *Britanniæ pars interior ab iis incolitur quos natos in insulâ ipsâ, memoriâ proditum est. Maritima pars ab iis, qui prædæ ac belli inferendi causâ, ex Belgis transierant, qui omnes ferè iis nominibus civitatum adpellantur, quibus orti ex civitatibus eò pervenerunt, et bello inlato ibi remanserunt, atque agros colere cœperunt. Hominum est infinita multitudo, creberrimaque ædificia, ferè Gallicis consimilia; pecorum magnus numerus. Utuntur aut ære, aut taleis ferreis ad certum pondus examinatis, pro nummo. Nascitur ibi plumbum album in mediterraneis regionibus, in maritimis ferrum; sed ejus exigua copia est; ære utuntur importato. Materia cujusque generis est, ut in Galliâ, præter fagum et abietem. Leporem et gallinam et anserem gustare, fas non putant, hæc tamen alunt, animi voluptatisque causâ. Loca sunt temperatiora, quam in Galliâ, remissioribus frigoribus.*

Ex his omnibus longè sunt humanissimi, qui Cantium incolunt; quæ regio est maritima omnis; neque multum a Gallicâ differunt consuetudine. Interiores plerique frumenta non serunt; sed lacte et carne vivunt, pellibusque sunt vestiti. Omnes verò se Britanni vitro inficiunt, quod cæruleum efficit colorem, atque hoc horridiore sunt in pugnâ adspectu, capilloque sunt promisso, atque omni parte corporis rasa, præter caput et labrum superius. Uxores habent deni duodenique inter se communes, et maximè fratres cum fratribus, parentesque cum liberis; sed, si qui sunt ex his nati, eorum habentur liberi, quo primum virgo quæque deducta est." [*Cæsar, Lib. V.*]

Britain, however, was but very imperfectly known to the Romans at the period of Cæsar's invasion, by means of those merchants who resorted to its ports for commerce. " *Omnia fere Gallis erant incognita; neque enim temerè præter mercatores illò adit quisquam; neque iis ipsis quidquam, præter oram maritimam, at-*

E

que eas regiones, quæ sunt contrà Gallias, notum est.*   Nor was their knowledge of our island much encreased by the short residence, and imperfect conquest of the Roman general ; who may be said rather to have discovered, than subdued it : *ostendisse potius quam tradidisse.*

From these records we may collect the following interesting particulars respecting the ancient Britons. That the interior part of Britain was inhabited by those said to have been born in the country, and who, I presume, were of Celtic origin ; and the sea coast by the warlike race of Belgæ, who had emigrated thither for the sake of plunder, and introduced with them the names of their own cities and tribes.+   We are informed that the population was great, that buildings were numerous, and cattle abundant, and that the houses resembled those of Gaul. The historian alludes to the commerce carried on in tin with the western parts of our island, and tells us, that the Britons had but little iron, and imported all articles of brass ; and that all kinds of wood grew there except the beech and fir tree. ‡   In speaking of the natives, he points out those of Kent as the most civilized, and mentions a similarity of manners with the inhabitants of Gaul. They had not applied themselves to agriculture, but led the life of *Nomades,* clothing themselves with skins, and subsisting on the produce of their flocks and herds. They shaved the whole of their bodies except the head and upper lip, and stained themselves with a certain paint. They lived in clans, and had their wives in common.

I shall not endeavour to trace the progress of the Roman armies that for many years were engaged in the conquest of Britain, nor to mark the immediate consequences of their victories ; § my present study is to consider Britain in its

---

* No more genuine account of the early population of Britain could be procured by the historian *Tacitus,* who, in his life of Agricola, says, " *Britanniam qui mortales initio coluerunt, indigenæ an advecti, parum compertum ; in universum tamen æstimanti, Gallos vicinum solum occupasse, credibile est.*

+ Thus we see the Attrebates from Artois, settled in Berkshire ; the Belgæ in Hampshire ; the Bibroci and Bibracte from Autun, in Berkshire ; the Brigantes in Yorkshire ; the Cenomani from the district of Le Manseau, in Norfolk and Suffolk ; the Ædui from Lower Burgundy, in Somersetshire ; and the Morini from Boulogne, in Devonshire. We have also Menapia in Pembrokeshire, and the Menapii on the opposite coast of Ireland, as well as on the shores of the Rhine, the Cimbri in the west of England, the Parisii in the north, &c. &c.

‡ In my notes on *Giraldus Cambrensis* I had occasion to notice fully this passage, and to quote the authority of Mr. Whitaker, who says, " that firs appear as early as the third century in the unromanized regions of Caledonia and Ireland, as the *acknowledged aborigines* of the country, being frequently mentioned in the poems of the ancient bards of each country. The fir is also often discovered in the mosses together with the birch and oak, and in such mosses as appear to the present period actually traversed by the roads of the Romans, particularly in that of Failsworth, where Mr. Whitaker himself dug it up three yards under the very gravel which formed the ridge of the Roman causeway.

§ In my introduction to the Itinerary of *Giraldus Cambrensis,* I have illustrated very fully the successive campaigns of the Romans in our island, from those of Julius Cæsar to that of Agricola.

earliest and most savage state; and perhaps a more just, spirited, and appropriate account could not have been given of our primitive Britons, than the following one given of the *Fenni*, by the masterly hand of the historian *Tacitus*. " *Fennis mira feritas, fœda paupertas ; non arma, non equi, non penates ; victui herba, vestitui pelles, cubile humus ; sola in sagittis spes, quas inopiâ ferri, ossibus asperant. Idemque venatus viros pariter ac fœminas alit. Passim enim comitantur, partemque prædæ petunt. Nec aliud infantibus ferarum imbriumque suffugium, quam ut in aliquo ramorum nexu contegantur ; huc redeunt juvenes, hoc senum receptaculum. Sed beatius arbitrantur, quam ingemere agris, illaborare domibus, suas alienasque fortunas spe metuque versare. Securi adversus homines, securi adversus Deos, rem difficillimam adsecuti sunt, ut illis ne voto quidem opus esset. [Tacitus Germania.]*

" Nothing can equal the ferocity of the *Fenni*, nor is there any thing so disgusting as their filth and poverty. Without arms, without horses, and without a fixed place of abode, they lead a vagrant life ; their food the common herbage ; the skins of beasts their only cloathing ; and the bare earth their resting place. For their chief support they depend on their arrows, to which, for want of iron, they prefix a pointed bone. The women follow the chase in company with the men, and claim their share of the prey. To protect their infants from the fury of wild beasts, and the inclemency of the weather, they make a kind of cradle amidst the branches of trees interwoven together, and they know no other expedient. The youth of the country have the same habitation, and amidst the trees old age is rocked to rest. Savage as this way of life may seem, they prefer it to the drudgery of the field, the labour of building, and the painful vicissitudes of hope and fear, which always attend the defence, and the acquisition of property. Secure against the passions of men, and fearing nothing from the anger of the gods, they have attained that uncommon state of felicity, in which there is no craving left to form a single wish." (*Murphy*)

Such, probably, was the way of life, and such the habits of those Britons who, in ancient times, resided upon our Wiltshire downs; and in treating of their towns and *tumuli*, I shall have an opportunity of marking the strong resemblance between them and the *Fenni*. The numerous and diversified *mausolea* of their dead, are every where apparent on the high grounds throughout England; but the habitations of the living have hitherto escaped unnoticed, and their discovery and investigation have, fortunately, been reserved for us. To the learned Dr. Stukeley we are much indebted for many interesting particulars respecting the stone temples at Abury and Stonehenge ; but practical experience has shewn us in how imperfect and unsatisfactory a manner his researches on barrows were conducted.   He has said but little on the fortresses and earthen works of the Britons, and the sites and remains of their towns have totally escaped his observation.   These will form a very prominent feature in my work, and must naturally excite the curiosity of the historian, and of every lover of antiquity.   To the general eye of observation, our Wiltshire downs appear as uninteresting as the moors in Yorkshire, or the fens in Lincolnshire; bleak, desolate, and shelterless; and affording only a scanty subsistence to the numerous flocks that are pastured on them: yet on these apparently barren and uninteresting spots we find the traces of an extensive British and Roman population; and the modern agriculturist confesses the superior excellence of those districts, heretofore inhabited, and which are still decidedly marked by a more verdant and fertile soil.

To the investigating eye and persevering hand of Mr. Cunnington, the discovery of these British towns is justly and solely due; a discovery totally new, and highly interesting; as by a certain and infallible index, we are enabled to trace the progress of British population from the rudest to the most civilized æra.

In traversing the extensive downs of Wiltshire, our attention is continually arrested by the works of the ancient Britons ; strong fortresses, circles, barrows, and other inequalities in the ground, which are evidently contrary to nature. Whoever has studied attentively the formation of our chalk hills, will observe, that all maiden downs, by which I mean all land untouched by the plough, bear a most even and smooth surface ; and whenever we find the appearance of that surface altered by excavations and other irregularities, we may there look with a prospect of success for the habitations of the Britons ; and especially if the herbage is of a more verdant hue, and the soil thrown up by the moles of a blacker tint.   There, on turning up the soil, will be found convincing proofs of ancient residence, such as animal bones, pottery, brick tiles, and coins of the lower Empire.   Such are the certain *indicia* which have led us to the discovery of numerous British towns and settlements ; and I flatter myself that the same *indicia* will lead to equally important discoveries in other counties where the plough has not annihilated them.

EARTHEN WORKS. Of these, our Wiltshire downs present a very numerous variety in camps, circles, and ditches.   It will be a very difficult matter to fix either the æra, or authors of the former, yet some general and probable rules may be laid down for ascertaining in some degree by what nation these camps were formed. When we find these works irregular in their form, simple in their construction, and with single and slight banks and ditches, we may, I think, safely pronounce them to be of genuine British origin, and the works of a barbarous and uncivilized people ; and when we find the intrenchments multiplied and distinguished by the vastness of their banks, the height of their keeps, and extreme depth of their ditches, we may suppose these to have been the works of people better versed in the art of castrametation. But whenever we meet with works of a square or oblong form, bounded by straight lines, and with rounded angles, we may indubitably pronounce them the work of the Romans. Of these latter works, which possess a superior degree of symmetry, our county has not yet afforded me one specimen, * though we have numerous proofs of the Romans having occupied the fortresses and towns of the Britons, first, probably, as victors, and afterwards as allies.

From a careful examination of these camps, I am of opinion that the greater part of them may claim a British origin ; but several of them bear the marks of innovation and alterations, which may have been made either by the Romans, Danes, or Saxons. The Danes were an active, predatory, and unsettled nation, always on the alert, continually flying from one part of the kingdom to another, and not remaining sufficiently long in any one place to erect such stupendous fortresses as some of those which have been vulgarly attributed to them. ✝ Besides, I meet with similar fortresses in the mountainous districts of Wales, where the Danes and Saxons were never known to penetrate. It occasionally happens that we hear of their battles in some spot adjoining these alpine fortresses; but we much oftener hear of them in the plains, and near cities, where none of these earthen works are to be found. I will not however deny, that, when hard pressed by the enemy, both Danes and Saxons might have occupied them, and might also have strengthened these British works with additional ramparts.

History enables us to speak with some degree of certainty about a few of our

---

* A fine example of Roman castrametation may be seen in the parish of Sodbury, Gloucestershire, and near the great road between Cross-hands and Petty France.

✝ Of the predatory and active excursions of the Danes, the annals of the year 1016 will furnish a singular example. We first find them at Cricklade in Wiltshire; then, about Christmas, in Warwickshire, Bucks, Bedford, Huntingdon, Lincoln, and Northumberland ; from whence they returned by the western coast to their ships before Easter. After Easter we find them in London ; then engaging with the Saxons at Pen, near Gillingham in Somersetshire; then at Sceorstan, London, and Brentford, and in Kent. They afterwards turned their arms against the East Saxons in Mercia, and were attacked by King Edmund at Ashdown. We hear of them afterwards in Radnorshire and Gloucestershire, before they returned to their winter quarters in London (*Chronicon Saxonicum*).

camps, though not of those within the limits of our county.   From the Saxon
Chronicle we learn, that in the year 901. King Edward the Elder, son of our
illustrious Alfred, encamped at Badbury, near Winbourn in Dorset: " *Equitavit
idcircò Rex cum exercitu, et castrametatus est apud Baddanbyrig juxtà Winburnam.*"
And as this fine camp, with its numerous and regular ramparts, clearly evinces
a great knowledge in the science of castrametation, we may with some degree
of certainty attribute it to the Saxons; though, from its commanding height,
and the barrows upon it, we have reason to suppose that an original British
work once existed on the same spot.

In the neighbourhood of Andover, in Hampshire, I find two other camps
mentioned by *Polydore Virgil*, which still exist.   The one, called Bury-hill,
is situated on an eminence west of Andover, and is strongly fortified by nature
as well as art; the other, called Barksbury camp, with a single *vallum*, is nearly
square, and situated in the plain: a small rivulet divides the two camps,
the former of which was occupied by Edmund the Saxon, and the latter by
Canute the Dane: " *Canuto festinante cum Edmundo confligere, quem intereà
audierat, Andoveram, qui est pagus ad XV. milliaria, prope Sarisberiam, reversum
esse ; quò ubi pervenit, castra in conspectu hostium plano loco posuit, suosque in aciem
eduxit.*

By an attentive examination of the numerous earthen works with which our
island abounds, and a competent knowledge of the Danish and Saxon histories,
much authentic information might be procured respecting these monuments of
antiquity, and in many instances their origin, as well as the alterations which
they have undergone, might be ascertained.

I have given these camps the first notice, as being the most conspicuous,
though not the most ancient of our earthen works; for the circles and *tumuli*
may certainly claim a much higher antiquity.   Of these circles, we find several dispersed about our downs, and almost generally on high and commanding
situations.   The slightness of the *vallum* and ditch that surround them, as well
as the smallness of their area, clearly indicate them not to have been constructed
for any military purpose, but most probably for some civil or religious object.
In countries abounding with stone, as in Wales and Cornwall, the circle was
defined by rude upright stones; but in our chalk hills, where nature produces
nothing larger than a flint, or an occasional sarsen stone, the circle is described
by a bank, and ditch.   At Abury and Stonehenge the two were united, and the
circles of stones encompassed by an earthen *vallum* and ditch.

The history of those numerous banks and ditches which intersect our island in various directions has never been clearly demonstrated : they have been generally called boundary ditches, and have been attributed to the Belgæ, Romans, and Saxons. Our county possesses, in the celebrated Wansdyke, the most stupendous of these ramparts, which we have traced in the most satisfactory manner from Maes Knoll in Somersetshire, to Savernake Forest near Marlborough in Wiltshire. But the experience I have lately gained by traversing our downs in search of British antiquities, enables me to make a distinction in these banks, and to divide them into two classes. Under the first may be placed the large ramparts of Wansdyke, and Bokerley ditch near Woodyates, which have a very high *vallum* on one side only, and were indubitably constructed for boundaries, like the celebrated dyke raised by Offa King of Mercia in Wales. I shall consider the second, as covered ways, or lines of communication from one British town to another : their formation is totally different from the former, and evidently not raised for barriers of defence ; the bank being of an equal height on each side, and the area of the ditch broader in proportion, and flatter. The frequent occurrence of these on our downs, has opened a wide field for reflection and conjecture ; much time was spent in doubt and uncertainty, till at length, their connexion with the British towns became apparent, and ascertained most clearly the original cause of their formation and destination.

TUMULI OR BARROWS. These are certainly the most conspicuous as well as the most ancient of our British antiquities ; and will become more interesting, as their history has never been sufficiently investigated. A very ingenious and elaborate work was published in the year 1793, by Mr. Douglas, under the title of NENIA BRITANNICA, in which he has detailed, with great perspicuity, the researches made by himself and others on this subject ; but these researches were confined to the southern coast of England, and chiefly to the county of Kent. When we compare the articles found by him, with those collected in our Museum, we shall evidently perceive them to be of a much more modern date ; and indeed the author fixes the æra of his barrows between the year 182 and 742. I shall have frequent occasion to observe in how imperfect a manner the operations of Dr. Stukeley were conducted.

" The most simple and natural kind of sepulchral monument, and therefore the most ancient and universal, consists in a mound of earth, or heap of stones, raised over the remains of the deceased. Of such monuments, mention is made in the book of Joshua, and in the poems of Homer, Virgil, and Horace ; and of such, instances occur in every part of this kingdom, especially in those elevated and sequestered situations, where they have been neither defaced by agriculture nor inundations.

" It has often been a subject of surprise to me, that in an age marked by its taste for antiquarian researches, greater attention should not have been paid to these most ancient and genuine records of past ages, so far at least, as to ascertain to which of the successive inhabitants of this island they are to be ascribed, or whether, in fact, they are the work of more than one people.* This can only be done by an examination of the contents of several of them in different counties, and in different situations, by persons whose learning, ingenuity, and attention qualify them for the task. In searching, however, into these rude memorials of our forefathers, the true antiquary will ever respect their remains; and whilst he enters into their views by endeavouring to revive their memory, he will also, as far as possible, consult their wishes, in leaving to their bones their ancient place of sepulture."✝

In our examination of this subject, we must not consider every barrow as a mere *tumulus*, or mound, loosely and fortuitously thrown up, but must rather view them as works of evident design, and executed with the greatest symmetry and precision.‡ That a correct idea may be formed of our barrows, and their great variety recognized, I have thought proper to describe them by a series of engravings, taken from existing specimens in the neighbourhood of Stonehenge, which district affords a far greater variety of sepulchral designs than any other I have yet observed throughout England.

I. The LONG BARROW, from its singular form and superior size, claims the first notice. They differ considerably in their structure, as well as dimensions: some of them resemble an egg cut in two lengthways, and the convex side placed uppermost; some are almost of a triangular form; whilst others are thrown up in a long ridge of a nearly equal breadth at each end; but we

* After the result of ten years experience and constant research, we are obliged to confess our total ignorance as to the authors of these sepulchral memorials: we have evidence of the very high antiquity of our Wiltshire barrows, but none respecting the tribes to whom they appertained, that can rest on a solid foundation.

✝ These remarks occurred to me in the 60th volume of the Gentleman's Magazine, for the year 1790, and coincide so truly with my own sentiments on the subject, that I have thought proper to insert them. In the numerous barrows we have opened, due reverence has been paid to the remains of the mighty dead: their bones and ashes have been carefully collected, and deposited again in the same tomb, together with a coin, marking the time when they were investigated.

‡ From the Celtic root *tumba*, we may trace the words, *tombeau*, and *tomb*. The word *Barrow*, is derived from the Saxon *Beorg*, *Beorh*, or *Byrig*, which may be applied. either to a town or fortress; a hill, or a mound. Hence, *Byrigenn, sepultura; borough* and *bury*. We find numerous places throughout England terminating with *bury*; and near such places, I have almost invariably found some ancient camp, or earthen work, which gave rise probably to such termination.

1. LONG BARROW.

3. BELL BARROW.   2. BOWL BARROW.

4. DRUID BARROW.

P. Crocker del.   Jⁿ Basire sc.

Published by W. Miller, Albemarle Street, London, Janʸ 1. 1810.

find more generally one end of these barrows broader than the other, and that broad end pointing towards the east: we also more frequently find them placed on elevated situations, and standing singly; though in some of the groups of barrows near Stonehenge, we find one long barrow introduced amongst the others. They differ very materially from the circular barrows in their contents, for we have never found any brass weapons or trinkets deposited with the dead, nor the primary interment deposited within the funeral urn. With a very few exceptions, we have always found skeletons on the floor of the barrow, and at the broad end, lying in a confused and irregular manner, and near one or more circular cists cut in the native chalk, and generally covered with a pile of stones or flints. In other parts of the *tumulus* we have found stags horns, fragments of the rudest British pottery, and interments of burnt bones near the top. These *indicia* attest the high antiquity of the long barrows; and though we clearly perceive a singularity of outline in the construction of them, as well as a singularity in the mode of burial, we must confess ourselves at a loss to determine, or even to conjecture, for what particular purpose these immense mounds were originally raised.

II. Bowl Barrow. This is, I think, the most ordinary shaped barrow, and more frequently met with than any of the others. On Mendip Hills in Somersetshire they abound; they have a very slight ditch round them in some places, but in others none at all.

III. Bell Barrow. This, from the elegance of its form, seems to have been a refinement on the Bowl Barrow: they abound in the neighbourhood of Stonehenge, and are moulded with the greatest accuracy and symmetry.

IV. Druid Barrow. This species, so decidedly different from either of the preceding, having owed the above appellation to Dr. Stukeley, I shall continue it by the same title; but not because I can subscribe to his idea of their having belonged to the Druids; for I have strong reason to suppose that these *tumuli* were appropriated to the female tribes. The outward *vallum* with the ditch within, is most beautifully moulded: in the area we sometimes see one, two, or three mounds, which in most instances have been found to contain diminutive articles, such as small cups, small lance heads, amber, jet, and glass beads.

V. Druid Barrow. Second Class. In the external form these resemble the preceding, but their circumference is not in general so large: the *tumulus* within rises gradually to a point from the edge of the *vallum,* and this constitutes the principal difference.

G

VI. POND BARROW. I can form no conjecture about these *tumuli* that carries with it the least plausibility; they differ totally from all the others, and resemble an excavation made for a pond; they are circular, and formed with the greatest exactness; having no protuberance within the area, which is perfectly level. We have dug into several, but have never discovered any pottery or sepulchral remains: though I have heard that an interment of burnt bones was found within the area of one of them on Lake Downs. We generally find one or more of these barrows in the detached groups, and on Lake Downs there is a cluster of four or five of them all together. I once thought that the Britons might have adopted this method of preparing their barrows for interment, by thus marking out the circle, and throwing out the earth on the sides, but the very great regularity of the vallum militates against this idea.

VII. TWIN BARROW. This fine specimen is taken from the neighbourhood of Everley, and is the most perfect I have met with. They are not very common, and by their being enclosed within the same circle, seem to denote the interments of two people nearly connected by the endearing ties of friendship or consanguinity.

VIII. CONE BARROW. This singular specimen is also taken from the neighbourhood of Everley, and is the only one of the sort I have yet seen. The *tumulus* rises immediately from the ditch, and the *apex* is higher and more pointed.

IX. BROAD BARROW. This resembles in a great degree the Bowl Barrow; but is considerably broader and flatter at the top. This example is taken from the group on Wilsford Down, and is most probably the very barrow on which the French prophets harangued the multitude.

X. DRUID BARROW, No. 3. This very singular barrow, between Amesbury and Everley, may be classed as a Druid Barrow, but it differs very materially from any *tumulus* I have yet seen, the outward *vallum* being much higher.

XI. DRUID BARROW, No. 4. This *tumulus*, adjoining the former, may be also deemed an unique. The area is perfectly flat, and rises beautifully from the *vallum;* indeed, I have seen no barrow formed with greater exactness.

XII. LONG BARROW, No. 2. This *tumulus*, in shape, resembles a small Long Barrow, but differs from the larger kind, by having a ditch all around it. This specimen also is taken from the neighbourhood of Everley.

The nature of our barrows having been hitherto so very imperfectly described, I have thought it necessary to enter rather minutely into the subject. Many of my readers will be astonished to see so great a variety of design in the sepulchral memorials of the ancient Britons; and will regret, with me, that their

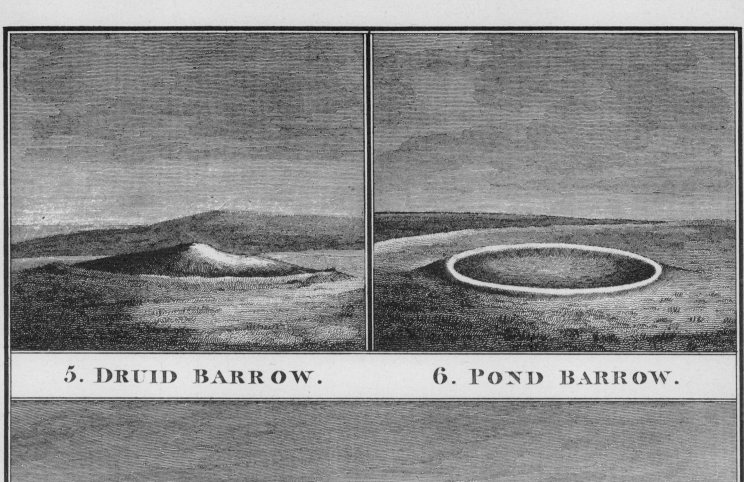

5. DRUID BARROW.   **6. POND BARROW.**

7. TWIN BARROW.

8. CONE BARROW.   **9. BROAD BARROW.**

P. Crocker del.   J.ᶠ Basire sc.

Publiſhed by W. Miller, Albemarle Street, London. Janʸ 1.1810.

10. DRUID BARROW.

11. DRUID BARROW.

12. LONG BARROW.

P. Crocker del.

J^s Basire sc.

Published by W. Miller, Albemarle Street, London, Jany 1. 1810.

history cannot be more satisfactorily ascertained. In the engravings, I have marked the decided forms, and the most prominent varieties, but many more of the latter might have been given.

Having described the external form of the sepulchral mounds, I shall now investigate their interior, and point out the different modes of burial adopted by the Britons. It has been the established opinion both of ancient and modern writers, that the custom of burying the body *entire* was the most primitive. Mr. Whitaker, in his *History of Manchester*, observes, " that the mode of interment among the primitive Gauls and Britons was either by consigning the remains entire, and undefaced to the ground; or by previously reducing them to ashes. The former mode is undoubtedly the most natural and obvious, and must therefore have been the original form of sepulture in the world. The latter is evidently a refinement upon the former, introduced at first, in all probability, to prevent any accidental indignities, or to preclude any deliberate outrages upon the venerable remains of the dead.

The classical authors are also of opinion, that the most ancient mode of interment was that of depositing the body *entire* in the earth. *Pliny* informs us, that the custom of *cremation* was adopted at a subsequent period, and originated from the fear of having the bones disturbed : as was the case in the Cornelian family at Rome, when *Sylla* the Dictator ordered his body to be burned, lest the friends of *Caius Marius*, whose bones he had ordered to be taken up, should retaliate on him by the same mode of revenge.* By the laws of the XII. Tables, we learn, that the two ceremonies of burying and burning were practised at the same period : " *In urbe ne sepelito, neve urito.*" But according to *Herodotus*, the custom of burning the dead did not prevail either amongst the Persians or the Ægyptians. The former venerated *fire* as a deity, and therefore thought it profane to feed a divinity with human carcases : the latter abhorred it, being fully persuaded that *fire* is a voracious animal, which devours whatever it can seize, and when saturated, finally expires with what it has consumed.

* *Ipsum cremare apud Romanos non fuit veteris instituti : terrâ condebantur. At postquam longinquis bellis obrutos erui cognovere, tunc institutum. Et tamen multæ familiæ priscos servavere ritus : sicut in Corneliâ nemo ante Syllam Dictatorem traditur crematus. Idque voluisse, veritum talionem, eruto C. Marii cadavere. Plinius, Lib. vii. cap. 54.*

" *At mihi quidem antiquissimum sepulturæ genus id fuisse videtur, quo apud Xenophontem Cyrus utitur. Redditur enim terræ corpus, et ita locatum ac situm, quasi operimento matris obducitur. Eodemque ritu regem nostrum Numam conditum accepimus : gentemque Corneliam usque ad memoriam nostram hâc sepulturâ scimus esse usam. C. Marii sitas reliquias apud Anienem, dissipari jussit Sylla victor ; quod haud scio an timens suo corpori posse accidere, primus e patriciis Corneliis igni voluit cremari.*" *Cicero de legibus*, Lib. ii.

From the researches made in our British *tumuli*, we have every reason to suppose that the two ceremonies of burying the body entire, and of reducing it to ashes by fire, prevailed at the same time. In each of these ceremonies, we distinguish a variety in the particular mode adopted. In the first, we have frequently found the body deposited within a cist, with the legs and knees drawn up, and the head placed towards the north. This I conceive to be the most ancient form *of burial*, and the same alluded to in the Holy Scriptures; " And when Jacob had made an end of commanding his sons, he *gathered up* his feet into the bed, and yielded up the ghost, and was *gathered* unto his people."

The second mode of burying the body *entire* is evidently proved to be of a much later period, by the position of the head and body, and by the articles deposited with them. In this case we find the body extended at *full length*, the heads placed at random in a variety of directions, and instruments of iron accompanying them.

Two modes of *cremation* seem also to have been adopted; at first, the body was burnt, the ashes and bones collected, and deposited on the floor of the barrow, or in a cist excavated in the native chalk. This, being the most simple, was probably the most primitive custom practised by the ancient Britons. The funeral urn, in which the ashes of the dead were secured, was the refinement of a later age. The bones, when burnt, were collected, and placed within the urn, which was deposited with its mouth *downwards*, in a cist cut in the chalk. Sometimes we have found them with their mouth *upwards*, but these instances are not very common: we have also frequently found remains of the linen cloth which enveloped the bones, and a little brass pin which secured them.

Of these different modes of interment, I am of opinion that the one of burying the body entire, with the legs gathered up, was the most ancient; that the custom of cremation succeeded, and prevailed with the former; and that the mode of burying the body entire, and extended at full length, was of the latest adoption.✝

* Before the arrival of *Odin*, the Scandinavians did nothing more than lay the dead body together with his arms, under a little heap of earth and stones; but he introduced into the north new customs, attended with more magnificence. In succeeding ages the Danes were wont to raise funeral piles, and reduce the bodies to ashes, which were collected together into an urn, and deposited under a little mound of earth. But this foreign custom was never quite universal, and the old rite took place according to conjecture, within five or six hundred years. These two funeral ceremonies have distinguished two distinct æra in the ancient northern history. The first was called the AGE OF FIRE, and the second the AGE OF HILLS, which last prevailed till Christianity triumphed in the north. *Mallet's Northern Antiq. Vol.* I. p. 341.

Sepulchral Urns. Of these, our barrows have produced a very great variety; and as I have strong reason to suppose that they were appropriated to distinct purposes, it is necessary they should be discriminated.

The first that claims our attention, is the large urn in which the bones of the deceased, when burned, were deposited, and which we find sometimes in an upright, but much more frequently in a reversed position; and this I shall call the sepulchral, or funereal urn.

The second differs from the former both in shape and design, and being found with skeletons, and containing neither ashes, burned bones, or trinkets, we may conclude that they were appropriated to some other purpose. A very ancient custom prevailed, and even still is practised amongst savage nations, of depositing articles of food with the dead. And as I think the Britons very probably destined these vases for the same purpose, I shall denominate them Drinking Cups. These vases are most frequently found with skeletons, and are placed at the head or feet. They are always neatly ornamented with varied patterns, and hold about a quart in measure.

The third species of vase differs very decidedly from either of the other two; is smaller in its proportions, and more fantastic in its shape and ornaments. It is in general too diminutive to have contained the ashes, or even the *viaticum* of the deceased. We frequently find them perforated on the sides, and one of them in the bottom, like a cullender, which circumstance induces me to think that they were filled with balsams and precious ointments, and suspended over the funeral pile. I shall therefore distinguish these vases by the title of Incense Cups, as in the description of the numerous *tumuli* we have opened, it is absolutely necessary that these urns, so different in their nature, should be properly and distinctly discriminated.

The name of *Thuribulum* might also be given to this small vase, as containing the *thus*, or frankincense, which was burned at funerals. *Lucan*, in recording those of *Pompey*, says,

> " *Non pretiosa petit cumulato thure sepulcra*
> *Pompeius, fortuna, tuus: non pinguis ad astra*
> *Ut ferat e membris Eoos fumus odores.*"

The same ceremony is mentioned by several other ancient authors.

> " *Cur nardo flammæ non oluere meæ!*"   *Propertins.*
> " *Sparge mero cineres, et odoro perlue nardo*
> *Hospes, et adde rosis balsama puniceis.*"   *Ausonius.*

This custom was continued to so late a period as the time of the Emperor *Justinian*, whose funeral rites have been thus commemorated:

> " *Thura Sabæa cremant, fragrantia mella locatis*
> *Infundunt pateris, et odoro balsama succo.*
> *Centum aliæ species, unguentaque mira feruntur,*
> *Tempus in æternum sacrum servantia corpus.*"

In the poems of Homer we find numerous allusions to sepulchral *tumuli*; and on the shores of the Hellespont many of them still exist. In recording the funeral obsequies of Patroclus, ordered by Achilles, the poet says,

> " The Greeks obey! where yet the embers glow,
> Wide o'er the pile the sable wine they throw,
> And deep subsides the ashy heap below.
> Next the white bones his sad companions place,
> With tears, collected in the golden vase.
> The sacred relicks to the tent they bore;
> The Urn a veil of linen cover'd o'er.
> That done, they bid the sepulchre aspire,
> And cast the deep foundations round the pyre:
> High in the midst they heap the swelling bed
> Of rising earth, memorial of the dead."   Iliad, Book xxiii.

Propertius, in one of his elegies, thus alludes to the custom of cremation, and to the sepulchral *earthen* urn:

> " *Deinde ubi suppositus cinerem me fecerit ardor,*
> *Accipiat manes parvula testa meos.*"

Of the SEPULCHRAL URN we have a fine specimen in the Frontispiece to this work; of the DRINKING CUP, in Plate IX.; and of the INCENSE CUPS examples will be given, of the same size as the originals, in Plates XI. and XII.

Though we are informed by *Strabo*, that pottery was one of the articles of barter between the Britons and the Phœnicians, I cannot persuade myself that any of the vases found in our Wiltshire *tumuli* could have been transported thither from so civilized a region. They are composed of very coarse materials, rudely formed, before the use of the turner's lathe was known, and so imperfectly baked, that I have seen one of them taken entire out of a barrow, and shiver into a thousand pieces by the mere action of the atmosphere upon it. The patterns with which they are ornamented display a great variety of design; and are evidently worked by hand, not by a mould. They seem to be indented on the clay when in a moist state, by some pointed instrument, and to have been imperfectly baked, either in the sun, or the fire of the funeral pile.

Such, without exception, have been the urns found in our barrows; all claiming a rude and remote British origin. After the conquest of our island by the Romans, a new species of pottery was introduced amongst the Britons, beautifully moulded, finely glazed, and richly ornamented, numerous fragments of which are to be found in all the villages of the Romanized Britons, but not the smallest morsel in any of the *tumuli* we have opened.*

The extreme rudeness of our sepulchral urns, as well as the articles deposited within our barrows, evidently prove their very high antiquity, and mark them of an æra prior to the Roman invasion. In the earliest ages of population, each nation was obliged to make use of those articles which the nature of their own soil supplied, either for domestic or military purposes: thus we find arrow heads of flint and bone, and hatchets of stone deposited with the dead; all of which, we may fairly conclude, were made at home; but the beads of glass, jet, and amber, together with the numerous articles of brass, and the rare specimens of pure gold, must have been imported. Hitherto our researches have furnished very few instruments of iron, and those denote a much later period. Gold and brass were known before iron, as the poet *Lucretius* observes :

" *Sed prius æris erat quam ferri cognitus usus.*"

And *Cæsar* tells us, that on his arrival in Britain, he was informed that the island produced iron, but that brass was imported: " *Ferri exigua copia est; ære utuntur importato.*"

The custom of depositing the arms, &c. of the deceased in the sepulchral mound was practised by many nations of antiquity, and is thus recorded by the historian *Tacitus*, in his account of the German tribes : " *Funerum nulla ambitio; id solum observatur, ut corpora clarorum virorum certis lignis crementur. Struem rogi nec vestibus, nec odoribus cumulant; sua cuique arma, quorumdam igni et equus adjicitur. Sepulchrum cespes erigit.*" No vain pomp attends their funerals; but a particular kind of wood is made use of in burning the bodies of illustrious personages. The funeral pile is neither strewed with garments, nor fragrant

* The following abstract from the *Monumenta Kempiana*, giving an account of some sepulchral vases found in Goodman's Fields, London, very justly discriminates the Roman from the British pottery : " *Ante et post Cæsaris tempora ibi fuisse sepulchretum, ut credam, faciunt vasa hic reperta; quorum alia tenuia, firma, elegantia, rubentia, pulchrè nitentia, per omnia denique figulo Romano digna; alia è diverso, crassa, fragilia, malè tornata, colore fusco, surdoque, rudi manu subacto luto, et solibus excocto, potiùs quam rotâ formata, et fornaci imposita videntur.*"

spices. The arms of the deceased are committed to the flames, and sometimes his horse. A mound of turf constitutes the sepulchre."

Mr. Whitaker makes the following remarks on the same subject: " In all unlettered and uncommercial ages, when the disengaged activity of men ever carries a keen and military edge with it, and his great employ is necessarily war and the chase ; the weapons of both would be universally reposited with the dead, and we have a striking passage of Scripture to this purpose, which shews the custom to have been as general as the spirit of ambition or the profession of arms. " They shall not lie with the mighty, which are gone down to hell with their weapons of war, and they have laid their swords under their heads."

Herodotus has recorded the following curious circumstances attending the funerals of the Kings of Scythia : " The body having been transported through the different provinces of the kingdom, they come at last to the Gerrhi, who live in the remotest parts of Scythia, and amongst whom the sepulchres are. Here the corpse is placed upon a couch, round which, at different distances, daggers are fixed ; upon the whole are disposed pieces of wood covered with branches of willow. In some other part of the trench they bury one of the deceased's concubines, whom they previously strangle, together with the baker, the cook, the groom, his most confidential servant, his horses, the choicest of his effects, and, finally, some golden goblets, for they possess neither silver nor brass : to conclude all, they fill up the trench with earth ; and seem to be emulous in their endeavours to raise as high a mound as possible."

Melpomene, lxxi.

Having explained in as brief a manner as the subject would admit, the nature and contents of our British *tumuli*, it becomes necessary to add a few words respecting their origin, and to endeavour to trace them from the earliest to the latest period of their existence in our island.

I have no doubt but that the greater part of our Wiltshire barrows, and more particularly those in the neighbourhood of Abury and Stonehenge, were the sepulchral memorials of the Celtic and first Colonists of Britain ; and some may be appropriated to the subsequent colony of Belgæ who invaded our island. From all the researches we have hitherto made, I am induced to think that few or any interments in barrows took place in our county after the Roman invasion. But this ancient custom seems to have prevailed at a much later period in other parts of England. Mr. Douglas, in his NENIA BRITANNICA, has most amply illustrated these later barrows, and fixes their æra between the years 582 and

742. Having never seen these *tumuli*, I cannot make a just comparison between them and those in Wiltshire; but on referring to his plans and descriptions, I am thoroughly convinced they were constructed at a much later period than ours. The barrows are placed much nearer to each other, and are uniform in their shapes;* whereas our groups are not so thickly crowded together, and present a very great variety of design and art in their construction.

History informs us that Hubba the Dane, who was killed in the year 878, was buried under a *tumulus*, which still retains the name of that chieftain: " *Dani verò cadaver Hubbe inter occisos invenientes, illud cum clamore maximo sepelierunt, cumulum apponentes quem Hubbelowe vocaverunt, unde sic usque in hodiernum diem locus ille appellatus est, et est in comitatu Devoniæ.*"†

In the ninth century, a law of Charlemagne ordered all the bodies of Christians to be taken to the cemeteries, not to the barrows of the Pagans: "*Jubemus ut corpora Christianorum Saxonum ad cæmiteria ecclesiæ deferantur, et non ad tumulos Paganorum.*"

As late as the year 1016, cremation was made use of after the battle fought at Assandun in Essex, between the Saxon king Edmund, and the Danish king Canute: " *Deinde altero die uterque exercitus per otium cibum capiunt, ac hesterno prælio interfectos in unum congestos cremant.*" *(Polydore Virgil*, p. 170.) And the historian of Essex (Morant,) speaking of Ashdon, the supposed scene of action, says, " Standing monuments of this victory are the four hills or barrows, commonly called Bartlow hills. They were erected over the bodies of those who fell in this battle, according to the Danish custom. Some of them being opened, there were found, in a stone coffin, two bodies, one of which lay with his head towards the other's feet; also two other stone coffins, with pieces of bones in them, and many chains of iron like those on horses' bits."

Mr. Douglas doubts whether these barrows should bear their date from this battle, saying very justly, " that as Canute, four years afterwards, in 1020,

---

* See his ground plan of a group of barrows on Chatham downs near Canterbury, consisting of nearly one hundred *tumuli*.

† In Risdon's Survey of Devon, the same fact is thus related. " There is a pretty tale delivered touching the assaulting of the castle of Kenwith, where the Danes were so valiantly repulsed, that they lost 1200 men, with their captain Hubba. After which their overthrow, they buried him on the shore, and, according to the manner of northern nations, *piled on him a heap of copped stones*, as a trophy to his memorial, whereof the place took to name Hubbastone. And though the stones were long since swept away by the sea's incroaching, the name still remaineth on the strand near Appledore, as I conjecture; for more than the shadow, yea, even the very substance, with small alteration, being to this day known by the name of Whibblestone."

dedicated a church to the memory of those slain in the battle of Ashdon,* it is evident that he was converted at this period, and in all probability was at the time of the battle; if so, it is not likely he should raise these immense hills, which would have employed an active army for a considerable time, engaged on more important business, and which savoured so much of a Pagan rite of burial, which the Christian rites interdicted."

Mr. Whitaker is of opinion, that the custom of burying under *tumuli* survived the introduction of Christianity, and continued beyond the departure of the Romans; and Mr. Borlase, in his history of Cornwall, instances some Roman coins found in Goldvadnek barrow. Mr. Douglas also notices coins of the Lower Empire being found in some of the barrows near Chatham.

My present researches will be confined to my own county; though it is both my wish and intention to trace, at some future period, the connection between the Wiltshire *tumuli*, and those of other counties. By investigating the barrows in Wales, Scotland, and Ireland, and by extending our enquiries to the opposite shores of Britany and Normandy, much real information might be gained, and we might then hope, by the assistance of our spades and pickaxes, to ascertain many important facts, and to prove with some degree of certainty, the original colonization of our Island.

* *Hoc anno Rex [Canutus] proficiscebatur Assandunum, et permisit ibi exædificari Ecclesiam de lapide et cæmento, ob eorum hominum animas qui ibi interfecti fuerant.*

THE

HISTORY

OF

ANCIENT WILTSHIRE.

THE

HISTORY OF ANCIENT WILTSHIRE.

AD QUÆ NOSCENDA, ITER INGREDI, TRANSMITTERE MARE SOLEMUS, EA SUB OCULIS
POSITA NEGLIGIMUS ; SEU QUIA ITA NATURA COMPARATUM, UT PROXIMORUM
INCURIOSI, LONGINQUA SECTEMUR ; SEU QUOD OMNIUM RERUM CUPIDO LANGUES-
CIT, CUM FACILIS OCCASIO EST ; SEU QUOD DIFFERIMUS TAMQUAM SÆPE VISURI,
QUOD DATUR VIDERE QUOTIES VELIS CERNERE. *Plinii Epist. Lib.* viii. *Ep.* 20.

I T is natural, though frequently not the case, that our attention should be more particularly excited, and our enquiries more generally directed, towards those objects of curiosity that are nearest our own home. *Pliny*, in his epistles, has observed, " that we undertake long voyages both by sea and land to behold those curiosities, which, if placed before our eyes, we totally neglect. Whether it is, that we are so formed by nature as to be incurious about the nearer, and intent only upon the more distant objects ; or that our desire grows languid to such things, as may be enjoyed without any difficulty ; or that we are apt to defer taking a single view of what we can at any time see as often as we please."

The above remark has been often exemplified with my countrymen. Many an Englishman has, when viewing the magnificent temple of St. Peter's at Rome, been put to shame, when interrogated about its rival building, St. Paul's. And indeed I feel myself most sensibly this remark, as for many years my attention was directed solely to the antiquities of foreign countries, whilst those of my own were overlooked. But the tide has ebbed, and the stream is diverted into its native channel.

K

I shall commence my History with a description of the district nearest my own residence, because it is situated at one extremity of the county where the line of chalk hills terminates.*   My first station, therefore, will be STOURTON, the ancient baronial residence of a noble family, settled there before the Conquest,✝ and deriving its name and title from the river Stour, which rises in the demesne lands attached to the estate.

STATION I. STOURTON.

THE Parish of Stourton is very extensive, and comprehends within its limits the hamlets of Bonham, and of Gasper, both in Somerset.   On the borders of the latter is the small village of Pen, near which several battles have been fought between the Danes and Saxons, and which have been thus recorded in the Saxon Chronicle.

A. D. DCLVIII.   *Hoc anno, Cenwallus pugnabat apud Peonne contrà Britannos, et eos fugavit ad Pedridan.* [Petherton on the river Parret.]

A. D. MI.   In this year there were violent contests between the Danes and Saxons, first in the county of Hampshire, and afterwards at Exmouth in Devonshire, from whence the former marched easterly towards Pen, and burned it. " *Perrexerunt deinde ad Exanmutham, ita ut proficiscerentur uno itinere usque dum pervenissent ad Peonho, ubi Cola regis summus præfectus, et Eadsigus regis præfectus adversum eos constiterunt cum copiis quas possent congregare, ubi autem fugati erant,*

---

* In giving the history of the chalk hills, in Wiltshire, I may be said to give the history of those in the other western counties, and indeed of all the high lands, throughout England ; for they naturally were the first occupied by the earliest inhabitants, at a period when the vallies were either encumbered with wood, or inundated by water.   On all of them we find earthen works, and barrows, the sure vestiges of ancient population.

✝ I find in *Turner's History of the most remarkable Providences*, the following account of this place. Stourton (the seat of Lord Stourton,) was belonging to his family before the conquest.   They say after the victory at Battaile, William the Conqueror came in person, into the west, to receive their reddition ; that the Lord Abbot of Glastonbury, and the rest of the lords and grandees of the western parts, waited upon the Conqueror at Stourton House.

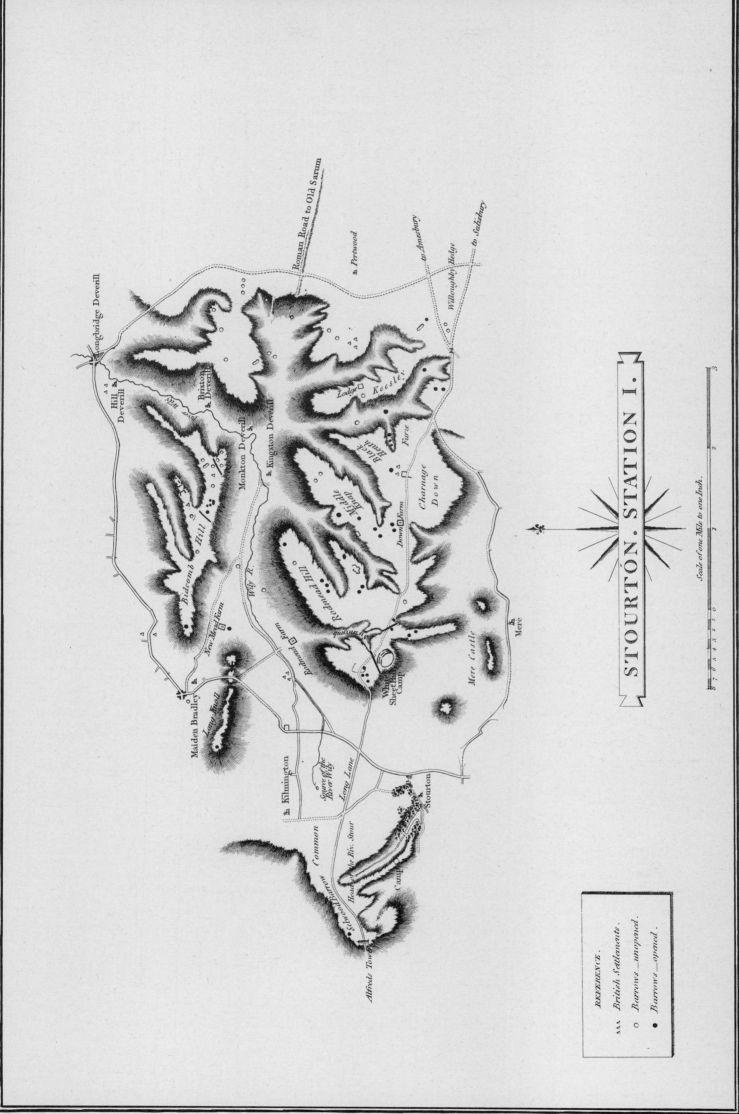

STOURTON. STATION I.

Scale of one Mile to one Inch.

REFERENCE.
ᴧᴧᴧ British Settlements.
 ○ Barrows — unopened.
 ● Barrows — opened.

Philip Crocker del.

London: Published by W.Miller. May 1811.

J.Cary. sculp.

Roman Road to Old Sarum

to Amesbury
Willoughby Hedge
to Salisbury

Longbridge Deverill
Hill Deverill
Brixton Deverill
Monkton Deverill
Kingston Deverill
Pertwood
Lodge
Keesley
Black Heath
Furze
Charnage Down
Down Farm
Middle Hill
Bidcomb Hill
New Mead Ham
Rodmead Farm
Rodmead Hill
Quarry
White Sheet Hill Camp
Mere Castle
Mere
Maiden Bradley
Long Knoll
Kilmington
Square of the Rever Way
Long Lane
Common
Headon the Riv: Stour
Schoodbarrow
Camp
Stourton
Alfreds Tower

Wily R.

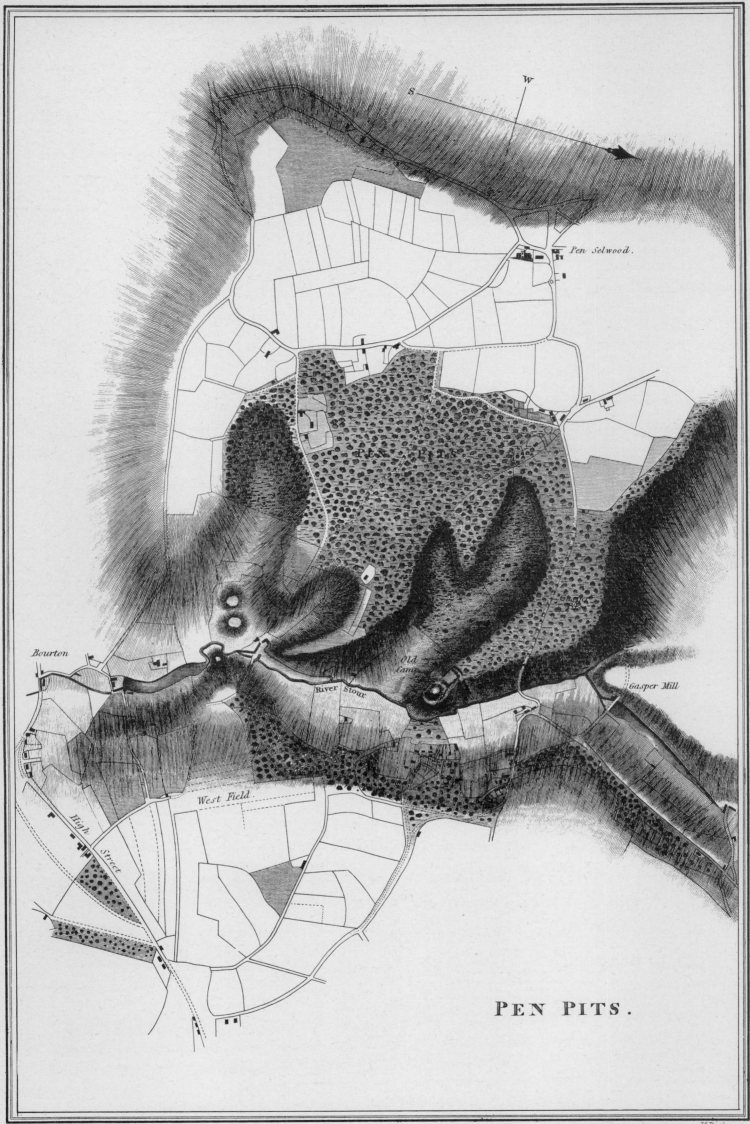

S

W

Pen Selwood.

PEN PITS

Bourton

Old Camp

River Stour

Gasper Mill

West Field

High Street

PEN PITS.

P. Crocker del.

J.ᵉ Basire sc.

Published by W. Miller, Albemarle Street, London, Jan.ʸ 1.1810.

et multi occidebantur, Danique loco stragis dominati sunt. Insequenti mane combus-
serunt villam apud Peonnho, et apud Clistune (Zeals Clevedon), *præter multas bonas*
villas quas nominare non possumus.

A. D. MXVI. *Eadmundus Rex invaserat occidentales Saxones, eique sese sub-*
didit omnis iste populus, nec multò post præliatus est cum exercitu [*Danorum*] *apud*
Peonnam juxta Gillingam.

Thus it appears that divers battles were fought at Pen, in the years 658,
1001, and 1016. The tradition of the last battle between Canute the Dane,
and Edmund the Saxon, seems to have been commemorated in the ancient door-
way of the parish church, where the heads of two crowned monarchs have
been placed as supporters to the arch, which is of the Saxon order, decorated
with zigzag ornaments, and a piece of rude sculpture in the centre. I should
not, however, have deviated from the plains of Wiltshire, merely to record the
desolating acts of a Danish or Saxon army, had not other objects of higher antiquity, and stronger interest claimed my attention. I allude to the very singular excavations called PEN PITS, which have been slightly mentioned,
but never sufficiently investigated, by former historians. The annexed plan
will best explain the situation of these extraordinary antiquities, which are
evidently the work of human art. It will be perceived, that the village of
Pen stands at the S. W. extremity of a large plain, surrounded on most sides
by steep and irregular ground; that part of the parish immediately adjoining
the village bears the most cultivated and improved appearance; some other
parts of the vale, watered by the river Stour, have also been brought into cultivation, but the greater proportion still remains in its wild and desert state,
covered with brush wood, though stripped of its oaks and timber.

The extent of land comprized within our plan, amounts to about seven hundred acres, of which nearly half have been brought into cultivation; but I
have no doubt but that the whole of this fine plain was originally excavated
into pits. In my own time the southern declivity of the hill, and another
large tract near it have been levelled, and a considerable allotment near Pen
Lodge is now undergoing the same process. These excavations seem also to
have extended along the eastern banks of the river Stour, as far as the farm
house at Bonham;* and from the appearance of the ground on the opposite

---

* In opening a stone quarry under Bonham hill, I found the ground had been moved before, and at a
considerable depth, were found some large pieces of charcoal, and some fragments of rude pottery. At a
short distance from the same spot, a labourer, in trenching his garden, found a small earthen vessel, which
was unfortunately destroyed; but from the description he gave me, it appears to have been British.

side, I have reason to think they were continued along the western banks of the said river.*

These pits are in their form like an inverted cone, and are very unequal in their dimensions; in some instances, we see double pits, divided by a slight partition of earth; and the soil in which they are dug, is of so dry a nature, that no water has been ever known to stagnate in them.

Various have been the opinions, and conjectures, of those who have examined these pits.

1. That the ground was thus excavated for the simple purpose of procuring stone.

2. That the Britons resorted to this spot for the querns or millstones, with which, in ancient times, they bruized their corn.

3. That they were made for the purpose of habitations, or a place of refuge, in times of danger. It would be ridiculous even for a moment, to suppose that so large a tract of land could have been excavated for the sole purpose of procuring stone; for these excavations in general cease with the upper *stratum* of sand, which covers a deep and fine bed of hard green stone. I have found this *stratum* of sand, perforated in some places, and fragments of stone dispersed about, which proves that the workmen could not have been ignorant of the *substratum*, and which they undoubtedly would have followed, had stone been the object of their research.

The conjecture, as relating to querns, is certainly ingenious, but will admit of some of the aforesaid objections; for, on finding a bed of stone suited to their purpose, would not the Britons, or indeed any being endued with common sense, have followed that *stratum*, instead of opening so many thousand pits over an extensive tract of land, in precipitous situations, and on the steep sides of hills? In every part of this district, where pits have been opened or levelled, these querns or millstones have been invariably found; they are made of the native green stone, and rudely formed: those which have holes perforated in the middle, were the upper stones, and were turned round the lower one by means of a handle fixed into the perforation. Similar stones, have been found at Knook, and in other British villages. These at Pen bear decided marks of the tool upon them, and appear never to have been used. The third opinion, as to their having been made for the purpose of habitations,

---

* When I built a kennel, some years ago, on this site, the ground bore evident marks of previous excavation.

carries with it much plausibility, but still furnishes objections. We know that the first houses were only pits covered over with sods of turf, and boughs of trees.* I am sensible also that no situation could be found better adapted to a British settlement: a dry, and healthy plain, gently elevated above a valley abounding with springs of never-failing water; yet we do not find a sufficient quantity of charred wood, animal bones, or pottery, to justify us in fixing this spot as a permanent residence of the Britons.

I have always been inclined to the latter conjecture, as being, in my opinion, less liable to objection than the other two; and this opinion has been strengthened by some circumstances which have lately transpired oo opening some of these pits in the parish of Zeals. At no great depth under the surface, the labourers found two querns, and in pursuing their work to the bed of native stone (about 18 or 20 feet), which they found in a great measure undisturbed, they discovered two large upright blocks of stone, and some smaller fragments piled up along-side of the pit, evidently the work of art, and probably so placed, in order to prevent the earth from falling into the pit.

In the further prosecution of their work in the same quarry, the labourers found several millstones, and a very singular archway of rude stone, at the base of which was placed a large flat stone as a threshold; and at the depth of above ten feet under the surface, they afterwards discovered several pieces of charcoal, some burned bones, and some fragments of the rudé as well as of the finer pottery of the Romanized Britons. Whatever may have been the original destination of these pits, the above circumstances clearly prove that they were known and frequented at a very remote period, not indeed by the first Celtic colonies, for there are no *tumuli* in the neighbourhood, but probably at a later period, when the custom of burying under barrows had ceased, and when our island had submitted itself to the Roman yoke.

The hill near which these quarries are now working, bears the name of *High-Street*, ✝ and lies near the S. E. extremity of the line of pits delineated in

* The custom of living under ground in pits, is of very high antiquity, and is thus alluded to by *Virgil* in his Georgics:

> *Ipsi in defossis specubus, secura sub altâ*
> *Otia agunt terrâ.*

and the same habits still continue in Kamskatka, and other countries.

✝ Whenever we find the word *street* (except in great towns and their immediate neighbourhood), we may expect to find traces of some British or Roman antiquities. This word, as well as *ystrad*, Welsh; the Latin *stratum*, and the Saxon *stræt*, are all derived from the Celtic root *Stread*: and our *High-Street* might have formerly been the approach to the British settlement at Pen.

Since I wrote this note, my statement has been justified with respect to this spot, for at *High-Street*, the workmen have just discovered several fine fragments of that species of pottery which we have assigned to the æra of the Romanized Britons.

L

our plan.   The western head of the extensive forest of Selwood is marked by the word *Pen*, which in British signifies *head;* as is also its eastern termination near Westbury in Wiltshire, where several places bear also the name of *Pen*. In the Saxon Chronicle it is called the *Coed Mawr*, or *Sylva Magna;* and in the Saxon language it would mean literally the *Wood of habitations*, from *Sel*, and *Sele*, *sedes*, *mansio*, *domicilium*, *habitaculum*, and *Wod*, wood.   The name of the adjoining villages of Zeals and Silton, in the former of which are many of these pits, may have been derived from the same root.

On the eastern side of these pits is an earthen work thrown up on a steep neck of land projecting over the river Stour ; it consists of an elevated keep, and an oblong out-work, unlike any of the camps on our chalk hills, and very similar to many I have observed in Wales.   It would be a difficult matter to determine whether this fortress was constructed before or after the pits were formed, or whether it was an appendage to them.

Having laid before my readers all the information I have been able to collect respecting these curious excavations, I must leave it to them to determine for what purpose they were originally made.   Each conjecture respecting their origin seems to have its objections ; and although I could wish to favor the idea of their having been used as British habitations, I must candidly confess, that the circumstance of finding so little charred wood and pottery within the pits, and no *tumuli* in their neighbourhood, militates forcibly against such a supposition ;* yet still they may have been connected with some British town in the neighbourhood, and may have been resorted to only in times of danger.

Iter I.   Before I enter the chalky regions of Wiltshire, the seat of our British antiquities, I must be allowed to make a short digression westward, into the neighbouring county of Somerset, in order to notice a few objects that deserve attention.   The first is a camp in Stourhead Park, double ditched, and of a form nearly circular, with entrances towards the east and west : it occupies the whole ridge of the hill, and is naturally defended on each side by steep and precipitous ground.   The area within the outer ditch contains seven acres : the circuit of the ditch is three furlongs 20 yards, and the sloping height

* Mr. Daines Barrington (Archaeologia, Vol VII. page 236), mentions some pits near Little Coxwell in Berkshire, which cover about fourteen acres of land, and are 273 in number.   He conceives the area to have been a considerable city of the Britons at the time of the earliest inhabitants.   Leland also takes notice of some pits in the Black Mountains, Carmarthenshire ; and I have been told of others near Honiton in Devonshire.

P. Crocker delt.

Js. Basire Sc.

Publiſhed for W. Miller, Albemarle Street, London, Jany. 1. 1810.

of the *vallum*, where deepest, is 27 feet.*   A little beyond this camp rises the river Stour, from six springs or wells, which the Stourton family take as their armorial bearings: the ancient park wall ran between them, and is thus noticed by Leland: " The river of Stoure risith thereof six fountaynes or springes, wherof three be on the northe side of the parke harde withyn the pale; the other three be northe also, but withoute the parke. The Lord Stourton gyvith these six fountaynes upon his arms."

At the head of the vale of Stour, a verdant terrace conducts you to a lofty tower, built in a most commanding situation to the memory of King Alfred. The name of this hill is KING SETTLE, and being most probably the pass of that monarch, when he issued from his retreat in the isle of Athelney, and marched to attack the Danes at Eddington, my predecessor, Henry Hoare, fixed on it for the above purpose.   Much hereafter will be said on this subject when I trace the march of the royal and illustrious Saxon; and many errors of former historians will, I hope, stand corrected.

A little to the west of Alfred's Tower is a large mound of earth, vulgarly called JACK'S CASTLE, and generally considered as one of those beacons, where in former times, fires were lighted to alarm the neighbourhood on the approach of an enemy:

> " And flaming beacons cast their blaze afar,
> The dreadful signal of invasive war."

Its elevated situation over the great forest of Selwood, commanding a distant view of the Severn, was well adapted to such a purpose, and might have been so used; but I always had considered its original destination to have been sepulchral, and so, on opening, it proved to be.

After digging for some feet through a soft sand, we came to a thick *stratum* of picked flints, under which was deposited an interment of bones very minutely burned, enclosed within a cist, and amongst them a small lance head of brass, and an axe or hammer of a species of stone, called Sienite; both of which are delineated of their natural size in TUMULI, PLATE I. The lance head had been esteemed valuable by the Briton its possessor, for it was protected by a sheath of wood.   The axe is one of the most perfect we have discovered, and is very nicely formed.   The high antiquity of this *tumulus*, which I shall call SELWOOD BARROW, is satisfactorily proved by the articles found within it.

---

* On New Park terrace there is another camp, not quite so large, but placed on the ridge of a hill, in a situation exactly similar.

I have strong reason to think that an ancient British way ascended this hill in its way from *Iscalis*, now Ilchester, to *Sorbiodunum*, or Old Sarum, and the barrow I have just described might have been placed there as an index or direction post to the travellers coming from the west; this road would have crossed Kilmington Common, and continued its course eastward towards the Deverills. An open lane still seems to mark this line, and some large barrows, in the valley between Rodmead farm and the village of Kingston Deverill, give strength to my supposition. One of these barrows, in a meadow on the right side of the lane, is remarkable for its size and fine shape: it has never been opened, and experience has taught us that our labour would be thrown away in attempting any barrows in similar damp situations. We spent considerable time in opening another large *tumulus*, in the common fields, nearer to Kingston Deverill; but the moisture of the soil obliged us to desist, and leave our work unfinished. In a meadow on the left side of the lane, and nearly opposite the first mentioned barrow, I was informed that two had been levelled, of which the marks are still visible.

From the village of Kingston Deverill I shall ascend a steep hill, which bears the three different names of Cold Kitchen Hill, Brimsdon, and Bidcomb.* In whatever point of view we consider this insulated hill, it proves a most interesting object; it abounds in British antiquities, and commands a variety of the most extensive and pleasing views: on all sides we perceive *tumuli*, ditches, and excavations, denoting ancient habitation. In the year 1803, Mr. Cunnington made some researches with the spade on this elevated summit, and on that part which intervenes between Bidcomb and Cold Kitchen, where there are several of those irregularities and verdant patches, noticed in my Introduction as never failing proofs of ancient population. There he found three Roman coins,+ fragments of stuccoed walls painted crimson and green, and a great deal of pottery of various sorts, with an ivory pin. The adjoining barrow had been opened before, as he found pieces of an urn, burned bones,

---

* All these names seem to be derived from a Celtic root. The world *cold* is frequently prefixed to places; Cold Arbour, Cold Berwick, Cold Henley, &c. &c. and is a corruption probably from the Celtic word *col*, signifying the head, chief, &c. &c. I imagine the word *kitchen* also, is a corruption from the Celtic word *kefn*, a ridge of hill, or *crech* and *crechen*, a hill, or summit: so that *col crechen*, or the chief summit, has by corruption been Anglicized into *Cold Kitchen*. The word Bidcomb is also probably derived from *bod*, habitation, and *comb*, a valley: and Brimsdown, from *brin* or *bren*, a hill, and *don*, an elevation. Each part of this hill answers to the above supposed derivations; for that part called *Cold Kitchen* is the most elevated; and Bidcomb bears several marks of ancient population.

+ The coins were of small brass, one of *Constantine*, another of *Gratian*, the third illegible.

and a pin or bodkin of bone, mixed indiscriminately with the soil. In the autumn of the same year, I attended the opening of five barrows situated towards the southern side of Cold Kitchen Hill; No. 1, 2, and 4, are nearly in a line from north to south; No. 3 points towards the east, and No. 5, the largest of the group, to the west. No. 1, elevated but a few inches above the ground, contained an interment of burned bones deposited in a neat circular cist. No. 2 had a deep round cist, filled with very black ashes, and charred wood, but no bones. In No. 3 we found nothing. In No. 4, a very small oblong barrow, we discovered a cist at the N. E end, very neatly cut in the chalk, containing only black earth and ashes; but at the S. W. end was another cist, 2 feet 4 inches deep in the chalk, containing a rude urn inverted, which being only 6 inches under the surface of the soil, was of course broken; the urn was 20 inches deep, eleven wide at the rim, and five at the bottom; it contained a complete interment of burned bones, and a brass pin. No. 5 had been opened before.

On the declivity of this same hill, pointing down to Whiteley farm, are several irregularities in the ground, denoting ancient habitations; and on the extreme western point of Brimsdon Hill, facing the village of Maiden Bradley, where the ascent is the easiest, is a solitary *tumulus*, which we opened in May, 1807, and found within it an interment of burned bones deposited in a cist, and amongst them a long pin of bone, perforated at the broad end, and a small lance head of brass, gilt.

Between Brimsdon Hill and the Duke of Somerset's park, there is a barrow in a meadow on New Mead farm, which contained a simple interment of burned bones. The regular connexion of the chalk hills is now broken, and they assume detached and fantastic forms. Bradley Knoll, in the Park, and Long Knoll, to the west of it, resemble in many points of view a gigantic bowl-shaped, and a long barrow. On the south side of the former are several inequalities; but on digging into them, I could find no marks of antiquity. These two hills are separated by a narrow ridge, over which the road passes to Frome, and where there are the vestiges of an ancient ditch. Here only is the ascent to Long Knoll gradual and easy. The distance from hence to the opposite extremity of the hill exceeds a mile; and those who visit this fine ridge will be amply recompensed, by the rich and extensive views which are on all sides presented before the eye. At the western and most elevated point of this hill is a low *tumulus*, which on opening, we found had once contained a skeleton;

M

but had been disturbed, probably when the boundary ditch between the counties of Wilts and Somerset was made across the barrow. Near it we found many fragments of ancient pottery, and in the ditch several small brass coins of the Lower Empire. From the very elevated and bleak situation of this hill, which is one of the highest in our county, being 973 feet above low water mark, this spot could only have been selected as a *speculum*, or beacon; for the ridge is too narrow to have admitted of any regular residence or settlement.

Iter II. Having mentioned the detached objects of antiquity, immediately adjoining this my first station, I shall now enter upon the wide and connected range of chalk hills, which extends across our own county into those of Hampshire and Dorsetshire. Immediately on ascending the hill called Whitesheet, we find ourselves surrounded by British antiquities. The road intersects an ancient earthen work, of a circular form, and which, from the slightness of its *vallum*, appears to have been of high antiquity. Adjoining it is a large barrow, which we opened in October 1807, and found it had contained a skeleton, and had been investigated before. On a point of land near this barrow are three others, all of which, by the defaced appearance of their summits, seemed to have attracted the notice of former antiquaries. No 1, the nearest to the edge of the hill, had certainly been opened, and appears to have contained a double interment. The primary one was an interment of burned bones deposited within a shallow cist,* in an urn rudely formed, and badly baked. Above it was a skeleton with its head laid towards the south, and which from its position and perfect preservation appears not to have been disturbed. Its mouth was wide open, and it " grinn'd horribly a ghastly smile," a singularity we have never before met with.

In the next barrow (the middle one), we found a simple+ interment of burned bones, which had escaped the notice of former investigators.

At the bottom of the third *tumulus* we discovered a cist cut in the chalk, but not a single fragment of either bone or pottery, so that probably the urn containing the relicks of the Briton had been taken out entire. But our researches in this barrow were not wholly unproductive; for a few inches under the turf, we found a skeleton laid on its side, the head turned towards the north-east,

---

* By the word *cist*, I mean an excavation cut in the soil or chalk, for the reception of the skeleton, ashes, or sepulchral urn.

+ By the word *simple*, thus applied, I mean an interment where the burned bones are piled up in a heap, and are unaccompanied by any arms or trinkets.

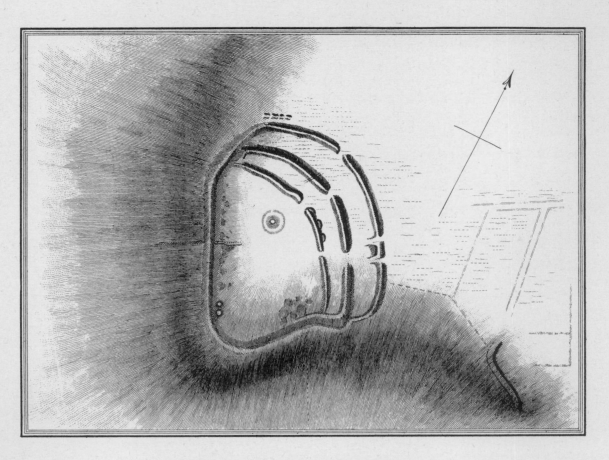

ON WHITE SHEET HILL.

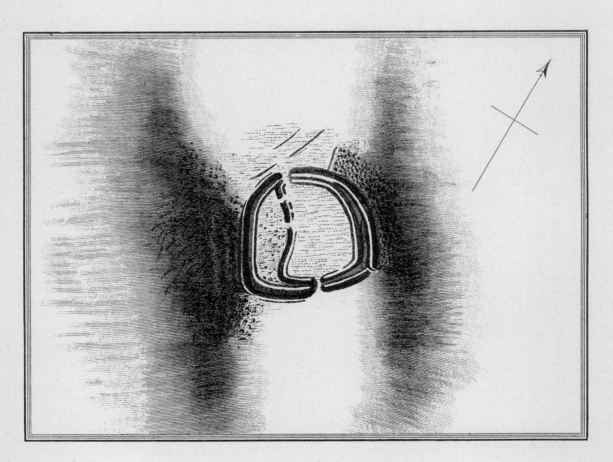

IN STOURHEAD PARK.

P. Crocker del.

Jᵉ Basire sc.

50   100   200   300   400

Scale of Yards.

Published by W. Miller, Albemarle Street, London, Janʸ 1.1810.

and a richly ornamented drinking cup at its feet, which, from its situation so near the surface, was unfortunately broken.

Following the line of down southward, we come to a large ditch, which intersects the whole ridge of the hill, which is very contracted at this point : and a little beyond it is a spacious camp, denominated, from the hill, WHITESHEET. This fine earthen work is placed on the brow of one of those hills where the chalky *stratum* terminates, and is strongly fortified on three sides by nature ; on the fourth, where it has no natural defence, and where the ground is level, it has been strengthened by the hand of art. On this side are all the entrances into the camp ; the first, through the outward *vallum*, has some additional works ; two other entrances through the second and third ramparts lead you into the area of the camp, which contains fifteen acres : the circuit of the outward ditch being four furlongs and 152 yards. Within this area is a circular mound resembling a barrow, but I am inclined to think it was thrown up for a clump of trees. The three different ramparts with which this work is fortified towards the plain, terminate with one on the side of the steep hill which forms its boundary on three sides ; within the area, and adjoining the S. W. rampart, are several irregularities in the ground, in which we found ashes, animal bones, and coarse pottery.

On the N. W. side of this camp, and close to the outward rampart, are some small mounds resembling *tumuli*, which on digging into, we found not to be sepulchral.

In my Introduction to this History, I had occasion to mention slightly these earthen works, our difficulty in ascertaining by what people they were constructed, and the probability that the greater part of them were originally British, and afterwards enlarged and strengthened by the succeeding people who took possession of them. From an attentive examination of this camp, I have reason to suppose it has had several masters. The works of the inner area are much slighter, broader, and more worn down by time than the others ; the second rampart is by far the deepest of the three ; and the outward ditch is considerably shallower, narrow, and irregularly formed. I am therefore inclined to think that the original fortress of the Britons who inhabited these hills, was confined to the inner work on the projecting point of the hill, in which we find the rude pottery ; and that the two additional ramparts were raised at a later period, perhaps by the Saxons, who, we know, fought many battles in this neighbourhood.

On a point of land southward, projecting over a deep valley called Great

Bottom, is another *tumulus*, in which we found a cist three feet deep, and the fragments of a very large rude urn, which must have filled up the whole of the excavation.   There are several other barrows in the neighbourhood, most of which, on trial, we found had been opened.   One, however, from its insignificance, and slight elevation, had escaped the notice of former antiquaries, and was reserved for my friend and fellow-labourer, Mr. Fenton, who discovered it, at a short distance beyond the second ditch that intersects this hill.*   At the depth of about three feet and a half he found a cist six feet in length, from east to west, containing the skeleton of a large man, with his limbs gathered up and crossed, and that of a younger person by his right side.   From the position of their heads, they seemed to have been placed in the affectionate attitude of embrace, as the two skulls nearly touched each other.   Close to them was a richly ornamented drinking cup; and near the left side of the adult was a small lance head of brass, and a piece of gray slaty stone, perforated at the ends.   He also found a small instrument of bone, and two circular ornaments of thin, but pure gold: these were also perforated, and used, like the blue stone, as ornaments of dress.   Towards the eastern side of the cist was a great deal of charred wood, the use of which it is difficult to conjecture, as the *tumulus* presented no apparent signs of burning.   The above articles are engraved in (TUMULI, PLATE II.) of the same size as the originals.

Continuing our ride over the down, we come to the shepherd's hut belonging to the Down farm, where another track-way bears off to the left, and leads to the villages of Deverill; but we shall continue the straight-forward line, towards Willoughby-hedge turnpike.

The first object worthy of notice is a small earthen work, apparently of high antiquity, which the track-way intersects; and near it are some irregularities in the ground, which contained pottery, &c.; here, therefore, was a small settlement of the Britons.   On the right and left of the valley, which I shall now follow, is a large tract of wild and uncultivated ground: that on the left is called Blackheath, that on the right, Charnage Furze.   On the former is a small

* Two ditches intersect the ridge of this hill, and each points into a deep valley, vulgarly called Swincomb. They might have been used as covered ways into the valley, where the inhabitants of the camp probably resorted for water : they resemble in their formation those ditches we generally find in the neighbourhood of British towns, and have a *vallum* of equal height on each side, with a broad area at bottom, and are too slight for works of defence.   As many battles were fought in these parts between the Danes and Saxons, might not the name of this valley, *Swincomb*, have been corrupted from *Swaine*, the Danish King? and might not Whitesheet camp have been enlarged and altered at that period? On the level part of this hill there are the traces of several walls of flint, which I cannot in any way account for: they continue for some distance along the track-way.

P. Crocker delt.

Js Basire Sc.

MERE DOWN.

Published for W. Miller, Albemarle Street, London, Jany 1. 1810.

barrow, under which we found an interment of burned bones within a rude urn.* On the latter are one large and two small *tumuli*, which I opened in October 1804. In the large one, at the depth of six feet, abundant signs of cremation appeared, which led to the expectation of shortly finding the interment, in which we were not disappointed; for a cist nearly circular, and overarched with flints was discovered considerably to the eastward of the centre of the barrow. It contained a vast quantity of charred wood, decomposed by the lodgement of water, and converted into a black kind of jelly, in which was bedded a very rude little vase (TUMULI, PLATE I.). It has four projecting knobs on the sides, that are perforated; which circumstance, added to its very black and smoky appearance, induces me to think it had been suspended over the funeral pile. We dug a great deal in this barrow, and I have still doubts whether we found the real and primary interment. The two adjoining small *tumuli* produced nothing.

From hence we proceeded towards Keesley Lodge, and on the declivity of the hill opened another barrow; on the floor of which we found large pieces of charcoal, and a simple interment of burned bones in a very shallow cist. Nearer the Lodge is another large *tumulus*, which from its superior size and form seemed to promise success; but after much labour we were obliged to abandon our researches, owing to the stiff and clammy nature of the soil, which we had no reason to expect on so dry and elevated a spot. There are some other barrows on the western declivity of the hill, but they produced nothing worthy of remark.

Continuing my route for a short distance along the valley which leads to Monkton Deverill, I shall ascend another ridge called in the map Middle Hill, and which will conduct us back again to the Down farm. The whole line presents *tumuli*, and other marks of ancient population. The first barrow worthy of notice is situated a little to the west of a clump of fir trees, on the declivity of the down; it is of the second class of Druid barrows, rising gradually from the *vallum* to the apex. On digging through a thin *stratum* of flints, and some vegetable earth beneath to the depth of two feet, we discovered an interment of burned bones within a cist cut in the chalk, and intermixed with

---

* Some singularity occurred both in the formation of this cist, and in the shape of the sepulchral urn, which was like a bowl. In the usual formation of cists, a cavity is made in the chalk, in which the burned bones are deposited, and over them the urn inverted; but in this instance the cist was not excavated, but a projection or knob of solid chalk was left to receive the inverted urn, and the bones were placed round it.

N

black mould, ashes, and charred wood.   Amongst the bones were found up-wards of forty amber beads of various forms and sizes, some of jet, others of the vitrified sort called pully beads, and two of horn.   Besides these articles, was a very curious ornament of amber, consisting of six separate pieces, which when strung together, formed a decorative part of the Briton's dress.   All these have been engraved of their original size in (TUMULI, PLATE III.).   There were also the fragments of a small ornamented cup, and a little brass pin. From the nature and size of the articles found in this barrow, we may rationally conclude it contained the relicks of some distinguished female.

On the same ridge, but nearer to the Down farm, is another circular *tumulus*, forty-two feet in diameter, and only fourteen inches in elevation.   On opening it, we found an oval cist, nearly three feet long, two feet wide, and about thirteen inches deep, containing an interment of burned bones closely piled together in a little heap, and amongst them some beads of amber, jet, and glass, with a pair of ivory tweezers, delineated in (TUMULI, PLATE III.).

A little beyond this barrow is an earthen work of an irregular form, with an entrance towards the east.

The next barrow on this line, which lies immediately upon the track-way, contained a rude British urn placed in an upright position, and an interment of burned bones.   This urn had two perforations on its sides.   On the south-west side of this track-way, are three other small barrows, disfigured by the plough ; the largest produced an interment of burned bones placed within a rude urn inverted;   the smaller nothing but charred wood.   Other insignificant bar-rows were opened in this neighbourhood, which afforded nothing worthy of attention.

We are now come back to that point near the Down farm where the two track-ways separated ;   but before I conclude this long Iter, I must make another digression to a hill called Rodmead, which contains some curious British anti-quities.   The site of two barrows is distinctly marked by some thorn bushes growing upon them, though the mutilated appearance of their surface gave us on great hopes of success.   Having, however, often proved the fallacy of exterior appearances, and that " *fronti nulla fides*," we commenced our operations with the spade, and were most amply repaid for our want of faith.   In the most northerly of these barrows, which I opened in October 1807, we discovered a skeleton extended at full length, with its head towards the north-east, and with it a variety of curious articles, which are engraved in (TUMULI, PLATE IV.).

P. Crocker del.ᵗ

KINGSTON DEVERILL.

Jⁿ Basire Sc.

Published for W. Miller, Albemarle Street, London, Janʸ 1, 1810.

P. Crocker delt.

Js. Basire Sc.

Published for W. Miller, Albemarle Street, London, Jany. 1.1810.

The brazen vessel is seven inches and a half in diameter, and was laid at the feet of the skeleton; the inside was gilt, and the outside protected by wood, and small strips of brass. The large cone of iron (somewhat smaller than the original), formed the *umbo* of a shield, and was certainly affixed to wood, some of which still adhered to it; near it were found two studs plated with silver, another small piece of the same metal, and a buckle and clasp of brass, all, most probably, appertaining to the shield. Besides the above articles, this warrior had a variety of iron arms buried with him, viz. a two-edged sword two feet six inches long, and one and three quarters wide: a knife eleven inches long, and one and a quarter wide: another knife three inches long; a spear head eleven inches long, and one and a half wide, and another six and a half long, and one and a quarter wide. This barrow bears a most striking resemblance to the first described by Mr. Douglas in his NENIA BRITANNICA; the only variation being an earthen vessel instead of a brazen one placed at the feet of the skeleton. He attributes similar barrows to the Saxons; though, as we well know that the Britons had the use of iron when *Cæsar* first invaded our island, I see no reason why this barrow might not have contained the remains of a Belgic warrior. In the adjoining barrow, which we opened very completely, we discovered no signs of any interment.

A little to the east of these barrows is a small and irregular earthen work, with an entrance towards the east. On digging into it, we turned up a great deal of very black earth, and fragments of rude British pottery.

Near Rodmead Penning we opened a small long barrow, in which were the remains of several skeletons that had been disturbed before. On the adjoining hill, projecting over the vale of Deverill, is a cluster of three small barrows placed in a triangular form, scarcely elevated above the surface, and seem to have been ploughed over in former times. One of these had been imperfectly explored, as the burned bones were found intermixed with the soil; but seve-ral pieces of amber, some beads, and a ring of jet had escaped the notice of former investigators. In the second we found an interment of burned bones, and a small brass pin enclosed within a rude urn and shallow cist, not exceed-ing four inches under the surface. In the third, we found no signs of any interment.

At the extreme point of this down, and on the declivity of the hill facing the village of Kingston Deverill, is a very large and conspicuous *tumulus*, which from its contents, we have denominated the FLINT BARROW. Its present base diameter is about seventy-six feet ; its elevation thirteen feet ; and the slope towards the north sixty feet. It is composed of large flints picked from the adjacent fields, and covered over with a thick coat of chalk. Our operations commenced by making a section to the south of the centre, and at the depth of six feet, we came to the loose flints ; we there expected to have met with the interment, but were completely disappointed ; and in pursuing our researches, were obliged to throw out from fifty to one hundred loads of large flints, and to begin fresh sections, but still without success ; yet from finding a great many animal bones, charred wood, ashes, as well as pieces of stag's horns, we were convinced that the mound was sepulchral. After all our labour and vexation, we were indebted to chance for the discovery of the history of this barrow. Some time after the cessation of our labours, we were informed that one side of the barrow had fallen down, and exposed three urns standing together near the surface, the largest of which contained an interment of burned bones, and a spear head of brass ; but we could gain no intelligence whatever into whose hands this relick or the two smaller urns had passed. There are a few other low barrows upon this down, which appear to have been opened in former times.

ITER III. In my last Iter I diverged to the left from the Down farm, to notice some barrows on Blackheath, Charnage, and Keesley downs ; I shall now continue my line straight to Willoughby-hedge turnpike. On a fine piece of down attached to West Knoyle farm, are two very low *tumuli*, which I opened in October 1807. In the smallest of the two we discovered the skeleton of a robust man, extended on his back at full length in a large cist. Between his knees was the iron *umbo* of a shield, exactly similar to the one before described on Rodmead down ; on his left side was a spear-head of the same metal, about seven inches long, and not quite an inch wide ; also an iron knife. The articles found in this barrow, as well as the mode of interment, mark it to be of the same æra as the one at Rodmead. In the adjoining mound we found a very imperfect interment of burned bones, so intermixed with the soil, that I doubt if it was the primary one. A little further on the same track, and in a paddock to the left, is another barrow, which Mr. Cunnington opened in November 1803, and found an interment of burned bones within a cist, and well secured by a great pile of flints. At the distance of about one mile south of Keesley Lodge is a neat circular barrow on the brow of the hill, thirty-nine feet in diameter, and five feet high. This was also opened at the same time, and produced, a few inches under the turf, the skeleton of a large man, and under it an oval cist cut in the chalk five feet long and three wide, containing a few large beads of jet, and some of amber.

There are a few other *tumuli* in the arable land adjoining Willoughby-hedge turnpike, which, I believe, have not been opened ; and on a piece of down between Pertwood farm and Keesley Lodge, the traces of a very ancient British settlement are marked by the unusual blackness of the soil thrown up by the moles. On digging we found fragments of the rudest pottery, and animal bones. All the down adjoining Keesley is intersected by banks and other strong marks of an extensive cultivation ; and the superior quality of its pasture affords another evident proof of its ancient population.

I shall now continue my Iter along the turnpike road leading from East Knoyle to Warminster, where, at MILE IV. from the former, and MILE VI. from the latter, we traverse a Roman road leading eastward to Old Sarum, through the thick woods of Great Ridge and Grovely. Several barrows are discernible on each side of the road on the downs belonging to the parishes of Monkton and Brixton Deverill, some of which have been opened by Mr. Cunnington, but contained nothing worthy of remark.

At a short distance from the road, leading to Longbridge Deverill, is the little sequestered village of Hill Deverill, where, in two fields immediately behind the parish church, the usual irregularities in the ground mark the site of a large British settlement, and where on digging, we found the pottery, brick flues, &c. &c. of the Romanized Britons.

STATION II. WARMINSTER.

Before I settle myself in my head-quarters at Warminster, it will be necessary to mention a few detached objects on the west side of this station, which deserve notice.   There are evident traces of a British village on the right side of the road leading from Maiden Bradley to Longbridge Deverill, and near a farm called Baycliff, marked upon the map.

Following the road to Longbridge Deverill, which forms the boundary between this and my last station, we find on the left, near the intersection of two roads, a mutilated barrow, which contained an interment of burned bones. This *tumulus* is placed exactly opposite the track leading to Bidcomb Hill; and I have before noticed another on the other extremity of the same hill, both of which I could almost suppose were placed there as indexes or guides to the British settlements on that hill.   A little beyond the village of Longbridge Deverill is Southley Wood, between which and the road to Heytesbury, is a very curious little earthen work resembling an amphitheatre in miniature. Though unfortunately much mutilated by the plough, its original shape may still be distinguished, as well as an approach to it from the road over a slightly elevated ridge or causeway.   It was encompassed without by a neatly formed *vallum*, from which you descend through a ditch to the inner work, which rises above the ditch, and presents a level area, containing less than half an acre. The depth of the outward *vallum* from the ditch is eighteen feet; the breadth of the ditch seven feet; the height of the inner work from fifteen to sixteen feet, and the length of the area of the inner work on its longest side (for it is of an oval shape) is one hundred and eleven feet.

Within the adjoining wood of Southley is another small earthen work of a squarish form, and containing in its area within the ditch three quarters of an acre of land. It is called Robin Hood's Bower. There is also another small earthen

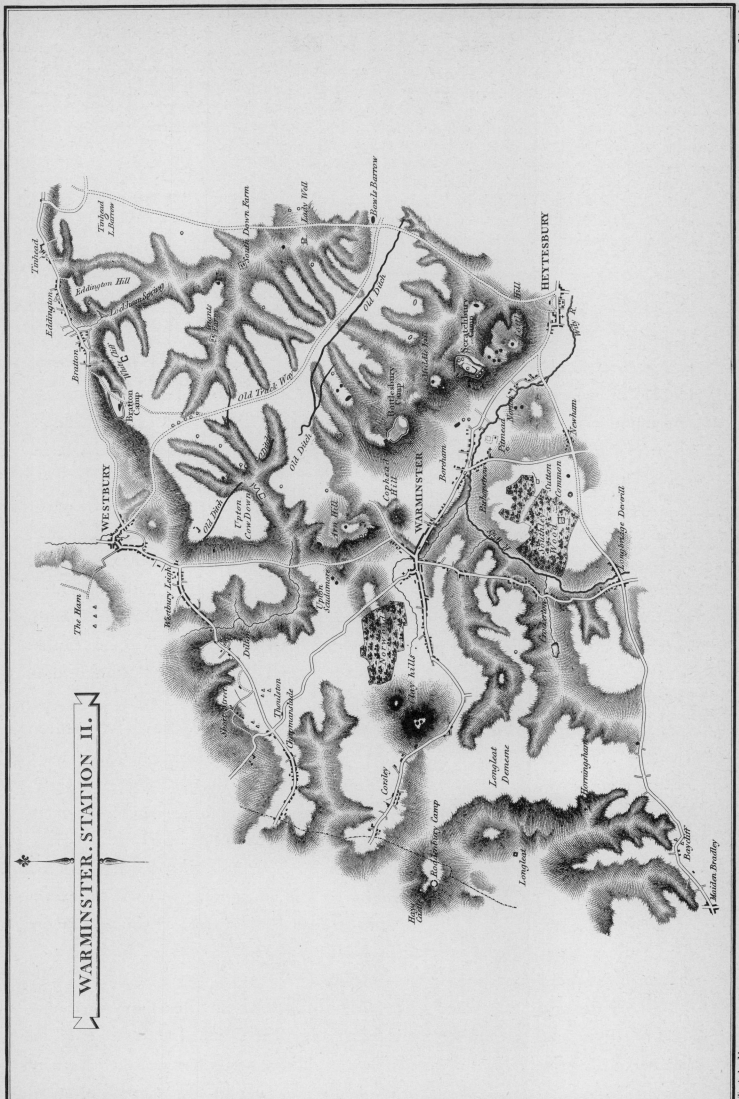

WARMINSTER STATION II.

Tinhead
Tinhead L. Barrow
Eddington Hill
Eddington
Bratton
Lodshan Spring
White Cliff
Bratton Camp
South Down Farm
Sandy Well
Bowls Barrow
Old Ditch
HEYTESBURY
Scratchbury
Battlesbury Camp
Old Ditch
Old Track Way
WESTBURY
Upton Cow Down
Old Ditch
Arn Hill
Cop heap Hill
Boreham
WARMINSTER
Newham
Pitmead
Bishopstrow
Sutton Common
Wood
Common
Longbridge Deverill
The Ham
Westbury Leigh
Dilton
Upton Scudamore
Norwood
Ley hills
Rockerton
Thoulston
Charmanslade
Corsley
Longleat Demesne
Horningsham
Hayes Castle
Rodsbury Camp
Longleat
Baycliff
Maiden Bradley

Philip Crocker del.

London: Published by W. Miller. May. 1811.

J. Cary sculp.

work on Sutton Common, and several barrows dispersed over the country as far as Bishopstow. All these circumstances are strong proofs of some large British village having existed near this spot, though we have not as yet been able to ascertain its exact situation. A little beyond is the village of Horningsham; and between that and Warminster is Crockerton, where a large pottery is at present established. The names of many adjoining places, such as, Pottle-Street near Horningsham, Potters-Hill, Crockerton, and the numerous fragments of various kinds of pottery, which are continually dug up in the grounds near the latter place, sufficiently prove that an extensive manufacture of earthen ware has been carried on for many centuries upon that spot.

On the western side of Longleat Park, near the confines of the counties of Wilts and Somerset, is a small earthen work called RODDENBURY CAMP. It is situated on the brow of a hill, has two entrances to the east and west, and is single ditched. Beyond it, towards the north, is a smaller circular work called HAY's CASTLE. Further eastward, and nearer Warminster, are two very singular knolls, which form a very conspicuous and beautiful object from every part of the adjacent country. They bear the name of CLEE or CLAY HILLS.* They differ considerably in size, and rise very boldly from the surrounding plain. The larger hill is surrounded by a ditch and rampart, bearing the marks of high antiquity.+ Its form is like that of a cone with an obtuse head; that of the lesser hill is drawn more to a point. On the summit of the larger hill are two barrows, both of which I have caused to be opened. The largest produced no evidence of its having been destined to sepulchral purposes. Near the bottom of it we found some ears of wheat undecayed, and the soil of which the barrow was composed had fragments of pottery, charred wood, and ashes intermixed with it, which may be accounted for, by supposing that this eminence was inhabited by the Britons previous to the formation of their mound, which, perhaps in later times, was made use of as a beacon. The adjoining barrow was certainly sepulchral, and originally contained an interment of burned human bones, which, on opening it, we found had been disturbed.

* I imagine their appellation is derived from the *Celtic* word *Cleis*, which signifies *Chalk*, of which material these hills are formed. There are also in Shropshire hills bearing the name of *Clea*, and upon them the remains of an ancient camp, and beneath them the village of Cleybury.

+ Bishop Gibson, in his edition of Camden, says, that " Clay-hill shews no marks of any trenches," a proof that he, like many other writers on topography, never visited the place he described; which will be evidently proved by the annexed view of Clay-hill, in which the ramparts are decidedly and correctly marked.

ITER I. From Warminster I shall proceed to the village of Upton Scudamore, where some inequalities in a field near the church, commanding a most delightful view, mark the site of the ancient residence of the Scudamore family. In the arable lands between Upton and Warminster are two large barrows, which we opened in November 1809. They stand east and west of each other ; the largest, to the west, is ninety-four feet in base diameter, and thirteen in elevation. At the depth of five feet we found the remains of a human skeleton, which had been deposited nearly east and west in a wooden box, or trunk of a tree ; but the bones were nearly decomposed, owing to the wetness of the soil : amongst them was found a small brass dagger, but so corroded that it would not bear removing. On the floor of the barrow, at the depth of thirteen feet, was a great quantity of wood ashes ; and a few feet from the centre a sepulchral urn standing upright, and containing a very complete interment of burned bones in high preservation.

The second barrow had been opened partially several years ago, and a skeleton discovered. We commenced our operations by a large section, and at the depth of eight feet came to a regular floor covered with black ashes, but found no interment near them ; at the depth of two feet and a half more, viz. ten and a half from the top, we came to the real floor, and on the northen verge of it found a large oblong cist nearly five feet deep, containing a skeleton with the head towards the north ; underneath it was a little well, as if designed to draw the moisture from the body. The opening of these barrows, as in all others in similar low situations, was attended with much labour and expense.

At a short distance to the north-west lies Dilton, a chapelry attached to Westbury. The church is placed in a retired and picturesque situation, and has a singular steeple of stone. A little further is Highsomley ; and not far from the farm house is a large stone quarry, near which many vestiges of the Romanized Britons have been found. In cultivating the fields, numerous fragments of all kinds of pottery are continually thrown up, and I have got one small vase entire, of which an engraving will be given in the course of my work. On the great road leading from Westbury to Frome, is a place called Short-Street : and I have before had occasion to remark, that whenever we find the word *Street*, we have reason to expect either British or Roman antiquities. This little village, consisting of a few scattered habitations, is situated on an elevated plain, commanding a fine view of the rich vale beneath ; and the residence of the Britons, and their conquerors the Romans, on this spot, is sufficiently proved by the coins and pottery dispersed over the adjacent fields.

But these *indicia* of ancient population are not confined to this spot, for the whole tract from Highsomley to this place seems to have been inhabited by the Romanized Britons.   In a field near Row turnpike, as well as in the grounds of Thoulston, the same remains have been discovered ; in short, all this neighbourhood seems to have been thickly peopled ; not perhaps in the early ages of Celtic or Belgic colonization, but after the coming of the Romans, when the Britons, partaking of the luxuries and comforts introduced amongst them by their conquerors, quitted their rude and exposed huts on the chalk hills, and sought a more sheltered situation on the gentle eminences of the sandy vale.

Leaving Short-Street, I shall steer northward towards Westbury Leigh, a hamlet of the greater town of Westbury, which has acquired its name from being situated west of the great camp of Bratton ; for, with very few exceptions, when we meet with the name of a place terminating with *bury*, we usually find some ancient camp or earthen work either on the very spot, or in its neighbourhood.   Hither extended the great forest of Selwood, noticed in my first station.   In Domesday book the lords of Westbury are stated to have had twenty-nine hog-keepers " *Ibi* 29 *porcarii*," to attend the herds of swine that fed in that great forest.   Here also, we have several places bearing the name of Pen, viz. Penleigh, Pen-knap, &c. &c. which denote the eastern head of the forest, as we have also Pen Selwood, on the western side of it.

To the north-west of Westbury is a large unenclosed common field, known by the name of HAM, where we find a continuation of British and Roman antiquities. Vulgar tradition reports that Old Westbury stood on this spot, and was battered from the adjoining camp at Bratton ; such was the account given me by a rustic lapidary whom I found working at the quarry, who informed me also, that on a little piece of ground lately ploughed up, called Compton's plot, was the town well, into which all the valuables had been thrown.   In the field between this plot and Heywood-house, the same man had assisted in digging up the foundations of a large building of well hewn stone ; and a labourer at Highsomley stone quarry, told me, that a tessellated pavement had been dug into near the well.

I shall defer the description of Bratton Camp, which, with the White Horse on its side, makes a very conspicuous appearance from this quarter, to a future Iter ; and return to my head-quarters at Warminster.

ITER II. Leaving the village of Upton Scudamore on the left, I shall now ascend the down belonging to that parish, following the windings of the hill,

P

which from a fine verdant terrace present a continued succession of rich and extensive views over the fertile vale beneath. On the first projecting point of hill is a small earthen work, with a slight *vallum*, and entrance towards the south, and near it a mutilated barrow. Shortly afterwards I crossed OLD DITCH, bearing westerly towards Westbury, or more probably to the British village at HAM. Cultivation of corn now commences, and with it all vestiges of British antiquities cease. On the eastern declivity of Upton down, overlooking a valley, is a small oblong earthen work, with an entrance at the south-west corner; it measures about two hundred and seven feet in length, and one hundred and twenty-nine in breadth. At first sight it appears to have a double *vallum*; but on examination, I found that the inner supposed rampart was only a bank, which is extended beyond the lines on the eastern side. Near this work are several irregularities on the declivity of the down, which mark the hand of art; and still further to the north, in a line leading from hence to the great trackway, is a circular barrow, about sixty feet in diameter, and four and a half in elevation; it is not encompassed, as usual, by a ditch, but has several almost circular excavations around it, from whence earth was taken to raise the sepulchral mound. On opening it, we found its interior corresponding in a great measure with the Long barrows, and differing from any of the circular *tumuli* hitherto examined; for amongst several large sarsen* stones and flints, we discovered seven or eight skeletons lying in every direction; the thigh bones of one by the head of another, a skull on the breast of a second, &c. &c. but no trinkets or warlike or domestic instruments.

I shall now return to the western ridge of hill, and direct my course towards Bratton Camp, where the White Horse+ presents its uncouth and ill-proportioned

---

* Dr. Stukeley says that the word *Sarsen* is Phœnician, signifying a rock; but what is commonly meant by this word, is a rough unhewn stone. Many of these are found on the chalk *stratum*, unconnected with any stone quarry; and of these the great trilithons at Stonehenge are formed. They are particularly numerous in the neighbourhood of Marlborough and Abury.

+ The Horse was the standard used by the Saxons both before and after their coming hither; and the celebrated one cut on a hill in Berkshire, from which the district bears the name of *Vale of White Horse*, has been universally considered as an historical memorial of the signal victory gained on that spot by King Alfred against the Danes in the year 871. Mr. Wise, who has written amply on this subject, doubts if the horse at Bratton can boast of the same relation, or the same claims to antiquity. He thus mentions it: " In the neighbourhood of Edingdon in Wiltshire, the place where Alfred gained the second most remarkable victory of his life, is a *White Horse* cut on the sides of an high and steep hill, and under a large fortification called Bratton Castle, so that in this respect it is not unlike the Berkshire horse. Bratton Castle is likewise the very place whither, as antiquaries agree, Alfred pursued Guthrum the Danish king, and after a siege of fourteen days, brought him to surrender; and this was another strong reason for refer-ring it to the time of that prince. Notwithstanding which, I must give my readers a caution about it: for did not the fabrick discover it to be modern, yet the inhabitants of Westbury, a borough town about a

BRATTON CAMP.

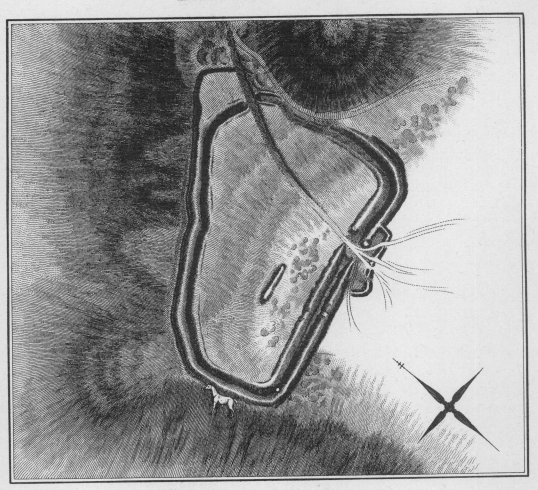

50 100   200   300   400
Scale of Yards.

VIEW OF CLAY HILL.

P. Crocker del.   Jᵉ Basire sc.

Published by W. Miller, Albemarle Street, London, Janʸ 1.1810.

figure on a steep declivity to the left ; a level plain leads us to the southern entrance of the camp.

BRATTON CASTLE. This strong fortress (a ground plan of which is here annexed) is situated on a point of land projecting to the north-west, over the rich vale that separates the chalky districts of North and South Wiltshire. On three sides it is naturally fortified by steep and precipitate hills; on the south side, where the ground is level, and the approach weak, art has been employed to strengthen it by double ramparts and a large outwork. The intrenchments of this camp, as in all our hill fortresses, humour the form of the hill; on the sides difficult of access one rampart was found sufficient, but where the approach was easier, two were raised. On the eastern side the very perpendicular declivities of the hill rendered any artificial fortifications unnecessary. On the north-east point there is an additional outwork, like a detached camp. The area within the ditches contains above twenty-three acres, the circuit on the top of the outer *vallum* is one thousand five hundred and forty yards, and the greatest height of the rampart is thirty-six feet.

I have remarked in my Introduction, that in all probability the camps placed on high situations, and bold points of land, were originally of British construction, and that they were successively occupied, as circumstances required, by the Romans, Danes, and Saxons ; and this, I think, was the case with Bratton, the projecting rampart afore-mentioned on the north east-side being apparently additional, and a more modern work. In a field beneath the north side of the camp, near the turnpike road, Mr. Cunnington found a great deal of Roman pottery of various kinds, and was informed that Mr. Whitaker, the late schoolmaster at Bratton, had once in his possession several Roman coins which had been picked up on the same spot. The same person also found within the area of the camp some querns or mill-stones, and nearly a cart load of large pebbles. As you enter this camp from the south, a large oblong barrow appears on the left, which has excited the attention of different people, and given rise to various reports; but as I cannot depend upon any researches, but those made immediately under our own eyes, I shall not repeat those handed down by uncertain tradition. Mr. Cunnington made two attempts on this *tumulus;* at first he cut

mile from it, who made it, and instituted a revel or festival thereupon, might inform them as much, it having been wrought within the memory of persons now living (1742), or but very lately dead. Yet still I think it may deserve the enquiry of others, who have more leisure than myself, How the common people came to be so fortunate in their choice of the ground? And whether the authors of it had not preserved the tradition of some older Horse, now obliterated, and of some more ancient festival now forgot?" *Wise. Further Observations upon the White Horse,* page 48.

a section nine feet long, and five wide, and found black vegetable earth for the depth of five feet, intermixed with pottery and animal bones. On one side of the section, at the depth of four feet, he discovered a pile of pebble stones * similar to those before mentioned, and a large stone bead. The area of this camp having been for many years under tillage, a great check is thereby put to any further discoveries. At a subsequent period Mr. Cunnington employed his men for several days in examining the large end of this barrow, but he only discovered the remains of three skeletons near the top.

BATTLE OF EDDINGTON.

The battle of Eddington, fought in the year 878, between King Alfred and the Danes, is so important an event in the annals of our English history, and the circumstances attending it have been so misrepresented by topographical writers, that, for the honor of our county, I feel it incumbent on me to enter fully into the subject ; to endeavour to distinguish truth from fiction, and by clearly stating the line of march pursued by our Saxon monarch, prevent, if possible, any future doubt or controversy. And when we consider that this battle decided in a great measure the fate of Britain, and secured its future liberty and independence, which, thanks to Providence and a well-regulated constitution, still remain sound and inviolate, whilst the greater portion of Europe has been obliged, through dire necessity, to sacrifice its freedom, privileges and riches ; this digression will, I flatter myself, be pardoned by my readers, and not be considered as tedious or nugatory. But in order to explain the circumstances leading to this battle, it will be necessary to give some short account of the life of Alfred, and of the events preceding this memorable engagement.

Alfred, king of the Anglo-Saxons, was born in the royal villa at Wantage

* These pebbles are not natural to this spot, but were probably brought from a hill near Codford, and were used in slings.

in Berkshire, A. D. 849, and succeeded to the monarchy on the death of his brother Ethered A. D. 871, at a period when the kingdom was distracted and harassed by a powerful army of foreign invaders. In this same year, the Danes, under the command of Hinguar and Hubba, had fixed their head-quarters at Reading in Berkshire. Hither Ethered and his brother Alfred repaired with their army, and giving battle to the Danes, were repulsed, with the loss of Ethelwulph their leader. Within four days another battle was fought at Æscesdun,* which terminated in favour of the Saxons; and in fourteen days afterwards a third engagement took place at Basing in Hampshire, where the Danes were victorious. After a temporary cessation from arms for two months, the royal brothers again took the field against their inveterate enemies the Danes, and a battle was fought at Meretune,+ where the Danes remained masters of the field. A. D. 871, hostilities ceased during the following summer, and the Danes continued in their quarters, at Reading. After Easter, king Ethered died, and was buried in Winbourn Minster, Dorsetshire.

The government of the kingdom of the West Saxons, and the command of its army, now devolved upon king Alfred. Hitherto he had acted only as second to his brother Ethered, on whose death, he was invited by the universal acclamation of his subjects, to assume the reins of government, which he at length, though unwillingly " *quasi invitus*," consented to do. But within one short month, the turbulent spirit of the Danes again summoned him to the field of battle, at Wilton, on the banks of the river Wily. Alfred engaged the enemy with inferior numbers, and by the impetuosity of his attack, compelled the Danes to fly; but having unfortunately followed them too far in their retreat, they rallied, and repossessed themselves of the field of battle. Conscious however of the military abilities of Alfred, they proposed terms of accommodation, which were accepted, on condition that they should quit the territory of the West Saxons.

In the year 872, the Danes quitted Reading, and wintered in London, which place they left in the following year, and marching into Northumberland,

---

* The scene of this battle, has been fixed at Ashdown in Berkshire, where there are the remains of two camps, supposed to be those occupied by the hostile armies. The standard used by the Saxons was a horse, and it is said that the White Horse on the hill, under one of these camps, was cut there, in order to commemorate the victory of Alfred over the Danes. *See Wise's Letter to Dr. Mead on some Antiquities in Berkshire.*

+ The site of this engagement (which is not mentioned by Asser) has not been ascertained. Bishop Gibson in his notes on the Saxon Chronicle, mentions Merton in Surrey, Merdon or Marden in Wiltshire, and Meretun or Merton in Oxfordshire.

wintered at Lindsey, in Lincolnshire. In 874, they proceeded to Repton, in Derbyshire, and there wintered; and in 875, they divided their forces into two armies; the one marched into Northumberland, under the command of Healften, and wintered near the river Tyne, having reduced all the adjoining country to subjection; the other division of the army, under the direction of three leaders, Gothrum, Osscytil, and Amund, took up its winter quarters at Cambridge. In this same year, Alfred fought a naval battle against six of the enemy's vessels, took one, and dispersed the remainder. In the year 876, the Danes, quitting their post at Cambridge secretly, and in the night, marched to Wareham in Dorsetshire, invading again the territory of the West Saxons, contrary to their late treaty; but another was made between the contending powers, hostages of the most distinguished nobles of the army were delivered as pledges for the due fulfilment of it, and the most solemn oaths administered, that they would immediately quit the territory of the West Saxons. Upon this occasion the pagans swore by their bracelets, (as it was the custom of the northern nations to swear by their arms,) which they had never done before to any other people; but this treaty, like the former, was no sooner made than broken, and a part of the hostile army, taking advantage of the night, marched into Devonshire, and took possession of Exeter.

In the year 877, the Danes, in conveying their forces from Wareham to Exeter, experienced a very disastrous calamity by the loss of one hundred and twenty vessels in a storm, on the coast of Dorsetshire at Swanage. Alfred pursued a part of their army by land as far as Exeter, and forcing them into the citadel, obliged them to capitulate, and enter into terms: upon which they retreated into Mercia, and there spent the winter. In the year 878, we find the Danes again invading our county; they took possession of the royal villa at Chippenham, made themselves masters of the whole surrounding country, and by their cruelty and extortions, obliged many of the natives to leave their habitations, and seek refuge across the seas, " *trans mare*."

The situation of our Saxon monarch became every day more critical and perilous; he with difficulty escaped falling into the hands of the enemy, and having for some time wandered about the rugged parts of Somersetshire, in the greatest distress, with a few of his faithful vassals, was obliged at length to seek refuge in the cottage of a neat-herd. His biographer Asser informs us, that one day, the king was sitting by the fire trimming his bow and arrows, when his rustick hostess perceived that the cakes, which she had placed before the fire to be baked, were burning, upon which she rebuked Alfred for his inattention in not turning them, and exclaimed,

" *Urere quos cernis panes, gyrare moraris*
Cum nimium gaudes hos manducare calentes ?"

Another anecdote of the Saxon monarch, during his retreat in Somersetshire, is recorded by the historian Speed; but as no notice is taken of it by his biographer, too much reliance should not be placed on it, particularly as it bears the character of romance.*

We are now come to that period of history,.which is the particular object of my inquiry, namely, the BATTLE OF EDDINGTON. The circumstances attending it, have been thus detailed by Asser: " *Eodem anno* (A. D. 878,) *post Pascha Ælfred rex cum paucis adjutoribus fecit arcem in loco, qui dicitur* AETHELINGAEG, *et de ipsâ arce semper cum nobilibus vasallis Summurtunensis (pagæ) contrà Paganos infatigabiliter rebellavit; iterumque in septimâ hebdomadâ post Pascha ad* PETRAM ÆGBRYHTA, *quæ est in orientali parte saltus, qui dicitur* SELWDU, *Latine autem sylva magna, Britannicè Coïtmaur (Coed mawr) equitavit; ibique obviaverunt illi omnes accolæ Summurtunensis pagæ, et Wiltunensis; omnes accolæ Hamtunensis pagæ, qui non ultrà mare, pro metu Paganorum navigaverant; visoque rege, sicut dignum erat, quasi redivivum post tantas tribulationes recipientes, immenso repleti sunt gaudio, et ibi castrametati sunt unâ nocte. Diluculo sequenti illucescente, Rex inde castra commovens, venit ad locum qui dicitur* ÆCGLEA, *et ibi unâ nocte castrametatus est. Inde sequenti mane illucescente vexilla commovens ad locum, qui dicitur* ETHANDUM, *venit; et contrà universum Paganorum exercitum cum densâ testudine atrociter belligerans, animoséque diù persistens, divino nutu tandem victoriâ potitus, Paganos maximâ cæde prostravit, et fugientes usque ad arcem percutiens persecutus est, et omnia, quæ extrà arcem invenit, homines scilicet, et equos et pecora, confestim cædens homines, surripuit, et ante portas Paganicæ arcis cum omni exercitu suo viriliter castrametatus est, cumque ibi per quatuordecim dies remoraretur, Pagani fame, frigore, timore, et ad extremum, desperatione perterriti, pacem petierunt.*"

* But this Prince, the very mirrour of princes, more minding the wealth of his subjects, than the majesty of state, disguised himselfe in the habite of a common minstrell, and in person repaired to the Dane's campe, who lay like Senacheribs wallowing in wantonnesse, and secure in their owne conceit, from impeach of danger, which Elfred, a most skillful musitian, and an excellent poet, did not a little egge on by his sweet musicke, and songs of their valour, so that he was suffered to passe uncontrolled into the company of their Princes at banquets, or elsewhere; whereby he both saw their negligent security, and by diligent observance learned the designes that in their counsels they intended. Returning to his comfortlesse company, he told them the condition of the hostile campe, and how easie it was to recover againe their decaied estates; whereupon showing himselfe to his subjects, unto whose sight nothing could be more joyous, on the suddaine he set upon the carelesse campe of the Danes, and made thereof a very great slaughter, to the great terrour of others in other parts, that had accounted him dead longe since. *Speed's Chronicle,* page 357.

Such is the account given of the battle of Eddington by Asser, the biographer and cotemporary of king Alfred ; by which we learn, that about Easter, in the year 878, the Saxon monarch, with the assistance of a few of his followers, constructed a fort at Athelney, from which he made continual excursions against his enemies the Danes.   The seventh week after Easter, he quitted his retreat in Somersetshire, and marched to a place called PETRA ÆGBRYHTA, or the STONE OF ÆGBRYHT, which is situated on the eastern side of the great forest of Selwood.   There he was met by all the inhabitants of Somerset, Wilts, and by those of Hampshire, who, through fear of the Danes, had not been obliged to cross the sea for safety, and whose joy, in seeing their beloved monarch alive, and safe after such severe trials and disasters, was very great.   There they encamped for one night.

On the morning of the following day, the king removed his camp to a place called ÆCGLEA, where he also encamped for the night.

On the next morning, he proceeded to ETHANDUM, and having there fixed his standard, commenced a vigorous attack upon the whole Danish army, which he completely defeated.   He then pursued them to their fortress, before which he remained encamped for the space of fourteen days, at the end of which term, the enemy, worn out by hunger and fatigue, surrendered at discretion.   A treaty of peace was proposed and agreed to by the Danes, many of whom embraced Christianity, and Godrum their king, with thirty of his most distinguished followers, were baptized by the hands of Alfred, at Auler in Somersetshire.   The Danish king and his attendants were afterwards most honourably received, and hospitably entertained by the Saxon monarch, for twelve days, in his royal villa at Wedmore.

Topographical writers have differed very widely in opinion respecting the line of march taken by Alfred, from Athelney to Eddington.   Camden and his annotator, Gibson, agree in fixing the scene of action at Eddington, near Bratton. The latter also thinks that CLAY HILL, near Warminster, might have been the ÆCGLEA, recorded by Asser under that title, and by the Saxon Chronicle, under that of IGLEA, but gives the preference to a village in the neighbourhood called LEIGH, meaning Westbury Leigh before mentioned.

Mr. Milner, in his *History of Winchester*, places the scene of action at Heddington between Devizes and Calne, and supposes that the fortress, to which the Danes were compelled to retreat, was Oldbury.

Mr. Lysons in his *Britannia, (Berkshire*, p. 162), upon the authority of Dr. Beke, a learned professor at Oxford, has transferred this battle to a third

Heddington, in the neighbourhood of Hungerford in Berkshire, making the English army take a forced march of thirty-five miles from PETRA ÆGBRYHTA, (which he allows to have been BRIXTON, in Wiltshire,) to ÆCGLEA, which he also places in Berkshire.*

A third, and still more extraordinary opinion respecting this battle, has been started by the late learned antiquary Mr. Whitaker, in his *Life of St. Neot.* In his usual decisive tone, he says, " to settle all this, I shall not cite the opinions of others, but produce my own. Others have almost uniformly agreed to fix the central point of the whole, the place of the engagement, at Heddington near to Bratton Castle, and not far from Westbury, in Wiltshire. Camden began, Gibson followed him, and Mr. Gough has followed both. Yet this is apparently wrong. The battle was fought at a place much further to the north. The Danes seized Chippenham when Alfred fled, and at Chippenham we find them when defeated by him. Near Chippenham therefore the battle certainly was."

I shall now analyze the above discordant opinions, and endeavour, if possible, to extract the truth. Of the spot fixed upon by king Alfred, for his retreat, no doubt has been entertained, and all historians have agreed in fixing it at Athelney in Somersetshire, where the event has been recorded on an obelisk, by the following inscription:

KING ALFRED THE GREAT, IN THE YEAR OF OUR LORD 879, HAVING BEEN DEFEATED BY THE DANES, FLED FOR REFUGE TO THE FOREST OF ATHELNEY, WHERE HE LAY CONCEALED FROM HIS ENEMIES FOR THE SPACE OF A WHOLE YEAR. HE SOON AFTER REGAINED THE POSSESSION OF HIS THRONE, AND IN GRATEFUL REMEMBRANCE OF THE PROTECTION HE HAD RECEIVED UNDER THE FAVOR OF HEAVEN, ERECTED A MONASTERY ON THIS SPOT, AND ENDOWED IT WITH THE LAND CONTAINED IN THE ISLE OF ATHELNEY. TO PERPETUATE THE MEMORIAL OF SO REMARKABLE AN INCIDENT IN THE LIFE OF THAT ILLUSTRIOUS PRINCE, THIS EDIFICE WAS FOUNDED BY JOHN SLADE, ESQ. OF MANSEL, THE PROPRIETOR OF ATHELNEY FARM, AND LORD OF THE MANOR OF NORTH PETHERTON, A. D. 1801.

All the writers also agree in terminating the first day's march of the Saxon army at PETRA ÆGBRYHTA, or Brixton Deverill, but they differ widely as to

---

* I shall hereafter have occasion to shew how very erroneous is the opinion of this author respecting some of the stations on the Roman roads in our county, published in the Archaeologia for the year 1806.

that of the second day; Camden and Gough having fixed the ÆCGLEA in the neighbourhood of CLAY HILL; Bishop Gibson at WESTBURY LEIGH; Dr. Beke, having transferred it into Berkshire, and Mr. Whitaker to HIGHLEY COMMON, near Whaddon, and to the south-west of Melksham, in North Wiltshire. A variety of opinion also has prevailed with respect to ETHANDUM, and indeed with some reason, as we find two places in Wiltshire, and one in Berkshire bearing the name of Eddington, and Heddington. Camden places it near Bratton; Mr. Milner, at Heddington beyond Devizes; Mr. Lysons in Berkshire, and Mr. Whitaker at Yatton in North Wiltshire. The opinion of the latter is so singular, and so unreasonable, that I think it right to lay it before my readers. He says, " the present YATTON, about five miles to the north-west of Chippenham, is the fair representative of ETHANDUN in the history. But the battle itself was a little lower, on the Avon, even at SLAUGHTENFORD; the very name of which denotes what the tradition of the inhabitants has handed down, concerning a great slaughter of the Danes in this place. So happily do the local circumstances accord with the historical representation! Yet where was the fortress to which the routed Danes fled? It was undoubtedly that double entrenchment in Bury Wood, betwixt Colern and North Wraxall." (*Life of S. Neot*, p. 269.)

I shall now endeavour to trace, with accuracy and impartiality, the line of march pursued by king Alfred, from his retreat at Athelney, in Somersetshire, against the Danes, who were stationed at Eddington, in Wiltshire: and I should hope that more reliance would be placed on one who has frequently examined the ground, than on those who, strangers to the country, have made use of maps as their guides, and the vague traditions of former historians, as the basis of their assertions.

If we look at the map of Somerset, and examine the line of country between Athelney and Brixton Deverill, we shall plainly see that the direct course from one to the other would pass near Somerton, Castle Cary, Bruton, and Maiden Bradley. Between the two latter places was the spacious forest of Selwood, extending from the village of Pen, to the town of Westbury. Two ancient roads, the one Roman, the other British, passed through this forest; the former leading from *Sorbiodunum*, or Old Sarum, through Grovely and Great Ridge Woods, Monkton and Brixton Deverill, and pointing across the Mendip Hills, to the Bristol Channel: the latter pursuing in some degree the same course, but diverging more to the south-west towards the British city of ISCALIS, now Ilchester. This was the road which king Alfred would naturally have chosen.

From Castle Cary or Bruton, he would have penetrated through Selwood by the road now bearing the name of HARDWAY, which leads to the summit of a hill called KINGSETTLE, upon which a lofty tower was built by my predecessor and grandfather Henry Hoare, Esq. in honour of king Alfred. A tablet placed under the Effigy of the Saxon Monarch bears the following inscription:

ALFRED THE GREAT, A. D. 879, ON THIS SUMMIT ERECTED HIS STANDARD AGAINST DANISH INVADERS. TO HIM WE OWE THE ORIGIN OF JURIES, AND THE CREATION OF A NAVAL FORCE. ALFRED, THE LIGHT OF A BENIGHTED AGE, WAS A PHILOSOPHER, AND A CHRISTIAN, THE FATHER OF HIS PEOPLE; AND THE FOUNDER OF THE ENGLISH MONARCHY AND LIBERTIES.

From this eminence the British road would have led him in a direct line over Kilmington Common, by Rodmead farm, to the Vale of the Deverills, and to Brixton, or the PETRA ÆGBRYHTA, where his first day's fatiguing march terminated.

On the second day he marched to ÆCGLEA, and there rested for the night. If this halting-place is fixed at Clay Hill, or in its neighbourhood, the army must have diverged considerably to the north-west; from a desire, probably, of following the wood-land tract, and avoiding the more open and exposed country. Silence and secrecy were the watchwords of the day; and the chief object of King Alfred was to surprise the unsuspecting Danes, who thought him secure in his retreat at Athelney. And here it will be necessary for me to answer some of the objections made by former writers, to this line of march. I shall not take any notice of the fanciful positions of Dr. Beke and Mr. Whitaker, but confine myself to those of the learned Camden and his annotator Bishop Gibson. The latter thinks " that Westbury Leigh would be a fitter situation for the ÆCGLEA of Asser and the Chronicle; and says that Clay Hill bears no marks of intrenchments, and is too far from the spot where the battle was fought on the following day near Eddington." Though on each of the first days march Asser tells us that Alfred encamped, " *castrametatus est*," we are not to imply that he raised military intrenchments, for the safety or convenience of his army for one night. There are indeed evident signs of raised earthen works round Clay Hill, as may be seen in the annexed plate, but they bear marks of much higher antiquity, and cannot possibly be attributed to the Saxon Monarch, whose object was to proceed slowly and secretly towards his enemy; slowly, that he might afford an opportunity for his friends from distant parts to join him; and secretly, that the enemy might gain no previous intelligence of his hostile intentions, all of which plans would have been counteracted, had he (according to Bishop Gibson), encamped at Westbury Leigh, a place adjoining, and within sight of Bratton Castle. I think, therefore, ÆCGLEA ought to be placed somewhere in the neighbourhood of Clay Hill or Bucley.

Let us next consider the events of the third day, which at length decided the superiority of the Saxon monarch over his inveterate enemies the Danes. The village of Eddington corresponds so well both in name and situation with the ETHANDUM of Asser, and the ETHANDUNE of the Saxon Chronicle, that I shall not hesitate in placing the scene of action at that place. It is situated at a short distance from Bratton, under the ridge of chalk hills, upon a bold point of which stands the fortress to which the Danes were driven for a temporary refuge. The original entrances to this camp are still used as a thoroughfare for the road to Bratton; and in a valley to the eastward is a fine perennial spring called Lockham, near which the residence of the Danes is still commemorated in the name of a field called Danes Ley.

Less would have been written or said on this memorable subject, had authors taken the pains to examine personally the local situation, or line of country through which King Alfred would naturally have directed his march. In the course now laid down before my readers, we find nothing improbable, and even etymology need not be tortured in order to explain the names of places recorded on this occasion; for we find the PETRA ÆGBRYHTA re-echoed in Brixton; the ÆCGLEA, in Clay, Clea, or Bucley; and the ETHANDUNE in Eddington. But the Cornish historian, Mr. Whitaker, disregarding the records of Asser and the Chronicle in this instance, (though in others he has held them forth as of the highest authority,) seeming to differ merely for difference sake, and in his dictatorial tone exclaiming,

" *Sic volo, sic jubeo, sit pro ratione voluntas,*"

has transferred ÆCGLEA and ETHANDUNE to HIGHLEY and YATTON, because, in looking over Mr. Gough's Additions to Camden's Britannia, he has found a place named SLAUGHTENFORD, and a camp adjoining. Such topographical and historical misstatements should stand corrected, even though made by so intelligent and seducing an author as Mr. Whitaker.

Leaving Bratton, I shall return to my head quarters by the great track-way. Barrows are thinly scattered over these downs, most of which appear to have been investigated, and therefore have not been attempted by us. Leaving the track-way, which continues its course along the ridge, I shall turn off to the right, and pursue my ride to Warminster, over a fine piece of level turf, which is marked by some clumps of fir-trees. And here it is necessary to correct an error in the great Map of Wiltshire, which has noticed an old camp, whereas it is only an oblong enclosure. On this hill we again meet with OLD DITCH, steering westward to Upton-cow down, where I have before mentioned it (page 54), and further on is a circular barrow, which from its singularity deserves notice. It is surrounded by a ditch, having a *vallum* without, through which are two entrances pointing east and west. On making a large section in it, we discovered at the depth of about eighteen inches, an article of iron resembling the head of a spear or halberd, and near it the halves of two horse shoes. In our progress to the floor of the barrow, we found a great many flat-headed nails, and pottery similar to what we find in the British towns, together with charred wood ; and on the floor of the barrow was a small circular cist containing a very few black ashes. We also met with considerable quantities of stiff clay, which is remarkable, as none is produced by nature on this down. A little further on the extreme point of this hill, immediately above Warminster lime-kilns, is a mutilated camp, which, when complete, was nearly of a square form. On digging a few years ago near one of the excavations made by quarrying, Mr. Cunnington discovered some pieces of Roman pottery.

On the edge of this same down, (called Arn Hill), overlooking the Westbury road, is a long barrow, newly planted, and which was partially opened by Mr. Cunnington in the year 1802. At the south end was a sarsen stone five feet high, terminating almost in a point, and placed in an upright position. Near it lay the bones of three skeletons, which appeared to have been deposited on the south and south-east of the stone, with the heads towards the east. They were all placed on a rude pavement of marl, and over them was thrown a pile of large loose stones. There are probably other, and more ancient interments in this *tumulus* ; but the contents of the long barrows have proved in general so very uniform and uninteresting, that we have not been tempted to make any further investigations in it.

In whatever light we view the tract of country presented to us in this Iter, it must prove highly interesting, as affording objects suited to each taste, and pleasing to each eye. The antiquary will find ample matter for reflection in the *tumuli* and other earthen works ; the military man will behold a fine specimen of ancient castrametation in the camp at Bratton ; the historian will contem-

s

plate with enthusiasm on the important consequences of the battle of Eddington, and retrace the character and noble exploits of our illustrious King Alfred ; and even the most indifferent stroller must feel a certain degree of pleasure in beholding the great variety of rich and extensive views which this ride will produce, and, with his horse, enjoy the verdant turf which accompanies his steps throughout it.

ITER III. From Warminster, I shall again ascend the downy district, where a continual supply of British antiquities is every where to be met with. Leaving the bold fortress of Battlesbury on the right, and reaching the summit of the hill, the attention is attracted by a long barrow on the left, which on opening, produced an interment of a skeleton near the centre, in a cist cut in the native soil beneath the floor of the barrow ; and over it, near the surface, was a small cup of rude British pottery. Near the above are two circular barrows, which were opened by Mr. Cunnington. In the one, situated to the east, was an oblong cist, at the depth of five feet from the surface, in which was deposited a skeleton with its head towards the north-east. This interment was protected by a prodigious quantity of flints thrown over it. The adjoining barrow also contained, at the depth of three feet, a skeleton, with its head lying exactly north, and covered with the chalky earth.

On the next projecting point of down is a circular earthen work, with one entrance to the south-east, and apparently another, but not so decisive, towards the west: its diameter from the entrance is about two hundred and eighty feet.

From hence I shall return to the great track-way, and continue my ride towards Bratton. There are some few barrows on these downs, one of which Mr. Cunnington opened. It is situated near Grant's farm, on the right side of the track-way, upon some newly broken up land, is large, though flat. It contained two rude urns, the one placed within the other, and an interment of burnt bones. The large urn was broken in pieces; the small one, containing about three pints, is still preserved in our Museum, and is rather particular in its shape, having a perforated and projecting handle.

Quitting the track-way, and leaving Bratton Camp to the left, I pursued my ride over a fine verdant down, and descended into the vale at a spot marked White Cliff in the large Map of Wiltshire. In my way I noticed a small earthen work nearly square, with an entrance towards the south-east ; it is very perfect and neatly formed, and measures eighty-seven by seventy-eight feet within the area. A little beyond it are some other irregularities and slight banks at the head of a little valley. From White Cliff I descended into the vale on the left, to see the picturesque church of Brattton, placed in a solitary and retired situation, though tradition reports that the village once stood near it. From thence I pursued the valley leading to South Down farm, passing by Lockham Spring, which rises under an eminence that presents a bolder outline than the generality of our chalk hills. Adjoining this farm, towards the north, is a large circular barrow, which Mr. Cunnington began to explore ; but a lantern enclosing three halfpence, and a glass bottle, appeared as evidences of its prior opening. In the ploughed ground to the south of the aforesaid farm is another large mutilated barrow, called Row Barrow, which Mr. Cunnington opened in the year 1801, and at the depth of four feet found an interment of burned bones, with which were deposited a spear, lance, and arrow-head of brass ; and these, contrary to the usual custom, were found two or three feet above the floor of the barrow ; from which circumstance, and further experience, we may reasonably conclude that this was a subsequent interment, and that the primary one still remains undiscovered. Adjoining Row-Barrow is a valley where several track-ways meet, and a well called Lady Well. At a short distance from the last mentioned barrow, and on the road leading to Imber, which will be described in my next station, there are two other long barrows on points of hills overlooking the vale, the one facing Scratchbury, the other opposite to Middle Hill, which, from the difficulty attending these *tumuli*, and the general similarity of others of the same model, we have not been induced to open. The same road by which we ascended the down at the commencement of this Iter, will conduct us back to Warminster.

ITER IV. A very interesting line of detached hills which bounds the left side of the Vale of Wily, between Warminster and Heytesbury, will form the basis of this Iter. Each eminence bears its military or sepulchral memorial, and opens to us a wide field for inquiry and conjecture.

The first of these, COP HEAD HILL, and situated at the back of the town of Warminster, is by nature of a conical shape, but rendered more so by art, as its *apex* has been evidently formed into a *tumulus*. Like many of the barrows on our plains, it was encompassed by a ditch and bank which are still apparent. Its summit presents a most beautiful and extensive *panorama* of wood, hill, and vale, and the interest of the antiquary is encreased by the numerous British works which may be distinguished from this elevated point. We opened this barrow, which is only three feet in elevation, in October 1809, and at the depth of two feet on the south-east side, discovered a skeleton lying nearly north and south, the head towards the latter point; but several of the bones had been disturbed by planting a tree at the top of the barrow. With the skeleton were deposited some pieces of flint, which appeared to have been polished by use, some fragments of stag's horns, the butt end of one of which had been cut off and perforated, and from its appearance used as a hammer. On the west side of the *tumulus*, at the depth of about three feet, and a little below the floor, was another skeleton, with the head towards the west, but unaccompanied by any arms or trinkets. On the north side we found a cist nearly two feet deep, in which were two skeletons, and an interment of burned bones; but I conceive these interments had been disturbed by planting, as towards the feet of the skeletons there was a great deal of vegetable earth intermixed with the bones. In this cist we discovered the remains of an infant, and by its side those of a female adult, probably its mother, both lying from north-west to south-east. In examining the cist near the body we met with burned bones, and a few ivory beads of the pully form; and on the floor of the barrow was a little heap of burned bones, nearly half the original interment. There were six beads, and a sea shell (a nerite): the former certainly belonged to the interment of burned bones; the latter probably to the infant skeleton.

The next hill has its summit crowned by the bold and extensive fortress of BATTLESBURY, and is the most conspicuous feature in the whole vale. This camp occupies the summit of an irregular point of down, and is by nature almost inaccessible on the west and north-east sides. The area of it within the intrenchments contains twenty-three acres and a quarter; the circuit of the outer *vallum* is seven furlongs and sixty-six yards, and the greatest height of the ramparts is sixty feet. You will observe by the annexed plan, on the north and south sides, where the ground is the most accessible, additional ramparts have been raised: and that the entrances to the east and west are guarded with outworks. The south-west angle of this camp is a point deserving particular attention. There the whole space of the inner ditch is occupied by a large circular barrow, which Mr. Cunnington opened, but found no interment. A few feet further to the west are two other barrows, over which the great inner rampart passes; these on opening, proved to be sepulchral: in the largest was found a cist containing burned human bones at the depth of two feet; and in the smallest, two skeletons lying from south to north, the head of the smallest reclining on the breast of the other. On the breast of the largest skeleton there was a small ring or bead of stone, which was probably worn as an amulet.

BATTLESBURY CAMP.

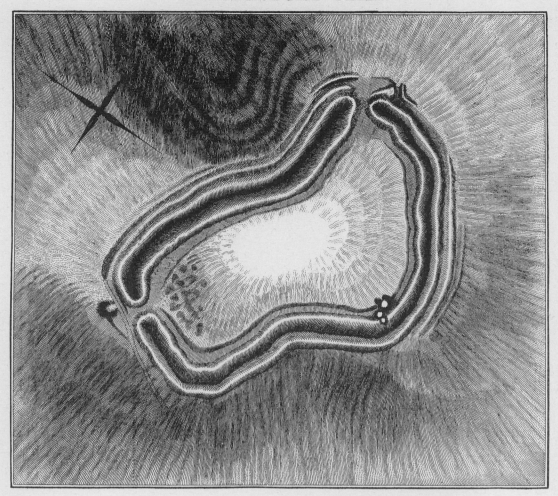

SCRATCHBURY CAMP.

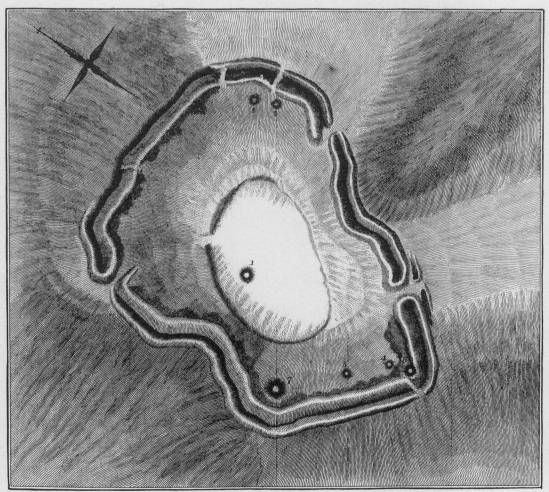

P. Crocker del.

Jⁿ Basire sc.

50   100   200   300   400

Scale of Yards.

Published by W. Miller, Albemarle Street, London, Janʸ 1.1810.

These circumstances tend to throw some light upon the æra of this camp, and evidently prove to us that the *tumuli* existed previous to the construction of that part of it where they are situated; for we still see them untouched and respected, and the ground taken from excavations near the large barrow, to raise the rampart, rather than disturb these ancient memorials of the dead. I doubt if the barbarous Saxons would have paid such a tribute of respect to their British predecessors.

Towards the north-west end of this camp are some small stone quarries, amongst which several human skeletons have at different times been found. Mr. Cunnington, observing some black earth amongst these excavations, dug there, and found at the depth of two feet, a human skeleton with its head to the north, and near it the greater part of the skeleton of a horse. The whole area of this camp has been in tillage for many years, and several Roman coins have been found; amongst them a large one in brass of *Trajan*, which is in the possession of Mr. Cunnington.

Those who are fond of elevated and commanding points of view, will be highly gratified in visiting our ancient camps; and few of them will be found more interesting than Battlesbury, whether we consider it in a military light, and admire the boldness of its situation and the strength of its ramparts, or whether in tracing its circumference, our attention is more particularly directed to the rich and extensive scenery that surrounds it. On the north side of the camp, where the hill is the most precipitate, the lynchets* have a very singular appearance, like a continued line of broken ramparts.

The next eminence that attracts our notice is called MIDDLE HILL. It has one large barrow on its summit, and two smaller on its declivity facing the vale of Wily. We fully investigated the former in the autumn of 1809, but found it had been opened before; the two smaller barrows contained interments of burned bones. In the fields beneath this hill, a great deal of ancient pottery has been found.

We now come to another strongly fortified eminence called SCRATCHBURY, a name derived probably from *Crech*, or *Crechen*, signifying a hill, or summit. This fine camp differs very materially from Battlesbury in the formation of its ramparts, which consist chiefly of one high *vallum* and a deep foss; but where the access is easier, there is another slight rampart. It appears to have had three entrances: the principal one to the south-east is approached by a narrow neck

---

* This word *lynchet*, is a corruption from land-sheare, a shred or strip of land; they are frequent at the declivities of our chalk hills, and are produced by the natural effect of the plough on sloping ground.

T

of land called Barbury : another entrance lies nearly east, and the third faces Middleton farm and Battlesbury camp. Near the first of these, a broken flint celt, with British and Roman pottery were dug up ; and a stone celt, with pottery and animal bones, was found by Mr. Cunnington amongst some loose earth and stones which had been recently excavated. These circumstances prove the very high antiquity of this camp, and bespeak a British origin. Its area exceeds forty acres : the circuit of the outer rampart is one mile eighty-six yards, and the greatest height of it is sixty-six feet.

But this camp is rendered particularly interesting by several *tumuli*, and another earthen work within its area. This latter inclines to a circular form, and occupies the *apex* of the hill ; but the whole of the area having been formerly in tillage, its shape has been much mutilated. On the north-west side, which is the most perfect, there is some appearance of an entrance ; the opposite side has been much defaced by the plough. Within this work is a large circular barrow, No. 1, but not above three feet in elevation. It contained an interment of burned bones, with which were deposited a small lance head of brass, a large amber ring, above fifty beads of the same material, a piece of brass two or three inches long, resembling a screw, and another bit of twisted brass, all of which are preserved in the museum of Miss Benet at Norton-house. Close to the above interment was a pile of ashes intermixed with fragments of burned bones. No. 2 contained within a cist in the chalk, an interment of burned bones, and some articles of bone, two of which were about two inches long, and flat, and the third was either a pin or arrow head, neatly polished to a very sharp point. No. 3 was unproductive, as well as the very small barrow No. 4. No. 5 contained a few burned bones at a considerable distance from the centre. No. 6 was also unproductive. No. 7 is a large barrow nearly one hundred feet in diameter, and twelve feet and an half in elevation, and is a very conspicuous object from the turnpike road below. Much labour and time were employed upon this *tumulus*, but without success, as the interment was not found. The various fragments of stag's horns, teeth of wild boar, charcoal, as well as an immense quantity of stones which had undergone the action of fire, seem to indicate this to have been a sepulchral barrow, in which the ceremony of cremation had been performed.

As we proceed eastward on this fine eminence, we are still accompanied by British remains. On the brow of the hill, overlooking the vale of Wily, and near some large chalk quarries, there are several barrows of various sizes, but many of them so mutilated as to be scarcely distinguished as such : some of them have been opened by Mr. Cunnington, but as they produced no important discovery, I will not take up the time of my readers by unnecessary detail. I shall only notice that these *tumuli* contained chiefly interments of burned bones, and that a great deal of rude British pottery has been found on this hill. On a more elevated part of the same down is a flat circular barrow, fifty feet in diameter, and eighteen inches in elevation, which produced a large rude urn inverted, containing an interment of human bones very imperfectly burned. Near it is another small circular barrow about forty feet in diameter and two and a half feet in elevation, which contained within a cist, a deposit of burned bones.

We now come to another eminence called COTTLEY HILL, whose summit is rendered conspicuous by a large *tumulus*. Mr. Cunnington opened it in the year 1801, by making a section of considerable length and width, but he could not find any interment within it : the only articles discovered were animal bones, iron nails, and broken pottery of different sorts ; some pieces very thick, and half burned, others of the fine black and red Samian species. This barrow is surrounded by a circular *vallum*, of small elevation ; and from the circumstance of the ditch being within the bank, we may pronounce this to have been originally a work destined for religious purposes. The south-west side is tolerably perfect, the remainder has been much defaced by the plough. The diameter of this circle, when complete, would have been about one hundred and sixty yards. On the north side of it are some trifling cavities in the soil, which on examination, produced black mould to the depth of three feet, intermixed with fragments of Roman pottery ; also four small pieces of brick flues similar to those found in the Roman Villa at Pitmead. On other parts of this hill, within the circle, there are depressions in the ground about four feet deep, containing pottery, animal bones, charred wood, &c. These circumstances, especially as no sepulchral *indicia* were discovered in the barrow, would almost lead one to suppose that this eminence had been fixed upon by the Romans as an exploratory post, and used by them for that purpose.

In Heytesbury north field, on the back of Scratchbury Camp, and Cottley Hill, is a long barrow, which Mr. Cunnington investigated at two different periods. The first trial took place in the year 1800, when a large cross section was made in the centre, and at the depth of twelve feet he discovered a little mound of black earth which extended along the middle of the barrow, but nothing was found except some pieces of stag's horns.

The second trial commenced with a section at the broad end. At the depth

of eight feet, he came to the black earth, which increased in height as he proceeded, and on working about three feet further, he found it rise into the form
of a circular barrow, and the soil was intermixed with large flints, marl, and a
few sarsen stones, which by their frequent falling down, made a continuation of the operations on this spot dangerous ; he therefore made another section
immediately over the conical mound of black earth, and after removing a great
quantity of earth, found a large circular cist about five feet wide, and two and
a half deep, cut very neatly in the chalk, which contained nothing but black
earth intermixed with stones and marl.   By the side of this cist, and further
to the south, lay the remains of a great many human skeletons crossing each
other in every direction, but the decayed state of the bones prevented his ascertaining the number of bodies.

On returning to Warminster through the vale, another barrow occurs, which
deserves particular notice.   It is called KING BARROW, and excepting those
near Tilshead, is the largest we have met with : it is situated about two hundred
yards north of the village of Boreham, and a little to the south of Battlesbury
Camp.   It stands nearly north and south, and the large end faces the former
point.   It now measures in length on the north-east side two hundred and six
feet ; and fifty-six feet in width at each end ; its elevation is from fifteen to
sixteen feet, and it appears originally to have been much larger.   It was first
opened in the year 1800, by a section of twenty-eight feet in length from the
N. E. edge to the centre, from which the men worked from right to left : the
soil composing the *tumulus* was chiefly marl, amongst which were intermixed
pieces of stags' horns, animal bones, boars' tusks, and very rude pottery. The
floor of the barrow was lined with a yellowish clay, and was about two feet
and three quarters lower than the adjoining ground ; nearly the whole of the
floor that was uncovered, had the appearance of rusty iron, and was strewed
with animal bones of birds and beasts, charred wood, ashes, and the coarsest of
pottery ; and near the edge of the section, was found the skeleton of a horse.
It is remarkable that this floor should extend several feet from the barrow on
the north-east side, and more than two feet below the present surface.   This
first operation having proved unsuccessful as to finding the interment, an
opening was afterwards made on the top of the barrow, and at the depth of
eighteen inches, three human skeletons were found, lying from south-west to
north-east ; and on the thigh of one of them was an iron sword, which originally had a handle of oak wood ; the blade is about eighteen inches long,
two wide, and single edged.   Near these skeletons was found the fragment of

an urn, very rude yet prettily ornamented, which probably contained an interment of burned bones, that was disturbed by the deposit of the above bodies. I should have observed, that on the floor of the large section we found a piece of a very hard stone of a violet colour, and neatly polished; the end of which now broken off, probably terminated in an edge. Since our first trials on this barrow, the present occupier of the land has carried away a great deal of it, and intends, as I have heard, to level the whole of it.

Not satisfied with our former researches, we have lately made another section in this *tumulus*, where we also found the floor of it full two feet and a half lower than the adjoining ground, and covered with black ashes, as in the first section; and the soil, as before, in some places had the appearance of iron when decomposed. In uncovering this floor, we were much surprized to find, that, as we approached towards the edge of the barrow, the clay and earth which covered the floor, rose three feet in height like another *tumulus*, and ten or twelve feet in diameter; amongst this clay and earth was an immense quantity of animal bones, some of oxen, but mostly of swine: among these bones and ashes were several pieces of burned human bones, and fragments of an urn and other British pottery, some specimens of which are curiously ornamented. After exploring a great many feet of this barrow within a barrow, we made a large section from top to bottom, but found nothing but a few animal bones, and a little charred wood. Thus, after infinite labour, we were again foiled, and the primary interment still remains undiscovered; for the position of the skeletons so near the surface evidently proves them to have been a subsequent deposit; and from the circumstance of finding so much charred wood, together with fragments of burned human bones, and rude British pottery, we have reason to think that the rites of cremation had been here practised. The urn on the top of the barrow was appropriated probably to one person, but from the appearance beneath, several bodies must have been burned.

U

STATION III. HEYTESBURY.

ITER I. From Heytesbury, which probably derived this name from its situation
east of the great camp of Scratchbury, I shall proceed a short way on the turnpike road leading from thence to Salisbury, and passing through the village of
Lower Knook, ascend the down to the left over Knook Foss Hill, erroneously
called *Horse Hill* in the old county map. When the present turnpike road
was forming, the workmen found a great many human bones on the slope of
the hill; and with them a long iron sword with a brass handle, a pair of brass
spurs, with long necks, and large rowels; also arrow heads, and quivers made
chiefly of twisted brass wire; small brass or copper money, and a drinking
glass, which was broken in two pieces. The old man from whom Mr. Cunnington gained this information, described the latter as having been stained
like the old glass in church windows. These articles were sold to a travelling
pedlar.

We now come to a fine piece of level maiden down belonging to the parish
of Upton Lovel, on which are six barrows. No. 1, a circular barrow, situated
on the west side of Upton Lovel Down, was opened by a labourer in order to
procure flints; and Mr. Cunnington hearing by accident of his operations,
attended on the spot, just as he had discovered a large rude urn, which was
broken in taking out of the cist; it was full of burned human bones, and amongst
them was found the elegant pair of nippers engraved in (TUMULI, PLATE IX).
In turning the barrow completely over for the sake of flints, he found at about
six feet from the central interment, a small urn imperfectly baked, and full of
red earth and vegetable mould. This urn is engraved also (above the nippers)
in the afore-mentioned plate. About the same distance from the centre, but
in different directions, were found two other small rude urns, which were

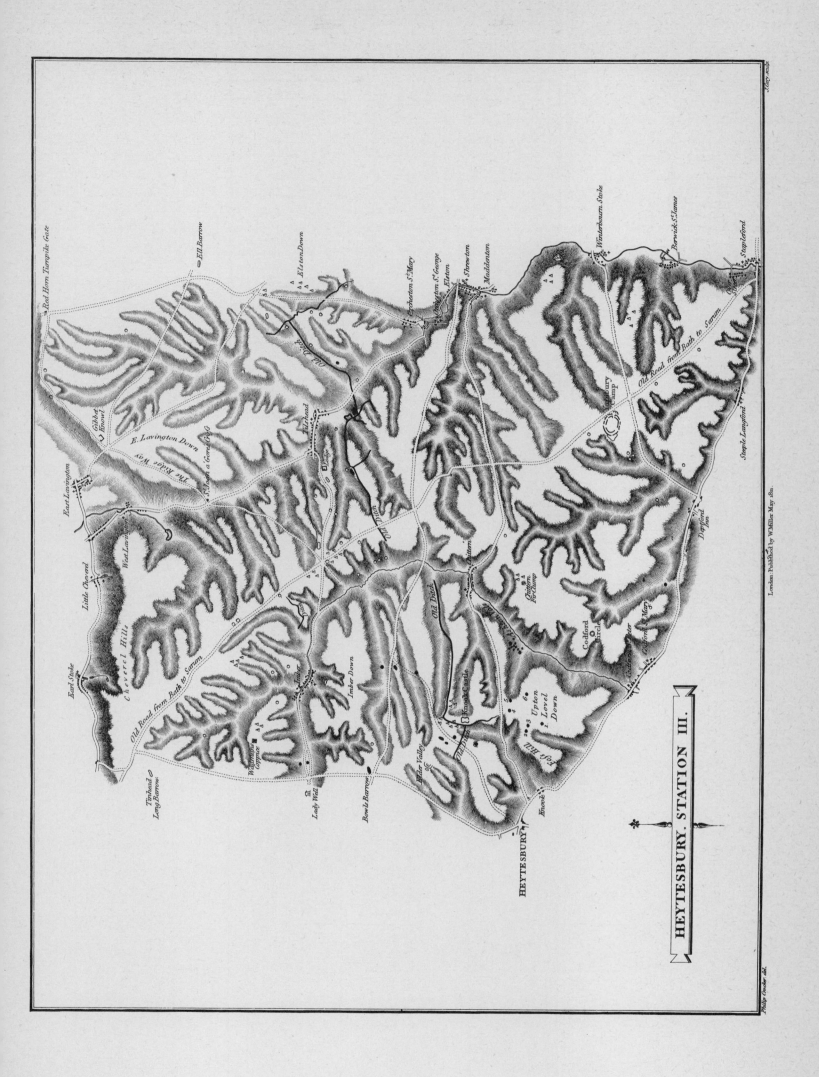

HEYTESBURY. STATION III.

Philip Crocker del.

London. Published by W. Miller May 1811.

Heath sculp.

unfortunately broken ; one of them contained black ashes, the other vegetable mould. On the floor of the barrow there was a thin *stratum* of clay.

Following the declivity of the hill, in a parallel line with the road leading to Amesbury, is another low barrow (No. 2,) which, like the former, was opened by a laboruer in search of flints. The primary interment of burned bones was deposited in a cist, unaccompanied by any urn or other memorial ; but on turning over the whole barrow, he discovered five urns of different sizes, forming a circle round the cist at the distance of about four feet : two of them contained ashes and very black earth ; the others vegetable mould of various colours. We have to regret that all these urns were broken to pieces through carelessness.

At a short distance from the above is another low barrow (No. 3,) which contained the bones of a skeleton, with its head deposited towards the north, and a fine ornamented drinking-cup placed near its legs, which was unfortunately damaged by the pick-axe.* Beyond this, on a higher part of the hill, is a low circular barrow, very neatly formed, and bearing marks of high antiquity. (No. 4). It was opened by Mr. Cunnington in the year 1801, and at the depth of nearly three feet in the native chalk, produced one skeleton lying on its back with the head towards the north ; and another in a sitting posture, the head and hands of which were within ten or twelve inches of the surface. The first, from the largeness of the bones, appeared to have been a stout man ; the latter, being much smaller, was probably a female, and perhaps his wife. The cist in which they were interred, was nearly of an oval form, excepting a small variation to the left of the larger skeleton, in order to make room for the other. On removing the earth from the feet of the largest skeleton, he found more than three dozen instruments of bones pointed and perforated, specimens of which are given in TUMULI, PLATE VII. Adjoining these lay three celts of flint or stone, two of which are engraved in PLATES V. and VI. and two other stones, which are also engraved in PLATE VI. One of these stones was evidently made use of for sharpening or bringing to a point the arrow heads of bone ; another stone of a larger size (not engraved,) served probably as a whetstone in forming and polishing the celts and other instruments.

On clearing away the earth from the legs, some boars' teeth were found perforated, and several *ætites*, or eagle stones, of white flint, which had been cut or broken in two, so as to form a rude kind of cup. Near the breast of this

* This cup is engraved in *Tumuli*, Plate IX.

skeleton was an axe of stone, engraved in Plate V. and a circular stone, Plate VI. which was probably used in a sling, and about two dozen more arrow or lance heads of bone. After discovering the latter, a considerable quantity of the bones of the small skeleton fell upon the large one, which caused a difficulty in ascertaining to which of the bodies the large ring engraved in Plate VII. belonged. It is made of jet, or canal coal, and has its outside ornamented with imperfect circles, which appear to have been formed by some rude instrument; it was worn probably as an amulet, not as a ring, for the inside has rather a sharp edge. Besides these articles, there were several stones and pebbles of different sorts, not to be found in the neighbourhood, a small brass pin, some beads of jet, and one of ivory or bone.

The contents of this small *tumulus* have been so numerous, and various, that I have been rather minute in my description of it, as they throw a strong light on the customs of our rude ancestors at a period when they lived in savage and pastoral wildness, and before the use of metals was known to them. The nature of the articles found in this barrow proves its very high antiquity, and will, I think, justify me in calling it a Celtic sepulchre.

No. 5 is situated still higher upon the hill, and was opened in the year 1801. At the bottom, and nearly in the centre, was a circular excavation, about two feet in diameter, and a few inches deep in the native soil, which contained half a peck of burned human bones, and under them a spear head of brass. About two feet to the south of this cavity was a sepulchral urn with its mouth downwards, containing three parts of a bushel of fine ashes, charred wood, and small fragments of bone; but it is rather remarkable, that among the bones, not one tooth was found. It is also singular, that, contrary to the usual custom, the ashes should have been deposited within the urn, and the interment of burned bones within the cist.

No. 6, the last barrow which I have to describe on this Down, from its superior size and commanding situation, has been called Upton Great Barrow. It is bell-shaped, well formed, and surrounded with a deep ditch and small *vallum*. This was also first opened by a labouring man who was often employed to dig up flints on these downs for the turnpike roads, and who had hopes of finding a treasure; but on meeting with nothing but bones and ashes, he sent for Mr. Cunnington, who, on coming to the barrow, found at the depth of eleven feet, a cist like a shallow bason, cut in the native chalk, and containing the burned bones of one person. With this interment were deposited forty-eight beads, sixteen of which were of green and blue opaque glass, of a long shape,

P. Crocker delt.

Js Basire Sc.

Publifhed for W. Miller, Albemarle Street, London, Jany 1,1810.

P. Crocker del.t

J.s Basire Sc.

Published for W. Miller, Albemarle Street, London, Jan.y 1, 1810.

P. Crocker del.

J.ᵒ Bafire Sc.

Published for W. Miller, Albemarle Street, London, Jan.ʸ 1. 1810.

and notched between so as to resemble a string of beads ; five were of canal coal or jet ; and the remaining twenty-seven were of red amber ; the whole forming a most beautiful necklace, and such as a British female would not in these modern days of good taste and elegance disdain to wear.* On a supposition that this large *tumulus* could not have been appropriated to the remains of a single person, Mr. Cunnington made several sections in it, but found only fragments of rude pottery, pieces of stags' horns, animal bones, and vast quantities of ashes and charred wood.

When we consider the diminutive size of many of these barrows, the nature of the operations commenced upon some of them by the rustic labourer, and the ease with which the remainder of them might have been explored, we have great reason to exult in the success of our researches, and to congratulate the public on having rescued from oblivion the history of these very ancient *tumuli*, so few in number, but so truly interesting and productive in their contents. Following the same ridge of down, which is intersected by a bank that runs towards Old Ditch on the left, I shall diverge to the right into a little secluded vale called Ashton Valley, in which is a group of eleven barrows, whose position is described in the annexed plate.

No. 1, a large bowl-shaped barrow, ditched round, and rather flat at top, is about eighty feet in diameter, and six in elevation; when Mr. Cunnington opened it in the year 1801, he discovered five urns, containing burned human bones, immediately under the turf, which from the pressure of cattle had been crushed to pieces. At a subsequent period he found four more urns, and also the interment of a skeleton lying on his face with its head towards the north, and its legs gathered up, deposited at the depth of three feet four inches from the surface. A little to the right of this skeleton was a kind of tunnel leading to the south, and large enough to admit a slender man : he examined it to the length of six feet, when it separated into two lesser branches to the right and left. Subsequent experience having induced him to think, that the primary deposit was still undiscovered, he again, in 1803, employed his men for two days upon it, and in the floor of the barrow found a cist containing a simple interment of burned bones. This *tumulus* had appeared to me so very singular in its contents, that I was anxious to make some further trials on it ; accordingly, in January 1808, we made another section in it on the south side, and found the skeleton of an infant, apparently not above twelve months old, in a

* Engraved in TUMULI PLATE IX.

X

small cist on the floor; and on continuing the section in a northern direction, we discovered the remains of a large urn, with the burned bones scattered about in a cist where they were originally deposited. This was certainly the primary interment, which had probably been disturbed by the men employed in opening the barrow some years ago; who, according to the vulgar, and indeed general opinion when we first began these researches, thinking that these urns contained coin instead of bones, made this discovery, and gave no information of it to Mr. Cunnington. This is one of the most remarkable barrows we have ever opened, and may be denominated a family mausoleum, as it seems to have contained eleven interments of burned bones, and two skeletons.

The adjoining *tumulus*, No. 2, has a deeper ditch than is usual round barrows of such small dimensions. Immediately under the turf we found some fragments of a coarse urn, and a few burned bones scattered about; and at the depth of five feet in the chalk, was a circular cavity, more than two feet in diameter, with a very even floor of marl; at the edge of which, but one foot deeper, was a circular cist containing an interment of burned bones.

The mound, No. 3, does not exceed eighteen inches in elevation. On making the first section in it, Mr. Cunnington was struck with the singularity of finding two pieces of fine Roman pottery at a considerable depth in the soil; and in prosecuting his researches, instead of a sepulchral urn, as he expected, he perceived that the earth and chalk had been excavated to the depth of eleven feet in order to form a room, and the soil being chalk, the sides were nearly as hard as a stone wall, and the angles quite sharp. Towards the centre lay a human skeleton, nearly south and north, extended at full length, and on its back, contrary to the general custom. In opening this place, when within two feet of the bottom, the men frequently found pieces of charred wood and iron nails of various sizes from half an inch to five long, and generally with flat heads. The circumstances attending this mound, are very particular; but the mode of burial, as well as the nails and fragments found in the soil which composed it, evidently prove, that it was an interment of a much later date to the others in this group.

No. 4, is a large flat circular barrow, in which, at the depth of two feet and a quarter, we found the floor covered with black ashes and charred wood, intermixed with human bones half burned.

No. 5, is a very flat and wide circular barrow, about eighteen inches in elevation, in which no interment could be found, although the greater part of it was opened.

BARROWS IN ASHTON VALLEY.

P. Crocker del.

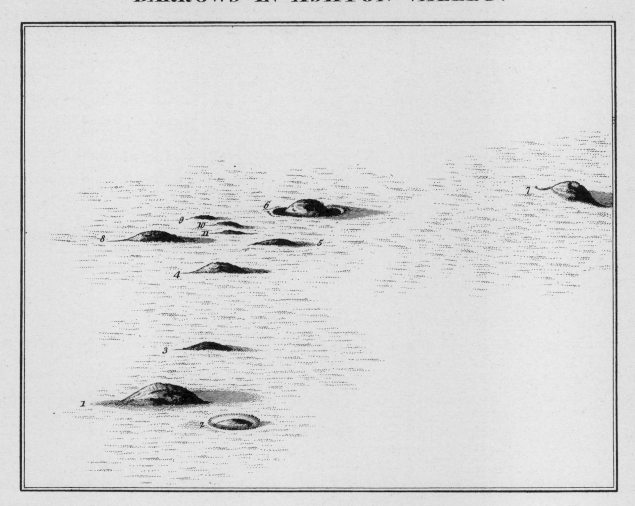

J.ˢ Basire sc.

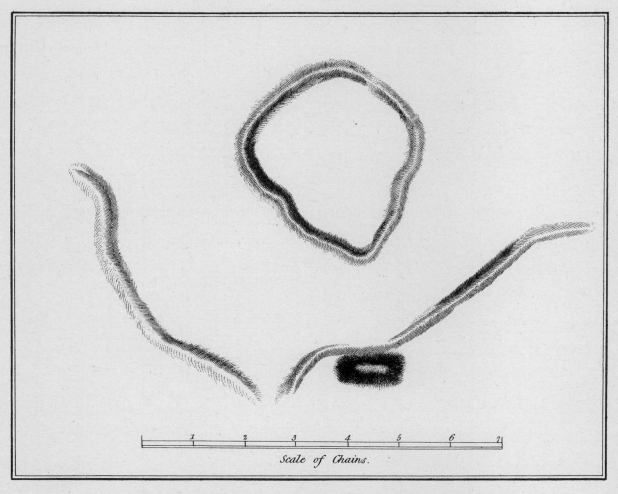

Scale of Chains.

EARTHEN WORK IN ELDER VALLEY.

Published by W. Miller, Albemarle Street, London, Jan.ʸ 1.1810.

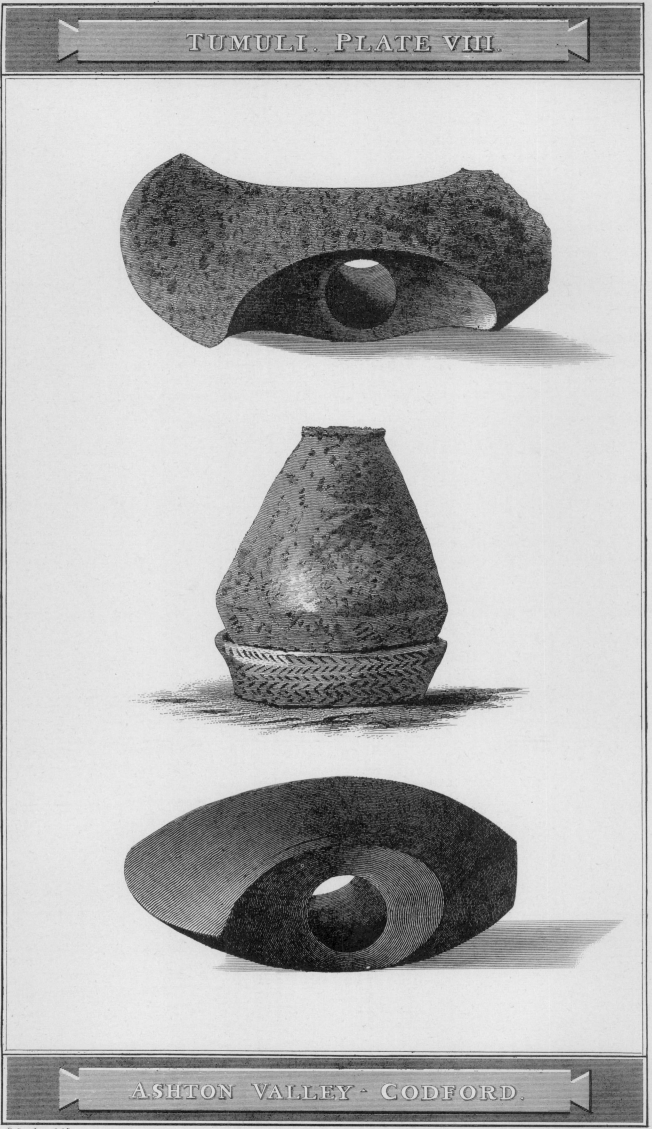

P. Crocker del.ᵗ

Jˢ Baſire Sc.

Published for W. Miller, Albemarle Street, London, Janʸ 1. 1810.

No 6, is a handsome bell-shaped barrow, sixty-three feet in diameter and eight in elevation, neatly ditched round, and placed on higher ground than the others before described. In this barrow, at the depth of eight feet, was found a large sepulchral urn inverted over an interment of burned bones, and a fine black stone celt or battle axe:* the ashes were piled up in a heap and placed near the urn.

No. 7. This circular barrow is placed on the declivity of a hill, and contained a skeleton interred from south-west to north-east at the depth of three feet nine inches under the surface. The position in which we found this skeleton would naturally lead us to suppose it to be the remains of some warrior slain in battle. The head was reclined upon the breast, one of the arms thrown backwards, and some of the fingers were scattered about, yet there were no indications to lead us to suppose it had ever been disturbed. We found a part of the shield of the deceased lying by its side ; it had been made of fir, and strengthened by slips of brass rivetted through, and though not thicker than a quarter of an inch, was quite firm, and had splinters remaining at the end where it was broken off. By the right side of the skeleton lay a considerable quantity of corroded iron, which probably was once the sword or spear of the warrior, and with it some small bits of cloth, so well preserved, that we can distinguish clearly the size of the spinning, and that it is what we now term a kersey cloth. Every circumstance attending the finding this skeleton induces us to think that this interment was subsequent to the original construction of the barrow ; especially as we afterwards, near the bottom of it, discovered a cist of little depth containing the burned bones of the primary deposit.

No. 8, is an old flat barrow, not ditched round, and five feet in elevation. In opening it, we were obliged to make several sections before we discovered the interment, which lay considerably to the south of the centre, on the native marl. The burned bones were piled into a little heap, without either ashes or charred wood, and close to them were a fine stone hatchet,+ and an arrow head of bone.

No. 9, 10, 11, are remarkably small barrows, elevated only a few inches above the native soil ; each contained an urn with human bones, but being deposited so near to the surface, they were of course crushed to pieces.

From hence I crossed the vale leading from Chittern to Codford, to a clump

* This axe is engraved at the bottom of the page in TUMULI PLATE VIII.
+ This stone hatchet is engraved at the top of the page in TUMULI PLATE VIII.

of trees, which is a conspicuous object on this eminence. Near it are some quarries, which are singular in their produce; for here, as well as upon most of the high points of land on the chalky *stratum*, we find a strange assemblage of sand, gravel, clay, and pebbles; and all these articles have been deposited within the compass of a few yards. From hence probably came the pebbles mentioned in my account of Bratton Camp as found there, and used by the Britons in former times for slings.

At a short distance to the south of this clump of trees, are the remains of a very extensive British town, covering several acres of ground, in which on digging, we have found the usual and undoubted *indicia* of ancient population. On a high point of the same hill, but nearer to the vale of Wily, is a very interesting monument of antiquity, and by far the most complete of any we have yet met with. I have taken notice of these circles amongst the earthen works in my Introduction, and have slightly mentioned one on Whitesheet Hill, and another on Rodmead Down, in my first Station (pages 42 and 47). A third also occurs near Mancum Wood, in my second Station; but the one on Codford Hill so far exceeds all these in symmetry of form, and beauty of situation, that I have purposely reserved my description of similar antiquities for the present occasion.

This earthen work, is situated on the summit of a hill commanding a most extensive and interesting prospect. It forms nearly a complete circle, the area of which contains above nine acres, and the circuit amounts to three furlongs and one hundred and ten yards. It is surrounded by a neatly formed *vallum* and foss, which, together with the area, have been much defaced by the plough. It is vulgarly called OLDBURY CAMP, but the smallness of the enclosure, as well as the slightness of the ramparts, evidently contradict the idea of its either having been made or used for military purposes; it has no signs of any entrance, nor is the ditch within, as we frequently find to be the case in the earthen works appropriated to religious purposes. That this work was dedicated to some juridical or religious ceremonies, the nature of its plan, its size, and elevated situation seem to indicate. Its vicinity to the large British town before mentioned, from which there is a fine gradual ascent, seems also to point out the connexion of the circle with it; for I can produce frequent examples of such circles existing in the neighbourhood of the British settlements.

We learn from the highest authority, that a very general and ancient custom prevailed of worshipping upon high places, which originated from the very natural idea of approaching as near as possible to the Deity on these holy occasions. In the *Book of Kings*, we are told, "nevertheless the high places were not taken away, for the people offered and burned incense yet in the high places;" upon which passage a modern writer has made the following note: " Many of old worshipped upon hills and the tops of high mountains; imagining that they thereby obtained a nearer communication with heaven. *Strabo* says that the Persians always performed their worship upon hills. Some nations, instead of an image, worshipped the hill as the Deity. In Japan most of the temples are at this day upon eminences, and often upon the ascent of high mountains, commanding fine views, with groves and rivulets of clear water; for they say, that the Gods are extremely delighted with such high and pleasant spots. This practice in early time was almost universal, and every mountain was esteemed holy. The people who prosecuted this method of worship, enjoyed a soothing infatuation, which flattered the gloom of superstition. The eminences to which they retired, were lonely and silent; and seemed to be happily circumstanced for contemplation and prayer. They who frequented them were raised above the lower world, and fancied that they were brought into the vicinity of the powers of the air and of the Deity who resided in the higher regions. But the chief excellence for which they were frequented was, that they were looked upon as the peculiar places where God delivered his oracles. *(Burder's Oriental Customs*, vol. ii. p. 156.)

This down is connected with another called Lamb Down, on which are several barrows, the greater part of which appear to have been opened in former times. One small *tumulus* had been overlooked, and produced a fine sepulchral urn inverted over a pile of burned bones in a cist, which is engraved in Tumuli, Plate VIII.

Descending from this hill, the turnpike road conducts us back to our headquarters at Heytesbury.

Iter II. In this second ride, I shall ascend the down, on the back of Sir William A'Court's grounds, to some large chalk quarries, and from thence, by a green trackway pursue my course towards Knook Barrow, which presents itself as a conspicuous object on the brow of the hill. It will, however, be necessary to notice two remains of British antiquity that occur on the road; the first, a slight earthen work, of an irregular shape with the *vallum* without, which has suffered so much from the continued operations of the plough, that it is difficult at present to ascertain its original form. A few yards within the work,

Y

towards the north-east, but not in the centre, is a small *tumulus*, in which, at the depth of about a foot and a half, was found a human skeleton, lying with its head towards the north, and its legs gathered up. On digging about three feet further towards the south, we came to a circular cavity, which contained a simple interment of burned bones. In this barrow we find both rites of burial practised, but no proof that these persons were buried at the same time.

Continuing along the track towards Knook Barrow, we perceive a small mound, which intersects a part of the road; and which I wish particularly to notice, as being the first barrow which Mr. Cunnington ever opened, and which, from the success he there met with, encouraged him to proceed in similar researches, and thus laid the foundation of my present work. It contained an interment of burned human bones deposited within a rude sepulchral urn inverted; and with it a spear head of brass in high preservation, having been secured from the wet by its situation within the urn. It was broken in two pieces, and the smallest of them was only discovered at the first time of opening, when several gentlemen attended; but at a subsequent period Mr. Cunnington found the remaining fragment.

On a piece of down to the left of the road we are now pursuing, called Conegar Hill, are two small barrows, in one of which was found a skeleton in its usual position, with an ivory or bone pin; in the other adjoining, which is not more than five feet in diameter, was a cist, containing, at the depth of two feet, an interment of burned bones, and with it a long brass pin. Adjoining to this hill, is ELDER VALLEY, a most retired spot, in which there is a very singular earthen work, unlike any other we have yet discovered. Its plan and dimensions will be best explained by the annexed engraving. Mr. Cunnington opened the mound, but found nothing in it but a few animal bones, a small piece of pottery, and a nail. As it did not prove to be sepulchral, and as the ditch of the outward work was within the *vallum*, as in many religious works, may we not, without being too fanciful, suppose this work to have been raised as an altar? That such were made use of in primitive times, we have the authority of the holy writings. " An altar of earth shalt thou make unto me, and shall sacrifice thereon thy burnt offerings, and thy peace offerings, thy sheep, and thine oxen" (*Exodus* xx. 24). Upon which we find the following note by the same author lately quoted: " Such altars (Tertullian observes) were among the ancient Romans in the days of Numa; when, as they had no sumptuous temples, nor images, so they had only *temeraria de cespite altaria*, altars hastily huddled up of earth, without any art."

On a declivity of the hill leading from the above work into the vale, are several small patches of ground of a brighter verdure than usual, in digging into which we discovered ancient pottery.

Crossing OLD DITCH, we now approach to Knook Long Barrow, which is about ninety feet long, fifty feet wide, and eight feet high   In the year 1801 Mr. Cunnington explored it, and in digging near the centre, about eighteen inches below the surface, discovered four headless skeletons lying from south to north, which appeared to have been deposited with very little ceremony, as two of them had their legs laid across each other.   Not having sufficient time to prosecute his researches, he reinterred the bones, and closed up the barrow In the year 1802 he repeated his operations, beginning by a large section from the centre to the east end.   Having proceeded to the depth of one foot, they came to a ridge of flints and large marl stones, which widened till, at the depth of five feet nine inches, they found a regular paved floor of flints which extended fifteen feet in length and six feet or more in breadth, but narrowed as it approached the east end.   This floor was covered with human and animal bones, and charred wood, but the fragments of bones were so small, that it was difficult to ascertain the number of human bodies that were burned.   Mr. Cunnington conjectured that there might have been seven or eight. Amongst these bones, were those of birds; and on the top of the barrow, immediately under the turf, were several pieces of stag's horn, and part of the head and horns of an ox, which a butcher pronounced to have been larger than ever he saw of that species of animal.   At the west end of the pavement, which was near the centre of the barrow, was a cist of a semicircular form, neatly cut in the solid chalk, similar to one in another long barrow at Tilshead, and containing only vegetable mould, charred wood, and two bits of bone.   The ridge of flints and stones was piled over the burned bones in this barrow, in the same manner as over the skeletons in Boles-barrow.

At a short distance from this long barrow, is a small and low circular *tumulus*, which was opened in the year 1800, and contained an interment of burned bones within a large rude urn imperfectly baked, and the point of a brass spear or dagger. The urn, from its position so near the surface of the soil, was crushed to pieces.

Having hitherto dwelt chiefly amongst the dead, let me now conduct my readers to the habitations of the Britons, when alive.   I have had occasion in my Introduction, to mention the numerous towns and villages, which our researches on the Wiltshire downs had enabled us to discover;   and

I have slightly noticed a few of them in my first and second stations; but as the British settlement on Knook Down bears a far more decided and perfect character, than either of those that have hitherto occurred, I shall illustrate it by a plan, and be more minute in my description of it. We have undoubted proofs from history and from existing remains, that the earliest habitations were pits or slight excavations in the ground, covered and protected from the in-clemency of the weather by boughs of trees, or sods of turf. The high grounds were pointed out by nature, as the fittest for these early settlements, being less encumbered by wood, and affording a better pasture for the numerous flocks and herds, from which the erratic tribes of the first colonists drew their means of subsistence; but after the conquest of our island by the Romans, when, by means of their enlightened knowledge, society became more civilized, the Britons began to quit the elevated ridge of chalk hills, and seek more sheltered and desirable situations. At first, we find them removed into the sandy vales immediately bordering on the chalk hills; and at a later period, when the improved state of society under the Romans ensured them security, the vallies were cleared of wood, and towns and villages were erected in the plains near rivers, which, after the departure of the Romans, became the residence of the Saxons. But a considerable period must have elapsed before these important changes took place, for on our bleakest hills we find the luxuries of the Romans introduced into the British settlements, flues, hypocausts, stuccoed and painted walls, &c. &c. Yet not a single inscription has ever been discovered in any one of these British villages, that can throw any positive light upon the æra in which they flourished, or were deserted, for a more temperate and less exposed climate.

If we refer to the plan of this ground, we shall perceive two British towns, situated at some considerable distance from each other, and seemingly connected by the means of OLD DITCH; we must also observe that at A, this ditch has been evidently broken through, and the line of habitations continued across it; from which circumstance we may reasonably conclude, that the ditch existed prior to the construction of the village; or perhaps, if the ditch served as a communi-cation between the upper and the lower villages, it might have been broken through in order to extend the limits of the latter.

The site of these villages is decidedly marked by great cavities and irregu-larities of ground, and by a black soil; when the moles were more abundant, numerous coins were constantly thrown up by them, as well as fragments of pottery, of different species. On digging in these excavations we find the

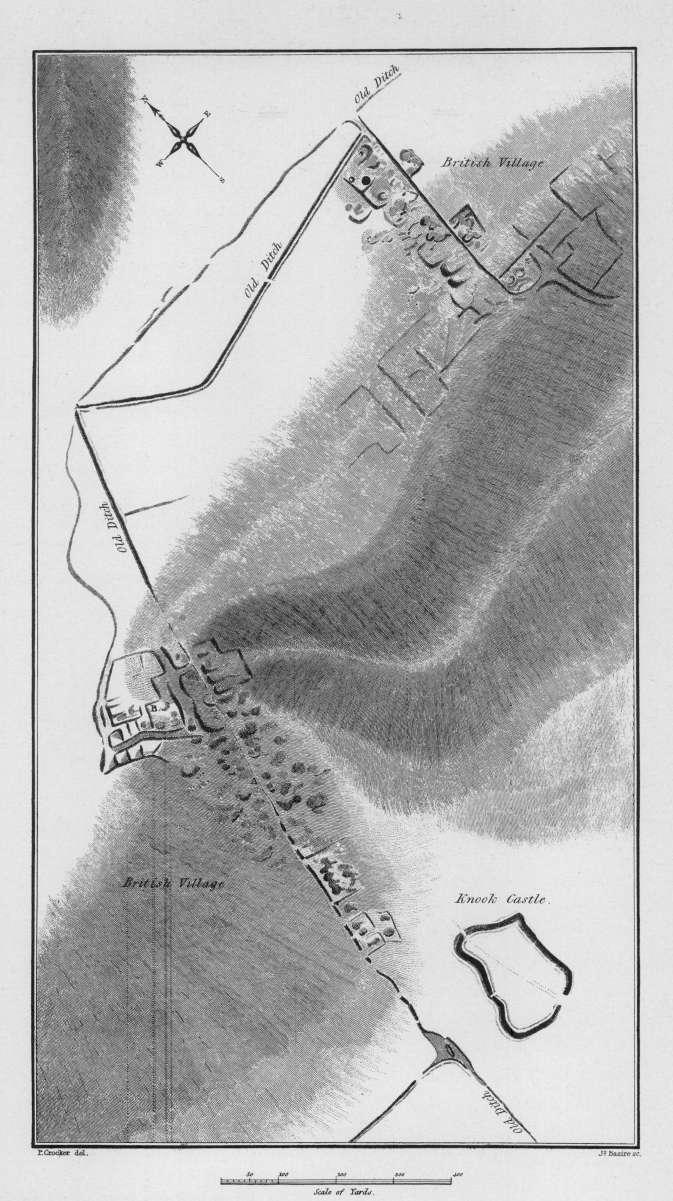

N

W———E

S

Old Ditch

Old Ditch

Old Ditch

British Village

British Village

Knook Castle

Old Ditch

P. Crocker del.

J.º Basire sc.

50   100   200   300   400

Scale of Yards.

Published by W. Miller, Albemarle Street, London, Jan.ʸ 1 1810.

KNOOK · UPTON LOVEL.

P. Crocker del.

J? Basire Sc.

Published for W. Miller, Albemarle Street, London, Jan.Y 1. 1810 .

coarse British pottery, and almost every species of what has been called Roman pottery, but which I conceive to have been manufactured by the Britons from Roman models ; also *fibulæ*, and rings of brass worn as *armillæ* or bracelets, flat-headed iron nails, hinges of doors, locks and keys, and a variety of Roman coins, of which the small brass of the Lower Empire are the most numerous, and particularly those of the Constantine family. Of the larger and first brass we have coins of Vespasian, Nerva, Antoninus, Trajan, Julia Mammæa, and Posthumus ; of the *denarii* we have Caligula, the elder Faustina, Julia Mammæa, the elder Philip, Gallienus, and Gratianus : the small brass are too numerous to particularize, but some of the smallest are remarkable, having only a radiated head (often very rude), and one or two Roman letters, which perhaps may have been struck during the latest struggles between the Britons and Saxons.

In digging within these British villages, we have but rarely discovered any signs of building with stone or flint ; but we have several times found very thin stones laid as floors to a room. The fire places were small excavations in the ground, in which we have frequently found a large flat hearth stone ; and in two parts of this extensive village we have discovered hypocausts similar to those in the Roman villa at Pitmead near Warminster. These are regular works of masonry, made in the form of a cross, and covered with large flat stones well cemented by mortar. We have also, during our investigations of this spot, repeatedly found pieces of painted stucco, and of brick flues ; also pit coal, and some fragments of glass or chrystal rings, beads, &c.

In one of the banks raised for the old habitations at B, we discovered a skeleton with its head laid towards the north ; at its feet was a fine black celt, and at the distance of a few feet was a bead, both of which are engraved in Tumuli Plate IX. In this, as well as in the generality of other British villages, the attentive eye may easily trace out the lines of houses, and the streets, or rather hollow ways conducting to them ; these are particularly visible in the upper village on these downs, as well as the entrance to it. The whole adjoining country is also strongly marked by the intersection of slight banks along the sides of the hills, which point to us the limits of ancient British cultivation ; and in many instances the smallness of them will shew the contracted scale on which agriculture was at that time carried on.

That this ground was known and occupied by the Britons at a very early period, the interment of the skeleton with the black celt will amply prove ; and that it continued as a settlement of the Romanized Britons, for a considerable length of time, will be equally substantiated by the numerous articles of iron, pottery, flues, glass, and coins, that have been dug up on this spot.

Following the line of the track-way which points towards Lavington, and intersects the British village near Tilshead, we find a low circular barrow adjoining the road, which produced an interment of burned bones within a neat circular cist. A brass buckle was found near it, and near the top was the skeleton of a horse. Deviating to the left in a direction towards Imber, we perceive a small long barrow on a declivity of the down, which was opened in 1801. At the depth of eighteen inches was a layer of white marl four or five inches thick, and the usual *stratum* of black earth at the bottom. At the depth of about three feet from the real centre, was an entire skeleton with its head laid to the north-east, probably that of an elderly man. The skull was very thick, the teeth were all gone, and one of the arms had been fractured, and set in such a manner as would not convey to us in modern times any favourable opinion of the ancient Britons' skill in surgery. Four feet further to the east of this skeleton were three others lying in the same direction ; and a few feet west from the first skeleton, was a circular cist nearly three feet deep, but containing no ashes nor bones.

Having crossed this hill, and pursuing the track towards Imber, we find another low barrow near the base declivity of the down, and a little to the right of a well and a clump of fir trees. This produced, at the depth of five feet, a human skeleton lying on its face, with the head towards the north. At its feet was a drinking cup of red pottery, which was unfortunately broken, but afterwards mended.

Having crossed the vale in which the little sequestered village of Imber is situated, and ascended the opposite hill, we perceive a clump of trees, which forms a very conspicuous and useful land mark to the traveller over these unfrequented downs : it bears the name of WADMAN'S COPPICE.

Between it and the village of Imber, are the remains of another large British village, placed in an elevated and commanding situation, and producing all the usual *indicia* of the residence of Romanized Britons. In the centre of this village, two banks running parallel from east to west, are very visible, which a neighbouring farmer observed were streets, and the ground between them was intended to secure the cattle. His first conjecture was well founded, for we meet with similar lines and streets in the generality of the British towns we have discovered upon our downs. In digging on this spot, we found fragments of pottery, animal bones, and some large pieces of yellow stone resembling that found in the quarries near Bath; and in one hollow place we discovered the remains of a human skeleton deposited with his drinking cup. A question may here arise, whether this interment had originally been made under a *tumulus*, and whether that *tumulus* had been levelled when the village was built. A similar instance has already been mentioned in the British village on Knook Down (page 85); and in a future part of my work, I shall have occasion to notice another interment near Stonehenge, over which certainly no mound was raised. I am inclined to think, that the Romanized Britons would not have removed the sepulchral memorials of their Celtic predecessors; that numerous interments might be found in similar situations; and that those deposited under barrows, form but a very small proportion, when the population of the country is duly considered.

ITER III. In this ride I shall ascend the hills at the back of Sir William A'Court's demesne, and proceed over Nanny Down towards Bowls Barrow. At the upper end of Heytesbury field and near the summit of the hill, is a flat barrow ploughed over, which Mr. Cunnington opened in 1800, and found about a foot under the surface, a layer of flints that extended nearly over the whole *tumulus*, intermixed with fragments of thick and coarse pottery; and was much surprized in finding ten small brass Roman coins of the Emperors *Constantine*, *Valentine* I. and II. and *Arcadius*, together with some pieces of the fine red Samian pottery. From the discovery of these articles, viz. first, the rude pottery, and afterwards the fine Samian ware, and coins, we may conceive this to have been occupied both by the Celtic and Romanized Britons.

On the summit of the hill we meet the great track-way, and crossing it come to a large *tumulus* named BOWLS BARROW; its length is one hundred and fifty feet at the base; its width ninety-four feet, and its elevation ten feet and a half, though it appears to the eye much higher; the broad end points towards the east. This large barrow was opened by Mr. Cunnington in 1801, and attended with much labour. He began by making a section of considerable width and length across the barrow near the east end, and at the depth of two feet nine inches found a human skeleton lying south-west and north-east, and with it a brass buckle, and two thin pieces of the same metal. Towards the centre of the barrow, were two other skeletons interred, with their heads towards the south, and one of them lying on its side. The interior parts of the barrow were composed entirely of white marl stone to the depth of four feet and a half: this was succeeded by a ridge of large stones and flints, which extended wider as the men worked downwards. At the depth of ten feet and a half, which was the base of the barrow, was a floor of flints regularly laid, and on it the remains of several human bodies deposited in no regular order. It appeared therefore, that they had been thrown together promiscuously, and a great pile of stones raised length-ways along the centre of the barrow over them. This pile (in form like the ridge of a house), was afterwards covered with marl excavated from the north and south sides of the barrow, the two ends being level with the plain. Although four men were employed for three days, they could not explore more than the space of about six feet by ten; yet in this small portion they found fourteen skulls, one of which appeared to have been cut in two by a sword. It is rather singular, that no fragments whatever of pottery, charred wood, or animal bones, were found in the course of the above operations.

At a subsequent period Mr. Cunnington made a second attempt on this *tumulus*, by opening more ground both at the east as well as west end; at the former he found the heads and horns of seven or more oxen; also a large cist close to the skeletons; but owing to the great height of the barrow, and the large stones continually rolling down upon the labourers, he was obliged to stop his operations.

From Bowls Barrow, I shall continue my ride along the track which forms the boundary of the last and the present station, and leads in nearly a direct line to another very conspicuous *tumulus*, called TINHEAD LONG BARROW. Crossing a valley, where several track-ways meet, we find near the one leading on the right to Imber, two barrows; one of which to the south, produced the deposit of a skeleton, and in the other the interment was not discovered. The country from hence to Tinhead Long Barrow now becomes cultivated, and unproductive of British antiquities. Near this *tumulus* we join the ancient track-way and old great road of communication between Bath and Salisbury before the establishment of turnpikes took place; the greater part of the mile-stones, still existing on it mark the distance to be XXXVI. miles. The map will best shew how ably the line was carried over this long ridge, and how few hills and vales impeded the traveller in his journey. On a very narrow part of this ridge, where a road leads from the down to the village of Imber, there is a low mutilated barrow, exactly similar to the one I have described on Warminster downs, (page 65,) and bearing the same peculiarities of an entrance over the ditch exactly east and west. At the next mile stone, viz. XXI. from Bath, and XV. from Salisbury, the unnatural inequalities of the ground, and the superior

YARNBURY CAMP.

From Deptford to Amesbury

Scale of Yards.

CODFORD CIRCLE.

P. Crocker, del.

J.ª Basire sc.

Published by W. Miller, Albemarle Street, London, Jan.ʸ 1. 1810.

verdure of the soil, announce the vicinity of a British settlement. On an elevated part of West Lavington Down, and a little to the south-west of the Great Penning, is a British village of considerable extent, situated at the inter-section of two ancient trackways ; the one, which a farmer called the Foss-way, leading from Old Sarum, by Yarnbury Camp to Tinhead, and from thence to Bath ; the other from the British village on Knook Down, by St. Joan A'Gores Cross to the Ridge-way, and from thence towards Casterley Camp, &c. &c. Near the Great Penning, are two barrows, one circular, the other oblong ; the former did not prove sepulchral, and contained only animal bones, and an abundance of Roman pottery, nails, &c.

On the western side of the trackway, before you descend into the vale of Imber, are the remains of a ditch and bank leading towards the British village ; but they cannot be traced for any great distance. On the eastern side of the said trackway is a large barrow of an oval shape, differing from the generality of Long Barrows, in not being ditched on the two long sides; and you may plainly perceive the marks of a ditch bending round, as it were to avoid it, which becomes much more decisive on the down, and points towards the village of Tilshead.

Returning to the great trackway, near the next mile stone we find a large circular barrow on the left side, and soon afterwards cross OLD DITCH. Leaving the villages of Chittern on the right, we then traverse the turnpike road leading to Amesbury at the eighty-seventh mile stone, and direct our course towards Yarnbury Camp. A little beyond the tenth mile stone from Sarum, is a fine circular *tumulus* on the right of the trackway ; and on the left, the remains of an earthen work. Its ramparts are slight, and its shape irregular, the east side approaching to the pentagonal, and the west to a circular form.

YARNBURY CAMP, which may have derived its name from the Cornish word *yein*, cold, presents a very fine specimen of ancient castrametation. Like the generality of those on our downs, it is placed on elevated and commanding ground, and from its vicinity to the great trackway, was most probably of British origin, though occupied and strengthened in later times by the Romans and Saxons. It contains within its area twenty-eight acres and a half ; the circumference of the outward ditch is one thousand seven hundred and sixteen yards, and the greatest height of the *vallum* is fifty-two feet.

In its present state it appears to have six entrances, several of which most certainly did not appertain to the original work. The principal approach is marked by a strong and detached outwork to the east ; and on the western side,

A A

where there appears to have been another entrance, there is an outwork of an irregular form, which I am inclined to think existed prior to the formation or enlargement of the camp. The inner rampart is very strong, and constructed in a much bolder, and at the same time more regular manner than the outward one, which, from its rudeness and want of neatness, seems to indicate haste in its formation. Within the area of this camp, several slight excavations mark the site of ancient residence, which is confirmed by the various articles we have found on opening the ground ; such as coarse British, as well as fine Roman pottery, querns, or mill-stones, brass *fibulæ*, Roman coins, iron, &c. &c.: and a few years ago, on digging near the centre of the area, an entire human skeleton was found, laid with its head towards the north, and having round one of its fingers a plain brass ring ; and amongst the bones there was another nearly of the same size. From an impartial review of these works, their vicinity to the great British trackway, the blackness and richness of the soil, and the numerous articles which have been discovered within them, I can have no hesitation in pronouncing this ground to have been originally occupied by the Britons, and afterwards, *pro tempore*, by the Romans and Saxons.

All the adjoining country produces evidences of ancient population, of which traces may be seen on the declivity of a hill to the west of Yarnbury Camp. There are several detached barrows about the neighbouring downs, most of which bearing the marks of prior investigation, have not attracted our attention.

ITER IV. In this ride, I shall direct my course to Knook Castle, and pursue the line of OLD DITCH, which nearly traverses the whole of this station in a direction from south-west to north-east. Near the British village at Knook it forms some very singular angles ; from thence towards Tilshead it pursues a gentle serpentine line till it reaches a long barrow situated on the north side of it, and where the ditch makes a decided curve in order to avoid the *tumulus*, and which is a certain proof of the superior date of the barrow. This long barrow is the largest we have met with, and very uniform in its construction ; it is three hundred and seventy-seven feet long, ninety-nine feet wide, and eleven feet high. This immense mound was investigated for the first time by Mr. Cunnington in the year 1802, who began his operations by making a considerable section at the east end. The barrow was composed chiefly of white marly soil, but near the bottom there was a *stratum* of black sooty earth from nine to eighteen inches thick, which appeared, like a ridge, to extend the whole length of the barrow, and decrease in thickness as it reached the edge.

Having advanced about thirty-two feet, he met with charred wood, small pieces of stag's horns, a few animal bones, and numerous bones of birds, particularly in one place, about two feet deep in the barrow, where there was nearly a shovel full of them deposited together. On continuing the section towards the south, the different *strata* bore the appearance of a circular barrow within the long one, as if there had existed one of the former on the spot, before the construction of the latter; but nothing was found except an additional quantity of charred wood at the bottom. On proceeding westward with the section, he discovered two interments of burned human bones at the top of the barrow, and at the depth of about a foot; the first of these was dispersed by the workmen, and unnoticed; the second was found immediately under the turf, within three feet of the former, deposited in a large circular cavity, and close by it were several very large pieces of stag's horns and some charred wood. Having proceeded about eighty-five feet from the east end, and finding nothing but the black line of earth at the bottom, the operations were transferred to the western end of the barrow, where, at the depth of eight feet, three human skeletons were found lying on a pavement of flints about a foot and a half above the floor; two of them side by side, with their heads to the north, the third lying at the heads of the former, and by its side was an oval cist, cut with as much exactness in the chalk as if it had been done with a chissel. It was three feet long, one foot nine inches wide, two feet and a half deep, and contained nothing but vegetable mould and charred wood. A great deal more of the pavement was examined, and nothing found but black earth, ashes, and remains of bones.

Following the line of OLD DITCH, we come to another mound on the brow of the hill, marked in the large map by the title of WHITE BARROW. But before we ascend the hill to it, we should notice, that there is an evident outwork of a bank and ditch branching out from OLD DITCH at the bottom of the hill, and joining it again on the top. This *tumulus*, which has lately been covered with a plantation, measures two hundred and fifty-five feet in length, one hundred and fifty-six feet in width at the broad or east end; and ninety-two feet at the west; its elevation does not exceed seven or eight feet, and in form it resembles a wedge. Though two large sections were made in this barrow, nothing was found but a few pieces of stag's, horns, and a line of black earth similar to that described in the former barrow.

The next trial was made upon another of these angular or wedge-like *tumuli*, situated at a short distance to the west of Tilshead Lodge. Its length is one hundred and seventy-three feet, its width sixty feet at the east, and forty-nine feet at the west end, and its elevation about five. This was also composed of marly soil, and produced the same black sooty earth at the bottom. Towards the east end, a skeleton was discovered just under the turf, lying from west to east, but unaccompanied by any arms, or sepulchral urn. Nearly opposite to each of these long barrows, I observed traces of a ditch branching off in a south-east direction, but I could not follow it for any distance.

In no part of our county are the Long Barrows so large or so frequent as in this station, and particularly in the neighbourhood of Tilshead; yet notwithstanding our expensive and continued researches in them, we are obliged to confess our ignorance for what purpose they were originally constructed. They have been thus mentioned by OLAUS WORMIUS, " *Diversi ab his quidam cernuntur tumuli, figurâ oblongiori, congerie depressiori, &c.*; and have been called by Mr. King in his *Munimenta Antiqua*, ship barrows, owing to their extended length. Others have supposed them to have been battle barrows, from the circumstance of finding the bodies thrown promiscuously together, without any attention to the usual revered rites of sepulture; but I can hardly suppose that such immense mounds would have been raised for that purpose, as the interments are in general confined to the broad end of the *tumulus*. I wish I could account for these particularities as rationally, as for the *stratum* of black earth which has been observed at the bottom of many of them,* and which has caused much conjecture amongst some of my friends; for it can be nothing but the decayed turf upon which the sepulchral mound was raised. Their high antiquity is confirmed by the fragments of rude British pottery, stag's horns, &c. found in the soil that composes them, and from the circumstance of cremation having been practised near the top of some of them. The cist near which the skeletons are generally found is another peculiarity which we cannot account for, and denotes some particular ceremony that was practised in these *tumuli*. Other barrows

* Various have been the conjectures respecting this *stratum* of black earth, which is so commonly found on the floors of the long barrows. A friend of mine was so convinced that it arose from the decomposition of numerous human bodies by means of fire, that he sent some of the soil to two of the most able chymists of the day, Mr. Hatchett, and Dr. Gibbes, to be properly analyzed. They both reject the idea of this black earth being the *residuum* of decomposed animal or human bodies; and Dr. Gibbes is of opinion that it arises from the decomposition of vegetable matter. If it had undergone the process of fire, the colour would have been converted into red, and not black. The most rational conclusion is, that in forming the outline of the intended *tumulus*, the turf was turned up as a guide for the workmen, in its construction; and thus the *stratum* of black vegetable mould is found to pervade the whole floor of the barrow; yet it is singular, that this circumstance should be confined to the long barrow; for in those of a circular form we find no such accompaniments, and the earth certainly appears to be of a darker colour than that of the adjoining soil.

display such a variety in their external design, and internal deposits, as to confound all system, provided we were inclined to form one; but the long barrows are so uniform in their construction, and uninteresting in their contents, that we have at length given up all researches in them, having for many years in vain looked for that information, which might tend to throw some satisfactory light on the history of these singular mounds of earth.

Following the line of OLD DITCH, and crossing the vale leading to the village of Tilshead, we perceive a *tumulus* on the apex of the opposite hill, and on the south side of OLD DITCH. It is vulgarly called SILVER BARROW: and was opened in the year 1801, by Mr. Tucker and Mr. Bartlett, inhabitants of Tilshead. It is not circular, but resembles an egg cut lengthways, with the convex side upwards, the widest base being sixty-nine feet. The earth for raising this barrow had been excavated from the sides, each end being level with the down. In making a large section through layers of chalk and vegetable earth to the depth of nearly seven feet, they discovered the bones of about seven persons who had been interred on a pavement of rude stones, and lying very irregularly, as in Bowls-barrow and other long barrows. The only articles found with them was an iron knife, a bone handle, and a small urn broken in two, which was made of a clay intermixed with stony particles, was turned in a lathe, and was rounder, better burned, and different in fashion from the British urns: the knife resembled those found in Knook Castle, and in the Roman villa at Pitmead. All these circumstances tend to prove that this *tumulus* was not of Celtic origin, but probably the sepulchral mound of some Romanized Briton.

Still pursuing the course of OLD DITCH, we meet with an occasional barrow on the high grounds, and at length come to another bank and ditch running from north to south, which meets OLD DITCH at right angles. The northern branch is soon totally lost in a vale nearly opposite to a fine long barrow on a hill to the right; the southern branch continues visible for some miles, leading to the large British village on Orcheston Down, and afterwards pursuing its course towards those on Winterbourn Stoke Down.

I shall now return to Tilshead, from whence, by the friendly hospitality and guidance of Mr. Lowther, the worthy owner of Tilshead Lodge, I was enabled to explore with comfort this widely extended chalky district, which we may justly call the deserts of Wiltshire, once the seat of a numerous British population, and till lately the solitary and last retreat of the majestic bustard.*

---

* *Bustard.* The following very curious and authentic account of two bustards, was published in the *Gentleman's Magazine* for the year 1805, by Mr. Tucker, School-master at Tilshead. " A man about four

The richness and superior verdure of the fine down near Tilshead, added to the *tumuli* dispersed about it, are sufficient marks of an ancient population, which extended probably over the whole plain from Tilshead to the British village last mentioned.

From this British village, I shall continue my ride on the trackway to the Great Penning, and from thence across a valley to St. Joan A'Gore's Cross, where we ascend the ridge-way, enjoying from an elevated terrace a most delicious view of the rich and extensive vale beneath. A little beyond the road which leads to East Lavington, are the mutilated banks of a square earthen work, and still further on is a barrow; the only two objects of antiquarian notice; but others of a more captivating kind are amply furnished by nature in the rich scenery of the prospect below. The downs on this side Lavington, viz. the Cheverell hills, and East Lavington down, being in tillage, furnish no British antiquities; nor, from the paucity of *tumuli*, do I think this tract was much inhabited in early times: but at a later period, I have strong reason to suppose that the whole line of country immediately under the chalk hills, became the favourite residence of the Britons, before they settled themselves deeper in the vallies, and near the banks of rivers.

We now come to Red Horn turnpike, and to the limits of this my third station: an uninhabited and desert region, * which, from the numerous flocks of sheep scattered over it, I could almost imagine was still possessed by Nomades. Leaving Ell Barrow at the xiv. mile stone on the left, I shall

o'clock in the morning, on some day in June 1801, was coming from Tinhead to Tilshead, when, near a place called Askings Penning, one mile from Tilshead, he saw over his head a large bird, which afterwards proved to be a bustard. He had not proceeded far, before it lighted on the ground immediately before his horse, which it indicated an inclination to attack, and in fact very soon began the onset. The man alighted, and getting hold of the bird endeavoured to secure it; and after struggling with it nearly an hour, succeeded, and brought it alive to the house of Mr. Bartlett, at Tilshead, where it continued till the month of August, when it was sold to Lord Temple for the sum of thirty-one guineas.

" About a fortnight subsequent to the taking this bustard, Mr. Grant, a farmer residing at Tilshead, returning from Warminster market, was attacked in a similar manner near Tilshead Lodge, by another bird of the same species. His horse being spirited, took fright, and ran off, which obliged Mr. Grant to relinquish his design of endeavouring to take the bird. The circumstance of two birds, (whose nature has been always considered, like that of a turkey, domestic,) attacking a man and horse, is so very singular, that it deserves recording; and particularly, as it is probably the last record we shall find of the existence of this bird upon our downs."

* This district may justly be denominated *desert*, for between Salisbury and the aforesaid turnpike, (a long tract of 16 miles,) and the great road of communication with Devizes, there is only one house, viz. the Druid's hut. A most evident advantage would arise to the public, if the line of road was conducted through the villages of Shrewton and Tilshead to East Lavington. Relays of horses might be established at one of the numerous villages in the vale; the rich traveller would thereby feel the tedium of his journey lessened, and the more indigent pedestrian would find that shelter and accommodation which at present are denied to him; and from the want of which, many a life has been lost.

pursue a direct line southward over the downs, leaving the long barrow before mentioned (page 93), on the right, towards a valley thickly strewed with the villages of Orcheston, Elston, Shrewton, Maddenton, and Rolston, and terminate my iter at Winterbourn Stoke. In this tract nothing worthy of note occurs in the line of antiquity, till we come to a fine piece of down on the right or west side of the vale leading from Maddenton to Winterbourn Stoke. Here we find another British village, with all its usual *indicia* of excavations, pottery, coins, &c. and at the south-east extremity of it, an interesting group of barrows, the description of which will be deferred till I come to the Station of Amesbury, as they appear to be connected with another group on the opposite or eastern side of the valley.

P. S. Since the printing of these last pages, some new discoveries have been made in the district allotted to this Station, which I shall here insert. At page 86, I noticed the remains of a British village on the down between Wadman's coppice and Imber; and we have lately discovered another in that neighbourhood. It is situated a little more than a mile north of Imber, on a piece of down called Little Cheverell, and in a direction towards the old road or trackway from Bath to Salisbury. It occupies the declivities of two hills which terminate in a vale leading towards Imber, and produces all the accustomed marks of an extensive British village, the entrance into which, between two slight banks, is very evident. It is truly interesting thus to trace with certainty, the early residences of our ancestors, and to find them so unexpectedly amidst the dreary regions of our extensive downs: and the district included within this Station, now the most defective in modern cultivation, proves the most abundant in ancient population, for we have found in it vestiges of six large British settlements.

The old track-way from Bath to Salisbury skirts the northern ramparts of Yarnbury camp, crosses the turnpike leading from Deptford to Amesbury, and pursues its course in a direct line over a fine extent of turf to Over-street, a name denoting British antiquity. On the right of this track-way are two barrows, each of which appears to have been opened; and at no great distance to the left of it, are the remains of a large British village, much defaced by tillage, but abounding in fragments of pottery, and all the usual marks of a remote British population. The site of all these villages is delineated on the map annexed to this Station.

B B*

STATION IV. WILY.

I HAVE allotted rather a larger district than usual to this Station, that I might be enabled to give a more detailed, and at the same time a more connected account of the VALE of WILY, a most interesting tract of country, abounding with Antiquities of every description, and the favourite residence of the Britons.

The true and original source of this stream is but little known, and has not been duly noticed in our large map of the county; for it is there marked as rising in the parish of Kingston Deverill, whereas its real source lies much farther to the westward, and in the adjoining county of Somerset. This circumstance would have escaped the observation of the most able geographer if he made his survey of this district in the summer months; for during that season there is no appearance of a river till you come to the villages of the Deverills. The Wily rises from a perennial spring called Bratchwell, in the parish of Kilmington, adjoining to that of Stourton,* and from thence runs easterly towards the vale of the Deverills, leaving a farm called Rodmead on the right, and the line of chalk hills above it. The barrows and earthen works on the down belonging to that farm, which have been described in my first station, attest the early residence of the Celtic Britons; and since the publication of that account, we have discovered traces of their successors, the Romanized Britons, amongst the arable lands belonging to Norton parish, in a field belonging to me, called Blacklands. Here probably the Britons had a settlement; not in the period of early colonization, when they resided on the highest hills, but at a later time, when they gradually descended from a bleak, to a more sheltered

* This spring is accurately laid down in the Map of Stourton Station.

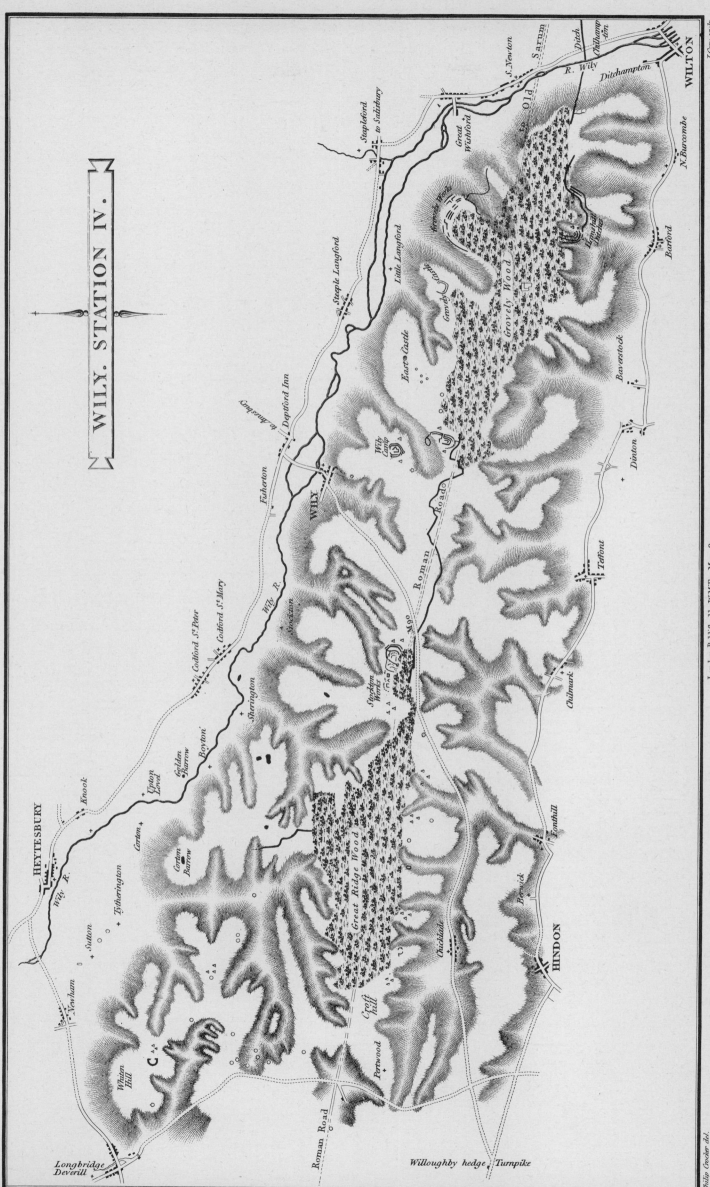

WILY. STATION IV.

WILTON

J.Cary sculp.

London: Published by W. Miller May 1811.

Philip Crocker del.

situation. This British village adjoins an open lane or track-way which conducts us into the unenclosed lands belonging to Kingston Deverill; and I have strong reason to suppose that this was an ancient British road leading westward over Kilmington common, by Alfred's Tower, and a road beneath called HARD-WAY, either to the strong British camp at CADBURY, or to the British city of ISCALIS, now ILCHESTER, the county town of Somerset. JACK'S CASTLE, to which I have given the more dignified title of SELWOOD BARROW, might in that case have been placed on its elevated and commanding situation, as a guide or landmark to those who were travelling from west to east.* This road, or rather track-way, is accompanied by *tumuli* in the vale leading to Kingston Deverill. Two have been levelled in a large meadow to the left of the road; a most beautiful maiden barrow remains untouched in another meadow on the right; and a third appears in the centre of the vale amongst the arable fields, all of which have already been noticed in my first station (page 40.)

We now come to the first village bearing the name of DEVERILL, a corruption from DIVE-RILL, and acquired by the eccentrick character of this spring, which during the summer months takes a subterraneous course, and appears only as a permanent stream at Kingston Deverill. In the very dry autumn of 1787, it ceased to flow in this and the adjoining parish of Monkton, and burst forth in that of Brixton Deverill.

On the left of this valley, we have the bold hill bearing the three appropriate names of Bidcomb, Brimsdon, and Cold Kitchen,+ the ancient residence of the Celtic as well as Romanized Britons; and further on, behind the church of Hill Deverill are considerable remains of another large British settlement; and I have lately been informed by John Parker,‡ our labourer, that in examining the ground between the villages of Hill and Brixton Deverill, he dug up in the meadows a great deal of rude British pottery. There are five villages bearing the termination of Deverill, and closely adjoining each other, viz. Kingston Deverill, or the King's town; Monkton, or the Monk's town; Brixton, the town

---

* Described page 39.—It has been supposed that the Romans erected *tumuli* on high points of land, to guide their legions and travellers to their respective stations, at a time when the low lands were encumbered with wood. I have observed many of them in similar situations, and adjoining to Roman roads, but have as yet opened none of them, in order to ascertain whether, by their contents, they were Roman or British. The barrow I here allude to, was certainly British, and the stone hatchet found within it, proves its very high antiquity.

+ See first Station, page 41.

‡ John Parker and his father Stephen, natives of Heytesbury, have been constantly employed by us in all our operations; and to the former we feel much indebted for many interesting discoveries of British settlements and other antiquities. Dr. Stukeley has recorded the merits of Ruben Horsall, the town-clerk of Abury; and why should I not do equal justice to those of our Heytesbury pioneers?

or stone of Brithric, or Egbert, and the *Petra Egbryhta* of Asser and the Saxon Chronicle ;* Hill, and Longbridge Deverill. From hence the river Wily continues its course N. E. towards Warminster, and near Boreham-mill receives the waters of the little river Ware ; it is still accompanied by British memorials of antiquity, at Crockerton on the left, and at Southley wood and Sutton on the right. At the village of Boreham the river makes a sudden angle and a deviation in its course from north-east to south-east, and is still accompanied by *tumuli* even in the low lands.+ Some of these I have already noticed near Boreham. There are two others in the meadows near Norton-house, each of which produced an interment of burned bones, and one was accompanied with an urn. In a large meadow between Norton and Bishopstrow, called PITMEAD, are the remains of two Roman villas ; and in another meadow on the other side of Norton-house, a beautiful little black cup was lately found in high preservation,‡ and is now in the Museum of Miss Benet. The interesting range of fortified hills on the north-east side of the Vale having been already described, I shall conduct my readers along the south-west side of the river WILY, following its course to our county town of WILTON, to which it has given its present appellation.§

In Heytesbury south field is a barrow nearly levelled by the plough, which contained a skeleton, with a spear head of brass. Pursuing the course of the stream, we come to the parish of UPTON LOVEL. I have already, in my account of the Heytesbury station, described the very interesting *tumuli* on the down attached to this parish ; yet that interest is not confined to the elevated district, but is continued along the vale. On the northern banks of the river WILY is a barrow, which from the nature and richness of its contents we have denominated the GOLDEN BARROW. It was opened for the first time in the year 1803. At the depth of two feet we found a little pile of burned human bones placed in a shallow bason-like cist, and at the distance of one foot from the bones was a considerable quantity of ashes intermixed with small fragments of burned bones.

---

* This village may have owed its appellation either to Brihtric, who succeeded to the kingdom of the West Saxons on the death of Cynewulf in the year 784, and reigned over it till the year 800 ; or it may have been so called from his successor Ecbryght, or Egbert: the latter bears the greatest affinity to the *Ecgbyrhtes-ston* of the Chronicle.

+ Though *tumuli* are most frequently to be met with on high ground, yet they are not by any means confined to that situation : but I must observe, that I have as yet found them in no part of our county so numerous, or large, as in the Vale of Wily between Boreham and Upton Lovel.

‡ A description of these antiquities will be given when I treat of the Roman Æra of our county.

§ Camden in his Britannia informs us, that the ancient name of this place was *Ellandunum* or *Ellandune,* and that Weolsthan, or Wulstan, who was Earl of it, founded a monastery at Wilton.

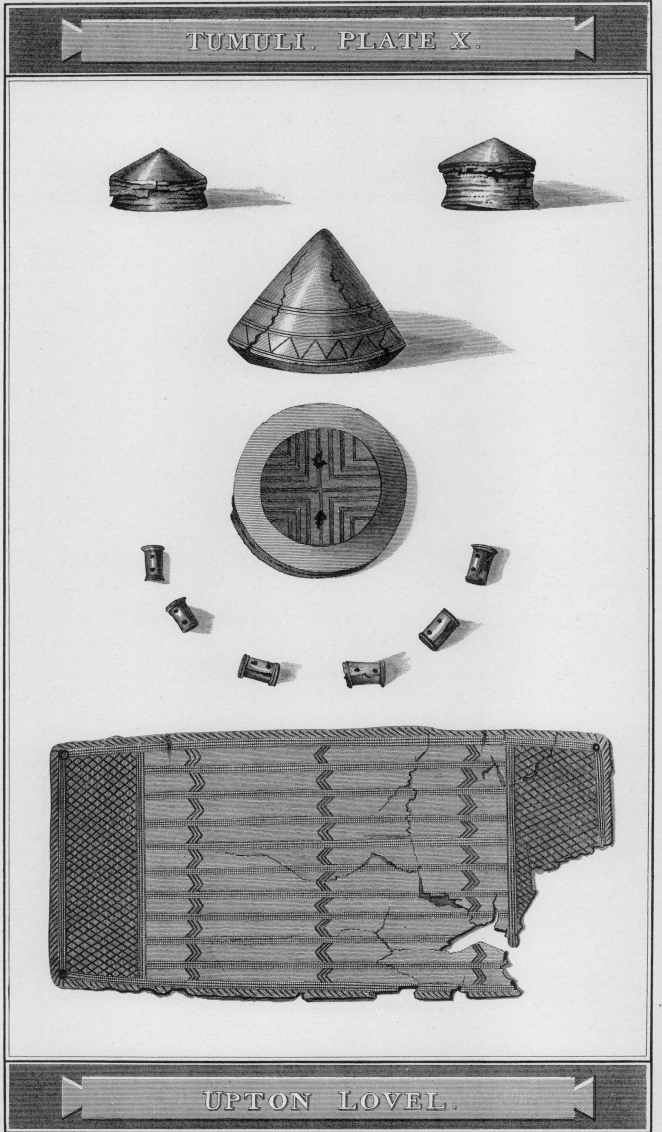

P. Crocker del.   J. Basire Sc.

UPTON LOVEL.

Published for W. Miller, Albemarle Street, London, Jan. 1.1810.

TUMULI. PLATE XI.

UPTON LOVEL.

P. Crocker del.t   J.º Basire Sc.

Publifhed for W. Miller, Albemarle Street, London, Jan.ʸ 1. 1810.

About two feet from the pile of bones, the following articles were discovered. 1. Thirteen gold beads made in the form of a drum, having two ends to screw off, and perforated in two places on the sides for the purpose of stringing. 2. A thin plate of the same metal, six inches in length, and nearly three in width, richly wrought, and perforated at the four corners. 3. Another ornament in form of a cone, decorated with circles and zigzags, and fitted closely to a piece of dark wood, like ebony, on which the marks of the pattern still appear impressed; the bottom part of this article is also perforated. The above are all of pure but thin gold, neatly worked, and highly burnished. The large flat plate must have been, like the cone, strengthened by a strip of wood behind; and the whole, by their several perforations, are strongly marked as forming the decorative accoutrements of some distinguished British chieftain. Besides the above, were two small articles in gold, resembling little boxes, about an inch in diameter, with a top, in the form of a cone, to take off. I cannot conjecture to what purpose these were appropriated, as they bear no sign of perforation. The whole of these have been correctly drawn of their original size, and form the interesting contents of TUMULI, PLATE X. Besides the above precious articles of gold, we discovered some large plates of amber, similar to those delineated in TUMULI, PLATE III. and above a thousand beads of the same substance, and of different sizes; also a curious little cup, studded over with projecting knobs, which appear to have been first made in the form of glass stoppers to a bottle, and afterwards inserted into the circular holes of the cup, which had been previously drilled for receiving them: between these grape-like protuberances are other perforations, which still remain open.

Such was the result of our researches in the year 1803; but not being completely satisfied, and still thinking that the primary interment had escaped our vigilance, I was anxious that a further trial should be made, which took place in July, 1807, and was attended with success; for, on the same level, and within a few inches of the very spot where the golden trinkets and the amber beads had been found, we discovered two cups, the one placed within the other. The largest of these was covered with a profusion of zigzag ornaments, but on taking out, was unfortunately broken to pieces; the smaller one, containing about a pint, is quite plain, and in good preservation. These cups, together with the necklace of amber beads, and a small lance head, and pin of brass, which were found near the pile of ashes in the same barrow, form the contents of (TUMULI, PLATE XI.) Still pursuing our excavations to the floor of the barrow, we there found an oblong cist, about eighteen inches deep, which contained a simple interment of burned bones, unaccompanied with either arms or trinkets. This was certainly the primary funereal deposit; but, however rich in materials, or elegant in form, the articles found nearer the surface of the barrow may be deemed, their high antiquity cannot be disputed; for although the grape cup exceeds in beauty and novelty of design any we have as yet discovered, the other two cups of unbaked clay, and rude workmanship, bespeak the uncivilized æra to which the construction of this sepulchral mound may be justly attributed. The next village in the Vale of Wily, is Boyton, the residence of my friend A. B. Lambert, Esq. a most zealous investigator of British antiquities. By his particular desire, Mr. Cunnington explored the barrows on his several manors of Corton, Boyton, and Sherrington, in the year 1804, and the result of those researches was published in Volume XV. of the Archæologia, for the year 1805. It is however necessary that in this general survey of the antiquities of our county, I should repeat the communications given to the Antiquarian Society on the subject of these barrows, otherwise my work might be justly thought deficient.

SHERRINGTON BARROW. The parish in which this *tumulus* is situated, adjoins that of Boyton, and is nearly opposite to Codford, on the other side of the river Wily. This barrow may be compared in shape to an égg cut in two; the convex side placed upwards, and the broad end to the W.N.W. Its length is one hundred and eight feet; its width, at the broadest part, eighty feet, and its elevation fourteen feet: it is composed of gravel dug near the Wily, from which river it is distant about a hundred yards. This barrow was opened by a large section at the broad end, and on the highest part, and at the depth of about sixteen inches were found four skeletons, lying from south to north. At the depth of fourteen feet we came to the floor, and native soil, which was covered with charred wood and ashes; on the south side was a neat circular cist, made in the original soil, about two feet in diameter, and sixteen inches in depth, in which were deposited the head of an ox, and one small horn of a deer. Not finding the primary interment, we made two other large sections, and in the first, which was near the centre of the barrow, we discovered, at the depth of eighteen inches, a skeleton lying from west to east; and on its right side was a spear head of iron; we pursued our researches to the floor, but made no further discovery. The next section was made still further towards the low end of the barrow, and produced at the same depth in the soil, the skeleton of a stout man lying in the same direction as the former. On its right side, close to the thighs, was a two-edged sword, the blade two feet long, with rather an obtuse point, and no guarded hilt; it had been enclosed in a scabbard of wood, a considerable quantity of which still adhered to it. On the right side of the head lay a spear head of iron, and on the left, the *umbo* of a shield of the same metal, with which was found an iron buckle, a piece of leather, a stirrup of brass perforated in several places, a thin bit of silver, and an iron knife, with several pieces of corroded iron.* To the east of this skeleton, and in the same direction, we discovered two others, one of an adult, the other of a child four or five years old, and with them a small knife, and a piece of corroded lead. Here ended our researches: the fragments of rude British pottery, deer's horns, and animal bones dispersed in different parts of this *tumulus* will prove its high antiquity ; experience has taught us that skeletons found near the surface of barrows were interments of a later date ; and in this instance we have reason to lament that the primary deposit still remains undiscovered.

I now quit the immediate vale of Wily, where no further discoveries of British antiquities have been made ; and return to the parish of Boyton, where there are two barrows, at no great distance from the Vale. They were opened by Mr. Lambert and Mr. Cunnington. The first stands on the edge of Boyton Downs, and at a short distance from the Long Barrow at Sherrington before described. It is circular in its form, seventy-six feet in its base diameter, and fourteen feet in elevation above the plain ; and being situated on high ground, commands extensive views towards the north and east. The operations were begun by a large section from north to south. In the first *stratum*, which was about two feet thick, and composed chiefly of vegetable earth, nine skeletons were discovered, lying in every direction, and in no regular order. A few years ago, the labourers employed to plant some trees on this barrow, found four skeletons, which were interred in Boyton church-yard ; therefore the whole number of bodies found on the top of this *tumulus* amounted to thirteen. The next *stratum* was one of small loose flints, similar to those now picked off the arable land in this neighbourhood for repairing the roads ; this was more than four feet thick ; a line of black vegetable earth then succeeded, and continued for eight feet more to the floor of the barrow. Here, and nearly in the centre, were deposited the burned bones of a Briton, piled up in a small heap, within a shallow cist in the native soil. In this barrow, as in many others, we find the two different modes of interment ; the primary one

---

* These articles bear a striking resemblance to those found in a barrow on Rodmead Down, which have been described in the Stourton Station, and engraved in (TUMULI, PLATE IV). These interments may certainly be attributed to the same æra, though the date of that æra cannot be satisfactorily ascertained.

at bottom, and the subsequent one near the top.   The other barrow in Boyton manor, is situated on a neck of land projecting from the great ridge wood to Stockton sheep pond, having Dean valley on the right.   It is forty feet in dia-meter, and three feet nine inches in elevation.   At the depth of four feet beneath the floor was the skeleton of a young person lying with the head nearly east, which is rather an unusual circumstance with primary interments deposited at so great a depth in the native chalk, in which case the head gene-rally lies towards the north.   Near the feet of the skeleton, lay the fragments of a very handsome drinking-cup, and at the distance of about one foot was another very small cup, both of which have been repaired, and are engraved in the Archaeologia, Vol. XV. p. 343.   The large cup is nine inches high, and the small one three inches and a quarter.

This district furnishes another long barrow, situated to the south of the river Wily, on an eminence, which from it has derived the appellation of Barrow Hill.   Corton Long Barrow stands exactly east and west, with its broad end towards the former point.   The plough has diminished its size both on the sides, and at the east end ; at this time its extreme length is two hundred and sixteen feet, its width at the east end twenty-five feet, and its highest elevation nine feet above the adjoining ground.   Mr. Cunnington at first conceived it to have been a double barrow, from the circumstance of finding a rude urn containing burned human bones at the west end.   The discoveries however made at the east end, prove it to have been originally a long barrow, and the sinking or apparent division in the middle was occasioned probably from the removal of earth by the farmers from that spot.   The next section was made in the highest part of the east end, but finding nothing, Mr. Cunnington was induced to consider it as a long barrow, and therefore commenced another section nearer the eastern extremity, where, after clearing away the earth for the depth of two feet, he came to a large stone, which required the strength of three men to lift out.   This proved to be the top of a pyramid of loose flints, marl stones, &c. which became wider near the bottom, where the base of the ridge measured more than twenty feet in length, and about ten feet in width.   Beneath this ridge were found eight skeletons, lying promiscuously in various directions.   Seven of them were adults, the eighth a child : they had been deposited on the floor of the barrow, between two excavations in the native soil, of an oval form, and seven feet apart.   These oval cists or pits were about four feet long, and two and a half deep ; they were cut in the chalk, and, with the skeletons, were covered with a pyramid of flints and stones.

P. Crocker delt.

J.º Basire Sc.

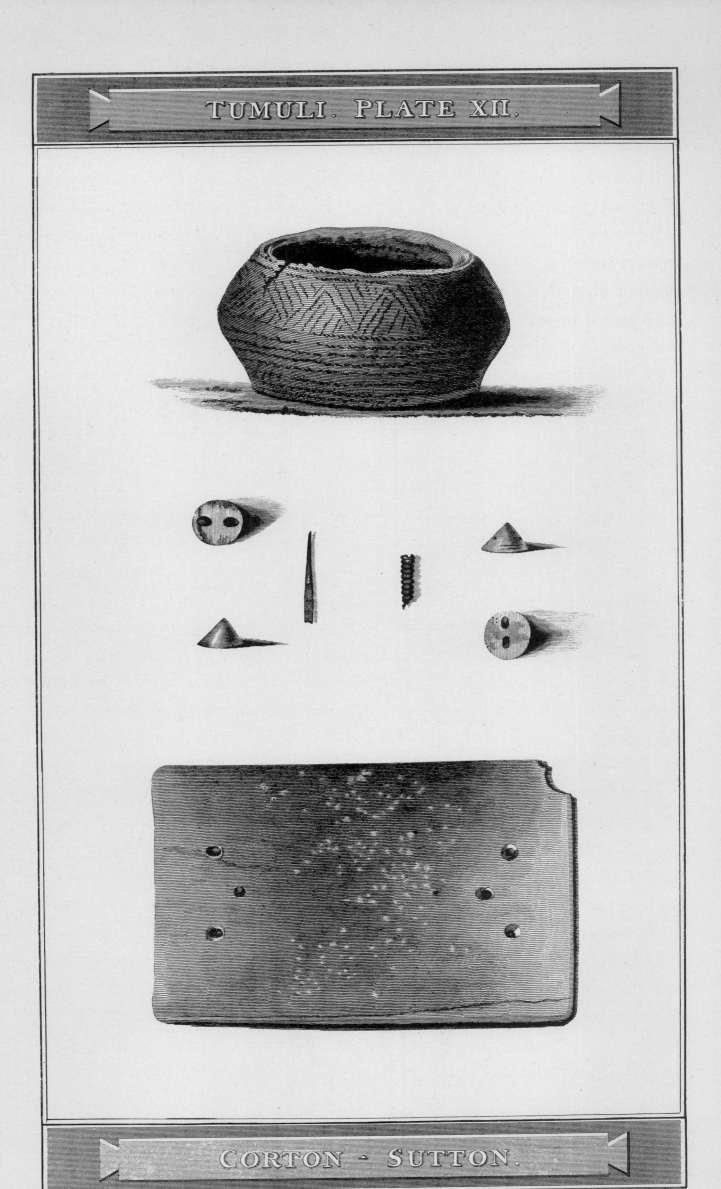

Published for W. Miller, Albemarle Street, London, Jan.ʸ 1.1810.

CORTON ∘ SUTTON.

The next village west of Corton is Tytherington, and beyond it are Little and Great Sutton. There were formerly several barrows dispersed about this neighbourhood, but several of them, since the enclosure of the commons, have been levelled. In one of these on the right of the road, between Sutton and Longbridge Deverill, was found the curious oblong piece of blue slate, engraved in TUMULI PLATE XII. In this article we see an humble imitation of the golden plate found at Upton Lovel, and described (page 100), and the perforations in it shew that it was destined for the same purpose, and suspended probably from the neck of a Briton. It was placed immediately under the right hand, and close to the breast of a skeleton, which had been interred with its head towards the north, and its legs, according to the primitive custom, gathered up. A few inches from this ornament were two boar's tusks, and close to the knees of the skeleton was a drinking-cup, which was unfortunately broken by the pressure of the earth over it. On the same side of the road, and nearer to Southley wood, is a small earthen work, on a common, nearly obscured by fern and furze. Another of the small barrows in this neighbourhood produced the interment of a skeleton, with a drinking cup at its feet. The little cup engraved in the same Plate, of the original size, was found in a small *tumulus*, on the edge of Corton Downs, adjoining Tytherington, together with an interment of burned bones in a circular cist. The other articles engraved in this Plate, were found with an interment of burned bones in a Druid barrow, on Sutton Veney Downs, not far from Pertwood. The cones are either of bone or ivory: the notched bead is of tin, and the only article of that metal we have ever found in a barrow; the little pin is of copper.

From Longbridge Deverill I again ascend the chalky district, to an insulated eminence, called in the Map of Wiltshire, WHITEN-HILL, where we again find ourselves amongst the Britons. Near the north-west point of this hill, is a small earthen work of a very singular form, resembling the letter D, with an entrance on the straight side, and towards the east. Its area contains about one acre and a quarter, and the ditch of the rampart is on the inside. On the east side of this work, we have found the usual marks of British population, and in the ditch on the left side of the entrance to it, we dug up some rude fragments of coarse pottery, together with a large piece of the fine red Samian; but the whole of this ground having been in tillage, few important discoveries can be made without the use of the spade. On the opposite point of this same hill, and adjoining the track way leading from Tytherington to Pertwood, and Hindon, the remains of another large British village appear in the most

D D

unequivocal manner.   On the north edge of these excavations, I discovered a
very low barrow bearing marks of high antiquity, and which, on opening, contained a skeleton lying on its left side, with its legs drawn up, two rude arrow
heads of flint near its head, and a drinking cup at its feet.   The irregularities of
ground extend over a large tract of the hill towards the south and south-east :
the excavations produce the same marks of antiquity as those in the other British villages before described, such as pieces of iron, flat headed nails, pottery,
&c and in one of them we discovered a fire place, or *hypocaustum*, in the form
of a cross, similar to those before mentioned at Knook, page 85.

Descending from this hill, and crossing a valley, we approach a neck of
land leading from Boyton to the Great Ridge wood, where I observed an
irregular bank and ditch pursuing their course over the downs towards the
wood, in which, owing to the thickness of the copse, I lost them.   The
numerous lynchets all around this spot, evidently point out some British
village in the neighbourhood, but which as yet I have not been fortunate
enough to discover.

This great range of wood extends in a line from Upper Pertwood west, to
South Newton east, and is divided about half way by the London road.   The
western part of it bears the name of GREAT RIDGE, the eastern part of it that of
GROVELY.   Its total length extends about sixteen miles, and probably in ancient
times formed one undivided forest.   The projecting points of land on each side
abound with remains of British and Roman antiquities ; and a Roman road
leading from SORBIODUNUM, or Old Sarum, to Monkton Deverill, and from
thence over the Mendip hills in Somersetshire to the shores of the Bristol channel, has been most judiciously carried along the highest part of the ridge.   Little
did I think when traversing, in my juvenile days, this woodland district in pursuit of a fox, I should at a more mature age find so much food for inquiry and
reflection in this apparently desert region : yet we must not judge of its pris-
tine by its present state ; for when occupied by the Britons, the greater part of
this woody ridge, and the high lands projecting from it, were in cultivation.
This is evidently proved by the numerous marks of old enclosures which are
visible on the sides of the hills, and are continued through the present coppice
to the very summit of the ridge.   When the early Britons first fixed upon this
elevated and healthy spot for their station, there was most probably a certain
quantity of wood dispersed over it, which they naturally cleared away,
and kept unincumbered as long as it continued a place of residence.   On the
arrival of the Saxons, these alpine situations were deserted, and more shel-

tered habitations were sought for in the valleys near rivers. Then the oak, the monarch of the forest, began to reassume his reign, and regain his long-lost privileges. We know the seeds of trees and herbaceous plants will lie for many years dormant in the soil until called forth to vegetation by some particular manure, or by the removal of some particular obstruction : and if we wish to see a striking example of the rapid working of nature in raising a forest, we need only observe how the fir-trees on Bagshot-heath, near Hertford-bridge, have extended their limits by the spontaneous scattering of the seeds from the original plantations. In short, what was once wood, will, if not checked by browsing of cattle, or other such like impediments, return to wood again:

" *Naturam expellas furcâ, tamen usque recurret.*"

I must now conduct my readers to the southern side of this great wood, in order to notice some British remains which have been lately discovered on its borders. The numerous marks of an extensive population on the northern side of the Ridge wood already investigated, induced me to think that the southern and more genial side would not have been neglected. I therefore ordered our *explorator* to examine it well with his spade and pick-axe ; and his researches were crowned with success ; for he discovered the remains of four British settlements between the western end of the wood, and the great road leading to Wily and Deptford.

The first is on an eminence called Croft Hill, marked by a clump of fir-trees, and facing the village of Chicklade ; it is bounded on the north by a bank, and I observed an old ditch near the fir-trees pointing east towards a little cottage in the vale.

On the next hill eastward, is an irregular earthen work with an entrance to the south : and on the adjoining eminence, we picked up pottery, with fragments of millstones, &c. &c. but the site of this British village being in tillage, the proofs were not so decisive as I could have wished. Still pursuing an easterly course, I observed an old earthen work, in a valley, nearly worn out, of an irregular form, with an entrance to the south-east. It is situated in a retired meadow between the hills.

On the next hill, called High Park, we found by digging, pottery, and all the *indicia* of British population, together with some barrows. But the fourth village is the most conspicuous. It is situated nearly opposite the New Inn in Chicklade bottom, and is marked by the usual irregularities, and excavations in the ground, which extend to a considerable distance. On digging we found rude British pottery, and a great deal of Roman, with some of the fine red Samian; also a small brass coin of the Emperor Carausius.*

Skirting the boundaries of the Ridge wood, we come to the great London road, and may observe an old bank, and ditch going off to the right, which on following, I found led into a British village on Hanging Langford Down; and had a fresh confirmation of my supposition that these banks and ditches, so numerous in our county, were lines of communication from one village to another; for such this ditch evidently appears to have been. Near the nine-tieth mile-stone we cross the line of the Roman road leading easterly to Sorbiodunum, or Old Sarum; and turning round the corner of Ridge wood, we again recognize the works of the Britons.

Stockton Works appear to have been originally surrounded by a ditch and a single rampart of earth, of which a considerable part towards the east still remains; but the western boundary, and many of the interior works have been much defaced by a great waggon track, which for many ages has passed through the works. The original entrance (a) was on the eastern side, near the head of a steep valley; but many other adits of a more modern date have been made for the accommodation of waggons frequenting the wood. At (b) there is also an entrance to an inner work, where we see numerous excavations, &c. and near the centre is a singular little work of a pentagonal form (c), and beyond it, the irregularities and cavities continue deep and numerous for a considerable distance to the westward. These works cover, according to Mr. Crocker's observations, the space of sixty-two acres, and extended probably much further towards the west, and into the wood on the south; but they are so defaced in many places, and in others so very doubtful, that what now remains can only be considered as a very imperfect specimen of the original works. We have dug in various places within the area, and found both large and small Roman coins, pieces of brass, iron nails, fragments of millstones, brick flues, tiles, and both British and Roman pottery; also the neck of a glass bottle of a sea-green colour; in short, all the vestiges of a numerous population. These works answer in a great degree, the account transmitted to us by the classical authors of the ancient towns of the Gauls and Britons. Cæsar in speaking of the capital of the British chieftain Cassivellaunus, says, " *Oppidum autem Britanni vocant, quum sylvas impeditas vallo atque fossâ munierunt.*

* A similar medal is figured by Dr. Stukely in his History of Carausius, Plate VIII. *in area* B. E. (*Britannicus exercitus*), in exergue mlxxi. which, the learned Doctor says, was struck at the imperial mint in London, A. D. 290, for gifts to the soldiery.

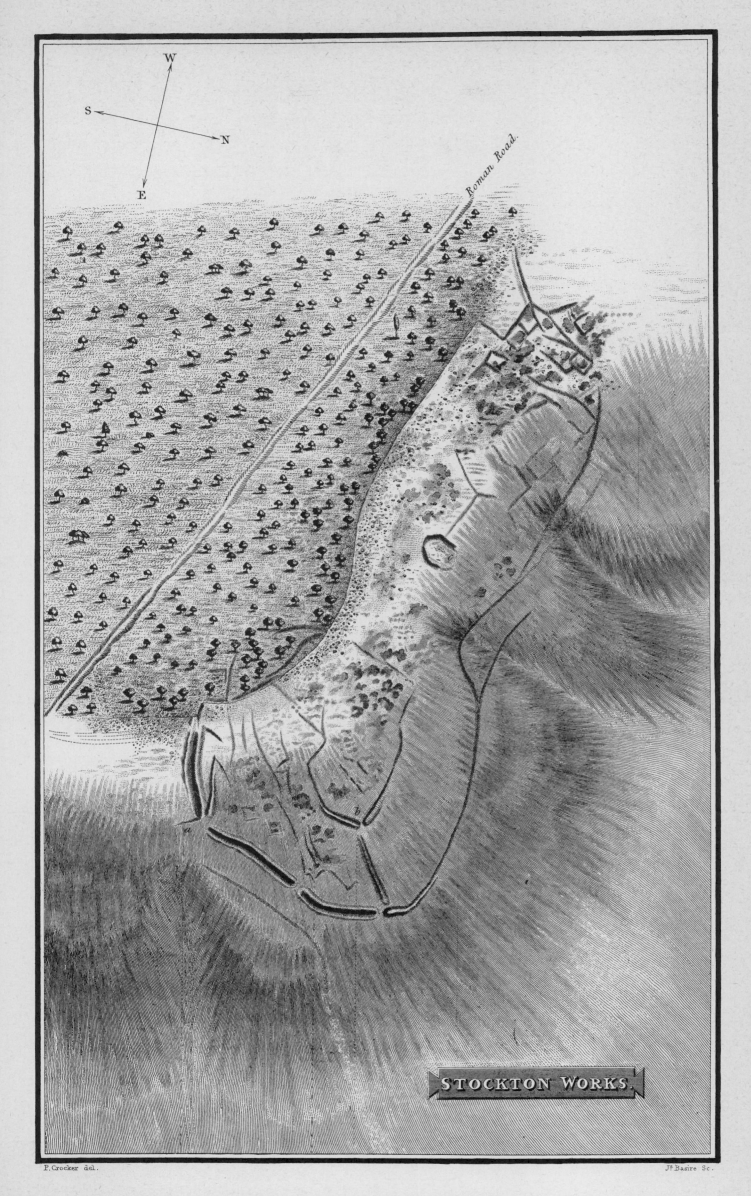

W

S

N

E

Roman Road.

STOCKTON WORKS.

P. Crocker del.

Jᵉ Basire Sc.

Published for W. Miller, Albemarle Street, London, Janʸ 1.1811.

A town amongst the Britons is nothing more than a thick wood, fortified with a ditch and rampart: and the geographer Strabo, speaking on the same subject, says, *Eorum urbes sunt nemora: latissimos enim circos, dejectis obstruunt arboribus, ubi constructis tuguriis, et ipsi pariter et armenti stabulantur.*" Their towns are woods, where they cut down the trees, build huts, and live there together with their herds.*

Its elevated and wild situation mark it as originally a British settlement, not a camp or strong hold, for the ramparts are too slight and unconnected to answer the purpose of a work of defence; nor till the æra of the Danes and Saxons do we find those gigantic intrenchments and multiplied lines of fortification, which abound in our county. After the invasion of Britain by the Romans, and the subjection of our capital at SORBIODUNUM, a road of communication was made from it through the extensive line of population with which this ridge was frequented; the transalpine victors here found a convenient station, and associated themselves with the conquered Britons. A series of coins from the first Claudius to Theodosius, mark also their continued residence on this spot for a long period; they are so numerous, and common, that the labourers employed to dig flints, throw them up, and leave them amongst the stones: twice on visiting these works, I found coins in this situation, one of which was a large brass in good preservation, of the Emperor M. AN-TONINVS. AVG. TR. P. XXV. The reverse of the coin bears this inscription enclosed within a wreath; PRIMI DECENNALES, COS. III. S. C.† The smaller one was a coin of DECENTIUS; on the reverse two figures of Victory holding a shield on which is inscribed VOT V. MULT. IO. i. e. *Votis quinquennalibus, multiplicatis*, or *multis decennalibus.*‡

In the arable lands between this ridge and the village of Stockton, is a long barrow, which we opened, and found similar to those of the same class. Adjoining the village of Stockton, is that of Wily, and near it Deptford Inn, where

* During a tour made this summer, 1810, in Caernarvonshire and Anglesey, I had great satisfaction in tracing the ancient residences of the Britons in the mountainous regions of Cambria, and in finding so great a similarity between those in Wales and those in Wiltshire. In each country an exalted situation was chosen: in Wales the outward line of enclosure was made with stone: in Wiltshire with earth; there the huts were circular, and surrounded with upright stones; here, the want of that article forbade such a shelter; in both places the roofs were probably formed by poles covered either with turf or boughs of trees twisted; and in Wales a large stone perforated in the middle for the admission of a pole to support the roof, is frequently found in the centre of these huts.

† This coin is engraved by Musellius in his Collection of medals, Table CXVII.

‡ Decentius was brother to the Emperor Magnentius, who being conquered by Constantius fell on his sword A. D. 351. Decentius had been raised to the rank either of Cæsar or Augustus by his brother, and followed his example by strangling himself on hearing of his death. He had several medals struck with his name, but as yet I have not been able to find an engraving of the one here alluded to.

I shall fix my quarters, and from thence continue my researches through the remainder of this Station.

Iter II. Passing through the village of Wily, I once more ascend the down, and soon again recognize the handiwork of our British ancestors, in a fortification vulgarly called Bilbury Rings, or Wily Camp.

This earthen work is little more than a mile distant from the village from which it derives its name, and is situated on a point of down that projects from the great ridge, and occupies a gentle declivity to the north. It is nearly of a circular form. The area within the ramparts includes seventeen acres and a quarter; the circuit of the outer *vallum* is four furlongs, and one hundred and ninety yards; and the height of the ramparts twenty feet. So many adits have been made through this work for the accommodation of waggons, and cattle, that it is difficult to ascertain which was the original entrance. It is fortified on the east by double, and on the west by triple intrenchments, the outward one, particularly on the east side, being very broad and flat. Within the area of this camp, we find the remains of another work, of a very irregular form, having the ditch within. This, I conclude, was the original work, connected with those on another adjoining hill, and the circular and more extended ramparts which enclose it were added probably at a subsequent period. The excavations within the inner work have produced every species of pottery, both rude British as well as fine Roman, small brass coins, part of a brass armilla, flat headed nails, pieces of iron, paving-stones, fragments of millstones, and black vegetable earth to the depth of three feet. On the south side, where there is the appearance of an entrance into the camp, is a small oblong barrow covered with furze and heath, in which, near the centre, and at the depth of about three feet, we found in a shallow excavation, an interment of burned human bones. I am doubtful if the mound on the north side is a barrow.

Continuing our ride in a southerly direction towards Grovely wood, we have a deep valley on our left, on the opposite declivities of which we plainly perceive a very singular and irregular circle, having its ditch within, and connected with some extensive works on the hill above. These are known by the name of West Down, or Hanging Langford Camp, in which parish they are situated. Their very great irregularity and want of symmetry evidently point them out to us as originally British; and the articles found on digging within the area, such as nails, pottery, &c. prove this spot to have been inhabited after the arrival of the Romans in our island: the whole is in tillage, and thereby

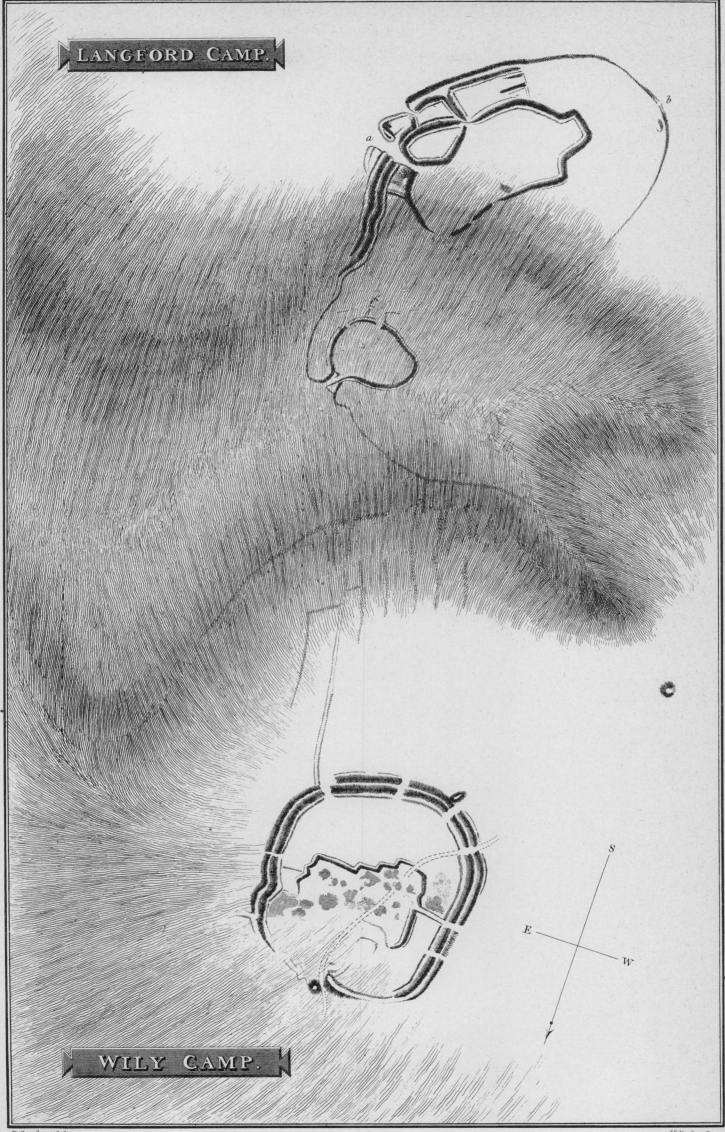

LANGFORD CAMP.

WILY CAMP.

P. Crocker del.

J^{s.} Basire Sc.

Publiſhed for W. Miller, Albemarle Street, London, Jany. 1 1811.

GROVELY CASTLE.

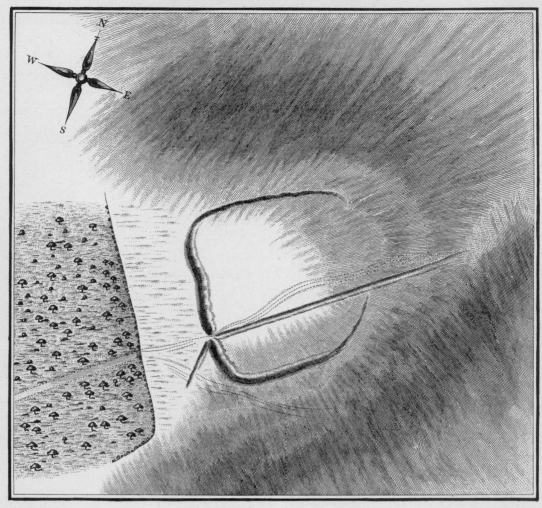

HAMSHILL DITCHES.

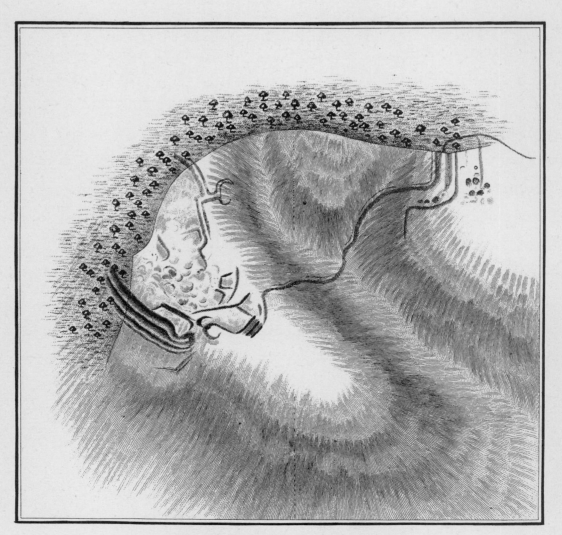

P. Crocker del.

J.ⁿ Basire Sc.

Published for W. Miller, Albemarle Street, London, Jan.ʸ 1.1811.

much defaced. The principal entrance was towards the east, at *a* ; and a ditch encompasses nearly the whole work, through which, at *b*, there seems to have been an approach to the interior works. As I may not probably be able to produce so decisive an example of ancient and modern castrametation, I wish to call the eye of my readers to the annexed map of Wily and Langford camps. He will at first sight perceive in the centre of the former, the vestiges of a rude and irregular work, with the ditch *within* the *vallum*, surrounded by a regular and circular entrenchment, strengthened with a double row of ramparts, and evidently of a more modern construction. In the latter, he will again recognize the British character, which pervades the greater part of the whole work, and in the small circle between the two, he will trace a resemblance in one particular with the minor work of Wily camp, each having their ditches *within* the *vallum*. There are several small barrows dispersed about the environs of these two camps, and the lynchets on all the adjoining hills attest an extensive and ancient cultivation. At a short distance from Langford camp, we come to the edge of Grovely wood, and are led to it by a ditch, entering the works at *b*. In this ditch I find a fresh confirmation of the idea I have before started respecting these relics of antiquity ; for you will perceive by the map, that it comes in a line from the British villages on the south side of Great Ridge, leaves Stockton works a little to the left, and having crossed the Roman road twice, forms an acute angle near a clump of trees called DINTON BEECHES ; then continuing along the northern side of Grovely wood, directs its course towards the British towns at Grovely, &c.; and this idea is corroborated by the circumstance of another ditch branching off from it, and pointing directly to the entrance of Langford works before mentioned at *b*, in the annexed plan.

I now cross the Ridge and Roman road, and skirt the southern undulations of Grovely wood, in a line with the old turnpike road from Chicklade to Salisbury. Though at different places, near the copse, I observed the marks of ancient enclosures, nothing decided attracted my attention, till I came to a point of hill projecting from the wood, opposite the village of Barford. There, on a piece of fine down belonging to that parish, are the evident traces of another large British village, of which I have given a ground plan. It is known by the vulgar name of HAMSHILL DITCHES, and is situated on the declivity of a high point of down projecting from the south of Grovely wood towards the village of Barford, to which parish it belongs.

Following the windings of the copse, we find a large ditch entering it at the eastern corner, and steering its course westerly through the wood towards the last mentioned British village : in the opposite direction it passes through the village of Chilhampton, crosses the vale of Wily, and then proceeds across the turnpike road from Salisbury to Devizes, towards the vale of Avon, opposite to Little Durnford. The village of Ditchampton below Chilhampton derived its name most probably from this ancient ditch.

Having turned the east corner of Grovely wood, we soon recognize very evident traces of the Roman road issuing from it in a raised and straight causeway; and having with some difficulty traversed the deep vallies that insinuate themselves into the wood, we at length come to a bold point of hill, facing the vale on the other side of the river, in which the villages of Stapleford, Berwick St. James, and Winterbourn Stoke are situated. On this commanding spot we find the skeleton of a large British town, hitherto unnoticed in any map, or by any writer. It bears the name of GROVELY WORKS, and occupies, in the form of a crescent, the high point of a hill, projecting from Grovely wood towards the vale of Wily, opposite the villages of Stapleford and Great Wishford, or rather between the two ; it extends nearly a mile in length, and covers a space of ground little less than sixty acres, commanding a very extensive and diversified prospect; towards the west, a long range of the vale of Wily, terminated with that conspicuous eminence Clay Hill, presents itself, and the view is rendered still more interesting to the antiquary by the numerous camps, circles, and *tumuli* which crown the surrounding hills. A thick copse wood, intermixed with fine beech trees, forms on the opposite side a good contrast to the expanded prospect across the vale, which is terminated by the distant hills in Hampshire, on which we recognize a continuation of British fortresses.

In point of situation, and in some other respects, these works bear a strong resemblance to those before described at STOCKTON, and agree with the description given by the Roman historian Cæsar, of the towns in Britain ; yet in some parts of them we may distinguish the intended alterations of a more modern engineer ; particularly near the centre, where there are some strong ramparts, much more regular in their plan, and of a very different character from the original part of the works. From their small extent, I am at a loss to conjecture for what purpose they could have been constructed. A little to the east of them are some marks of an entrance, and one of those small pentagonal enclosures, which are peculiar to British towns, and similar to the one before mentioned in the works at Stockton. Still further on, a bank and ditch issue from the body of the works, and point towards the vale below. The raised lines now become fainter for a short distance, but on turning round

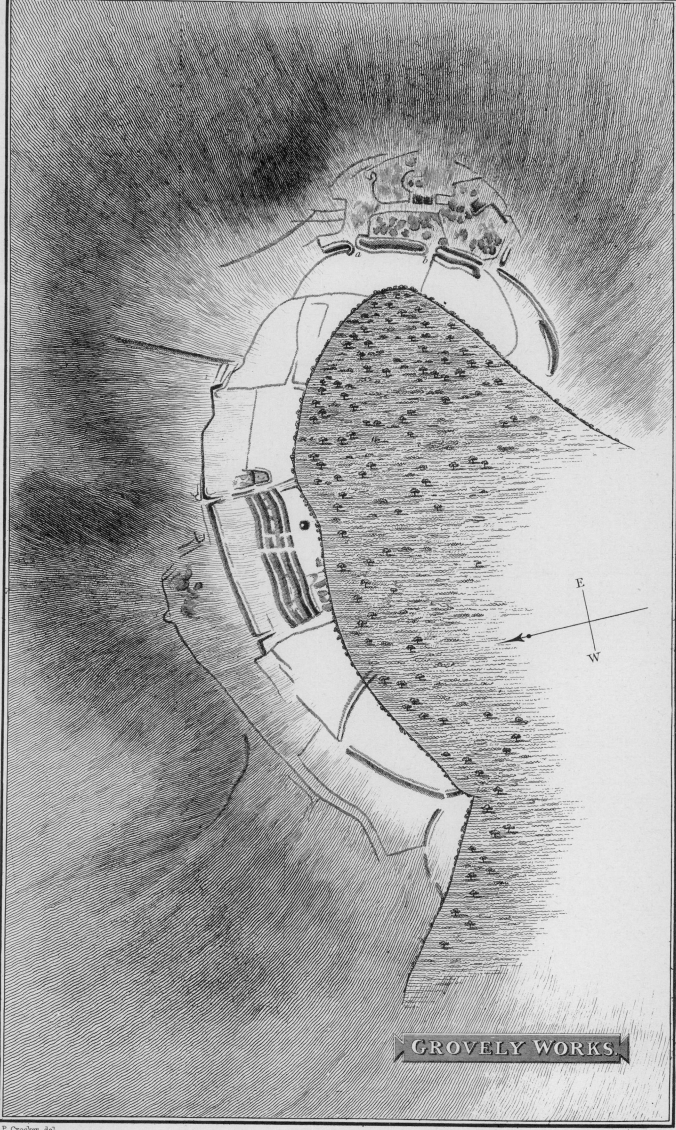

E

W

P. Crocker del.

J.ᵉ Baſire Sc.

Publiſhed for W. Miller, Albemarle Street, London, Janʸ.1.18n.

the eastern angle of the hill and wood, they reappear in a very decided and conspicuous manner. Here also the original works seem to have been interrupted by the addition of ramparts of a stronger construction, and of a more modern æra, which, as well as those before mentioned, near the centre of these works, will appear very evident upon the annexed plan. On the outside of these ramparts, the excavations are very numerous, covering a large tract of ground, and producing all the usual marks of a mixed British and Roman population. At *a* and *b* in each of these more modern additions, there are appearances of entrances, and from the eastern side of the excavations, there are traces of a ditch descending to the vale, and winding along the opposite hill eastward. Still following the boundaries of the wood, and crossing a deep valley, I observed a ditch leading up the opposite hill to an earthen work, called GROVELY CASTLE, but I do not think it ancient. This intrenchment is placed on an elevated spot, and is fortified by a single rampart, extending from the south-west towards the east: on the north and north-east sides there are none, which induces me to think that the camp was never completed; it was certainly never made use of as a permanent residence, for on digging in it, we could find no pottery, charred wood, animal bones, or any proofs whatever of habitation. Its form does not denote any high antiquity, and the bank and ditch running through it are modern. The area within the intrenchments, if complete, would contain about fourteen acres, and the circuit would be four furlongs and one hundred and thirty-two yards; the height of the rampart is thirty-three feet. The next hill also has its antiquities. Besides several barrows dispersed about a rough tract of furze and heath, we find a curious little earthen work, vulgarly called EAST CASTLE, which at first sight bears the appearance of a Druid barrow, having a small mound raised within its area; but on opening it, we could discover no sepulchral deposit, and found only fragments of British pottery, and a rude bodkin made of bone. Its circumference is two hundred and four yards, and the contents of its area three quarters of an acre.

From this hill I descend into the vale of Wily, and passing through the village of Hanging Langford, proceed to my quarters at Deptford inn, having completed an Iter rich in food for the antiquary, and interesting to every eye that is not totally indifferent to the many varied and beautiful views which this circuit of Grovely wood continually affords.

I have before had occasion to mention that it would be a very difficult matter to ascertain the original constructors of our camps and earthen works, but that the greater portion of them might be attributed to the Britons, though in later times, they may have been altered, strengthened, and inhabited by the Romans, Saxons, and Danes. This ITER will in some degree confirm my opinion on this subject. In STOCKTON works we recognize the simple British character throughout the greater part of them, and call to mind the description before quoted, of Cæsar, respecting the British towns, " *Oppidum autem Britanni vocant quum sylvas impeditas vallo atque fossa munierunt.*"

In the works of HANGING LANGFORD we observe the same British character ; a ditch, slight ramparts, and great irregularity in the plan of the different enclosures.

In WILY CAMP, on the adjoining hill, we recognize in the inner area the same British irregularity, with the ditch *within ;* and in the outward circle we clearly trace a more regular and modern style of castrametation.

In GROVELY WORKS we also see the handiwork of different engineers ; and it appears that the later innovations, tending apparently to add strength to the camp, were never brought to a termination.

But before I quit the subject of this interesting vale of Wily, let me briefly review the numerous antiquities that accompany its boundaries on each side. They may be said to commence at the village of Kingston Deverill, where the Wily becomes a permanent stream. Here we find *tumuli* dispersed about the plain, as well as on the hills. To the left we have Bidcomb hill, the ancient and aerial residence of the Britons ; between Brixton and Hill Deverill, we find traces of the same nation near the banks of the river, and at the latter, the decided remains of a large settlement. Earthen works and *tumuli* still attest the residence of an ancient people in the neighbourhood of Sutton, and Southley wood, and are continued along the vale to Boreham, Bishopstrow, Norton, and as far as Upton Lovel, where they cease. The antique honors are then claimed by the hills. They present themselves in a most conspicuous degree on each eminence, from Warminster to Heytesbury, along the northern side of the valley, and are continued on the bordering hills of Upton Lovel, Codford, &c. as far as the village of Wily. From thence the opposite side of the vale seems to assume the superiority, and to retain it undisputed for several miles, viz. from Stockton works to those at Grovely. I question if any part of England, and I am sure that no part of our own county, that I have yet examined, can produce so rapid a succession of interesting British remains, all tending to prove that the Wily was a favourite stream, the *dilectus amnis* of the Britons, for many succeeding centuries.*

* The Wily derives its name from the Celtic word *Gwy*, water ; and from the same root we may trace the county town Wilton, and Wiltshire.

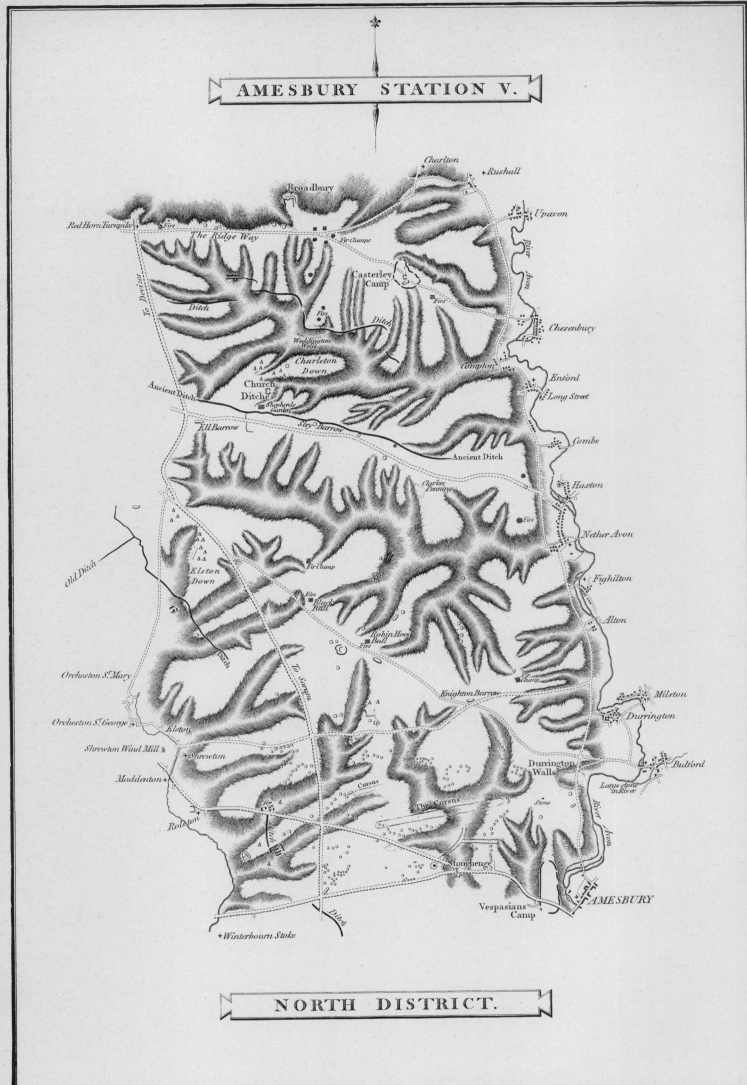

AMESBURY STATION V.

NORTH DISTRICT.

Philip Crocker del.   London: Published by W. Miller. May 1811.   J. Cary sculp.

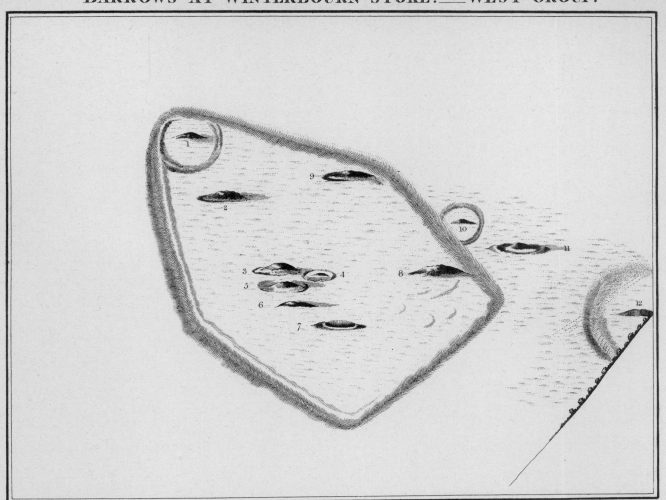

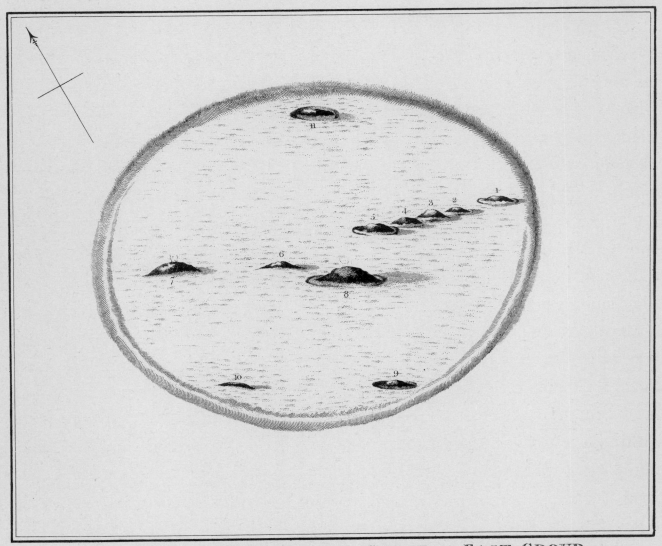

BARROWS AT WINTERBOURN STOKE. — EAST GROUP.

P. Crocker del.

Jᵒ Basire Sc.

Published for W. Miller, Albemarle Street, London, Janʸ 1. 1811.

STATION V. AMESBURY.

NORTH DISTRICT.

Iter I. In my description of the last Station, Wily, I slightly noticed a group of barrows on the west side of the valley leading from Shrewton to Winterbourn Stoke. They are situated at a short distance from the latter village, on a gentle eminence, and are twelve in number; nine of them are surrounded by a ditch and *vallum* enclosing an area of about four acres, but certainly of a period subsequent to the barrows within it. All these *tumuli*, excepting one, were investigated in the month of July 1809, and the following is the result of our researches.

No. 1 is a large and wide Druid barrow, in which it appeared that the primary interment had been moved to make room for the subsequent deposit of a skeleton, which also had been disturbed at some still later period. In examining the cist which contained the skeleton, we observed that the feet had not been displaced; near them was an iron knife; and in our further researches we found at the bottom of the cist several fragments of burned bones, belonging to the remains of the original interment. No. 2, like many of the others in this group, is much mutilated, and of large diameter, but not more than four feet in elevation. It contained an interment of burned bones secured within a very large brown urn rudely ornamented, which was broken by taking out. A considerable quantity of linen cloth was perceptible among the bones. No. 3, a flat barrow, mutilated, and about the same elevation as the last, contained within an oval cist, a simple interment of burned bones, and shreds of linen cloth. No. 4 afforded no sepulchral remains, and probably was not intended for a barrow. No. 5, a circular flat barrow, contained a double cist; the smallest of which produced a little dagger of brass, and a variety of beads, amongst which were two joints of the vertebral column of a petrified *encrinus*. The beads, in number about four dozen, were neatly made of clay, but not well burned, except two of the largest, which had been ornamented with faint *striæ*. Besides the above were a great quantity of curious little shells, in shape like the Hirlas horn used by the Britons, which were perforated lengthways, and formed probably the necklace of some female. (TUMULI PLATE XIII.) The large cist contained only the bones of a sheep. No. 6 is a flat circular barrow, in which we found an oval cist, containing burned bones, and a rude little cup, resembling a saucer, which was broken. No. 7 is a small pond barrow. No. 8, a very irregular flat barrow, three feet high, produced near the centre a large urn standing upright within a circular cist, and containing, amongst an interment of burned bones, a small brass dagger, with a bone top to it, neatly finished, with five holes on the side for so many rivets, by which it was fastened to a wooden handle. The urn found in this *tumulus* was very large, and elegantly formed; (TUMULI PLATE XIII.) it contained a few black beads that had undergone the action of fire, and was so closely cemented to the chalk, that we had great difficulty in detaching it from the cist. No. 9, a flat circular barrow, contained two small round cists, in each of which was deposited an interment of burned bones; in one we found a curious little double cup;* in the other, no articles whatever. No. 10 was opened by Mr. Cunnington in the year 1804. In its form, it resembles the second class of Druid Barrows, is neatly ditched round, having the *vallum* without, and the *tumulus* rising gradually to its apex from the ditch. It contained an urn inverted over the burned bones, which had been wrapped up in a linen cloth, to protect them; and with the bones were found a small brass pin, employed probably for fastening the cloth, five rings of a dark brown colour, one of which was perforated for suspension, (TUMULI, PLATE XIII.) a small cone of the same materials perforated also for the same purpose, and several pully beads of glass, with one of jet, and another of amber. No. 11. This barrow, more perfect in its external form than the rest, contained within an oblong cist, a simple interment of burned bones. No. 12. The *vallum* of this large Druid barrow is so much defaced, and the elevation of the mound so very trifling, that it might easily escape general notice. It contained a very large rude urn, sixteen inches and a half deep, inverted over an interment of burned

* This cup has a division in the middle, which renders the hollow on each side equal: it is unlike in this particular to any we have yet found, and is very neatly ornamented in the usual rude style, with the Vandyke pattern. An engraving of it, full size, is given in TUMULI Plate XIII.

P. Crocker del.

Jᵉ Basire Sc.

Published for W. Miller, Albemarle Street, London, Janʸ 1. 1811.

bones, and within it a smaller vase. With them were found two black rings similar to those before described, but not perforated for suspension, a large amber bead perforated, four pully beads, and three of a black colour. The three last mentioned barrows are situated on the outside of the bank and ditch, which, at first sight, bear an equivocal appearance from their singular shape, resembling a pentagon, which I have before stated as being a favourite form with the Britons; but on a close investigation of them, they appear decidedly of a more modern date than the barrows. The name of the hill, CONIGAR, and the vulgar tradition of this spot having once been appropriated to a rabbit-warren, will corroborate this conjecture, and ascertain the origin of this earthen enclosure. On the adjoining hill, called HIGH DOWN, and to the N. W. of the group of barrows, are the decided remains of a British village, in which we found coins of the Lower Empire, pottery of various sorts, with animal bones, and all the usual *indicia* of an ancient British and Roman population.

On the eastern side of the valley, and nearly opposite to the cluster of barrows which I have just described, is another group situated on the southern declivity of a projecting point of the downs; and commanding a fine view southwards of the vale of Winterbourn, bounded by the woody district of Great Ridge; and of the vale of Shrewton northwards. They are enclosed in an area of about seven acres, within an oval earthen work, surrounded by a bank and ditch of slight elevation, are eleven in number, and are attended with some novel and peculiar circumstances. By the annexed plan, we perceive that No. 1, 2, 3, 4, 5, 6, 7, run nearly in a parallel line from east to west. No. 8 is a little to the south of the above lines, and No. 9, 10, 11, placed at equal distances from the outward ditch and bank, form a triangle. In the barrows No. 1 and 2, the rites of cremation had been practised, but no circumstances worthy of any particular detail occurred. No. 3 and 4 had been opened by shepherds, and contained interments of burned bones. In the former was found a little cup, which Mr. Cunnington purchased. No. 5 contained an urn very imperfectly baked, and within it an interment of burned bones, and a very small arrow head of bone. In No. 6 the ceremony of burning had been adopted. No. 7. This large barrow produced three interments. At the depth of four feet and a half, we discovered the skeleton of an infant, with its head laid towards the south; and immediately beneath it, a deposit of burned bones, and a drinking cup, which was unfortunately broken. At the depth of eight feet, and in the native bed of chalk, we came to the primary interment, viz. the skeleton of a man lying from north to south, with his legs gathered up according to the primitive custom. On his right side, and about a foot or more above the bones, was an enormous stag's horn. This was certainly the original deposit; though we find the same mode of interment, as well as cremation adopted at a subsequent period near the surface of the barrow. No. 8 is a large old-fashioned bowl-shaped *tumulus*, the base diameter being nearly one hundred feet. It contained a skeleton lying on the floor with its head towards the north, and much decayed from its having been covered with vegetable earth. Mr. Cunnington, supposing that this barrow contained more interments, made a second trial, but procured no further information. The remaining three barrows within this enclosure, viz. 9, 10, 11, which I have before mentioned as being placed nearly at equal distances from the *vallum*, and forming a kind of triangle, afforded, on opening, no one appearance of sepulchral remains; and for what purpose they could have been raised, it is impossible for me to determine; it is rather singular that eight out of the eleven *tumuli* which are enclosed within this work should have each proved sepulchral, and these not so.

Continuing our ride in an eastern direction over this rich down, we meet with a ditch and bank traversing it, and leading on each side directly into a British village. I have before started the new idea that these banks and ditches, of which there are so many in different parts of our county, were not boundaries, like Wansdyke, &c.* but roads of communication from one village to another, in which the passenger could walk both sheltered, and almost unperceived: and here we have a convincing proof that this my supposition has solid grounds of support, for we find one of these ditches issuing from one village, and leading across the valley immediately into another; and as far as we could trace them, we perceive by the map, that the ditch and bank which are visible on Wilsford and Lake downs, pointed directly to these British villages, and still further northward we find another bank and ditch proceeding towards the great British village on Elston down. The general character of these towns is so similar, and their produce so uniform, that a repeated description of each of them would be tedious to my readers. Those on Stoke downs are interesting specimens, and the southern village presents a greater degree of regularity than

* Whoever views these banks and ditches with an attentive and unprejudiced eye, will easily perceive a decided distinction between them, and those evidently formed for boundaries; the *valla* of the former being thrown up with a great deal of symmetry, and equally on both sides, with a wide and flat surface left between them at bottom; the latter having an elevated *vallum* on one side only, with a deep and narrow ditch on the other. Of these the districts comprehended within my work, will afford striking examples in Wansdyke, North Wiltshire, and in Bokerley ditch, near Woodyates in Dorsetshire.

usual: for in it we may trace the favourite square form of the Romans, which they almost universally adopted in the formation of their camps : the northern village bears a more decided British character.

The first barrow that occurs on leaving the British villages, is No. 1, situated at a short distance from the bank and ditch before mentioned, and near the road leading to Shrewton ; it contained a very large interment of burned bones. No. 2 appeared to have had a prior opening. No. 3 is a long, or rather triangular barrow, standing nearly east and west, the broad end towards the former point ; it measures 104 feet in length, 64 feet in width at the large end, 45 feet at the small end, and does not exceed three or four feet in eleva-tion. This *tumulus* has been much mutilated, partly by former antiquaries, and partly by cowherds or shepherds, who had excavated the eastern end, by making huts for shelter. Our first section was made at the western end, but produced nothing. On making a second, we perceived the earth had been disturbed, and pursuing the section, found two or three fragments of burned bones. We next observed a rude conical pile of large flints, imbedded in a kind of mortar made of the marly chalk dug near the spot. This rude pile was not more than four or five feet in the base, and about two feet high on the highest part, and was raised upon a floor, on which had been an intense fire, so as to make it red like brick. At first we conceived that this pile might have been raised over an interment, but after much labour in removing the greater part of it, we very unexpectedly found the remains of the Briton below, and were much astonished at seeing several pieces of burned bones intermixed with the great masses of mortar, a circumstance extremely curious, and so novel, that we know not how to decide upon the original intent of this barrow. The primary interment might have been disturbed before, or we might have missed it ; the Britons might perhaps have burned the body by an intense fire on the spot, where the earth was made red ; and the calcined bones might then have been collected together, and mixed in the mortar, which, with flints, formed the rude cone over the fire-place. If this opinion is right, the Britons in this case adopted a very singular method for preserving the dead. We have left some of the mortar containing the burned bones, near the top of the barrow, to satisfy the curiosity of any person who might wish to examine it. Though nearly the whole of the bones had a slight tinge of green, we could not discover any articles of brass. On exploring this barrow further to the east, we found two deep cists containing an immense quantity of wood ashes, and large pieces of charred wood, but no other signs of interment. No. 4 had been opened by a shepherd, and its history is unknown. No. 5. This large circular barrow is situated a few yards west of the road leading from Salisbury to Devizes, is flat at the top, five feet in elevation, and 110 feet in base diameter. When on the top of this *tumulus*, you perceive several depressions on the surface, from which, and its large dimensions, we conceived it must have been a family sepulchre, and so it proved to be. We opened it by a large square section near the centre, and in digging down to within a foot of the floor, we found the skeleton of a young person, deposited over the north-west edge of a very large and deep oblong cist; and upon the same level, on the south side, we discovered an interment of burned bones. On clearing the earth to the depth of five feet, we reached the floor of the barrow, in which a cist of the depth of four feet was cut in the native chalk, and at the depth of two feet on the southern side of the cist, was deposited the skeleton of an infant, apparently but a few months old. From the positions in which these interments were placed, it is evident they had been deposited at different times, and were subsequent to the primary one, in search of which we next proceeded. On clearing away the earth from the large cist, we found the head of a skeleton lying on the north side, but to our surprise, no *vertebræ* or ribs; further on were the thigh bones, legs, &c. At the feet was a little rude drinking cup, nearly perfect, and two pieces of a dark coloured slaty kind of stone, lying parallel with each other, which are engraved in Tumuli Plate XIV. We also found a large black cone, and an article like a pully, both of jet, and a piece of flint rudely chipped, as if intended for a dagger or spear. This *tumulus,* if more minutely examined, might very probably produce other interments, but from its great width, the operation would be attended with a very heavy expense.

Pursuing the line of barrows, we cross the great turnpike road, leading from Salisbury to Devizes, at milestone VIII. from the former; nearly opposite to which stands No. 6, which we found had been explored by some prior investigator. No. 7 is a fine bell-shaped barrow, 122 feet in diameter, and 9 feet in elevation. After great labour in making a spacious excavation, we unfortunately missed the interment; but from finding the fragment of a very large urn, and a few burned bones, we have some reason to think the barrow might have been opened before. No. 8. This barrow, rather inclined to the bell shape, is 82 feet in diameter, and $7\frac{1}{2}$ in elevation. It contained within a shallow oblong cist, the burned bones (as we conceived) of two persons piled together, but without arms or trinkets. In excavating the earth from this barrow, our men found a piece of square stone polished on one side, having

Tumulus 5.

Tumulus 5.

Tumulus 10.

Tumulus 5.

Stoke Group Nº 15.

F. Crocker del.

Jᵉ Basire Sc.

Published for W. Miller, Albemarle Street, London, Janᵞ 1. 1810.

two marks cut into it, also a whetstone. No. 9, a small barrow not above sixteen inches in elevation, produced, six feet apart, the horns of two large stags, and between them a sepulchral urn inverted over a pile of burned bones. This urn is rudely made, yet elegant in its outline.* On digging deeper, we discovered the skeleton of an adult lying with its head to the south; and on pursuing our researches to the depth of four feet in the native bed of chalk, we found another skeleton with its head placed towards the north; but each of these interments was unaccompanied by any warlike or decorative articles. No. 10. In this small *tumulus*, which appears to have been partially opened before, we found an oblong cist, which was arched over with the chalk that had been thrown out of it; and in the further part of it, a few fragments of burned bones, and a large glass bead, of the same imperfect vitrification as the pully beads so often before mentioned, and resembling also in matter, the little figures that are found with the mummies in Egypt, and are to be seen in the British Museum. This very curious bead has two circular lines of opaque sky blue and white, which seem to represent a serpent intwined round a centre, which is perforated. This was certainly one of the GLAIN NEIDYR of the Britons, derived from *glain*, what is pure and holy, and *neidyr*, a snake. Under the word *glain*, Mr. Owen, in his Welsh Dictionary, has given the following article: "The *main glain*, transparent stones, or adder-stones, were worn by the different orders of the Bards, each having its appropriate colour. There is no certainty that they were worn from superstition originally; perhaps that was the circumstance which gave rise to it. Whatever might have been the cause, the notion of their rare virtues was universal in all places where the Bardic religion was taught. It may still be questioned whether they are the production of nature or art." Mr. Mason, the poet, thus alludes to these stones,

. . . . But tell me yet
From the grot of charms and spells,
Where our matron sister dwells,
Brennus, has thy holy hand
Safely brought the Druid wand,
And the potent adder-stone,
Gender'd fore th' autumnal moon?
When in undulating twine
The foaming snakes prolific join;
When they hiss, and when they bear
Their wond'rous egg aloof in air;

* See TUMULI PLATE XVI.   H H

> Thence, before to earth it fall,
> The Druid in his holy pall,
> Receives the prize,
> And instant flies,
> Follow'd by the envenom'd brood,
> Till he cross the silver flood.

The serpent has ever been respected by the nations of antiquity, and noticed with peculiar marks of veneration. It was considered as an emblem of immortality, and from the circumstance of shedding its skin annually, a symbol of renovation. We find it introduced on the coins and altars of the ancients, and even temples, from their resemblance in form, assumed the title of DRACONTIA. Of these, we have a singular example in our own county, at Abury in North Wiltshire, which I shall describe minutely during the progress of my work.

The beads or rings, which are the present object of my attention, are thus noticed by Bishop Gibson, in his improved edition of Camden's Britannia: " In most parts of Wales, and throughout all Scotland, and in Cornwall, we find it a common opinion of the vulgar, that about Midsummer Eve (though in the time they do not all agree) it is usual for snakes to meet in companies, and that by joining heads together, and hissing, a kind of bubble is formed like a ring about the head of one of them, which the rest by continual hissing, blow on till it comes off at the tail; and then it immediately hardens, and resembles a glass ring; which whoever finds, (as some old women and children are persuaded) shall prosper in all his undertakings. The rings which they suppose to be thus generated, are called GLEINEU NADROEDH, i. e. *Gemmæ Anguinum*, whereof I have seen at several places about twenty or thirty. They are small glass annulets, commonly about half as wide as our finger rings, but much thicker; of a green colour usually, though some of them are blue, and others curiously waved with blue, red, and white. I have also seen two or three earthen rings of this kind, but glazed with blue, and adorned with transverse streaks or furrows on the outside. There seems to be some connection between the GLAIN NEIDYR of the Britons, and the ovum anguinum mentioned by Pliny, as being held in veneration by the Druids of Gaul; and to the formation of which, he gives nearly the same origin. They were probably worn as an *insigne*, or mark of distinction, and suspended round the neck, as the perforation is not sufficiently large to admit the finger. This bead, which I consider as a very interesting relic of antiquity, is engraved of its original size in TUMULI PLATE XIV. No. 11 is a pond barrow.

P. Crocker del.

J⁵ Basire Sc.

GROUP OF BARROWS ON WINTERBOURN STOKE DOWN.

Published for W. Miller, Albemarle Street, London, Jan.ʸ 1.1811.

WINTERBOURN STOKE GROUP OF BARROWS.

To the south of the last mentioned barrow, is a large group of twenty-seven *tumuli*, which, being so thickly clustered, could not be numbered sufficiently distinct on the general map: I have therefore had them engraved on a separate plate, which will explain, better than any verbal description, the different forms of the barrows which compose this group.

No. 1. The first of these is a long barrow, situated between the angle of the cross roads, which we did not open, being so well satisfied about the history of this species of *tumuli*.   No. 2 is a fine barrow, 93 feet in diameter, and 8 in elevation. The interment of burned bones which it contained, was piled up in a little heap upon the floor of the barrow, and amongst them was a small urn. No. 3 had been partly intersected in forming the turnpike road. Near the top of this barrow was an urn rudely formed, with an ornament on the rim in relief, like the shape of an horse-shoe, and enclosing a deposit of burned bones; we missed the primary interment. No. 4, as well as No. 5 and 6, produced simple interments by cremation. No. 7. At the depth of four feet from the floor of this barrow, was found the skeleton of a child, with a bason-like urn ; and in a cist cut in the native chalk was the primary deposit of an adult skeleton, lying from north to south, with a drinking cup at his feet. No. 8. This is one of that species we have styled Druid barrows of the second class. In the centre it had an oval cist, four and a half feet long, and two feet wide, with an even floor of chalk : and in the middle of it was a heap of burned bones, but no ashes. At the distance of a foot was a fine drinking cup, richly ornamented, but unfortunately broken on removing. No. 9 contained a simple interment of burned bones. It appears doubtful if No. 10 was sepulchral, as on making a large section in it, we could perceive no signs of interment. In No. 11 we found a deposit of burned bones, a small cup, of thick British pottery richly ornamented, but unfortunately broken, and a bone pin of a different form from any we have yet found, being bent in a semicircular form, and perforated at the head. No. 12, a very low barrow, produced only a simple interment by cremation ; in No. 13 nothing was found ; and No. 14 is a pond barrow.

No. 15. On clearing the earth from our section in this beautiful bell-shaped *tumulus*, and after four days labour, we came to an interment differing from any we had yet met with ; for instead of finding the burned bones of the deceased, enclosed within the native chalk, or in a sepulchral urn, we perceived they had been deposited in a box or coffin of wood, about three feet and a half long, by two feet wide, and placed upon the native turf ; the whole was then covered with a coat of blueish clay, and the mound constructed. On removing the clay, and the mouldering fragments of the wood,* we first discovered two small pieces of ivory, with rivets of brass through each, which I think appertained to the tips of a bow ; and afterwards a beautiful spear head of brass, the most perfect and the largest we have as yet found ;+ close to this was another lance head, which was unfortunately broken ; it lay above a foot from the bones, near which was a long pin of ivory, not perforated, but neatly polished and pointed at the thinnest end ; and another instrument of the same material, resembling the tweezers engraved in TUMULI PLATE III. The human bones had been piled up in a heap, and intermixed with them were some rivets, and small strips of brass, which probably belonged originally to the box. In making the section of this barrow, the workmen found the remains of five or more skeletons, at a short depth beneath the surface of the sepulchral mound.

No. 16. This, and the preceding barrow, both for superiority of size, and elegance of form, may be justly considered as the two finest *tumuli* in this group: they stand so contiguous to each other, that their circumvallations somewhat interfere. The first mentioned, is 89 feet in base diameter, and 14 feet in elevation: the one, now the object of our inquiry, measures in its base diameter 112 feet, and about 15 feet in elevation. On making our section, we were surprised to meet with a large and heavy piece of fossil wood, of a calcareous nature, resembling a bunch of twigs. I cannot learn that there is any substance of the kind in this neighbourhood, and I am sure the earth of which the barrow is composed, could never have generated it. At the depth of nearly 15 feet, and immediately under the spot where the fossil wood was found, we came to a shallow oblong cist, in which a skeleton had been deposited within the rude trunk of an elm-tree,‡ with its head lying to the north-east. On the left side of the head, a beautiful urn had been deposited, but crushed to pieces by the heavy pressure of earth upon it. We were however fortunate in collecting sufficient fragments to enable Mr. Crocker to make out an exact drawing of its form and outline. (TUMULI PLATE XV.) This sepulchral urn is different both

---

* This box was placed in a direction from north to south. The wood of which it was composed appeared to be elm, yet we found also some pieces of oak.

+ This fine spear-head, together with the two pieces of ivory, are engraved of their natural size in TUMULI PLATE XIV.

‡ The knots and bark still adhering to the tree, we were able to ascertain with certainty its distinct species: some naturalists, however, suppose, that the elm was introduced from the Continent into England, at a comparatively modern period.

N.º 1.

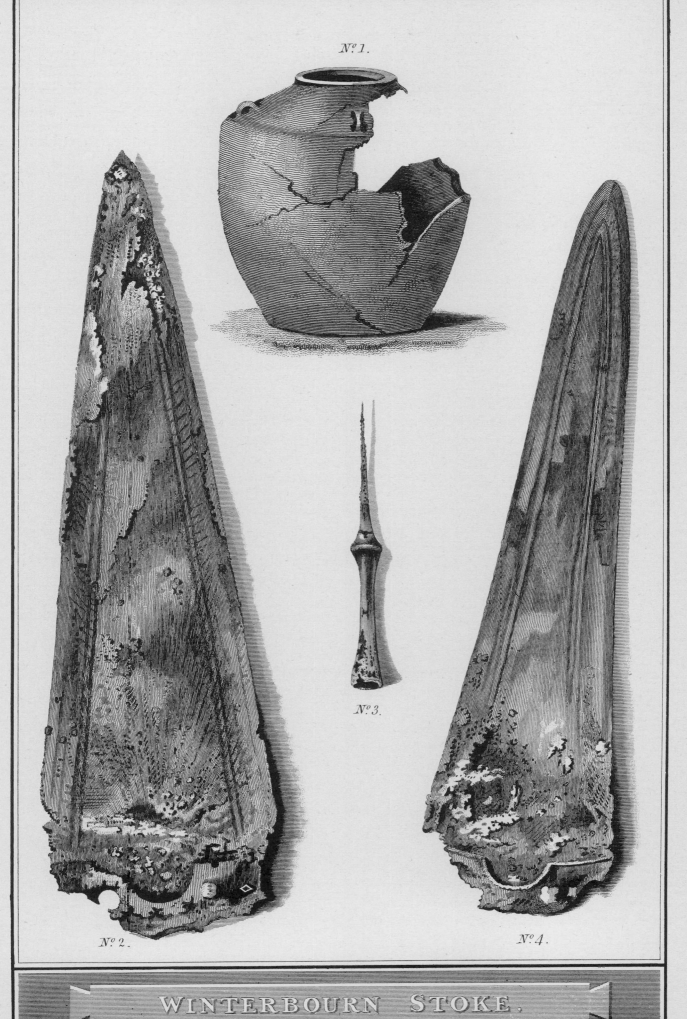

N.º 2.

N.º 3.

N.º 4.

P. Crocker del.

J.ª Bafire Sc.

Published for W. Miller, Albemarle Street, London, Jan.ʸ 1.1811.

in shape and colour to any we have ever found in the British sepulchres. It resembles in tint the fine red Samian pottery, and appears to have been turned in a lathe ; the form of the neck is neat, and the five handles are like those we see on the Roman vessels ; yet with all these appearances, we have one criterion to judge by, which, I think, will prove it to be of British manufacture, *viz.* that it is not more than half baked, and the fractures discover a black and sooty appearance within, not having been burned in a kiln, like the pottery of the Romans. Near the breast of the skeleton, lay the brass dagger No. 2. which had been guarded by a case of wood, part of which appeared to have been highly ornamented, as we found a bit of wood near it that had indentations which certainly had been gilt. The handle seems to have been made of box wood, and rounded somewhat like that of a large knife. Near it lay a brass pin with an ivory handle, No. 3. On the same side, but near the thigh, was a fine spear-head of brass, No. 4, very perfect, and most elegantly moulded, (for I have no doubt of these articles having been cast in moulds), and another article of ivory. The rich contents of this *tumulus* has induced us to crown it with royal honours, and to give it the title of KING BARROW. I have often been asked, if the largest barrows were not found, on opening, to be the most productive in their contents? The question is very natural, and I have rather wished to second that supposition ; but as yet I have not a sufficient basis for that hypothesis. In the present instance, indeed, there is some ground for the above remark.

No. 17. Adjoining the two last bowl-shaped barrows, are two of the Druid kind. The one produced a simple interment of burned bones ; the other, No. 18, contains within its area three small *tumuli*, in each of which, at the depth of 18 inches, we found interments of burned bones. In the largest, which is in the centre, was a small urn, and two or three large beads of amber, in the form of half a circle and half an oval. In the second we also found two or three beads, and in the third, only burned bones. No. 19. This *tumulus* measures 97 feet in diameter, and 7 feet in elevation. At the depth of nearly three feet, we discovered a sepulchral urn covering a little pile of burned bones,* and almost immediately under them, lay a skeleton ; but before the workmen came to the urn, they had found two interments of burned bones in the east and west corners of their sections. At the depth of seven feet, *viz.* on the floor of the barrow, lay a skeleton, with its head towards the west, and near it was a small oblong cist, without any deposit in it. Amongst the earth thrown out of

* See TUMULI, PLATE XVI.

I I

this barrow, we found a perforated pebble-stone, about two inches long, and very neatly polished; it has one corner broken off, and some cracks, as if it had been burned. It does not appear suited either to domestic or military purposes. The Britons seem to have attached particular qualities to certain stones; and this, probably, may have been suspended as an amulet from the neck. No. 20 is a pond barrow; and No. 21, from the fragments of burned bones dispersed promiscuously about the soil, affords sufficient evidence of a prior opening. No. 22. The interment which this barrow contained, presented some kind of novelty and variety. It appeared as if the native turf had been first taken off, the body placed on the chalk, and a large conical pile of flints raised over it. From finding some of the bones above the floor, and amongst the flints, we might almost be led to suppose, that the Briton here interred, had suffered a similar death to that of Achan.* The skeleton was laid from north to south, and from the size of the bones, appeared to be that of a young person, or a female. No. 23 and 24 turned out unproductive.

No. 25 is a large and rude bowl-shaped barrow, 107 feet in diameter, and 6 in elevation. Its surface being uneven, we were led to suppose it had been opened. In making a large section into it, the workmen threw out the bones of several dogs, and some of deer, and on the floor found a human skeleton, which had been originally interred from north to south, but many of the bones had been displaced, probably owing to a recent interment of burned bones, which had been deposited near the feet of this skeleton. On the right side of its head were two small earthen cups, one of which was broken; the other preserved entire; the first, though of rude materials, and scarcely half burned, was very neatly ornamented; the other, is of a singular form and pattern: it is of a yellowish colour, and perforated in several places. Near these cups was a curious ring or bracelet of bone or ivory, stained with red, which was unfortunately broken into several pieces. With the above articles were two oblong beads made from bone, and two whetstones; one of the silicious kind, almost as fine as a hone, and neatly formed; the other, of a fine grained white silicious stone. Near the above were a brass pin, a pair of petrified fossil cockle shells, a piece of stalactite, and a hard flat stone of the pebble kind, such as we frequently find both in the towns, as well as in the *tumuli* of the Britons. No. 26 is a fine bowl-shaped barrow, 97 feet in diameter, and nine feet and a half in elevation. Mr. Cunnington attempted to open it in the year 1804, but missed the interment, when, as it turned out, he was within one foot of it. Fortune

* " And all Israel stoned him with stones; and they raised over him a great heap of stones." Joshua, Chap. vii.

now favoured our researches, and discovered to us in an oblong cist, a skeleton lying from north to south, within a shallow case of wood, of a boat-like form. Round its neck were found a great variety of amber and jet beads, a lance head, and pin of brass, with a little urn of a very neat form, which was broken to pieces.

No. 27. This large *tumulus* is about 90 feet in its base diameter, and in elevation seven. It has several depressions on the top, from which, and the discoveries made in it, I am inclined to think it must have been a family sepulchre. We commenced our researches by making a large section from east to west, and at the depth of two feet (though at some distance from each other), found the skeletons of two dogs, as we conjectured, but being deposited in the vegetable earth, they were much decayed. At the depth of seven feet, we came to the floor of the barrow, where we discovered a large oblong cist, five feet long, four feet wide, and two and a half feet deep, neatly cut in the chalk; and on clearing away the earth round this cist, we perceived a sepulchral urn inverted in a half circle, cut in the side of the large cist, which, on taking out, we found had been placed in the lap of a skeleton, which lay at the depth of about a foot within the cist, its head towards the north. The urn contained burned bones, and was of a very rude make, but from the pressure of the earth was broken in two pieces. On removing it and the skeleton, we found five more skeletons lying almost side by side; two of which were young persons; and when we reached the floor of the cist, we found, what I consider to be the primary interment, *viz.* two skeletons lying by the side of each other, with their heads to the north, and both extremely well preserved. One of them (from the size of the bones), was a tall and stout man; all their teeth were very firm, and remarkably even. At their head was placed a drinking cup. From the manner in which these several bodies were interred, and from the position of the urn, containing the burned bones, we had positive proof that the two different modes of burial had been practised in this barrow at different periods; also that the urn was deposited at a period subsequent to all the other interments; for after interring the first bodies on the floor of the cist, the vast quantity of chalk dug out of it, was again thrown in to cover them, and this chalk would naturally rise above the level of the adjoining soil. When the other bodies were interred at a subsequent period, the vegetable mould, of which the *tumulus* was composed, was dug through, as also about a foot or more of the chalk out of the original cist; and after depositing the latter bodies over the original interment, the earth mixed with the chalk, would be thrown over, and being thus mixed, would make a line of distinction, being different in colour to the vegetable mould composing the *tumulus*, and the chalk out of the cist ; and this distinction was very obvious. That the urn containing the burned bones was the third deposit, we have also sufficient proof, as all the earth that covered it, as well as that corner of the cist in which it stood, was vegetable mould. To the north of this group, are two very small mounds scarcely elevated above the surface, which produced nothing worthy of notice.

Leaving the Winterbourn Stoke group, and proceeding in a line towards STONEHENGE, we find but few barrows, until we approach the precincts of that monument. No. 12 is a group of small *tumuli*, in one of which, immediately under the turf, we found a very rude urn, badly baked, and containing ashes, burned bones, and two pieces of twisted brass wire, which probably once formed a ring : this urn was not inverted. We attempted to open another, but finding that, together with the remainder of the group, it had been ploughed over, we gave up our researches, as, owing to the slight elevation of these barrows above the level of the ground, their contents would most probably have been destroyed by the continued operations of agriculture. No. 13 is a Druid barrow, which contained a simple interment of burned bones. No. 14 a group consisting of eight barrows of different sizes, and close to the road leading to Amesbury. The *tumulus* nearest that place produced the largest sepulchral urn we have ever yet found, it measures fifteen inches in diameter at the top, and is 22½ inches high ; it varies also most decidedly in shape and pattern from any others in our collection ; on which account we have distinguished it by the name of the STONEHENGE URN. It contained an interment of burned bones, and was not inverted ; but the deposit was secured by a large triangular stone, placed over the mouth of the urn. It is engraved in TUMULI PLATE XVI. Two of these barrows are superior in size to the rest ; the one nearest the road is large and bowl shaped ; eighty feet in base diameter, and eight and a half in elevation, though it appears to be much higher. The men made a large section, supposing the interment would be found at a considerable depth, but they met with it at eight feet and a half, in a shallow oblong cist, where the burned bones had been interred in a box of wood. The adjoining large *tumulus* produced an interment by cremation, which had in former times been disturbed by rabbits. Some others of this group, though scarcely elevated above the ground, produced deposits of burned bones ; in one of them, just under the turf, was found a brass spear head, and two of the others had been opened before.

P. Crocker del.

J.º Basire Sc.

Tumulus 9.

N.º 19. Stoke Group.

Tumulus 14.

Tumulus 42.

Tumulus 36.

Scale of Inches.

Published for W. Miller, Albemarle Street, London, Jan.ʸ 1.18n.

On approaching STONEHENGE, we come to a fine group of barrows, several of which have had their external appearance much defaced by rabbits. No. 15, is a Druid barrow, in which we found a deposit of burned human bones within a cist. It had been opened before, and some scattered fragments of bone, led us to suppose that a skeleton had been found, though the other interment had escaped unnoticed. No. 16 is a mutilated flat barrow, 76 feet in diameter, and only 3 feet in elevation. This appears to have been one of those opened by Dr. Stukeley, and thus mentioned by him in his account of STONEHENGE (page 46). " And in a very great and old fashioned barrow, west from STONEHENGE, among such matters, I found bits of red and blue marble chippings of the stones of the temple ; so that, probably, the interred was one of the builders." During our researches in this *tumulus*, we perceived that a long section had been made, and found the bones of two skeletons which had been interred on the floor, also several pieces of stag's horns, animal bones, &c. as well as some fragments of sarsen stones, similar to those which form the great trilithons of STONEHENGE. On clearing out the earth from this section, we observed a small heap of whiter soil, which having removed, we came to the primary interment of burned bones within a fine circular cist, and found a spear head of brass in fine preservation, and a pin of the same metal. It is somewhat singular, that these burned bones (a more than usual quantity) should have laid unmolested in a barrow where there were a hundred rabbit holes. On removing the earth from over the cist, we found a large piece of one of the blue stones of STONEHENGE, which Sowerby the naturalist calls a horn stone, which, with the sarsen stone, is a very singular occurrence, and decidedly proves that the adjoining temple was erected previous to the *tumulus*. Some persons acquainted with the soil in this part of Wiltshire, might think the finding of sarsen stones no uncommon event, and I should perhaps have thought the same, had these specimens been rounded by attrition ; but the stones found within this barrow, are pieces chipped off, (I am sorry to say) like those now daily knocked off from the great fallen trilithon. With regard to the blue stone, we are certain this species is not to be found in the southern district of Wiltshire. In opening the fine bell-shaped barrow N. E. of STONEHENGE, we also found one or two pieces of the chippings of these stones, as well as in the waggon tracks round the area of the temple. These circumstances tend to give a much higher æra of antiquity to our celebrated building, than some antiquaries would be willing to allow, and evidently prove that at the period when the *tumuli* adjoining STONEHENGE were raised, the plain was covered with the

K K

chippings of the stones that had been employed in the formation of the stone circle. No. 17 is a long barrow, in which we made no discovery. No. 18 is injured by rabbits. No. 19 seems to have been one of those opened either by Lord Pembroke, or Dr. Stukeley, who had been successful in finding the interment in an oblong cist. No. 20. This barrow had been opened before, and contained the interment of a skeleton. No. 21 and 22 were unproductive. No. 23. Mr Cunnington attempted to explore this fine bell-shaped barrow some years ago, but was unsuccessful. On a second trial, I found that in his former operations he had left off within a few inches of a large rude sepulchral urn inverted over a pile of burned bones, amongst which was an elegant pair of ivory tweezers.

Having described all the barrows within the triangle formed by the roads leading from Amesbury to Deptford on the south ; to Shrewton on the north ; and from Salisbury to Devizes on the west ; I shall endeavour to relieve my readers from the monotony, which the description of so many similar objects must naturally create, by introducing them within the precincts of STONEHENGE ; and shall defer my account of the remaining barrows in its environs, to a future Iter.

STONEHENGE.

THIS remarkable monument is situated on the open down, near the extremity of a triangle formed by two roads ; the one leading on the south from Amesbury to Wily, the other on the north from the same place, through Shrewton and Heytesbury to Warminster.*

A building of such an obscure origin, and of so singular a construction, has naturally attracted the attention of the learned, and numerous have been the publications respecting it ; conjectures have been equally various, and each author has formed his own. Before I venture to give any opinion on this

* Its precise situation will be more satisfactorily explained by the annexed engraving.

VIEW OF STONEHENGE FROM THE EAST.

CAMP NEAR AMESBURY.

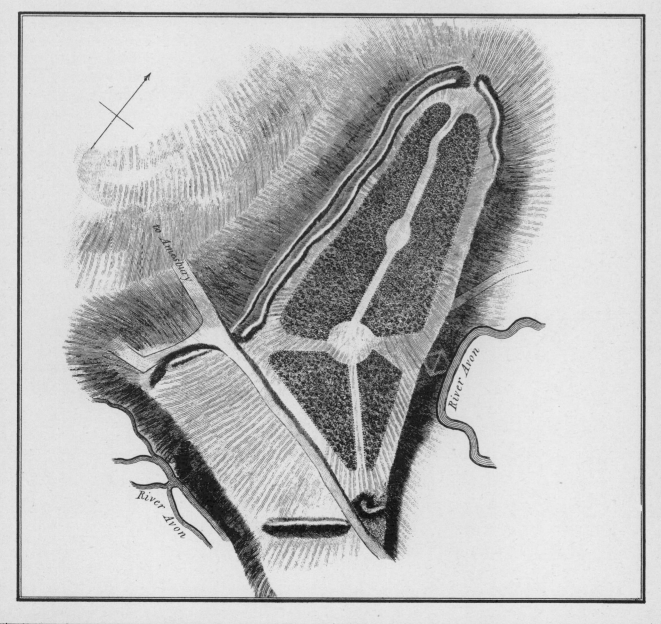

P. Crocker del.

J.ᵉ Basire Sc.

Published for W. Miller, Albemarle Street, London, Jan.ʸ 1, 1811.

mysterious subject, it will be necessary for me to lay before my readers those of preceding writers concerning it.

The earliest accounts of STONEHENGE, that have been transmitted to us by the monkish historians, are so deeply involved in the fable of antiquity and romance, that little reliance can be placed on them; they must not, however, be totally omitted, as it is the duty of every historian to take notice even of traditions, however apparently improbable; for some portion of truth is often intermixed with fable, and many important facts have been traced to a most obscure origin.

These writers inform us, " that there was in Ireland, in ancient times, a pile of stones worthy admiration, called the GIANTS' DANCE, because Giants, from the remotest parts of Africa, brought them into Ireland; and in the plains of Kildare, not far from the castle of Naas, as well by force of art, as strength, miraculously set them up; and similar stones, erected in a like manner, are to be seen there at this day. It is wonderful how so many and such large stones could have been collected in one place, and by what artifice they could have been erected; and other stones, not less in size, placed upon such large and lofty stones, which appear, as it were, to be so suspended in the air, as if by the design of the workmen, rather than by the support of the upright stones. These stones (according to the British History), Aurelius Ambrosius, King of the Britons, procured Merlin, by supernatural means, to bring from Ireland into Britain. And that he might leave some famous monument of so great a treason to future ages, in the same order and art as they stood formerly, set them up where the flower of the British nation fell by the cut-throat practice of the Saxons, and where, under the pretence of peace, the ill-secured youth of the kingdom, by murderous designs, were slain."

" *Fuit antiquis temporibus in Hiberniâ lapidum congeries admiranda, quæ et* CHOREA GIGANTUM *dicta fuit, quia Gigantes eam ab ultimis Africæ partibus in Hiberniam attulerant, et in Kildariensi planicie, non procul à castro Nasensi, tam ingenii, quam virium opere mirabiliter erexerant. Unde et ibidem lapides quidam aliis simillimi, similique modo erecti, usque in hodiernum conspiciuntur. Mirum qualiter tanti lapides, tot etiam, et tam magni unquam in unum locum vel congesti fuerint, vel erecti; quantoque artificio lapidibus, tam magnis et altis, alii superpositi sint, non minores; qui sic in pendulo, et tanquàm in inani suspendi videntur, ut potius artificum studio, quam suppositorum podio inniti videantur. Juxta Britannicam historiam lapides istos Rex Britonum Aurelius Ambrosius divinâ Merlini diligentiâ, de Hiberniâ in Britanniam advehi procuravit; et ut tanti facinoris egregium aliquod memoriale relinqueret, eodem ordine et arte quâ priùs, in loco constituit, ubi occultis Saxonum cultris,*

Britanniæ flos cecidit ; et sub pacis obtentu, nequitiæ telis, male tuta regni juventus occubuit."

Thus says Giraldus in his Topography of Ireland, which he wrote in the year 1187 ; by whose account we learn, that in his time certain stones placed upon each other, like those which now exist at STONEHENGE, were visible on the plains of Kildare ; but that these stones, originally brought from Africa, were conveyed to England by Merlin, and erected by Aurelius Ambrosius King of the Britons,* on the spot where some of his most distinguished subjects had been slain by the treachery of the Saxons. This event is thus recorded by LEWIS, in his *Ancient History of Britain :* " In the reign of Vortigern, a conference was appointed to take place, near the Abbey of AMBRI, with Hengist the Saxon, and it was agreed, that both parties should come without armour. But Hengist, under the colour of peace, devised the subversion of all the nobility of Britain, and chose out, to come to this assembly, his faithfullest and hardiest men, commanding every one of them to hide under their garment, a long knife, with which, when he should give the watch-word, every one should kill the Briton next him. Both sides met upon the day appointed, and treating earnestly upon the matter, Hengist suddenly gave the watch-word, and caught Vortigern by the collar ; upon which, the Saxons, with their long knives, violently murdered the innocent and unarmed Britons, at which time, there were thus treacherously murdered, of earls and noblemen of the Britons, four hundred and sixty."

After this massacre at STONEHENGE in 461, repeated battles were fought between Ambrosius and Hengist. In the year 464, the former was defeated by the latter, near Richborough in Kent ; but in 487, victory decided in favour of Ambrosius, who subdued his rival in a battle on the river Don, in the north of England ; and in the following year, took him prisoner, and put him to death.

Another old writer, Jeffrey of Monmouth, has entered more circumstantially into the history of the stones, and attributes the erection of them to the aforesaid British King. He says " that Aurelius wishing to commemorate those who had fallen in battle, and who were buried in the convent at Ambresbury, thought fit to send for Merlin the prophet, a man of the brightest genius, either in predicting future events, or in mechanical contrivances, to consult him on the proper monument to be erected to the memory of the slain. On being

* Aurelius Ambrosius succeeded to the kingdom of Britain, on the death of Vortigern, in the year 465. He was of Roman extraction, though educated in Britain. After a reign of thirty-two years he was poisoned by the contrivance of Pascentius, son of Vortigern. Cressy, p. 221.

interrogated, the prophet replied ; "If you are desirous to honour the burying-place of these men with an everlasting monument, send for the GIANTS' DANCE, which is in Killaraus (Kildare), a mountain in Ireland.* For there is a structure of stones there, which none of this age could raise without a profound knowledge of the mechanical arts. They are stones of a vast magnitude, and wonderful quality ; and if they can be placed here, as they are there, quite round this spot of ground, they will stand for ever." At these words, Aurelius burst out into laughter, and said, "how is it possible to remove such vast stones from so distant a country, as if Britain was not furnished with stones fit for the work?" Merlin having replied, that they were mystical stones, and of a medicinal virtue, the Britons resolved to send for the stones, and to make war upon the people of Ireland, if they should offer to detain them. Uther Pendragon, attended by 15,000 men, was made choice of as the leader, and the direction of the whole affair was to be managed by Merlin. On their landing in Ireland, the removal of the stones was violently opposed by one Gillomanius, a youth of wonderful valour, who at the head of a vast army exclaimed, "To arms, soldiers, and defend your country ; while I have life, they shall not take from us the least stone of the GIANTS' DANCE." A battle ensued, and victory having decided in favour of the Britons ; they proceeded to the mountain of Killaraus, and arrived at the structure of stones, the sight of which filled them both with joy and admiration. And while they were all standing round them, Merlin came up to them, and said, "Now try your forces, young men, and see whether strength or art can do more towards the taking down these stones." At this word, they all set to their engines with one accord, and attempted the removing of the GIANTS' DANCE. Some prepared cables, others small ropes, others ladders for the work; but all to no purpose. Merlin laughed at their vain efforts, and then began his own contrivances. At last, when he had placed in order the engines that were necessary, he took down the stones with an incredible facility, and withal gave directions for carrying them to the ships, and placing them therein. This done, they with joy set sail again to return to Britain, where they arrived with a fair gale, and repaired to the burial-place with the stones. When Aurelius had notice of it, he sent out messengers to all the parts of Britain, to summon the clergy and people together to the mount of Ambrius (Ambresbury), in order to celebrate with joy and honour, the erecting of the monument. A great solemnity was held for three successive days ; after which, Aurelius ordered Merlin to set up the stones brought over from Ireland, about

* This account is copied from Thompson's translation of Jeffrey of Monmouth.

the sepulchre, which he accordingly did, and placed them in the same manner as they had been in the mountain of Killaraus, and thereby gave a manifest proof of the prevalence of art above strength." page 250.

What then are we to think of these ancient accounts of STONEHENGE? In following the Iter of Giraldus through Wales, I never had reason to complain of his want of accuracy in the description of places, however he might have staggered my faith in some of his marvellous stories. He appears to have seen with his own eyes, during his tour in Ireland, about 1186, an immense pile of stones, on the plains of Kildare, consisting of upright stones, with their imposts, and corresponding exactly with those at STONEHENGE. " *Lapides quidam simili modo erecti, usque in hodiernum conspiciuntur.*" And he relates the wonderful voyage of the original stones brought from Africa to Kildare, and from thence into Wiltshire, on the credit of the British historians.

Jeffrey of Monmouth contradicts himself as to the placing of these stones; for he first says, " that Aurelius intended them as a memorial to those of his subjects who had been slain in the battle with Hengist, and who had been buried in the convent at Ambresbury; and afterwards tells us, they were set up round the sepulchre on the mount of Ambrius, which place (where STONEHENGE now stands) is two miles distant from the supposed site of the convent.

However strange and improbable these ancient accounts may appear, some truth may lie hidden under the veil of fiction. I never saw a more likely spot, or one better situated for a STONEHENGE, than the Curragh of Kildare, and I regret very much, that, when in Ireland, I did not examine this verdant and extensive plain more attentively. I observed earthen works and barrows, the *indicia* of ancient population, and if ever a temple existed on this spot, I have no doubt its site, even at this remote period, might be discovered. I cannot possibly attribute so modern an æra to the erection of STONEHENGE, as the time of Aurelius; otherwise we might suppose, that, under the story of Merlin and his arts, was designed the fact of some architect transporting the plan of such a temple from Kildare to Amesbury; or that one or two of the lesser circles, which now form a part of STONEHENGE, and which are of a totally different stone from the larger circle, and oval, had been removed. This, indeed, was possible, but by no means probable; nor can I nod assent to any of these stories, except that of my friend Giraldus, who states having seen a pile of stones resembling STONEHENGE, on the plains of Kildare.

Another monkish historian, Henry of Huntingdon, who wrote about the year 1148, in the reign of king Stephen, places STONEHENGE amongst the wonders of Britain ; but candidly confesses, that no one can imagine by what art, and for what purpose, such large stones could have been erected. *Apud Stanenges, ubi lapides miræ magnitudinis in modum portarum elevati sunt, ita ut portæ portis superpositæ videantur; nec potest aliquis excogitare qua arte tanti lapides adeo in altum elevati sunt, vel quare ibi constructi sunt."* (p. 299.)

All the information, therefore, that we have gained from the ancient authors respecting STONEHENGE, is, that a huge pile of stones was erected on a hill near Amesbury, and that it was considered as one of the wonders of Britain. Such indeed, it may still be justly denominated, for no such building exists, not only in our own island, but even in the known world. For its plan and manner of construction, we must refer to modern writers, of whom a numerous list have employed their pens in the description of it. The first of these is the learned CAMDEN, the father of British antiquities, who, in the first edition of his BRITAN-NIA, printed in Latin, A. D. 1586, thus expresses himself.

" *Septentriones versus ad* VI. *plus minus à Sarisburiâ milliari, in illâ planitie, insana (ut Ciceronis verbo utar) conspicitur constructio. Intrà fossam enim ingentia et rudia saxa, quorum nonnulla* XXVIII. *pedes altitudine,* VII. *latitudine colligunt, coronæ in modo triplici serie eriguntur, quibus alia quasi transversaria, sic innituntur, ut pensile videatur opus ; unde* STONEHENGE *nobis nuncupatur, uti antiquis historicis* CHOREA GIGANTUM *à magnitudine. Hoc in miraculorum numero referunt nostrates, unde verò ejusmodi saxa allata fuerint, cum totâ regione finitimâ vix structiles lapides inveniantur, et quánam ratione subrecta, demirantur. De his non mihi subtilius disputandum, sed dolentius deplorandum obliteratos esse tanti monumenti authores. Attamen sunt qui existimant saxa illa non viva esse, id est, naturalia et excissa, sed facticia ex arenâ purâ, et unctuoso aliquo coagmentata. Fama obtinet Ambrosium Aurelianum, sive Utherum ejus fratrem, in Britonum memoriam, qui ibi Saxonum dolo, in colloquio ceciderunt, illa Merlini mathematici operâ posuisse. Alii produnt Britannos hoc quasi magnificum sepulcrum eidem Ambrosio substruxisse eo loci, ubi hostili gladio ille periit, ut publicis operibus contectus esset, eâque extructione, quæ sit ad æternitatis memoriam, quasi virtutis ara.*"

" Toward the north, about six miles from Salisbury, is to be seen a huge and monstrous piece of work, such as Cicero termeth *insana substructio.* For within the circuit of a ditch, there are erected in manner of a crown, in three ranks or courses, one within another, certain mighty and unwrought stones, whereof some are 28 feet high, and seven feet broad, upon the heads of which, others like overthwart pieces, do bear and rest crosswise, with small tenons and mortises, so as the whole seemeth to hang, whereof we call it

STONEHENGE, * like, as our old historians term it, for the greatness, CHOREA GIGANTUM, the Giants' Daunce. Our countrymen reckon this for one of our wonders, and much they marvel from whence such huge stones were brought, considering that, in all those quarters bordering thereupon, there is hardly to be found any common stone at all for building ; as also, by what means they were set up. For mine own part, about these points, I am not curiously to argue and dispute, but rather to lament with much grief, that the authors of so notable a monument are thus buried in oblivion. Yet some there are that think them to be no natural stones, hewen out of the rock, but artificially made of pure sand and some gluey and unctuous matter, knit and incorporate together."

The common saying is, that Ambrosius Aurelianus, or his brother, Uther, did rear them up by the art of Merlin, that great mathematician, in memory of those Britons, who, by the treachery of Saxons, were slain at a parley. Others say, that the Britons erected this for a stately sepulchre of the same Ambrosius, in the very place he was slain by his enemy's sword ; that he might have of his country's cost such a piece of work and tomb set over him as should for ever be permanent, as the altar of his virtue and manhood."

We might naturally have expected better information respecting this singular structure from so learned a writer, and so zealous an antiquary as CAMDEN ; he merely tells us the situation of this *insana substructio*, and makes so palpable a mistake in the numbers of the circles, that I question if he ever visited them himself: if he had seen them, he never could have stated the number of their ranks as three, instead of four ; he also errs in their height; for none, as I shall shew hereafter, ever extended to the height of 28 feet. He retails the old and improbable tradition of their having been erected by Ambrosius Aurelianus.

In the year 1620, STONEHENGE attracted so much the attention of King James the First, that, being at Wilton, the seat of the Earls of Pembroke, during his progress in the year aforesaid, he sent for the celebrated architect INIGO JONES, and ordered him " to produce out of his own practice in architecture, and experience in antiquities abroad, what he could discover concerning this of STONE-HENGE." The result of his inquiry was not published till after the death of INIGO JONES, by his friend JOHN WEBB, Esq. who thus prefaces the work: " To the favourers of antiquity. This discourse of STONEHENGE is moulded off and cast into a rude form, from some few indigested notes of the late judicious architect, the Vitruvius of his age, INIGO JONES. That so venerable an antiquity might not perish, but the world made beholding to him for restoring it to light,

* This title is evidently Saxon, and derived from the words *stan*, stone, and *henge*, hanging.

the desires of several of his learned friends have encouraged me to compose this Treatise. Had he survived to have done it with his own hand, there had needed no apology. Such as it is, I make now yours. Accept it in his name."

His descriptions are much more satisfactory than any of those preceding, being illustrated with ground plans, elevations, and views; yet still he has committed errors, which it will be my duty to point out; but I will first lay before my readers his account of this singular structure.

" The whole work, in general, being of a circular form, is 110 feet in diameter, double winged about, without a roof, anciently environed with a deep trench, still appearing, about 30 feet broad. So that betwixt it and the work itself, a large and void space of ground being left, it had, from the plain, three open entrances, the most conspicuous thereof lying north-east; at each of which were raised on the outside of the trench aforesaid, two huge stones gate-wise, parallel whereunto, on the inside, were two others of lesser proportion. The inner part of the work, consisting of an hexagonal figure, was raised by due symmetry, upon the bases of four equilateral triangles, which formed the whole structure; this minor part likewise was double, having within it also, another hexagon raised, and all that part within the trench sited upon a commanding ground, eminent, and higher by much than any of the plain lying without, and in the midst thereof, upon a foundation of hard chalk, the work itself was placed; insomuch from what part soever they came unto it, they rose from an ascending hill."

He states the stones of the outward circle to be fifteen feet and a half high, and those of the greater hexagon, twenty. The order Tuscan, and the plan consisting of four equilateral triangles, inscribed within the circumference of a circle. He attributes the whole to the Romans, and the adjoining camps of Yarnbury and Ambresbury to Vespasian, when he conquered the Belgæ, who inhabited this district. He dates its origin from that period, when the Romans having settled the country under their own empire, and by the introduction of foreign colonies, reduced the natural inhabitants of this island unto the society of civil life, by training them up in the liberal sciences. Concerning the use to which STONEHENGE was originally destined, our author is clearly of opinion that it was a temple, it being built with all the accommodations properly belonging to a sacred structure. For it had an interval, or spacious court, lying round about it, wherein the victims for oblation were slain, into which it was unlawful for any profane person to enter; it was separated from the circumadjacent plain by a large trench, instead of a wall, as a boundary about the temple, most conformable to the main work, wholly exposed to open view. Without this trench, the promiscuous common multitude, with zeal too much, attended the ceremonies of their solemn, though superstitious sacrifices, and might see the oblations, but not come within them. It had likewise its peculiar CELL, with porticos round about, into which, as into their *Sanctum sanctorum*, none but the priests entered to offer sacrifice, and make atonement for the people. Within the CELL an altar was placed, having its proper position toward the east, as the Romans used. *Aræ spectent ad orientem*, says Vitruvius."

Our author thus concludes his treatise: " I suppose I have now proved from authentic authors, and the rules of art, that STONEHENGE was anciently a temple, dedicated to CŒLUS, built by the Romans, either in, or not long after those times when the Roman eagles spreading their commanding wings over this island, the more to civilize the natives, introduced the art of building amongst them, discovering their ambitious desire, by stupendous and prodigious works, to eternize the memory of their high minds to succeeding ages."

We might naturally suppose that a man of such a profession, and so distinguished in it, would have been both correct in his plans, and ingenious in his conjectures; but unfortunately he has erred in both: for in converting the two inner circles into an hexagon, he has adopted a plan which the building never could have assumed; and he has attributed its construction to a nation, amongst whom not a single model of the same kind can be found. He has told us that it was built by the Romans, after they had brought the natives of Britain to subjection, which could not have been earlier than the time of Claudius, and probably as late as Vespasian, under whom the celebrated Agricola completed the conquest of our island, and extended his victorious arm over the distant provinces of Caledonia. And can we for a moment suppose, that a people who had long before this period adopted the elegant architecture of the Greeks, and who had erected at Camalodunum, or Colchester, a temple to the Emperor Claudius, would on a sequestered plain, distant from any of their stations, have raised up a rude pile of stones, for which their own country could neither have furnished an idea, nor supplied a model?

Nor can I concur in opinion with this author about the entrances into the area of the work, which, he says, were three; or about the stones which he places near them. He has also erred in stating the situation, on which STONEHENGE stands, to be higher than any of the adjacent plain.

The publication of this treatise by INIGO JONES, produced a reply in the year 1662, by WALTER CHARLETON, a physician.

This writer, who differs *in toto* from his predecessor, attributes STONEHENGE to the Danes, and the æra of its construction to the beginning of the reign of King Alfred the Great, during the period of his adversity, and the prosperity of the Danes. He concludes his dissertation by saying, " that of all nations in the world, none was so much addicted to monuments of huge and unhewn stones as the Danes appear to have been for many hundred years together ; that they used to set up such, not only in their own country, but in all other places also, wherever the fortune of war had at any time made their adventures and achievements memorable, and more particularly in England and Scotland ; that in Denmark, at this day, there stand many stupendous heaps of stones, in most particulars agreeing with that I have now discoursed ; that upon a strict and impartial inquest, neither the ancient Britons, nor Romans, nor Saxons, are found to have any justifiable title to the honour of founding that of STONEHENGE ; that no one of our old historians made mention of any such work, until long after the Danes had acquired the sovereign power in this island, and left sundry memorials of their victorious armies ; that the great impairment of the fabric since that time of the Danish conquest, doth not evince it to be of greater antiquity ; that neither the magnificence of the same at first, nor the vastness of strength, and skill in engines, required to the transportation and elevation of stones of such prodigious weight, are sufficient arguments to the contrary. Considering these things, I say, why may I not conjecture, that the Danes, and only the Danes, were the authors of STONEHENGE ?"

This treatise called forth another author, JOHN WEBB, Esq. of Butleigh in Somerset, whom I have before mentioned as having published the posthumous work of INIGO JONES. In a tedious and uninteresting dissertation of 228 pages, entitled " *A Vindication of Stonehenge restored,*" he supports the Roman system laid down by his father-in-law, INIGO JONES, saying, that Mr. JONES's opinion, that the Romans, and only the Romans, were the founders of STONEHENGE, appears in all probability, valid, and decked in the lively colours, and plain livery of truth. Nor let it be deemed presumption in me to assert it, seeing it hath this advantage over all others, concerning the same obscure subject, that it stands impregnable, and is not to be refuted."*

AYLETT SAMMES, in his *Britannia antiqua illustrata*, printed in 1676, wrote a short treatise on STONEHENGE, in which he recapitulates the opinions of INIGO JONES, and others, on the subject, and adds, " why may not these giants (alluding

* The united works of Inigo Jones, Dr. Charleton, and John Webb, were published in the year 1725, in one folio volume.

to the name of CHOREA GIGANTUM given to STONEHENGE), be the Phœnicians, and the art of erecting these stones, instead of the stones themselves, brought from the furthermost parts of Africa, the known habitations of the Phœnicians?"

In speaking of Merlin, he says, " And yet, to look upon all things as fabulous and ridiculous concerning him, were perhaps too inconsiderately to wrong the virtues of so eminent a person ; for I cannot choose but look upon him as a man of excellent parts, far beyond any of his age, however rendered by fables suspected ; for considering how the British chronicles and fame, unanimously conspire in setting forth his actions, we may safely believe that his admirable skill, especially in mathematics, was the occasion and ground of these fictitious and impertinent things they make him perform in the behalf of Vortigern and other princes. So that, although we allow him not to be so great, or rather monstrous, as some, out of their love, would have him; yet we may reasonably suppose him wiser, and far above those sort of men that lived in his time, there being always something of truth to be found at the bottom of a fable." And he further adds " that the greatest disadvantage and unhappiness that can befal a great and generous spirit, is to be born in a dark, base, and ignorant age, who, looking on the actions of the brave through the magnifying glass of their own fears and simplicities, make them swell through a too forward, but injurious zeal, to that monstrosity and bulk, that their very greatness makes them suspected by posterity ; so that the infinite disadvantages that fame suffers by the suspicion of after ages, can never be recompensed by the overplus allowed in the age they lived in, or in the next succeeding."

In the year 1695, an improved edition of CAMDEN'S BRITANNIA was published in English by EDMUND GIBSON, afterwards made Bishop of Lincoln, in which our celebrated monument is thus recorded: " About seven miles north of New Salisbury, is STONEHENGE, a piece of antiquity so famous, as to have gained the admiration of all ages, and engaged the pens of some very considerable authors. It is of itself so singular, and receives so little light from history, that almost every one has advanced a new notion. To give the several conjectures, with some short remarks, is as much as the narrow compass of our design will allow ; but not to hunt after such uncertainties, and in the mean time pass over what lays before our eyes, we will premise a description of the place as it now stands, much more distinct than what Mr. CAMDEN has left us.

" It is situated on a rising ground, environed with a deep trench, still appearing, and about thirty feet broad. From the plain it had three entrances ; the most considerable lying north-east, at each of which were raised on the outside of the trench, two huge stones, gate-wise, parallel whereunto on the inside, were two others of less proportion. After one has passed this ditch, he ascends 35 yards before he comes to the work itself, which consists of four circles of stones.   The outward circular is about 100 feet diameter, the stones whereof are very large, four yards in height, two in breadth, and one in thickness. Two yards and a half within this great circle, is a range of lesser stones. Three yards farther, is the principal part of the work, called by Mr. JONES, the CELL, of an irregular figure, made up of two rows of stones, the outer of which consists of great upright stones, twenty feet in height, two yards in breadth, and one yard in thickness. These are coupled at the top by large transome stones like architraves, which are seven feet long, and about three and a half thick. Within this was also another range of lesser pyramidal stones of about six feet in height.   In the inmost part of the CELL, Mr. JONES observed a stone (which is now gone) appearing not much above the surface of the earth, and lying toward the east, four feet broad, and sixteen feet long, which was his supposed altar stone.

" After reciting the various people and nations, to whom the erection of these stones has been attributed, he adds, " That it could not have been built by the Romans, is evident from the rudeness of the whole work. So that (as Mr. AUBREY, in his MSS. *Monumenta Britannica*, has very well observed) while Mr. JONES pleases himself with retrieving a piece of architecture out of Vitruvius, he abuses his reader by a false scheme of the whole work."   For the cell is not of an exact hexagonal figure, but very irregular, and comes nearer an heptagon ; so that the whole work cannot be formed upon the basis of four equilateral triangles, as Mr. JONES supposed. Neither are the entrances into the trench so regular and so equidistant as that author would make them.   Nor could it have been built by the Danes, as, for many other reasons, so particularly because it is mentioned in some manuscript of Nennius, who, as every body knows, wrote almost 200 years before the Danes were masters of any considerable part of this island."

Having combated the opinions of Mr. JONES, and Mr. WEBB, as to its having been the work of either the Romans, or Danes, he adds, " I should think, one need make no scruple to affirm, that it is a British monument ; since it does not appear, that any other nation had so much footing in this kingdom, as to be authors of such a rude, and yet magnificent pile."

In the beginning of this description, the learned Bishop has copied the errors of INIGO JONES, with regard to the three entrances, and the stones near them : he states the height of the outward circle of stones at only twelve feet ; and the height of those of the CELL indiscriminately, at twenty feet ; both of which statements will be hereafter proved to be incorrect.   He says also, that the stone, supposed by INIGO JONES to be the altar, was gone ; but it still exists at this day in its original position, and nearly answers to the measurement, given of it by the said author.

In the year 1720, a work was published at Hanover, under the title of *Antiquitates Septentrionales*, by GEORGE KEYSLER, with plates. The author recites the opinions of the English writers respecting STONEHENGE, and adopts the ground plan of INIGO JONES, making the two inner circles of stones of an hexagonal form. He will not allow the credit of erecting this temple, either to the ancient Britons, or to their conquerors, the Romans ; but attributes it to the Danes, or Anglo-Saxons.

The work of Dr. STUKELEY, published in the year 1740, has rendered all former accounts of STONEHENGE nugatory and unsatisfactory. He differs widely in opinion and in plan, from his predecessors ; he saw with his own eyes, and dictated from his own good sense and sound judgment. The patronage and friendship of Thomas Earl of Pembroke, a great lover of antiquities, enabled him, from the vicinity of his Lordship's seat at Wilton, to visit STONEHENGE frequently, and to note down his observations on the spot ; and whilst the remarks of former writers have been confined to the sole building, and many of them retailed from others preceding ; those of STUKELEY have been extended to various other antiquities in the neighbourhood, and marked with accuracy and able discrimination.

As I shall probably have occasion to make frequent and ample quotations from his work, I shall not at present lay his opinion before my readers, but proceed to state the few remaining authors who have treated on this subject.

In the year 1747, STONEHENGE was described and illustrated with numerous plans, by JOHN WOOD, an architect, who had distinguished himself, particularly at Bath, by his skill and good taste in building. He is more minute in his ground plans, than any of his predecessors, from whom he differs materially in the lines of his third and fourth circles. He concludes his treatise, by giving it as his opinion, " that it was a temple erected by the British Druids, about a hundred years before the commencement of the Christian æra."

In the year 1754, *An Enquiry into the patriarchal and Druidical Religion, Temples, &c.* was published by WILLIAM COOKE, M. A. in which the stone temples at

ABURY and STONEHENGE are described; but in each of them, much is borrowed from Dr. STUKELEY. He supposes STONEHENGE to have been a place held sacred by the Druids, and appropriated to civil or religious assemblies; adding, " To the meeting of great assemblies, whether on civil or religious accounts, the place seems peculiarly adapted; for which purpose, I believe, the world does not. afford a nobler spot. Its situation is upon a hill, in the midst of an extended plain, in the centre of the southern part of the kingdom, covered with number-less herds and flocks of sheep, in which respect the employment, and the plains themselves are patriarchal; where the air is perfectly salubrious and exhilarat-ing, and the yielding turf fine as the surface of a bowling green. From almost every adjoining eminence the prospect is open into Hampshire, and Dorset-shire, and takes in all the lofty hills between Marlborough and Sandy Lane, sustaining the long range of Wansdyke, and the mother church of Abury."

In the year 1771, Mr. SMITH published, in one volume, extracts from all the preceding writers on STONEHENGE, with ground plans, and two perspective views of the temple. He is more minute than his predecessors, in describing the number, position, and state of the different stones which form the temple; and I think his plan is the most correct of any that have as yet been given. He considers it to have been a tropical temple, erected by the Druids for ob-serving the motions of the heavenly bodies.

Mr. KING, in his *Munimenta Antiqua*, has not suffered STONEHENGE to escape his notice; he supposes it to have been erected in the very latest age of Druidism.

Mr. DAVIES, a Cambrian, in his *Celtic Researches*, imagines that STONEHENGE, as well as SILBURY HILL in our county, were alluded to in the Welsh Triads, where it is recorded, that the three mighty labours of the island of Britain, were, 1. Lifting the stone of Ketti; 2. Building the work of Emrys; 3. Piling up the Mount of the Assemblies.

" The works of Emrys imply the sacred circles, such as STONEHENGE, which is known by that name; the MAIN AMBRES, in Cornwall, DINAS EMRYS in Snowdon, * and other PETRAI AMBROSIAI; and in SILBURY HILL we may con-template the Mount of the Assemblies; but what third kind of British monu-ment is there, which displays the effect of great labour in lifting a stone, unless it be the enormous Cromlech?"

The same writer thinks, that the massacre at STONEHENGE, in the year 472, is alluded to by the Bard Aneurin, in his poem of Gododin, as well as the stone circle itself; " from whence (he adds) it must follow, that this pile could not

* Mr. Davies very improperly places Dinas Emrys amongst the sacred circles, as it is only a round insu-lated hill, and evidently a fortified post.

have been erected, as fable has sometimes reported, in commemoration of the massacre; but that, on the contrary, it was a monument of venerable antiquity in the days of Hengist; and that its peculiar sanctity influenced the selection of that spot for the place of conference between the British and Saxon princes. It is equally clear, that the sacred building did not receive its name GWAITH EMRYS, from Emrys or Ambrosius, a prince who fought with Hengist, but that, on the other hand, it communicates to him its own name, as he was president and defender of the Ambrosial stones.

" That this structure was sacred to the Druidical superstition, is fully evident, from the language in which it was described, and the great veneration in which it was held by the primitive bards, those immediate descendants and avowed disciples of the British Druids. As the great sanctuary of the dominion, or metropolitan temple of our heathen ancestors, so complex in its plan, and constructed upon such a multitude of astronomical calculations, we find it was not exclusively dedicated to the Sun, the Moon, Saturn, or any other individual object of superstition; but it was a kind of Pantheon, in which all the Archite and Sabian divinities of British theology were supposed to have been present." *Celtic Researches*, p. 385.

By the above list of writers, it will be seen that STONEHENGE has by no means been overlooked; but till the time of Dr. STUKELEY, (the space of more than a century from the date of INIGO JONES's work on the same subject) nothing was done satisfactorily: each author seems to have blindly followed his leader, and to have retailed those errors which a personal investigation and accurate admeasurement of the building would have surely prevented; but in STUKELEY we find every thing we could desire or expect; great learning, sound judgment, minute investigation, and accuracy of description, added to the most enthusiastic zeal in the cause of antiquity; and if he had rested on sound British ground, instead of flying to Tyre for his Herculean hero, and adopted a measure more generally known than the cubit, his work would have been much more intelligible.

It is a melancholy consideration, that at a period when the sciences are progressively advancing, and when newly discovered manuscripts are continually drawn forth from their cloistered retreats, to throw a light on the ancient records of our country; it is mortifying, I say, that the history of so celebrated a monument as STONEHENGE should still remain veiled in obscurity. The monks may boldly assert that Merlin, and only Merlin, was the founder of our temple; and we cannot contradict, though we may disbelieve. The opinions of the

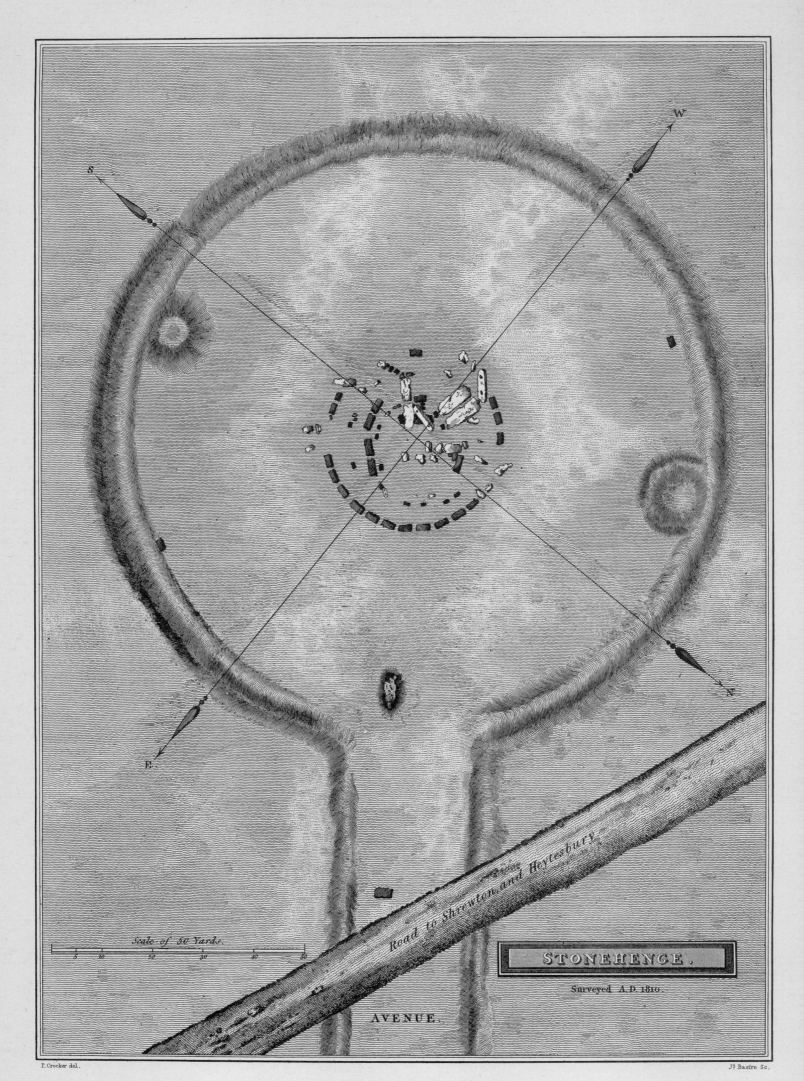

S

W

E

N

Scale of 50 Yards.
5   10   20   30   40   50

Road to Shrewton and Heytesbury

STONEHENGE.

Surveyed A.D. 1810.

AVENUE.

P. Crocker del.

J.º Basire Sc.

GROUND PLAN OF STONEHENGE.

Published for W. Miller, Albemarle Street, London, Jan.ʸ 1.1811.

learned have been so numerous and various (as I have already shewn), that I can hardly venture to give any of my own. I trust, however, I shall be able to correct the errors of some of my predecessors, and to throw some new light on the history of those Britons who inhabited the plains surrounding STONEHENGE, though I can neither inform my readers at what æra, or by what people this wonderful monument was erected. The revolution of ages frequently elucidates history, and brings many important facts to light ; but here all is darkness, and uncertainty ; we may admire ; we may conjecture ; but we are doomed to remain in ignorance and obscurity.

STONEHENGE. The construction and plan of this building are of so novel and singular a nature, that no verbal description, though drawn up by the ablest writer, can possibly convey to the reader a competent idea of it. If I talk to you of a Doric, Ionic, or Corinthian temple, you will readily form such an idea of the building in your mind, as not to be surprized on seeing it ; for each of these Orders has its fixed proportions, and each its appropriate ornaments ; but were I to describe to you a rude temple composed of four circles, one within the other, with upright stones twenty feet high, and others of an immense size placed across them like architraves, I fear my description would prove very unsatisfactory. The pen, therefore, must call in the assistance of the pencil ; for without a reference to plans and views, no perfect knowledge can be gained respecting this " Wonder of the West." In the plans now presented to you, I have endeavoured to correct the errors of others, and by the assistance of an able surveyor, repeated visits, and a strict attention to accuracy, to render them as complete as the great intricacy of the subject will admit.

The first Plate represents a general ground plan of STONEHENGE, surrounded by a ditch and slight *agger* of earth.* I cannot allow more than one entrance into the area of the work. This faces the north-east, and is decidedly marked by a bank and ditch called the AVENUE, which leads directly into it. On our approach to it on this side, the first object that arrests our attention, is a large rude stone in a leaning position, which by some has been called " *the Friar's heel*." Its height is about sixteen feet, and its original purport is totally unknown, though conjecture has not been idle in ascribing various uses to it. We now enter the area of the work, having the bank and ditch that encompassed the temple on our right and left. Writers have described this as a deep ditch, and thirty feet wide, and have not noticed the ditch being on the *outside* of the *vallum*.✝ According to our measurement, the ditch could not have exceeded

---

* The circumference of this ditch measures three hundred and sixty-nine yards.

✝ From the circumstance of the ditch being *within* the *vallum* at Abury, and from other similar examples

fifteen feet; in short, this whole line of circumvallation was a very slight work. Adjoining the *agger*, within the area, is a large prostrate stone, which has given rise to various opinions; the most prevailing of which is, that it was the stone on which the victims were slaughtered; but all these hypotheses are completely overturned by the circumstances of three sides of the stone bearing the same mark of tools as the large uprights of the temple, and the projecting part of the base, where it rested in the ground, remaining in its rude state, and unhewn; the fourth side, being uppermost, has been much defaced and excavated by the continual effect of water on it for a long succession of years. This we proved, by digging so completely under it, as to be able to examine the undermost side of the stone, where we found fragments of stag's horns. This stone measures in length twenty-one feet two inches, of which three feet six inches being under ground, the height of the stone, when upright, was seventeen feet eight inches. The distance from the first stone in the avenue to the second stone at the entrance into the area, was about one hundred feet, and the distance between that and the outside of the stone circle, was nearly the same. The distance from the *vallum* to the temple is also one hundred feet, as well as the inner diameter of the temple; so that the Britons seemed partial to the proportion of one hundred feet, having adopted it in so many important parts of their building.

There are two small stones within the *vallum*, and adjoining it, whose uses have never been satisfactorily defined. The one on the south-east side is near nine feet high, and has fallen from its base backwards on the *vallum:* the other on the north-west side is not quite four feet high; both rude and unhewn. There are also two small *tumuli* ditched round, so as to resemble excavations, adjoining the *agger;* they are very slightly elevated above the surface, and deserve particular notice, as they may give rise to some curious and not improbable conjectures. Dr. Stukeley supposes them to have been the places where two stone vases were set; and the stones before mentioned to have been two altars for some particular rites, which he does not, however, take upon himself to explain. Here our learned Doctor gets out of his depth, as do others, who suppose these cavities to have been destined to hold the blood of victims. On minute investigation you will plainly see, that the *vallum* of the *agger*

which I shall have occasion to mention hereafter, I have reason to agree with Stukeley, in thinking it a distinguishing mark between religious and military works; those of the latter nature, being made for the purpose of defence, would of course have their ditches on the outside of the bank, as we find in all the strong camps upon our hills.

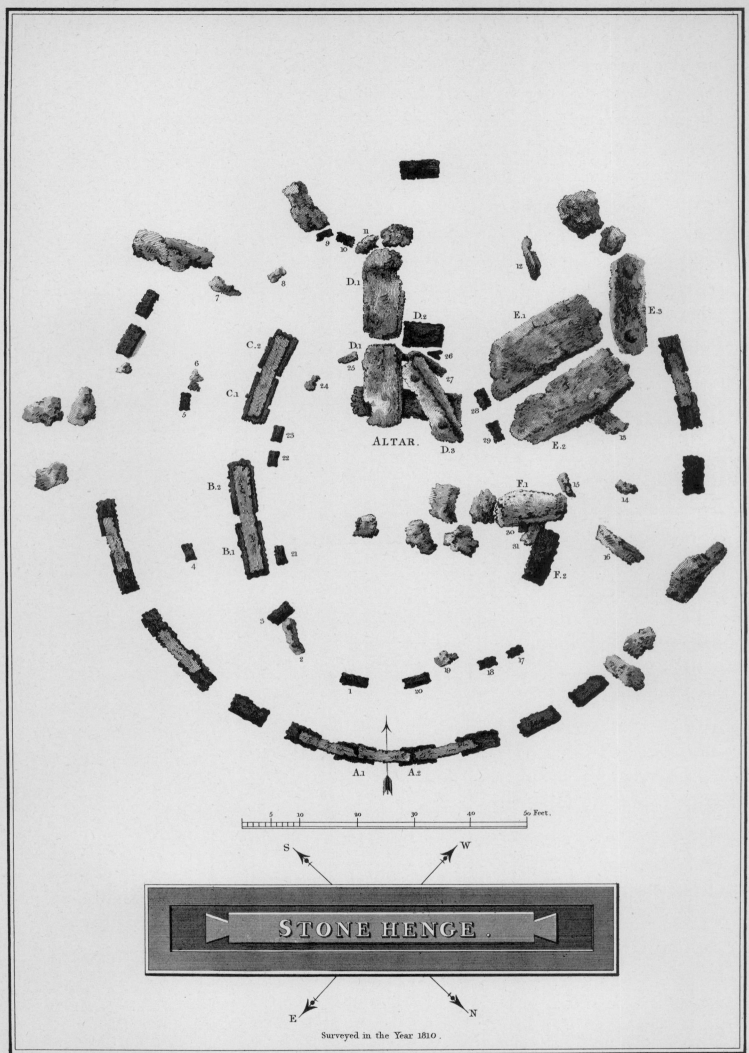

P. Crocker del.

Js Basire Sc.

ALTAR.

STONE HENGE.

Surveyed in the Year 1810.

Published for W. Miller, Albemarle Street, London, Jan.ʸ 1. 1811.

surrounding the work, has been evidently curtailed, by forming the *tumulus* on the north-west side of the circle, which induced us to open it, when, much to our surprise, we found within it a simple interment of burned bones; from whence we may fairly infer, that this sepulchral barrow existed on the plain, I will not venture to say before the construction of STONEHENGE, but probably before the ditch was thrown up; and I scarcely know how we can separate the æra of the one from the other. We also opened the other *tumulus* on the south-east side, but found nothing in it. You will perceive that I have marked only one *adit* to the temple on my plan; for I am satisfied with STUKELEY, that the other two supposed entrances are modern works, and made by the frequent intercourse of carriages.

The second Plate represents a ground plan of the temple, divested of all its appendages. To render it more intelligible, I have distinguished the fallen stones from those that remain in their original position, by representing the former as prostrate, and by engraving the latter with a darker stroke; and as, hitherto, the trilithons or imposts have never been represented in any plan, I have thought fit to insert those that remain; but I beg it may be understood, that by so doing, I have been obliged to deviate a little from true perspective, as, if drawn to a scale with the rest of the stones, they would totally cover the uprights on which they rest

Let us now approach this mysterious building, and enter within its hallowed precincts. " When you enter the building, says STUKELEY, whether on foot or horseback, and cast your eyes around upon the yawning ruins, you are struck into an extatic *reverie*, which none can describe, and they, only, can be sensible of, that feel it. Other buildings fall by piecemeal, but here a single stone is a ruin, and lies like the haughty carcase of Goliath. Yet there is as much of it undemolished, as enables us sufficiently to recover its form, when it was in its most perfect state: there is enough of every part to preserve the idea of the whole. When we advance further, the dark part of the ponderous imposts over our heads, the chasm of sky between the jambs of the CELL, the odd construction of the whole, and the greatness of every part, surprizes. We may well cry out in the poet's words, " *Tantum religio potuit.*" If you look upon the perfect part, you fancy entire quarries mounted up into the air; if upon the rude havock below, you see, as it were, the bowels of a mountain turned inside outwards." At first sight all is amazement and confusion; the eye is surprised, the mind bewildered. The stones begin now, and not before, to assume their proper grandeur; and the interior of the temple, hitherto blinded by an uniform exterior, displays a most singular variety and gigantic magnificence. But such is the dilapidation, and such the confusion of the displaced fragments, that no one, who has not, as I may say, got the plan by heart, can possibly replace them in imagination according to their original destination. To obviate these difficulties, and assist the antiquary in developing this labyrinth of stones, I have annexed a correct plan of them as they now stand, which would be rendered more perspicuous at first sight, if each circle, as well as each oval, were distinguished by a separate colour.

This temple consists of two circles, and two ovals; the two latter constituting the CELL or SANCTUM. The outward circle, about three hundred feet in circumference, is composed of huge upright stones, bearing others over them, which form a kind of architrave. Though they evidently shew the mark of tools, they are still irregular in their forms and sizes. The height of the stones on each side the entrance is a little more than thirteen feet, and the breadth of one, seven feet, and of the other, six feet four inches: the impost over them is about two feet eight inches deep. The space between the stones in this outward circle varies; that between the entrance stones is five feet, and rather wider than in the rest. This circle consisted originally of thirty stones, of which seventeen still remain standing. At the distance of eight feet three inches* from the inside of this outward circle, we find another composed of smaller stones, rude and irregular in their shapes. Dr. STUKELEY is certainly accurate in his conjectures, when, contrary to the opinion of preceding writers, he states the number of stones of which this circle consisted, to be forty, and not thirty; and this fact may be satisfactorily proved, by measuring the space occupied by the stones belonging to this circle, No. 17, 18, 19, 20, which stand, as well as No. 1, nearly in their original position, by which it will be clearly seen, that the number of the whole circle must have been forty. Some few particularities in this circle deserve notice. Dr. STUKELEY in his ground plan of STONEHENGE, has placed the two stones at the entrance into this circle, No. 1 and 20, a little *within* the range of the others, observing, " that the two stones of the principal entrance of this circle, correspondent to that of the outer circle, are broader and taller, and set at a greater distance from each other, being rather more than that of the principal entrance in the outer circle. It is evident too, that they are set somewhat more inward than the rest; so as that their outward face stands

* I have taken this measurement across from No. 4, to the south-east side of the temple, where the stones still remain in their original position; but this inner circle is not placed exactly in the centre between the trilithons of the outward and inner circle, as the distance between No. 4. and B. 1 is ten feet four inches.

in the line that marks the inner circumference of the inner circle." This remark is just, but the lines are rather exaggerated on his plan; and I doubt if it was originally intended that these two stones should retire within the adjoining circle. No. 1 retires nine feet ten inches from the outward circle; No. 20, ten feet; No. 18, nine feet; and No. 17, eight feet eight inches. No. 2 appears to have belonged to this circle, and to have been the impost of a small trilithon. Might there not have been another in the vacant space on the opposite side, to correspond with it? Of this circle, originally consisting of forty stones, traces remain only of twenty; and it is rather doubtful whether No. 15 belonged to it, being so far removed out of its line; but from the circumstance of its being a very rude stone, and those of the inner oval in general being better shaped, I am inclined to think it is properly numbered on our plan.

We now come to the grandest part of our temple, the CELL, or SANCTUM; in forming which, the general plan has been varied; for this inner temple represents two-thirds of a large oval, and a concomitant small oval, as in the outward temple we find a large and a small circle. The large oval is formed by five pair of trilithons, or two large upright stones, with a third laid over them as an impost. The placing of the imposts is also varied, for they are not continued all round, as in the outward circle, but are divided into pairs, thereby giving a great lightness to the work, and breaking its uniformity; neither are they like those of the outward circle, parallel at top; but they rise gradually in height from east to west, as will be seen by the following admeasurements. Trilithon B, is sixteen feet three inches high; trilithon C, is seventeen feet two inches high; and trilithon D, is twenty-one feet six inches high: thus we see the progressive height of the trilithons to be sixteen feet three; seventeen feet two; and twenty-one feet six inches. D. 1, being fallen, we are enabled to ascertain how deep they were fixed in the ground, and in what manner. A rude projecting portion of the stone was left at its base, by which it was secured in the soil, and small fragments of stone and pounded chalk were rammed in to steady it. This fallen stone is broken in two pieces; one fragment measures twelve feet four inches; the other nine feet five inches, and the part sunk in the ground four feet six inches, making a total height of twenty-six feet three inches; so that STUKELEY errs in making their length thirty feet. The impost of trilithon E, measures sixteen feet four inches in length; the distance between the mortaises being nine feet seven inches. The impost belonging to this trilithon, D. 3, likewise prostrate, was fifteen feet six inches long.

P P

The present age has to lament the fall of trilithon E, which took place on the 3d of January, 1797.*

> " *Recidit in solidam, longo post tempore, terram*
> *Pondus, et exhibuit junctam cum viribus artem.*"

One of these uprights measures twenty-one feet four inches, and the other twenty-one feet three inches: deducting from which four feet, or rather more, the length under ground, we still find this pair of trilithons correspond with those opposite C. 1, as we find also the trilithon F. 2, now standing, corresponding in height nearly with the opposite one B.; the one being sixteen feet three inches, and the other nearly the same. Thus we see a great degree of regularity pervading the plan of this building, and the approach to the altar rendered more striking by the trilithons rising gradually as you advance towards it. Before I conclude my account of this grand oval, let me call your attention to the leaning stone, D. 2, which is nine feet out of the perpendicular. This stone, in the artist's eye, from its singular position, and bold tenon, forms one of the most picturesque features of the building, by breaking the uniformity of the upright lines :

> " *Jam jam lapsura cadentique*
> *Imminet assimilis.*"

It is also singular how, with such a vast projection, and the bearing of only four feet and a half in the ground, it should so long have retained its situation, and continued unmoved at the great concussion which the foundation must have sustained on the falling of the three stones in 1797. The situation of this stone, with regard to the ribbed one, No. 26, deserves also notice : the large upright seems to be supported by the smaller one, but on close examination I almost doubted if it did : the adhesion or connection between them is just sufficient to swear by ; and that is all. The trilithons of this oval are evidently finer stones, and more regular in their forms, than those of the outward circle, and the leaning stone above the altar, exceeds all the rest in beauty. The third stone, C. 1, is next ; and the finest impost is the one over the trilithons C. 1, and C. 2. Some of these, as well as others in the outward circle, taper from their base towards the top.

It now remains for me to describe the inner oval, which, according to Dr. STUKELEY, consisted originally of nineteen stones, of which I still see traces of

---

* An account of the falling of this trilithon, with two views representing it in its original, and in its fallen state, was drawn up by Dr. Maton, and published in the Archaeologia, Vol. XIII.

eleven, viz. from No. 21, to 31. They are much smoother and taller than those of the inner circle of small stones, and incline to the pyramidical form. The most perfect of these is No. 23, which is seven feet and a half high, twenty-three inches wide at the base, and decreases to twelve inches at the top. The stone, No. 26, deserves notice from having a groove cut all down it; for what purpose, no rational conjecture has ever yet been formed; its shape also varies somewhat from that of its companions, as it bevils off almost to an angle on the inner side. The altar stone is fifteen feet long, and almost totally covered by the fall of one of the large upright stones, and its impost, across it. The inside diameter of this whole building is about one hundred feet; and the width of the entrance into the CELL, from the trilithons B. and F. forty-three feet; and the distance from the altar stone to the entrance into the temple, fifty-seven feet four inches.

Having described with accuracy the form and measurement of this celebrated temple, it may not be uninteresting to my readers, to hear something about the nature of the stones that composed it. The large upright stone close to the turnpike road, and the one lying flat on the ground, which has been called the " slaughtering stone ;" the two small stones near the *vallum*, as well as all the great stones composing the outward circle, and the five trilithons of the grand oval, are all sarsen stones, collected from the surface of the Wiltshire downs. Dr. STUKELEY informs us, that this word is Phœnician, and signifies a rock; what is now understood by *sarsen*, is a stone drawn from the native quarry in its rude state.* It is generally supposed that these stones were brought from the neighbourhood of Abury, in North Wiltshire; and the circumstance of three stones still existing in that direction, + is adduced, as a corroborating proof of that statement. They are certainly of the same nature as those in the neighbourhood of Marlborough, and are a fine-grained species of siliceous sand-stone.

---

* In regard to the natural history of these stones, says STUKELEY, the whole country hereabouts is a solid body of chalk, covered with a most delicate turf. As this chalky matter hardened at creation, it spewed out the most solid body of the stones, of greater specific gravity than itself; and assisted by the centrifuge power, owing to the rotation of the globe upon its axis, threw them upon its surface, where they now lie. A more modern naturalist has supposed that a stratum of sand, containing these stones, once covered the chalk land, and at the deluge this stratum was washed off from the surface, and the stones left behind. Certain it is, that we find them dispersed over a great part of our chalky district; and they are particularly numerous between Abury and Marlborough; but the celebrated field called from them, the Grey Wethers, no longer presents even a single stone; for they have all been broken to pieces for building, and repairing the roads.

+ The one in Durrington field; another in Bulford river; and another in Bulford field.

In the inner circle, the inner oval, and the altar, we find a material difference in the nature of the stones. No. 1, 2, 3, 4, 5, 6, 7, 8, 10, 12, 13, 14, 15, 16, 18, 20, 21, 22, 23, 24, 25, 26, 27, 28, 29, and 30, are an aggregate of quartz, feldspar, chlorite, and hornblende; No. 9, is a siliceous schist; No. 11, 17, 19, are horn-stone, with small specks of feldspar and pyrites. The altar stone is a micaceous fine grained sand-stone, and measures about fifteen feet in length.

The area of this temple has naturally excited the investigation of the curious, but no important discoveries have been made. STUKELEY tells us, that a tablet of tin was found there, in the time of King Henry VIII. inscribed with many letters, but in so strange a character, that the most learned antiquaries of the age could make nothing out of it. Some have called it Punic, others Irish; and the Doctor says, " it was no doubt a memorial of the founders, written by the Druids." Mr. INIGO JONES says, that the cover of a *thuribulum*, or incense cup, was found within the area; and STUKELEY tells us, that the heads of oxen and other animal bones were found there. In more modern times we have found, on digging, several fragments of Roman, as well as of coarse British pottery; parts of the head and horns of deer, and other animals, and a large barbed arrow head of iron. Dr. STUKELEY says, that he dug close to the altar, and at the depth of one foot, came to the solid chalk. Mr. CUNNINGTON also dug about the same place to the depth of nearly six feet, and found the chalk had been moved to that depth; and at about the depth of three feet, he found some Roman pottery, and at the depth of six feet, some pieces of sarsen stones, three fragments of coarse half-baked pottery, and some charred wood. After what STUKELEY has said of finding the marl solid at the depth of one foot, the above discoveries would naturally lead us to suppose, that some persons, since his time, had dug into the same spot; yet after getting down about two feet, there was less and less vegetable mould, till we reached the solid chalk; some small pieces of bone, a little charred wood, and some fragments of coarse pottery were intermixed with the soil. In digging into the ditch that surrounds the area, Mr. CUNNINGTON found similar remnants of antiquity; and in the waggon tracks, near STONEHENGE, you frequently meet with chippings of the stones of which the temple was constructed. Soon after the fall of the great trilithon in 1797, Mr. CUNNINGTON dug out some of the earth that had fallen into the excavation, and found a fragment of fine black Roman pottery, and since that, another piece in the same spot; but I have no idea that this pottery ever lay beneath the stones, but probably in the earth adjoining the trilithon, and after the downfall of the latter, fell with the mouldering earth into the excavation.

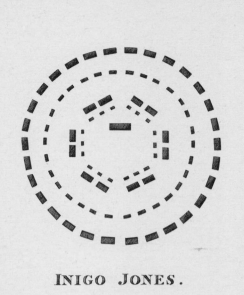

INIGO JONES.

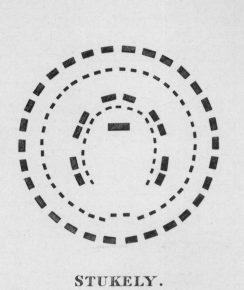

STUKELY.

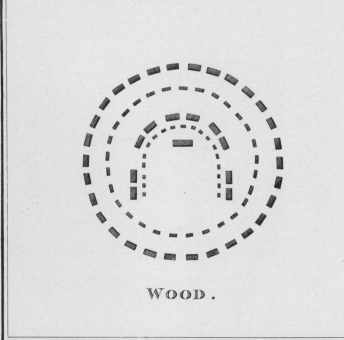

WOOD.

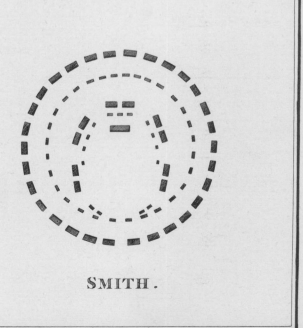

SMITH.

P. Crocker del.

J.ᵉ Basire Sc.

Published for W. Miller, Albemarle Street, London, Janᵞ 1 1811.

The only conclusion we can draw from the circumstance of finding Roman pottery on this ground is, that this work was in existence at the period when that species of earthenware was made use of by the Britons in our island.

The third Plate consists of four ground plans, and one bird's eye view, of Stonehenge, which I have arranged on one page, for the purpose of bringing them before the eye in one point of view, and thereby enabling my readers to make their comparisons betwixt them with greater facility. A striking difference will be perceived in the plans of Inigo Jones and Mr. Wood, both architects by profession. They agree as to the outward circle ; but Mr. Wood makes the second circle consist of only twenty-nine instead of thirty stones. They differ totally in the two next ranges ; the former giving the cell the form of an hexagon ; the latter making it partly circular and partly straight. The former states the number of large stones in the third range to be twelve, and the small stones to be eighteen : the latter (like Stukeley,) states the large stones to be ten, and the smaller nineteen ; but he places them in a very different form. It is somewhat singular, that of all those who have given plans of Stonehenge, the very two men, who from their profession, as architects, ought to have been the most accurate, should have been the most inaccurate ; for on comparing their plans, with our ground plan of the stones now remaining, you will immediately be convinced, that the third and fourth ranges of stones could never have assumed an hexagonal figure nor the figure, designed by Wood.

In the plans laid down by Dr. Stukeley, and Dr. Smith, we see a great concurrency of opinion, and a much nearer approach to correctness ; they agree as to the number of stones in the great circle, and great oval, and very nearly as to their position ; Dr. Stukeley makes the number of stones in the large circle to be forty ; and of the small oval, nineteen. Dr. Smith makes those of the small circle to be thirty, and of the small oval thirteen ; for he supposes a pair of small trilithons on each side, one impost only of which remains, and is marked No. 2 in the ground plan ; but Dr. Stukeley includes this impost in his second circle. The following letter, received from Mr. Cunnington, has induced me to add a fourth plan of Stonehenge, which forms the centre compartment of the plate.

" On viewing the remains of this monument of the Britons, I have been surprized that the following question never occurred to those writers who have considered this subject, viz. " Why did the Britons, in erecting Stonehenge, make use of two kinds of stone, which are totally dissimilar to each other ? " Any person versed in mineralogy, will perceive that the stones on the outside of the work, those composing the outward circle and its imposts, as well as the five large trilithons, are all of that species of stone called *sarsen*, which is found in the neighbourhood ; whereas the inner circle of small upright stones, and those of the interior oval, are composed of granite, horn-stone, &c. most probably brought from some part of Devonshire or Cornwall, as I know not where such stones could be procured at a nearer distance."

" In considering the subject, I have been led to suppose that STONEHENGE was raised at different æra ; that the original work consisted of the outward circle and its imposts, and of the inner oval of large trilithons ; and that the smaller circle and oval, of inferior stones, were raised at a later period ; for they add nothing to the general grandeur of the temple, but rather give a littleness to the whole ; and more particularly so, if, according to SMITH, you add the two small trilithons of granite."

I am much pleased with this new idea respecting STONEHENGE, which, to use a well known Italian proverb, " *Se non è vero, è ben trovato*." *If not true, is well imagined;* for it is not, like many others, founded on idle conjecture, but has some rational ground to rest upon. In erecting this mighty structure, its builders would naturally select for that purpose the materials nearest at hand ; such were the *sarsens*, which compose the grandest part of the work, viz. the outward circle, and large oval ; and why, with these materials, acquireable at no great distance (for at that early period, the plains adjoining STONEHENGE might very probably have furnished stones sufficiently large), should the architects have sought materials for the small circle and small oval, in such distant counties ? This difference in the stones is a strong argument in favour of Mr. CUNNINGTON's conjecture ; for had the Britons erected the temple at one and the same period, they would most naturally have made use of the native, not foreign materials. And in viewing this new supposed plan of STONEHENGE, divested of its unmeaning pigmy pillars of granite, and diminutive trilithons, we behold a most majestic and mysterious pile, unconfused in its plan, simple and grand in its architecture, most awful and imposing in its effect. Such indeed is the general fascination imposed on all those who view it, that no one can quit its precincts, without feeling strong sensations of surprize and admiration. The ignorant rustic will with a vacant stare attribute it to the giants, or the mighty arch-fiend ; and the antiquary, equally uninformed as to its origin, will regret that its history is veiled in perpetual obscurity. The artist, on viewing these enormous masses, will wonder that art could thus rival nature in magnificence and picturesque effect: even the most indifferent passenger over the plain

P.Crocker del.

J.Basire Sc.

WEST VIEW OF STONEHENGE.

Published for W.Miller, Albemarle Street, London, Jan'ʸ.1.1812.

must be attracted by the solitary and magnificent appearance of these ruins; and all with one accord will exclaim, " HOW GRAND! HOW WONDERFUL! HOW INCOMPREHENSIBLE!"

SINCE the foregoing pages were printed off, I have been gratified with a perusal of the curious manuscript, mentioned in page 139, and written about the year 1665, by JOHN AUBREY, Esq.* and am thus enabled to add another name to the list of authors who have delivered their opinions and conjectures respecting STONEHENGE. This work is entitled MONUMENTA BRITANNICA, and was prepared by its learned compiler for the press, but was never printed. It treats largely of the various British and Roman antiquities within our island, and most particularly of those two celebrated monuments which adorn our own county; ABURY, and STONEHENGE. He was the cotemporary of INIGO JONES, WEBB, and CHARLETON, who severally gave their opinions in print respecting STONEHENGE. In speaking of the work of the former celebrated architect, who in the year 1620, was ordered by King James the First to draw out a plan and description of this celebrated monument, and which was published in the year 1655, by his son-in-law, Mr. WEBB, he says, " There is a great deal of learning in it; but having compared his scheme with the monument itself, I found he had not dealt fairly, but had made a Lesbian's rule, which is conformed to the stone; that is, he framed the monument to his own hypothesis, which is much differing from the thing itself; and this gave me an edge to make more researches." He particularly points out the plan of the CELL, or inner temple, as false, INIGO JONES having laid it down as a *regular hexagon*, instead of the *part of an oval*, which it really is. " The ruines of it, he adds, doo clearly enough shew, without further demonstration, that it could neither be a hexagon, or heptagon; nor can all the angles be forced to touch a circle."

Mr. AUBREY informs us, that this ancient monument of STONEHENGE was mentioned by Caxton, in his Chronicle, as the second wonder in Britain; and that

---

* Mr. AUBREY was born at East Piers, in North Wiltshire, A. D. 162⅚, and resided for some time at Broad Chalk, not far from Salisbury, on an estate belonging to the Earl of Pembroke, of which he had a lease. He wrote the History of Surrey, the Life of his countryman Hobbes, of Malmesbury, a volume of Miscellanies, and reposited the collections he had made for a History of Wiltshire in the Ashmolean Museum at Oxford. The valuable manuscript here quoted, viz. *Monumenta Britannica*, is in the possession of William Churchill, Esq. of Henbury, in Dorsetshire, to whom I am happy thus publickly to acknowledge my thanks for his obliging loan of it.

it was a part of the inheritance of the wife of Lord Ferrers of Chartley, who was daughter of Lawrence Washington, Esq.* Upon what ground the writers call it Stonehenge, + he could not tell ; he had not seen the old deeds of this estate, but by the neighbourhood it was called Stonedge, *i. e.* stones set edgewise. He quotes some verses of Sir Philip Sydney concerning them :

> " Ne'er Wilton sweet, huge heepes of stones are found,
> " But so confus'd, that neither any eie
> " Can count them just, nor reason reason try
> " What force them brought to so unlikeley ground."

He retails the old and marvellous account (from Caxton's Chronicle) of Merlyn's transporting these stones from the hill of Kildare in Ireland, and placing them on the plains near Ambresbury, by desire of the British King Aurelius Ambrosius ; but he gives it only as a vulgar tradition. He says, the stones (of which this monument is composed) are of the very same kind with the Grey Wethers near Marlborough. He supposes that a circle of stones was continued all round the inside of the earthen *vallum* that encompasses the temple, as at Abury : " Witnesse yet, three pittes or signes of them, where the stones were heretofore pitch't, and equidistant." It will be seen by my plan, that two stones only remain at present in that situation.

From this manuscript we gain some curious information respecting one of the great trilithons of the CELL. This leaning stone, marked D. 2, in my ground plan of Stonehenge, adds, in the artist's eye, a great beauty to the general appearance of the temple, by varying the upright position of the surrounding trilithons. Its partial fall is attributed to the researches made in the year 1620, by George Duke of Buckingham, who, when King James the First was at Wilton, (the seat of the Earls of Pembroke) " did cause the middle of Stonehenge to be digged, and this under digging was the cause of the falling downe, or recumbencey of the great stone there, twenty-one foote long."‡ In the process of this digging they found a great many horns of stags and oxen, charcoal, batter-dashes, § heads of arrows, some pieces of armour eaten out

---

* This monument has again changed its owner, by the late death of the Duke of Queensberry, A. D. 1810.

+ I am rather surprized that so intelligent a writer should not have recognized a Saxon title in the words Stan-henge, or Hanging stones.

‡ Mr. Aubrey says he owes the above information to Mrs. Trotman, who then lived at the farm of West Amesbury (to which this monument belongs) ; she told him that the Duke of Buckingham would have given to Mr. Newdick (the owner of this place) any rate for it, but he would not accept it.

§ I am at a loss to conjecture what our author means by the word batter-dash; of which he has given a rude sketch in his manuscript, and which resembles the instrument made use of for churning butter.

with rust, bones rotten, but whether of stagge's or men they could not tell. He further adds, that Philip Earl of Pembroke, (Lord Chamberlayne to King Charles the First) did say, " that an altar stone was found in the middle of the area here, and that it was carried away to Saint James's."

This may have been the stone within the CELL, before alluded to in page 139, but the large flat stone, which has generally been considered as the ALTAR, still remains in its original situation, and is of a different species from any other in this temple.

Mr. AUBREY notices the SEVEN BARROWS, one of which, he says, is called PAN BARROW, and the others have likewise their names.*

In summing up his account of these antiquities, Mr. AUBREY thus expresses himself ; " when a traveller rides along by the ruines of a monastery, he knows by the manner of building, chapelles, cloysters, &c. that it was a convent ; but of what order, Benedictine, Dominican, &c. it was, he cannot tell by the bare view. So it is cleer, that all the monuments, which I have here recounted were temples. Now my presumption is, that the DRUIDS being the most eminent order of priests among the Britaines, 'tis odds, but that these ancient monuments, AUBURY, STONEHENGE, &c. were temples of the priests of the most eminent order, viz. DRUIDS ; and it is strongly to be presumed, that AUBURY and STONEHENGE are as ancient as those times. This inquiry, I must confess, is a gropeing in the dark ; but although I have not brought it into a cleer light, yet I can affirm, that I have brought it from an utter darkness to a thin mist, and have gone farther in this essay than any one before me." +

Having stated the modern traditions and opinions respecting STONEHENGE, I ought not to omit the very ancient account given by DIODORUS SICULUS, of a round temple dedicated to APOLLO, and from the following description of it, supposed to have been situated in Britain, and perhaps the very monument of which I have been lately treating. The historian says, " amongst the writers on antiquity, HECATÆUS, and some others, relate, that there is an island in

---

* Mr. AUBREY notices only one of the groups of seven barrows: whereas, on referring to the plan, you will perceive there are two groups, nearly in a parallel line, with an opening left between them, through which the avenue from STONEHENGE directed its course towards the river Avon.   In one of these seven barrows, Lawrence Washington, Esq. told Mr. AUBREY, in the year 1649, " that he had digged up coales, and pieces of goates horns or stagge's horns: " and in another of them, he says, " that by the Duke of Buckingham's digging, a bugle horn tipt with silver at both ends was found, which (according to Mrs. Trotman's report) his Grace kept in his closet as a great relique."

+ This assertion is more just with respect to Abury than to STONEHENGE ; for Mr. AUBREY was preceded at the latter by INIGO JONES and others ; but was the first in describing the former.

the ocean opposite to Celtic Gaul, * and not inferior in size to that of Sicily, lying towards the north, and inhabited by HYPERBOREI, who are so called because they live more remote from the north wind. ✝ The soil is excellent and fertile, the climate temperate, and the harvest is made twice in the same year. Tradition says, that LATONA was born here, and therefore APOLLO is worshipped in preference to any other deity ; and because the inhabitants celebrate him daily with continued songs of praise, and pay him the highest honours, they are considered as the Priests of APOLLO : to whom a magnificent *precint* ‡ is allotted, and a remarkable *temple of a round form*, and adorned with many votive offerings. The city is also dedicated to this deity ; many of its inhabitants are musicians, who striking up their harps within the temple, chaunt sacred hymns to their God, and honourably extol his actions. The government of the city, and the care of the temple, are intrusted to the BOREADÆ, the descendants of BOREAS, who inherit this government by an uninterrupted line of succession."

On reading this ancient record of HECATÆUS, the enthusiastic antiquary will recognize the island of Britain, the *sacred precinct*, the *round temple* of STONEHENGE, and the bards or *cytharistæ* § chaunting hymns in praise of their favourite God APOLLO : and I must confess, that such an hypothesis does not rest on unsubstantial ground. Two living writers have alluded to this passage in DIODORUS ; Mr. MAURICE, in the sixth volume of his *Indian Antiquities ;* and Mr. DAVIES, in his *Celtic Researches :* and each concludes that the *round temple* mentioned by HECATÆUS could be no other than our STONEHENGE.

The latter thinks that the Celtic deity, BEL, ‖ is identified with the Solar

* In the expression of *Celtic Gaul*, I have followed the translation of Mr. DAVIES, the author of *Celtic Researches*, who notices this passage of Diodorus ; which, in the original, runs this, εν τοις αντιπεράν της Κελτικης τοποις, *i. e.* in those districts opposite the Celtic ; by which was certainly meant that province of Gaul distinguished by the name of GALLIA CELTICA ; and thus it is interpreted both in the Latin and French translation of the Greek author.

✝ Previous to his description of these Hyperborei, the Greek author had been describing the Scythians and other people residing *nearer* the north pole.

‡ The Greek word τεμενος is thus defined in the Lexicon: " *agri portio seorsum ab aliis sita, et deo dedicata : ager sacer, nemus sacrum, &c.*

§ The Bards were both priests and poets : the harp was their inseparable attribute, and skill upon that instrument was an indispensable qualification for their office. (DAVIES's *Celtic Researches*, p. 191.)

‖ This deity, BEL, seems to have been known to the Romans under the title of BELENUS, and indentified with the god APOLLO. *Pitiscus*, in his Lexicon, says, " *Belenus erat idem qui Apollo.*" This deity was held in particular reverence by the inhabitants of Aquileia in Italy, and worshipped by them under the joint names of APOLLO BELENUS. The word BEL, in the Celtic language, has a variety of meanings: it signifies high, supreme, from whence, Prince, Lord. Mr. TOLAND, in his History of the Druids, says, that on May eve the Druids made prodigious fires on their carns, in honour of BEAL, or BEALAN ; Latinized by the Romans into BELENUS ; by which name the Gauls and their colonies understood the Sun ; and therefore to this hour, the first of May is by the aboriginal Irish called LA BEALTEINE, or the day of BELEN's fire.

divinity Apollo ; and says, that the first name of Britain, after it was inhabited, was Vel ynys, or the Island of Bel.   He also supposes, that the battle of Hen Velen, mentioned in a song of the Bard Taliesin, alludes to one fought near Stonehenge.   The massacre of the Britons in that neighbourhood is frequently alluded to by the Welsh Bards, * as well as the sacred precinct of Stonehenge. In song xii. of the Gododin, by Aneurin, we find the stone cell of the sacred fire noticed ; and in song xv. we find also the great stone fence of the common sanctuary.   In the songs of another Welsh Bard, Cuhelyn, we also find allusions made to Stonehenge, in the words mawr cor cyvoeth, the great circle or sanctuary of the dominion.

All these ancient documents tend to prove, that at a very early period + a stone temple existed at Stonehenge, which was considered as the great sanctuary of the dominion ; and confute, in the most satisfactory manner, the very idle and ridiculous idea of the town of Ambresbury having derived its name from the British King Ambrosius.

The next object that attracts our attention is the Avenue.   It is a narrow strip of land, bounded on each side by a slight *agger* of earth.   On referring to the map of the environs of Stonehenge, where its situation and form will be best seen, you will perceive that it issues from the N. E. entrance of the temple ; then crossing the turnpike road, proceeds in a straight line towards a valley, where it divides into two branches, the one leading in a gentle curve towards the cursus ; the other directing its course in a direct line up the hill between two rows of barrows, planted with fir trees.   The most northern group has been called by Stukeley, the old king barrows; the opposite group, the new king barrows; and under these titles I have distinguished them in my map. The former are lower and flatter in their construction than the latter, which increase in height with the ground towards the south.

In the eye of the antiquary, they are much disfigured by the clumps of Scotch firs planted upon them, though at the same time secured from the researches of his spade.   More than an usual regularity is preserved in the disposal of these *tumuli* ; and I must here call the attention of my readers to the map, where they will perceive them ranged in a semicircular line, and a passage

---

* " And the spot appointed (for the massacre) was in the precinct of Iôr, in the fair quadrangular area of the *great sanctuary of the dominion (Song of Cuhelyn)*. Perhaps this area was the *cursus*. Mr. Davies says, " that Iôr is a name sometimes applied to the Supreme Being, but borrowed from British mythology, where it seems to have meant the Sun moving within its orbit or circle.

+ The Bard Aneurin died about the year 570, and the Bard Cuhelyn flourished about the middle of the sixth century.

decidedly left for the AVENUE, of which traces are still evident as far as this spot; but it has afterwards been obliterated by tillage in its passage through Amesbury park. Here again we have another proof of STONEHENGE, and its AVENUE, having been formed prior to the surrounding barrows, and we see a rude attempt at symmetry in the seven barrows, arranged in two separate lines, which flank the AVENUE (like wings) on its ascending the summit of the hill. Dr. STUKELEY supposes that the AVENUE continued its course in a direct line to Radfyn * farm on the banks of the river Avon, and from thence to Haradon hill, a lofty eminence on the opposite side; but even in his time, the traces of it were not distinguishable much farther than at present. The length of the AVENUE from the ditch round STONEHENGE to the spot where it branches off, is five hundred and ninety-four yards; and from thence it is visible about eight hundred and fourteen yards up the hill.

The northern branch appears undoubtedly to lead towards the CURSUS, though its traces become very faint soon after it has quitted the eastern line up the hill: it seems to have pursued a bending course towards the CURSUS, but I could not perceive that it pointed to any decided opening in that work.

We are now led to the CURSUS, or the Race course of the Britons, a most interesting and perfect relict of antiquity. It is situated north of STONEHENGE, and extends in a line from east to west. According to Mr. Crocker's measurement, its length is one mile, five furlongs, and one hundred and seventy-six yards; its breadth one hundred and ten yards. The head f it, which is towards the east, is marked by a mound of earth, resembling a Long Barrow, which extends across the whole CURSUS. Here the spectators of the race were seated, and a more eligible post could not have been chosen; for the ground descends from hence at first in a very gentle slope, and then ascends a slight hill, affording to the spectators a most comprehensive view of the whole course.

Some few particularities attend this CURSUS, which deserve notice: at the distance of fifty-five yards from the eastern end, which is terminated, as I have before said, by an oblong elevated mound, you evidently perceive the termination of the course rounded off, as if the horses or chariots made a turn at this spot; and at the distance of six hundred and thirty-eight yards from this end, are two entrances into the area of the CURSUS, opposite to each other; and eight

* I imagine the word *Radfyn* is derived from the British word, *Rhyd,* a ford, and *fin,* a boundary, as it is situated on the banks of the river Avon.

hundred and twenty-five yards further on, the *vallum* has been much broken down by the continual track of waggons ; and to this spot Dr. STUKELEY supposes the northern branch of the AVENUE from STONEHENGE pointed.

At a short distance from the western extremity, a slight bank runs across the CURSUS ; and between it and the end, which is rounded off, there are two barrows irregularly placed within the area. This bank cannot be accounted for, satisfactorily ; for we can hardly suppose, that if the chariots started from the east end, they would drive *over* this bank, to the termination of the course at the west end. The elevated mound at the east end, seems to announce that to have been the seat of honour ; and the superior view which it commands of the whole extent of the course, fully corroborates that supposition. We are again assured, that a bank across the end of the CURSUS formed a part of the general plan of these places of amusement, by a second example in the smaller adjoining CURSUS ; and we also see that the barrows, within the area of the larger CURSUS, were not placed there as *metæ*, (as in the Roman CIRCUS,) for there are none within the area of the smaller CURSUS. They probably stood on that ground long before the formation of this course, and being between the bank and the end, could not have impeded the races, as I can never suppose that the chariots passed *over* the bank : they might, perhaps, have started from this end ; and in that case the bank would prove no impediment to their career.

The plan, both of the large and small CURSUS, corresponds so much with that of the Roman CIRCUS, that I feel inclined to think, that the formation of these on our Wiltshire downs, took place after the settlement of the Romans in our island, and that they cannot be deemed of British origin.

Quitting STONEHENGE, with its appendant antiquities, and pursuing the road to our quarters at Amesbury, we find three *tumuli* situate between the avenue and the turnpike road. No. 24 is a very flat barrow, in which were the skeletons of an adult and a child, deposited in a very shallow cist, and which had been disturbed by a prior opening. No. 25 is a wide bowl-shaped barrow, in which we found, within a shallow cist, a skeleton with its head towards the north, and a drinking cup by its right side, and near it a neatly formed pin or needle of bone. No. 26 is situated on the borders of the turnpike road, and produced a large interment of burned bones on the floor, with a cone of jet, two oblong beads of the same substance, eighteen of amber, and a very small cone of the same.

From hence the road to Amesbury leads us on the edge of the Duke of Queensberry's park, through an ancient earthen work, commonly called VESPASIAN's camp, which shall be described in my next Iter.

ITER II. VESPASIAN'S CAMP. This extensive work has been generally supposed to be Roman, and has, as well as the neighbouring camp of YARNBURY, been attributed by STUKELEY to the Emperor VESPASIAN. That this great General occupied one or both of them, during his conflicts with the Belgæ, is not unlikely; but that he constructed either of them, is very improbable, as they bear no resemblance whatever to the camps formed by the Romans. This was originally the strong-hold of those numerous Britons who inhabited the plains around STONEHENGE, an asylum in times of danger, for their wives, children, and cattle; such as our experience has taught us existed all over our downs, and especially near those districts selected by the Britons for their residence. Such we find at Yarnbury, Amesbury, and Everley, in this immediate neighbourhood, and such we find dispersed all over our county. These camps were afterwards taken possession of by the succeeding nations of Romans, Danes, and Saxons, as occasion and necessity required; and to the more modern conquerors we chiefly may attribute the immense ramparts and outworks added to the original and more simple works of the Britons.

This camp occupies the apex of a hill, surrounded on two sides, east and south, by the river Avon; it comprehends within its area thirty-nine acres, extends in length from south to north, and terminates in a narrow rounded angle at the latter point. It was surrounded by a single *vallum*, which has been much mutilated on the east side in forming the pleasure grounds of Amesbury park. The ramparts on the western side towards STONEHENGE, are very bold and perfect. It appears to have had two entrances, north and south; the former still remains perfect, and undoubted. The area is planted and fancifully disposed in avenues, walks, &c. near the principal one of which, and on the highest ground, is the appearance of a barrow, but much disfigured in its form.

From this camp, I shall direct my steps to the gap between the old and new King's barrows, near the former of which is a solitary *tumulus*, No. 27, which appeared to have had a prior opening, and to have contained originally, the skeletons of two adults, and two children. Round the arm of one of the former was an ornamented bracelet of brass, which the labourers unfortunately trod upon, before they perceived it, and broke it into three pieces, but it has been repaired, and preserved in our Museum.

On approaching the CURSUS, we find a numerous continuation of barrows, flanking the southern side of it; the first of which is No. 28, and one of those opened by Lord Pembroke, in the year 1722, as well as No. 29, of which I shall copy the account given by STUKELEY, in his description of STONEHENGE, page 44.

" In the year 1723, by Thomas Earl of Pembroke's order, I begun upon a barrow north of STONEHENGE, in that group south of the CURSUS. It is one of the double barrows there, and the more easterly and lower of the two; likewise somewhat less. It was reasonable to believe, this was the sepulture of a man and his wife; and that the lesser was the female; and so it proved, at least a daughter. We made a large cut on the top, from east to west, and after the turf was taken off, we came to the layer of chalk, then to fine garden mould. About three feet below the surface was a layer of flints, humouring the convexity of the barrow. These flints are gathered from the surface of the downs in some places, especially where it has been ploughed. This being about a foot thick, rested on a layer of soft mould another foot, in which was enclosed an urn full of bones. The urn was of unbaked clay, of a dark reddish colour, and crumbled into pieces. It had been rudely wrought with small mouldings round the verge, and other circular channels on the outside, with several indentures between, made with a pointed tool, (see Plate XXXII. where I have drawn all things found in this barrow.) The bones had been burned, and crowded all together in a little heap, not so much as a hat crown would contain. The collar-bone, and one side of the under-jaw, are graved in their true magnitude. It appears to have been a girl of about 14 years old, by their bulk, and the great quantity of female ornaments mixed with the bones, all which we gathered. Beads of all sorts, and in great number, of glass of divers colours, most yellow, one black; many single, many in long pieces notched between, so as to resemble a string of beads, and these were generally of a blue colour. There were many of amber, of all shapes and sizes; flat squares, long squares, round, oblong, little and great. Likewise many of earth, of different shapes, magnitude, and colour; some little and white, many large and flattish like a button, others like a pully; but all had holes to run a string through, either through their diameter, or sides. Many of the button sort seem to have been covered with metal, there being a rim worked in them, wherein to turn the edge of the covering. One of these was covered with a thin film of pure gold. These were the young lady's ornaments; and all had undergone the fire, so that what would easily consume, fell to pieces as soon as handled; much of the amber was burned half through. This person was a heroine, for we found the head of her javelin in brass. At bottom are two holes for the pins that fastened it to the staff. Besides, there was a sharp bodkin, round at one end, square at the other, where it went into a handle. I still preserve whatever is permanent of these trinkets; but we recomposed the ashes of the illustrious defunct, and covered them with earth, leaving visible marks at top, of the barrow having been opened, to dissuade any other from again disturbing them; and this was our practice in all the rest."

" Then we opened the next barrow to it, enclosed in the same ditch, which we supposed the husband or father of this lady. At fourteen inches deep, the mould being mixed with chalk, we came to the entire skeleton of a man; the skull and all the bones exceedingly rotten, and perished through length of time; though this was a barrow of the latest sort, as we conjecture. The body lay north and south, the head to the north."

Not dissuaded by the external appearances, and convinced by experience that all interments found near the surface were subsequent deposits, Mr. CUNNINGTON, in 1803, explored the second *tumulus*, by making a section rather to the south of the centre, when at the depth of six feet, he came to the floor of the barrow, which was covered with ashes; and on digging still further to the south, he found a fine oblong cist, about eighteen inches deep, fifteen-inches wide, and two feet long; and in it a complete interment of burned bones, and with them six beads apparently of horn, four of which were perforated; the other two were circular, and rather flat, but all appeared as though they had been burned. Dr. STUKELEY made the same observation respecting the articles found in the other barrow; but he must have been mistaken as to the amber, for we know that fire would entirely consume it.

No. 30. A beautiful bell-shaped barrow, and the largest of this group. It measures in diameter from ditch to ditch one hundred and thirty-one feet, and fifteen feet in elevation. The superior size and beauty of this *tumulus* particularly excited our curiosity, and raised our expectations of success; but alas! after immense labour in throwing out the earth, to the depth of fifteen feet, we found only a simple interment of burned bones, unaccompanied by any urn, arms, or trinkets; the relicts were piled up in a little heap upon the floor where the body had been burned, and close to a small circular cist or *cinerarium*, which contained black ashes, intermixed with some small fragments of bone. No. 31, a bowl-shaped barrow, one hundred and four feet in base diameter, and seventy-one and a half in elevation, produced on its floor an interment of burned bones, with a small spear head: and No. 32, a fine bell-shaped barrow, contained only a simple interment of burned bones. No. 33, is a kind of

Druid Barrow, presenting an area of seventy-eight feet diameter, surrounded by a fine *vallum* without the ditch, but having no elevation, as usual, in the centre. Deprived of this index to the place of interment, we expected much trouble in finding it; but our workmen luckily hit on the very spot; and at the depth of two feet, found a circular cist, containing a deposit of burned bones, together with a great many beads. Some of them were pully beads of glass, two of stone, another of a transparent horn-like substance; but the most were of amber, and much decayed. No. 34 has had a prior opening; and in No. 35 we could not find the interment. No. 36. The contents of this barrow, in some degree, recompensed us for our disappointment in the two last. It produced three human skeletons, laid from north to south, and immediately one over the other; the first about two feet deep; the second on a level with the adjoining soil. Close to the right side of the head of this last skeleton was a drinking cup, and with it a considerable quantity of something that appeared like decayed leather. Six feet lower lay the third, with which was found the drinking cup, engraved in Tumuli Plate XVI. When throwing out the bones of this skeleton, we had a strong proof how well they are preserved when deposited deep in the chalk, as they would bear being thrown for a considerable distance without breaking: the teeth were perfectly white, and not one of them unsound; but the most remarkable circumstance was, finding a piece of the skull, about five inches broad, that had been apparently sawn off, for I do not think that any knife could have cut it off in the manner in which this was done. No. 37. In this barrow we found only a large oblong cist, full of black ashes, and a few burned human bones; and in No. 38, after much labour, we missed the interment. No. 39 is a bowl-shaped *tumulus*, adjoining the south side of the cursus: it is seventy-eight feet in diameter, and at this time nearly seven feet in elevation, although it has been some years under tillage. This interesting barrow had experienced a prior, but a partial opening, and one skeleton, with a drinking cup, had been disturbed. On reaching the floor, we discovered another skeleton, lying with its head due north, which, from the size of the bones, and the great quantity of beads attending the interment, we conceived to have been that of a female; and several of these being found near the neck, confirmed, in some degree, this opinion. Close to the head stood a kind of bason, neatly ornamented round the verge, but unfortunately broken into several pieces. On removing the head, we were much surprised to find that it rested upon a drinking cup, that had been placed at the feet of another skeleton, and which was interred in an oblong cist two feet deep, and lying also from north to south. With the drinking cup was a spear head of flint, and a singular stone.

In this *tumulus*, three persons were interred; the primary deposit must, of course, have been the skeleton lying in a cist, excavated within the chalk ; the second was probably the wife of this person, lying with her head at his feet; and the third and last, might have been their son.　The drinking cup found at the feet of the primary interment, is large, and holds more than a quart; it resembles in form and manufacture many of the others; is made out of poor clay, intermixed with bits of chalk ; yet it is profusely ornamented, and in a different style to any we have yet seen.　How such a multitude of indentations could be put on the surface, while the clay retained its flexibility, is surprising; for it is very clear, that these ornaments were put on singly, and most probably by a bone instrument.　The sharpness and nicety to which this spear head of flint, as well as the arrows of the same material, have been chipped, must also strike the attention of every observer.　Yet we know them to have been made use of, by all barbarians, for destructive purposes.　Neither must the aforementioned stone be passed over unnoticed ; it is very neatly polished, feels silky, and, at first sight, looks something like fossil wood: it is striped irregularly, with dark green and white, and its proportions will be ascertained by the annexed engraving, PLATE XVII. which represents both the spear head and stone, of their natural size.　Mr. CUNNINGTON thinks it is of that species of stone called by KIRWAN, ligniformed asbestos, and that it may have been considered by the Britons as of high value, from its supposed virtues.

No. 40, in point of size, may be called the monarch of the plain, being evidently the largest barrow upon it; and its history still remains veiled in obscurity. The first time we opened it by a very large section, and examined well the floor; but though we perceived symptoms of cremation, in charred wood, &c. we could not discover the primary interment.　Nor were our subsequent researches more favourable, and we still remain in ignorance.　Perhaps some future antiquary may be more fortunate ; and such is the caprice of ancient sepulture, that the deposit may be found near the top, as in the instance of our flint barrow at Kingston Deverill, (p. 47.)　No. 41 produced an interment of burned bones.　No. 42. Nearly opposite the last mentioned barrow, but on the south side of the turnpike road, is a neat circular *tumulus*, sixty-six feet in diameter, and six feet in elevation, which was opened in 1803, and produced within a circular cist, an interment of burned bones, and a brass pin with part of its handle, deposited in a neat and perfect urn; the latter of which is engraved in TUMULI PLATE XVI.　No. 43 and 44.　These two barrows are included within the boundaries of the CURSUS, and very near the western end of it. In opening the first of these, our labourers discovered, at the depth of three

P. Crocker del.

Jᵉ Baſire Sc.

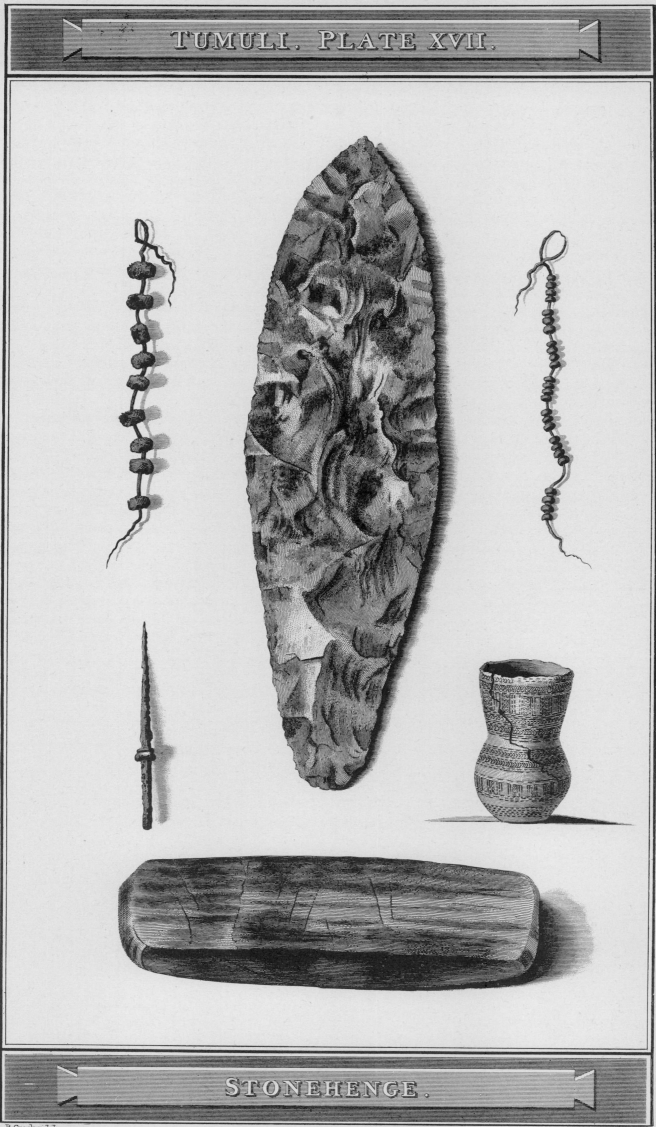

STONEHENGE.

P. Crocker del.

Jᵉ Baſire Sc.

Publiſhed for W. Miller, Albemarle Street, London, Janʸ 1.1811.

feet, the skeleton of an adult, with a drinking cup, and on the floor of the barrow, another of a child. We afterwards, in a shallow cist, found the third skeleton of a man, lying with his head to the north, and close to it, on the right side, was a curious pebble, and under his left hand was a dagger of brass. The pebble is kidney-formed, of the sardonyx kind, striated transversely with alternate spaces, that give it the appearance of belts; besides these *striæ*, it is spotted all over with very small white specks, and after dipping it into water, it assumes a sea green colour. In the adjoining barrow, No. 44, we found only a simple interment of burned bones. The next barrows that occur in our Iter westward, are three in number, placed nearly in a line parallel to each other. No. 45, 46, 47, all of which proved uninteresting in their contents. The first and last produced simple interments of burned bones; the second, a rude urn with cremation. No. 48, a Druid barrow, contained an interment of burned bones, with a brass pin. No. 49 is a long barrow. No. 50 is a circular bowl-shaped barrow, in the examination of which, we experienced much perplexity, although not uncommon, owing to the Britons having adopted so many modes of burial. At the depth of five feet, we found a regular *stratum* of flints, intermixed with black vegetable mould; on removing which, we came to the floor of the barrow, in which some excavations had been made, and channels formed. One of these was connected with the cist, which contained a skeleton lying from south to north; in another channel, we found a large branch of a stag's horn; and in a little corner, we took out a shovel-full of bones, intermixed with earth, which were broken almost as small as chaff. Near the feet of the skeleton lay a considerable quantity of very small bones of birds or mice. The day being far advanced, we did not pursue all the channels, and it is very probable that this barrow may contain other skeletons. No. 51, a fine bell-shaped barrow, ninety-five feet in diameter, and seven feet in elevation. At the depth of four feet and a half in the native soil, viz. eleven feet and a half from the summit, we found two skeletons with their heads laid towards the north; the one, an adult, the other, a young person, not more than about twelve years of age. No. 52 and 53. We were unsucessful in our attempts on these two large barrows. In the former, we perceived several marks of very intense fire, with some earth, quite black, and some burned to a brick colour. In the latter, near the centre, we found a circular cist containing only ashes, but missed the primary interment. An unusual quantity of small bones, probably of birds, was dispersed about the barrow. No. 54. A fine bell-shaped barrow, eighty feet in diameter, and seven feet in elevation, produced on the floor and near the centre, a circular cist, about eighteen inches wide, and one foot deep, full of wood ashes, and a few fragments of burned bones. About two feet to the north of the above was another cist, of an oblong form, much larger and deeper than the other, which contained an interment of burned bones, piled up in a heap in the centre of the cist. The next barrow, No. 55, was opened some years ago, and produced only a simple interment of burned bones. A little on the other side of the Devizes road is a mound, which being only a land mark, is not numbered. In the adjoining large flat barrow, No. 56, we discovered a cist, that had been previously investigated, but on opening it, the workmen found an arrow head of flint near the top.

I shall now direct my steps back towards Amesbury, over a beautiful down, abounding with *tumuli* of various descriptions. The first group that occurs, is situated near the northern limits of our map, and is numbered from 57 to 65, and consists of four Druid, and five circular barrows. As they all bore the marks of prior opening, I did not attempt any of them : some had been explored a few years ago, by Mr. CUNNINGTON, at a time when no idea was entertained of prosecuting his researches to the present extent, and when no very regular account was kept of his discoveries.* We now come to three large barrows on the declivity of the hill, 66, 67, 68. No. 66 is a low barrow, in which were fragments of a human skull, of a large sepulchral urn, and a drinking cup. No. 67 has a very irregular and mutilated surface : each seem to have had a prior opening. No. 68 is a pond barrow. On the opposite hill is a beautiful group of *tumuli*, thickly strewed over a rich and verdant down. Their perfect appearance raised our expectations of success, and the attendance of many of my friends from Salisbury, and a beautiful day, enlivened our prospects ; but we had again sad cause to exclaim *Fronti nulla fides*, Trust not to outward appearances. No arrow heads were found to mark the profession of the British hunter ; no gilded dagger to point out to us the chieftain of the clan ; nor any necklace of amber or jet, to distinguish the British female, or to present to her fair descendants, who honoured us with their presence on this occasion : a few rude urns marked the antiquity and poverty of the Britons who fixed on this spot as their mausoleum. Unproductive, however, as were the contents of these

* On referring to Mr. CUNNINGTON's papers, I find some account of these barrows. The Druid barrows had been partially opened : in one, he found an interment, with a broken dart or lance of brass ; and in another, the scattered fragments of burned bones, a few small amber rings, beads of the same, and of jet, with the point of a brass dart. In opening the large barrow, No. 57, he found in a cist, at the depth of twelve feet from the surface, the remainder (as he thought) of the brass dart, and with it a curious whetstone, some ivory tweezers, and some decayed articles of bone.

barrows, it may not be uninteresting to the antiquary, whom either chance or curiosity leads across these fine plains, to know their history.

No. 69 had been opened in former times by Mr. CUNNINGTON. No. 70 contained an interment of burned bones, deposited in an irregular cist. No. 71. A Druid barrow of the second class, or rather bowl-shaped within a ditch, produced the skeleton of a child near the surface, and lower down, two rude sepulchral urns, the one above the other, each containing burned bones. No. 72 had been opened before by Mr. CUNNINGTON, and produced a sepulchral urn. No. 73, a Druid barrow of the second class, contained near the surface, a skeleton with four wooden beads near its neck; and it appeared, that another interment of burned bones had been taken out. No. 74 is also a Druid barrow, but the elevated mound was not in the centre of the area. It produced a *cinerarium*, and ashes in a cist. No. 75 had been opened before, as well as No. 76 and 77, and in 78 we could find nothing. No. 79 had also experienced a prior opening. No. 80 is not sepulchral. In 81 we discovered a large rude urn, containing an interment of burned bones. No. 82 had a *cinerarium*, and two simple interments of burned bones, just under the surface. No. 83 contained a sepulchral urn, with a small brass pin. To the south of No. 80, on the opposite hill, is a Druid barrow (not inserted in the plan), which produced a large rude urn without an interment.

In the same easterly direction, but nearer to the CURSUS, is another fine group of barrows, equally inviting to the eye, but nearly as unproductive as the preceding.

No. 84 is the largest barrow in this group, and has been ploughed over. In making our section, we found pieces of stag's horns, pottery, and the remains of a skeleton and drinking cup, and two knives; but the primary interment was a skeleton, with its legs gathered up, and hands placed under its head. No. 85 contained originally an interment of burned bones, within a cist, but had been opened. No. 86 had also experienced the same investigation; it had a circular cist, and a *cinerarium*. No. 87, a Druid barrow of the second class, contained fragments of an urn and burned bones, in a shallow circular cist. No. 88. A similar, but finer barrow, produced near the surface, just under the turf, the fragments of a rude urn and burned bones, and lower down, a sepulchral urn reversed over a deposit of burned bones. No. 89 has been in tillage: it contained a skeleton, placed in a long circular cist, with its head towards the north. No. 90, in tillage, produced a large urn rudely ornamented, and inverted over a deposit of burned bones. No. 91 contained an interment of burned bones, deposited on the floor of the barrow; and beneath it was a deep cist, containing abundance of ashes and charred wood, intermixed with particles of bone. No. 92. In digging down to the floor of this barrow, we discovered the remains of a skeleton, with fragments of a funeral urn, burned bones, and some enormous pieces of stag's horns. Within a cist, excavated beneath the floor of the barrow, lay a skeleton with its legs gathered up, and head placed towards the north. No. 93 contained, near the top, an interment of burned bones, in a rude broken urn, with a small cup; also, the remains of a skeleton, charred wood, stag's horns, and flint apparently prepared for war-like instruments. The primary deposit was a skeleton, with its head placed towards the south-east, accompanied by a fine drinking cup, richly ornamented, and in the highest state of preservation, which I have had engraved in TUMULI PLATE XVIII. half the size of the original, in order to shew the pattern more conspicuously.

No. 94 being sown with wheat, could not be investigated. No. 95, 96, 97, 98, and 99, proved totally uninteresting, and contained, chiefly, interments of burned bones. On the opposite hill, eastward, is another group of nine barrows. No. 100 contained a simple interment of burned bones within a circular cist. No. 101, a similar interment, accompanied with two black rings of some bituminous substance, and one pully bead. No. 102, an interment of burned bones in a cist, with remnants of the cloth in which the relicts were enveloped. No. 103, a deep circular cist with ashes. No. 104 is a large flat circular barrow, which had been opened, and must have proved both interesting and productive to those who first investigated it. In the course of our examination, we found the bones of several skeletons, fragments of urns, and a rude instrument made from a stag's horn; there was also a large and deep cist. No. 105 and 106 had been opened by others. No. 107 produced a small interment of burned bones, with a pin of bone at top, and under it, a pile of ashes in a cist. No. 108 is a pond barrow.

On a rising ground to the north, and a little beyond the barn, is another group of seven barrows. No. 109, 110, and 111, had been investigated: on opening the first, we found the soil intermixed with the turf, which clearly indicated a prior opening. We were deterred from making any attempt on the second barrow, by a great cavity in its apex; and we found the third had been examined. No. 112 is a double barrow, rising towards the east, and somewhat resembling a long barrow, but ditched all around. The lowest part had been opened, and contained an interment of burned bones. In the

Tumulus 93.

P. Crocker del.

J⁹ Baſire Sc.

Publiſhed for W. Miller, Albemarle Street, London, Janʸ 1. 1811.

other mound, we found an interment of burned bones, secured by a linen cloth under a rude urn. No. 113 had been examined before, but we found in it fragments of an urn and skeleton. No. 114 contained a deposit of burned bones and ashes, in a deep cist. No. 115 contained also a similar interment, but had been opened before. I had for a long time viewed these two last groups of barrows with satisfaction, and anticipated much pleasure and success, in opening them. I had also reserved them for the gratification of some of my friends in the neighbourhood, who attended our operations: judge then of my mortification and disappointment, in finding that many of them, though with the most even, and apparently maiden surface, had been already investigated, and robbed of their contents; and the remainder either totally unproductive, or uninteresting. Poor indeed were the Britons who once inhabited these plains, unlike their rich neighbours, whose relicts were deposited in the vicinity, and particularly on the southern side of Stonehenge; but though disappointment attended our researches in this district, truth is obtained, and the history of these numerous barrows remains no longer involved in obscurity. Adjoining the cursus, and nearly in a line with it, are a few small barrows. No. 116 had been opened before. No. 117 contained a small rude urn, with an interment of burned bones. No. 118 is a small long barrow, and produced a deposit of burned bones and black ashes in a neat circular cist. No. 119 contained an interment of burned bones in a small cist. No. 120 is a pond barrow; and No. 121 produced a rude urn reversed over a deposit of burned bones.

From hence, I proceed towards the vale of the river Avon, where, adjoining the public road, we find the interesting remains of a spacious British town or village, called Durrington, or Long Walls. The first name is evidently derived from the Celtic word *dur*, water, and applies to the situation of the adjoining village of Durrington near the river. The site of this ancient settlement is decidedly marked by a circular embankment, partly natural, and partly artificial, which shelters it from the south-west winds: the view it commands in front, is delightful, facing the rich and well wooded vale, and the lofty range of Haradon and adjoining hills. Having been for many years in tillage, its form is much mutilated; but from what remains, it appears to have been of a circular form, and to have had a *vallum* all around it on the high ground, but not on the east side near the water. We picked up a great deal of pottery within the area of the works.

On viewing the country round Stonehenge, and remarking with surprise, the numerous memorials of the dead, so thickly scattered over these extensive plains; we are led naturally to inquire, " Where were the habitations of the living?" This question can be answered in part, but not so fully as I could wish, by the discoveries we have made in the British villages, on Winterbourn Stoke, Durrington, and Lake downs; many others would, probably, have been found in the environs of Stonehenge, had not the soil been turned up by the plough. We are fortunate, however, in having rescued so many from oblivion, and to have thrown aside the thick veil which, notwithstanding the active researches of a Stukeley, has, till this period, obscured them. On the south side of Durrington walls, is an elevated mound, bearing the appearance of a barrow, No. 122, in which we dug to the depth of eleven feet, but found no sepulchral marks whatever. A little further on the right of the road leading to Amesbury, we see the mutilated remains of an enormous Druid barrow, No. 123; and still further, on the same side of the road, a very singular *tumulus*, No. 124, appearing like three barrows rising from one large base, but certainly a long barrow. It stands from south-west to north-east, and has its wide end towards the west: on the small end, and also on the centre, are mounds resembling two circular barrows. We opened that on the small end, and found only a few ashes and charred wood; but in the central mound we discovered, near the top, a skeleton and a drinking cup, both of which had been disturbed. On reaching the floor of the long barrow, we found a circular cist like a little well, but it contained no interment; from this well-like cist, a tunnel, like a chimney, ascended nearly to the top. I imagine that, as in most of our long barrows, the primary interment would be found at the broad end. In this *tumulus* we have rather a singular instance of a circular barrow being raised upon a long barrow. No. 125, in tillage, appears to have been a barrow of very large proportions, and there are two others in the corn fields nearer the park, No. 126, 127, which we have not attempted to open. There are also near them, under the hill, some appearances of earthen works much mutilated, which I cannot account for: I once thought they formed part of a circle, but I cannot speak with any decision about them.

Before I conclude this Iter, let me call the attention of my readers to the annexed map of Stonehenge, and its environs, in which the hills, roads, antiquities, and barrows are accurately laid down, from actual measurement. In it you will find a striking picture of ancient times. You will see the spot selected by the earliest inhabitants of our island for their residence; you will behold that stupendous monument of antiquity, Stonehenge, the building set apart for their civil or religious assemblies: you will perceive its connexion, by

means of the AVENUE, with the CURSUS, a spot appropriated to their games, and races ; you will recognize also in the camp vulgarly attributed to the Emperor Vespasian, the strong-hold of the Britons, or the asylum for their families and herds in times of danger : at Durrington, and on Winterbourn Stoke Downs you will see the habitations of the Britons, with the lines of communication, from one village to another ; and in the numerous barrows dispersed over this extensive plain, you will distinguish the simple memorials of the mighty dead. In short, you will have clearly traced to your imagination's eye a most impressive history of our ancient Britons.

Yet I do not wish you to suppose that all these antiquities can boast the same remote æra of antiquity ; for in them we may clearly distinguish the marks of two distinct people, the Britons, and their conquerors, the Romans. To the first I would attribute the construction of STONEHENGE, and the raising of the barrows ; to the latter, the CURSUS,* and the principal remains of the villages ; for although we find in them fragments of rude unbaked pottery, yet the well burned Roman earthen ware preponderates : the villages also on Stoke down bear rather a more regular form in their plan, than we usually meet within the original British settlements. That STONEHENGE existed *before* some of the barrows adjoining it, has been clearly proved by the chippings of stone discovered within them : and that the custom of burying under *tumuli* ceased on our downs✝ after the arrival of the Romans, is, I think, also proved, by our never having found a single urn either well baked, or turned with the lathe, in any one barrow. At the period when these villages were inhabited by a mixed population of Britons and Romans, (whom I call Romanized Britons,) they certainly had dropped the custom of burying under barrows, and having no index to direct our spades, we have never been fortunate in discovering the cemeteries of the people who inhabited these British villages.‡ Such a discovery would be a grand and most satisfactory *desideratum*. for, instead of the rude and coarse urn of British pottery, we should then be gratified with specimens of that elegant earthen-ware for which the Romans (copying the Græcian models)

---

* The cursus so resembles in form the Roman circus, that I am inclined to think its plan was introduced by that nation.

✝ When I say that the custom of burying under *tumuli* appeared to cease on the mixture of the Romans with the Britons, I allude only to my own county : for Mr. Douglas, in his *Nænia Britannica,* has clearly proved that the same custom was continued in Kent later than the seventh century.

‡ If we refer on the map to the situations of the numerous British villages already described, we shall find only a few scattered barrows around them, a proof that other modes of interment must have been adopted by the inhabitants of them.

X X

were so justly celebrated. That, even in the rudest times, other modes of burial, besides the barrow, were adopted, we have an interesting proof in an interment which was lately discovered above Durrington Walls, by a shepherd, who in pitching the fold, found his iron bar impeded in the ground : curiosity led him to explore the cause, which proved to be a large sarsen stone, covering the interment of a skeleton, with whose remains the articles engraved in Tumuli Plate XIX. were deposited, viz. a spear head chipped from a flint, a small hone or whetstone, a cone and ring of jet like a pully, and two little buttons of marl or chalk, all bespeaking an interment of the earliest date.

It may also be naturally expected that, after quoting the various descriptions and conjectures of others respecting Stonehenge, I should give some opinions of my own. This I shall do with diffidence, and lament that the history of this celebrated " wonder of the west" will most probably ever remain unknown. I cannot for a moment hesitate in declaring it to be neither Roman, Saxon, nor Danish. We learn from the holy Scriptures that the earliest memorials were of stone ; and we find to this day single, double, and triple upright stones, as well as numerous circles dispersed about our dominions : we then find some attempt at architecture in the cromlech and kistvaen, in both of which we see immense stones laid incumbent upon others that are upright ; whether these gave the idea of the imposts at Stonehenge, or *vice versâ*, will-be a difficult matter to determine ; at all events I consider Stonehenge of a much more modern date than Abury, where there are no imposts, and no marks of working on the stones : but in the former we perceive a regular plan, a great degree of symmetry, and great knowledge in mathematics. We know also that many stone monuments exist on the Continent, and in that part of it, from whence our island probably received its earliest population, viz. Gallia Celtica.* I have before stated my opinion, that our earliest inhabitants

* The most remarkable of these monuments, and such as must excite our curiosity in the highest degree, is situated in the hamlet of Carnac, near Vannes and Auray, on the western coast of Bretagne, and in the department of Morbihan, in France. Monsieur Cambray, in his *Monumens Celtiques*, has given a very detailed and animated description of this interesting relict of antiquity. He tells us that some detached stones on the hills, and sand banks, announce the approach to this grand theatre, which consists of an immense heap of rude unhewn stones (amounting to four thousand or more) standing in an upright position on a sandy plain near the sea coast. They are ranged in eleven straight lines, which lines are separated from each other by a space of thirty or thirty-three feet, and the distance from one stone to another varies from twelve to fifteen feet. The highest of these stones measures twenty-two feet out of ground ; the width varies ; one of them is twenty-two feet high, twelve feet wide, and six feet thick, and many of them are moveable ; these stones present the most singular aspect : they stand alone on

P. Crocker del.

J? Bafire Sc

Publifhed for W. Miller, Albemarle Street, London, Jan.y 1, 1811.

DURRINGTON WALLS.

were Celts, who naturally introduced with them their own buildings, customs, rites, and religious ceremonies ; and to them I attribute the erection of STONE-HENGE, and the greater part of the sepulchral memorials that still continue to render its environs so truly interesting to the antiquary and historian.

The general title of DRUIDICAL has been given to all these stone monuments: and some of my readers may be surprized that I have not adopted it. That the Druids existed in our island, at a very early period, and officiated as priests, there can be no doubt, but as the learned Mr. Bryant, in his Mythology observes, " Under the sanction of their names we shelter ourselves, whenever we are ignorant and bewildered." And Mr. Borlase, with equal justness remarks, " that the work of STONEHENGE must have been that of a great and powerful nation, not of a limited community of priests ; the grandeur of the design, the distance of the materials, the tediousness with which all such massive works are necessarily attended, all shew, that such designs were the fruits of peace and religion."

ITER. III. Having described STONEHENGE, and the antiquities immediately connected with it, I shall now conduct my readers to the more distant ground allotted to this Station.

Following the turnpike road, that leads from Amesbury, through the vale of Shrewton to Heytesbury and Warminster, we find, at a farm-house in the little village of Rolston, a small square work with strong ramparts, and bearing marks of considerable antiquity. Ascending from thence to the high land, the greater part of which is under cultivation, we again encounter a numerous assemblage of barrows, formed into different groups, and assuming a variety of shapes. Of these I cannot give so detailed or satisfactory an account as I could wish. Some were opened by Mr. CUNNINGTON, during the early period of his re-searches, when no very regular account was kept of his discoveries, and not the most distant thought entertained of laying the result of them before the public. *

In one of the Druid barrows, which is intersected by a boundary ditch between the parishes of Rolston and Winterbourn Stoke, he discovered an interment of

---

an extensive plain, attended only by the sand that supports them, and the vault of heaven that surrounds them : not an inscription to explain, not an analogy to inform : the men whom you call, the traveller whom you interrogate, gaze at it, and either turn away their head, or recount follies. They recall to our memory those times which neither our calculation nor our history can ever attain.

* His ingenious researches are now, alas! at an end. Death, has deprived me of a worthy and intelligent coadjutor. He was the *Alpha* of this publication ; Fate forbad that he should be the *Omega*.

burned bones, and the fragments of a large coarse urn, which I mention, because the circumstance of finding a large sepulchral urn, within a Druid barrow, very rarely occurs.   In a small circular barrow, about three feet in elevation, attached to one of the groups nearer Durrington down, was found an interment of burned bones, accompanied with a beautiful little cup, which we had the good fortune to preserve entire, and which is engraved of the same size as the original in TUMULI PLATE XVIII. It is of a pale lead colour, and has been bent and cracked, probably by the heat of the funereal pile.

In the eastern part of Rolston field, is a group of circular *tumuli* of different dimensions, two of which Mr. CUNNINGTON opened some years ago.   The first is seventy feet in base diameter, and six in elevation.   At the depth of two feet and a half, he found three skeletons lying in different directions, on which discovery, he doubted whether he should make any further trial, but conceiving there was an unusual quantity of marle stones in this barrow, he pursued his researches, and after digging to the vast depth of twelve feet from the top of the barrow, six of which were in the native soil, he came to the primary interment, consisting of a skeleton, lying with its head to the north, and the legs and thighs drawn up as close as possible to the body.   On the right side of the head, lay a small black stone hatchet, [TUMULI PLATE XX.] which, added to the extraordinary depth at which the body was deposited, proves this to have been a very ancient sepulchre.   The other is a handsome bell-shaped barrow, one hundred feet in the base, and eleven feet and a half in elevation; but, notwithstanding a large section, we did not succeed in finding the interment.

As we pursue our ride northward, Shrewton windmill is a very conspicuous object to our left.   On erecting this building, the interment of a skeleton was discovered; it lay on its back; the brass articles engraved in TUMULI PLATE XX. were deposited by its left side, and the blade of an iron knife on its right; and between its legs was a drinking cup; but there was no appearance of a barrow.   Here we find an interment of a later æra, and of the same period as that before described on Rodmead down, p. 47, when the custom of gathering up the legs had ceased, and when the use of iron was more generally adopted; for in the early *tumuli*, none of that metal has ever been found.   After quitting the arable lands on this hill, we find an ancient ditch, running north-west and south-east over a fine piece of down; and in the first bottom, not far from a well-house, the signs of an irregular earthen work on the left; the bank and ditch then ascend the hill, making a sharp turn round a barrow, as if to avoid it from respect, and pursue their course nearly in a direct line, till they join OLD DITCH,

P. Crocker del.

J.º Basire Sc.

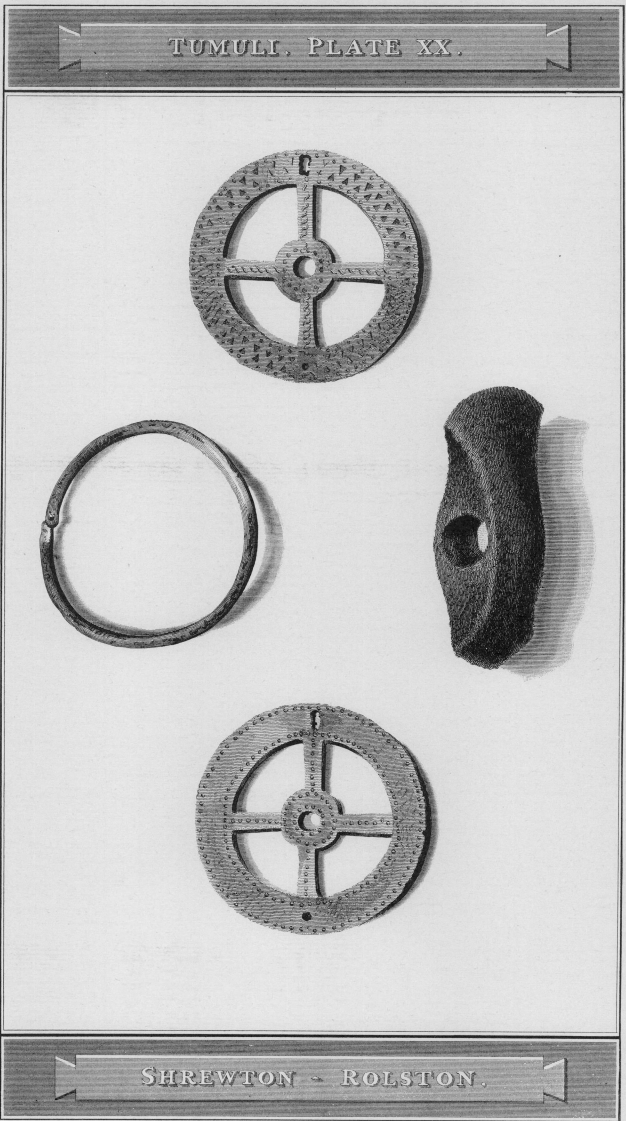

P. Crocker del.

J.º Basire Sc.

Published for W. Miller, Albemarle Street, London, Jan.ʸ 1.1811.

coming from Tilshead, which I have mentioned page 93. This ditch and bank, as in numerous other instances, seem to have formed a line of communication between the British villages already mentioned, on Winterbourn Stoke down, and another very extensive one on Elston down, near to which they pass, as my readers will perceive by the map of this station. This last British village occupies the summit of a beautiful down belonging to the parish of Elston, and owes its superior verdure to the ancient population which resided on it. A long avenue or street on the north side, leading to the village, the excavations for its huts, fragments of pottery, and all the usual concomitant *indicia*, evidently mark out the original occupation of this spot. This down leads us to the great road from Salisbury to Devizes, which once most probably was a British track-way. Crossing it near the twelfth mile-stone, and continuing upon it as far as the fourteenth, I then deviate to the right, and approach a large *tumulus*, called most appropriately ELL barrow, and still reserving its ancient British title of *Ell*, which signifies *conspicuous;* a title which it most justly deserves, for I know of no single object in this wild district, which so generally attracts the eye at a distance. Near this long barrow, we encounter a large and ancient bank and ditch, running nearly east and west, over a high ridge of land, and near it we again find its usual attendant, the British village: but though this bank points westerly towards the course of the others before mentioned, I could not find out its junction with either of them. It is called OLD DITCH in the Wiltshire map, but improperly ; as I have already stated where that ditch terminated. Close to the northern boundaries of it we begin to perceive traces of a British village, which continue in the most ostensible manner to the declivity of the hill facing Weddington wells, and occupy several acres of the richest down land I ever beheld. Adjoining these works is a little square intrenchment vulgarly called CHURCH DITCHES, with a regular entrance towards the east. Appearances of ancient population are still visible, though in a slighter degree, over Charleton down: the hills and vales are steep, and much intersected by each other, and the whole scenery is highly interesting to the antiquary, and the admirer of simple unadorned nature. On the northern side of this village, and on the brow of the opposite hill, we find several banks and ditches, one of which bears away in a north-east direction, to the great British town at CASTERLEY, the description of which must be reserved for a future Iter.

ITER IV. Starting once more from my head quarters at Amesbury, I shall direct my course towards KNIGHTON LONG BARROW, which, from its elevated

situation on a high ridge of land, rivals, if not surpasses, ELL BARROW in pre-
eminence of prospect.   The first object of our attention, near a clump of trees
called ROBIN HOOD BALL, is one of those ancient circles, which I have before
mentioned and described in the Heytesbury Station, p. 80.   This, like the
generality of them, is placed on an elevated and commanding situation, but has
this peculiarity, of having one circle within the other, with an entrance towards
the north.   We have to regret the great injury these circles have sustained by
the plough, as in their original state they must have been highly curious, and
are the more remarkable, from representing a double circle.

On the north-west side of this work are some barrows, one of which had been
opened before, but in exploring it our men turned out the fragments of burned
bones and a singular whetstone.   Lower down on the south are some other
barrows; in one of which, was found a brass dart or arrow head.   To the
east is a long barrow.   About a mile, to the south of Robin Hood Ball, and
on Knighton down, we find the undoubted remains of another small British
settlement, consisting of a square earthen work.   Its eastern side is bounded
by a bank and ditch, which taking a southern direction, intersect a Druid
barrow one hundred and thirty-two feet in diameter; another proof of the
prior antiquity of the *tumulus*.

Returning to the ridge, I continue my ride to another clump of trees called
BLACK BALL; and it is interesting on this spot to remark the actual progress of
nature in creating woods and forests; for on every side, except the south-west,
we see an increasing growth of young fir-trees, raised from the cones of their
parents which have been dispersed by the winds.   Nothing interesting occurs
between this spot, and Red Horn Turnpike, where the chalk hills terminate, and
form the boundary of a rich vale that separates the northern and the southern districts of our county.   Here I shall direct my course to the right, and follow the
same ridge-way, which, in a former Iter, I had ascended from JOAN A GORE'S
CROSS, and had examined as far as this turnpike.   The same interesting terrace,
the same rich view of the vale beneath, still continue to charm the eye, and arrest
the attention.   A few *tumuli* mark an ancient population adjoining it.   This
elevated trackway is still vulgarly called the PORT-WAY, and the RIDGE-WAY.
One of the barrows on the left side of it was opened by Mr. CUNNINGTON,
but he found no symptoms of interment, and only a broken glass bead: pottery
and coins are frequently dug up in the neighbourhood.   Continuing along the
ridge, we traverse an old bank and ditch, which steers southerly towards the
British village, described in my last Iter, and the verdure of the whole adjoin-

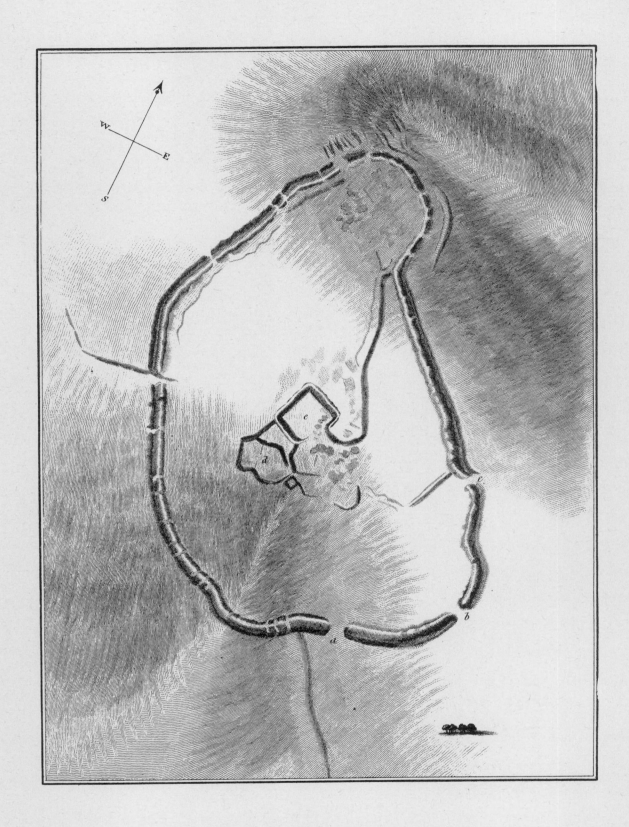

P. Crocker del.

J.º Basire Sc.

CASTERLEY CAMP.

Published for W. Miller, Albemarle Street, London, Janᵞ 1.1811.

ing downs seems to indicate the ancient residence of the Britons on these hills, though I could see no decided marks of any village. A little further, on the brow of a hill projecting towards the vale, are the vestiges of either an unfinished or a mutilated camp, called BROADBURY.* Proceeding a little further, I quit the ridgeway, and direct my course towards CASTERLEY CAMP. This earthen work bears the strongest marks of originality, and none of the modern signs of innovation. I consider it as a British town, but not so populous as either of those already noticed at STOCKTON and GROVELY. Here we find no deep or multiplied ramparts, but a simple ditch and *vallum* of no great elevation, enclosing an area of above sixty acres. The richness of its soil having induced the owner to devote it to tillage, many of the original works and excavations have been defaced, but we still in D. and E. recognize the works of the Britons; the former in its irregularity resembling others before noticed at STOCKTON and GROVELY: the other, E., by having the ditch *within* the *vallum* denoting probably a place appropriated to religious purposes. Many passages have been made through these works for the accommodation of waggons; it is therefore difficult to state the original entrances: I rather doubt if C. was one, but can speak, I think, confidently respecting A. and B., though we do not usually find two entrances so near to each other, and it would be reasonable to suppose there had been another entrance or exit at the northern end, where there are signs of some outworks, &c. The line of ramparts is most perfect and regular on the east side. On the south side, we may observe a bank and ditch issuing from the camp, which runs over the down, and bends towards the vale of Avon. The area of this camp contains above sixty-four acres; the circuit of the outer ditch is one mile and a quarter, and the depth of the *vallum* is twenty-eight feet. On the west side also, are the signs of another bank and ditch.

This camp from its elevation commands a very distant view; and upon minute investigation, will be found to be one of the most original and unaltered works of the British æra, which our county, amidst numerous antiquities of a similar nature, can produce.

On returning from CASTERLEY CAMP to my head quarters at Amesbury, I pursue a direct line to that conspicuous land-mark, Knighton long barrow: and find but little in that tract to arrest the attention of the antiquary. On a

* We often meet with the names of Bodbury, and Badbury, evidently derived from the British word *bod*, a dwelling; but in digging in the area of this camp, Mr. Cunnington, could not find any pottery, or other signs of residence.

piece of down to the south of Clarke's Penning, there is a large barrow, and near it an old bank and ditch with a few excavations; also a cluster of small *tumuli*, on the declivity of a hill. The barrows on Durrington down, over which our road leads us, having been already described, I shall now conclude my account of this Station, reserving for a future Iter the numerous antiquities which are situated in the southern district of Amesbury.

STATION VI. EVERLEY.

The remains of British antiquities having proved so abundant, and our subterraneous researches so productive in the neighbourhood of Stonehenge, I have thought proper to divide the Station of Amesbury, into two districts, the northern, and the southern. The former has been examined and completed; but as the Station of Everley, comprehending the tract of country between the river Avon, and the boundary line of our county, constitutes a more regular and natural junction with the northern part of the Amesbury district, I shall make Everley my Sixth Station, and, when completed, shall then return to the southern division of Amesbury, which will conduct me to the capital of the ancient Britons at Old Sarum, and the more modern county-town at Salisbury.

On leaving Amesbury, and deviating to the left from the great road leading through Andover to London, we see an almost uninterrupted succession of sepulchral memorials dispersed in numerous groups over the downs, in our track between Amesbury, and Everley. Here also we have rescued from oblivion the sites of many British villages which are still distinguishable over these widely extended plains. On the right is a high point of land called Haradon, and Beacon hill, which from its commanding view, has been fixed upon as one of the points in the general Survey of the kingdom now making by order of Government. Further on to our right we see the fortified hill of Chidbury, which is a most conspicuous land-mark from every part of the surrounding country

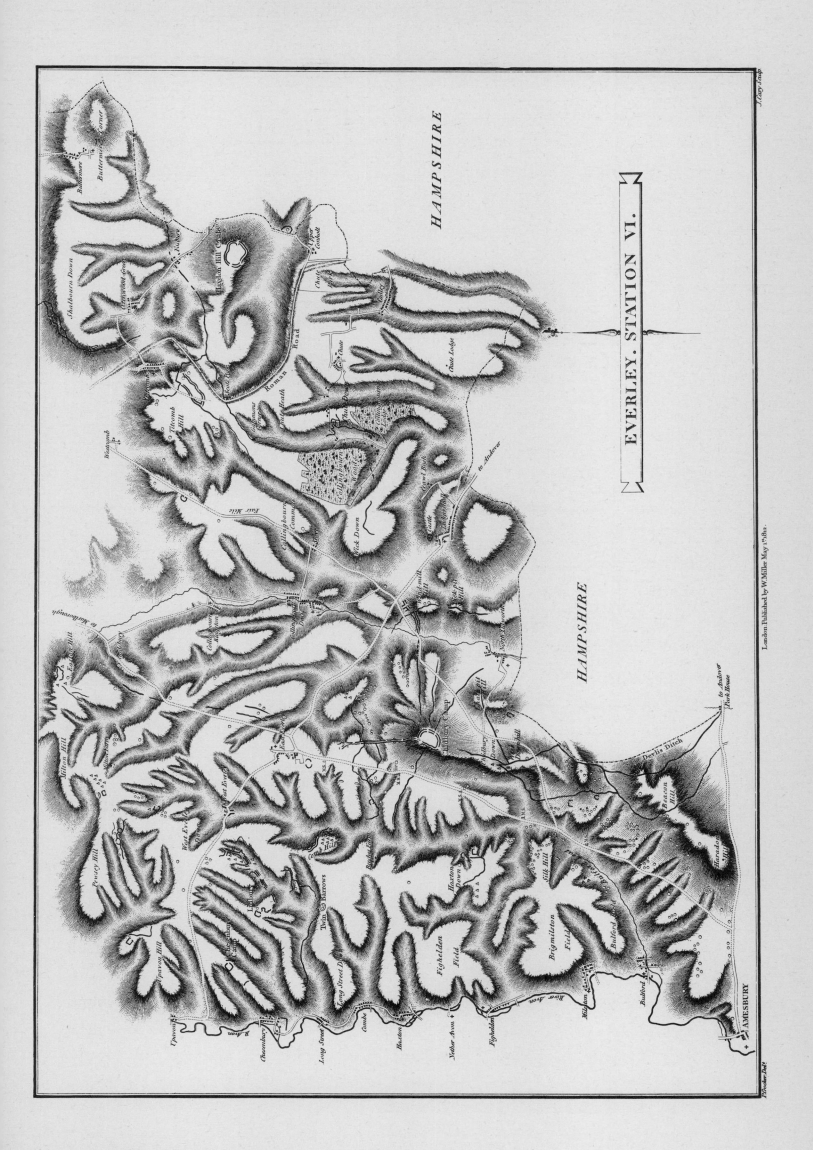

EVERLEY. STATION VI.

HAMPSHIRE

HAMPSHIRE

T.Foster Delt.

London. Published by W. Miller May 1st 1801.

J. Cary Sculp.

The first object which in this ride attracts our attention as antiquaries, is an ancient bank and ditch, which are seen on the right hand side of our track-way, descending from Beacon Hill, into the plain beneath, towards a thicket of furze, where they take a contrary direction, and point northerly to an eminence, noticed in the Wiltshire map by the name of West Down Hill. This line of road, leading across the downs from Salisbury to Marlborough, is still marked by mile-stones; and between the eleventh and twelfth, we find, adjoining the bank and ditch, one of those small earthen works, which so frequently occur on our downs, with an entrance towards the south, and measuring on that side 140 feet, on the west 120 feet, on the north, where it assumes a semicircular form, 176 feet, and on the east 160 feet: the entrance is 40 feet from the eastern angle. On West Down Hill the bank and ditch form an acute angle, and divide into two branches, one of which points directly up to Chidbury Hill, and the other to Chalk-pit Hill; the former branch, though levelled by the plough, is still discernible by the vivid colour of the grass, and is very visible on the sides of the hill; the other branch continues very perfect for some distance over the down, leaving Chidbury Hill on the left, and North Tidworth on the right; and in its course passes near a group of twelve barrows, which from being planted with various sorts of trees, tend to enliven the downy scenery around them. On the eastern side of these *tumuli* is a little square earthen work, bearing marks of antiquity, and having its ditch within the *vallum*, and an entrance towards the south : it measures about 200 feet in length, and 105 in breadth. The bank and ditch now take a north-east course across the arable lands, and have been nearly reduced to a level by the plough, but their line may still be traced with accuracy for some distance towards Chalk-pit Hill. Leaving the further prosecution of this bank to some future opportunity, I return to West Down Hill,* in order to follow the upper line of bank and ditch, which, by our map, you will perceive returns towards Beacon Hill, nearly in a parallel direction, but on a higher level: in its course it intersects a barrow, and for a short distance has been made use of as the boundary line between the two counties of Hampshire and Wiltshire ; but it soon again diverges, and separates into two branches, one of which descends the western side of Beacon Hill, and joins the bank before described in the plain; the other descends the eastern side of the same hill, and pursues its

---

* The numerous marks of old enclosures on the downs adjoining this spot, induced me to make some further researches with the spade, which discovered the well-known relicts of British population. All the excavations which lead us generally to the knowledge of British villages had been levelled by continual ploughing, but the surface of the soil abounded with fragments of very old and rude pottery.

course to the extremity of our county at Park House. At a short distance west of this place, and close to the 74th mile-stone, I observed another bank and ditch, which I followed up to the summit of Beacon Hill, near Old Hill coppice, and found to be a continuation of the one I before noticed as descending from Beacon Hill into the vale beneath. I continued my ride over the lofty and beautiful ridge of Haradon Hill, and returned once more to my old quarters at Amesbury.

ITER I. I shall now proceed towards the head quarters which I have fixed upon for the examination of this Station, at East Everley, where there is a good inn, situated on the verge of a very fine down, and from its retirement and tranquillity, most admirably suited to the studies of an antiquary. Passing over a verdant plain which is thickly strewed with the simple yet impressive memorials of the mighty dead, I deviate on the right to CHIDBURY CAMP, a strong fortress situated on an eminence, which forms a very conspicuous land mark to almost every part of our county, and with regard to extent of prospect from its summit, stands unrivalled in it. Its form resembles that of a heart, at the lower or narrow part of which, facing the north-west, is the principal entrance, protected by an outwork; and a little further towards the east is another entrance, but without any outwork. This camp is double ditched, and the ground rises gradually from the ramparts towards the area, which is on the highest part of the hill. The side easiest of approach is towards the south-west, where the adjoining ground, on the outside of the camp, is nearly on the same level ; the three other sides are steeper, and skirt the edge of the hill. The surface of the area is much defaced by brakes of furze, rabbit holes, and sundry excavations: it contains within the ramparts seventeen acres ; the circuit of the inner ditch is five furlongs and 101 yards, and the depth of the *vallum* is 46 feet. Independent of the very interesting and extensive prospect which from the ramparts of this camp, the eye commands over the wide tract of adjacent down, and extending as far as the Isle of Wight on one side, and terminating on the other with the ridge of hills on the western borders of our county, on which the Abbey at Fonthill, and Alfred's Tower at Stourhead are clearly discernible, this hill possesses a curious aggregate of natural curiosities ; for its soil produces fine gravel and pebbles, brick earth, chalk, and springs of water.

On quitting this fine eminence, and descending into the plain towards Everley, our attention is attracted by a very bold, broad, and straight raised causeway issuing from the principal entrance of the camp, and directing its

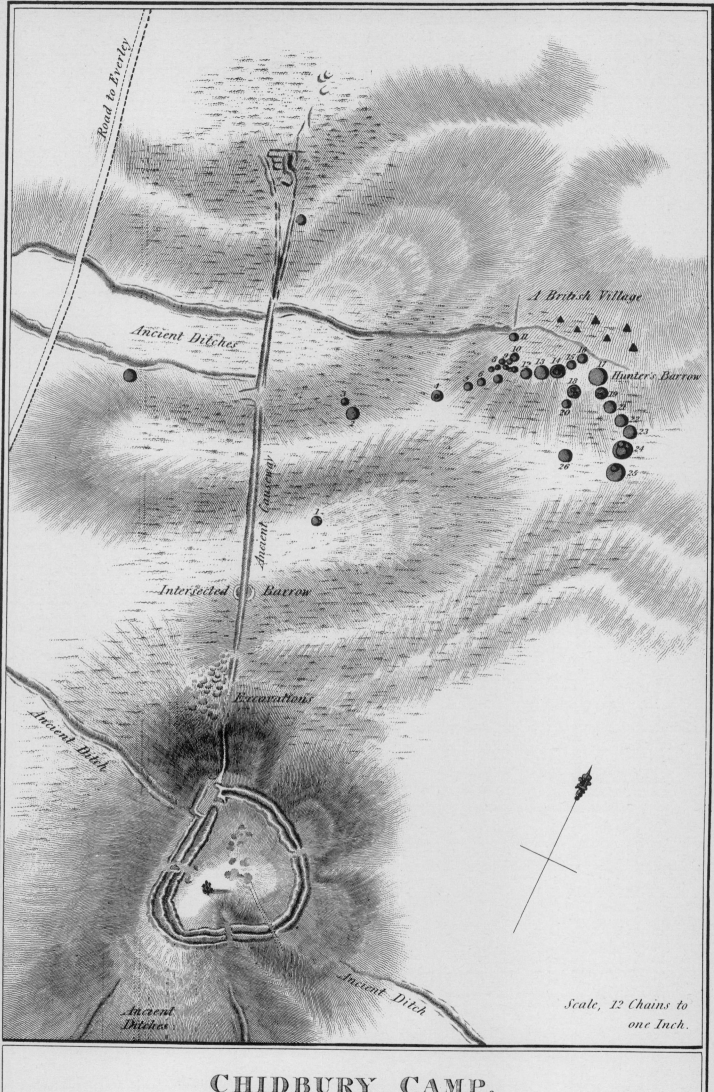

CHIDBURY CAMP.

Road to Everley

A British Village

Ancient Ditches

Hunter's Barrow

Ancient Causeway

Intersected Barrow

Excavations

Ancient Ditch

Ancient Ditch

Ancient Ditches

Scale, 12 Chains to one Inch.

P. Crocker del.

J. Basire Sc.

Published by Sir Rich.d Colt Hoare Bar.t Jan.y 1826.

course towards Everley. In its structure it resembles so much the Roman roads, that I could almost suppose it had been formed after their model. This causeway extends in length one mile and 88 yards, and in its progress intersects in half a large Druid barrow, as will be seen on our map. It terminates in a valley, and immediately at a spot where there are several irregularities and excavations in the soil. With all the ardour and fancy of a zealous antiquary, I once fondly thought that here I might discover the traces of King Ina's palace, who, according to tradition, had a country seat at Everley;* but on digging into several of the banks, as well as into the hollow places, I could find no fragments even of stone, or any *indicia* of habitations. The origin and cause therefore of this singular bank and ditch must remain to be developed by some future and more fortunate antiquary.

A little on the south side of these excavations we meet with two ancient banks and ditches, one of which crosses the trackway, and leads towards an extensive British village, and a large group of barrows. These, during my rides over the downs, had frequently attracted my attention, and so far excited my curiosity as to induce me to open them. Our researches commenced in July, 1805 ; and though they did not prove equally satisfactory with those in the immediate neighbourhood of Stonehenge, yet they did not turn out totally void of interest and novelty. My readers will find each barrow numbered on the annexed map, to which I shall refer in my description of them.

No 1. is situated at some distance from the main body of the group, on a declivity between it, and Chidbury Hill. On making our section, the first thing we discovered was the jaw, and a part of the thigh bone of a skeleton near the surface ; and on prosecuting our researches, we perceived the rim of a large sepulchral urn in an oblique direction, with its mouth upwards, and occupying nearly the whole space of the cist, so that we found some difficulty in extracting it ; but Stephen Parker, our veteran pioneer, succeeded much to his credit, and brought it home safe to Everley ; but from the rudeness

---

* In the year 688, Ina, King of the West Saxons, began his glorious reign, and in the year 692 enacted his laws, which are printed in *Wilkins's Concilia*, vol. i. p. 478. This event is thus recorded by the historian Cressy. " Ina, King of the West Saxons, being desirous to compose and settle his kingdom in good order, by rooting out such ill customs as had crepp'd in among the people, called an assembly of his bishops and nobility, and by common advice enacted those famous laws, called *King Ina's Laws*, which continued in force many ages, even till the coming and conquest of the Normans, and of which William of Malmsbury saith, " a mirrour of their purity remained to his time." These were seventy-five in number, and are extant in Sir Henry Spelman's *Collection of Councils*. According to the Saxon Chronicle, this prince succeeded to Ceadwalla, and reigned 37 years. Having constructed a monastery at Glastonbury, he made a journey to Rome, and there ended his days.

of its texture, and imperfect baking, it cracked and fell to pieces the following day: it measured 13½ inches in height, and 10½ inches in diameter, and contained a deposit of burned human bones. From the circumstance of finding only one half of the skull, and one piece only of the thigh bone, it appears that the greater proportion of the body was burned; and perhaps the skull, which had evident marks of a contusion, and which very probably occasioned the Briton's death, was reserved on purpose to denote to posterity the cause of it. In the intermediate space between this barrow and the group, we find a large and small *tumulus*, numbered 2, and 3. In the first we discovered a cist cut in the chalk, containing a variety of articles chiefly made of bone, and which form the contents of TUMULI PLATE XXI. The central instrument is of brass and fixed into a handle made of stag's horn: the other articles of bone that are here engraved, denote a very high antiquity, as well as a period when the use of metals was probably unknown. Besides these rude instruments, we found a whetstone, apparently never used, of freestone, and another with the indenture made in it by attrition, such as I have before noticed in TUMULI PLATE VI., and a hone of a blueish colour. It is singular that all these articles should have been collected within a cist, without either bones or ashes.* In the adjoining small barrow, we found the deposit of a skeleton, but no articles accompanying it.

No. 4. We now approach the large group of barrows situated in a retired vale, and on the gentle declivity of a hill. This is a low barrow encompassed by a circular ditch, and containing a cist within a cist. At the depth of one foot and a half we came to the first, which had been secured at top by a covering of flints; it was nearly circular, and about three feet in diameter. Within this was another cist, more contracted in its size, but nearly of an equal depth, about 14 inches. In this we found a most singular and novel interment of bones, very well burned; in throwing out of which with his shovel, our labourer surprized us with a beautiful and diminutive cup, which fortunately received no damage, and is engraved in TUMULI PLATE XXII. of its original size. On pursuing our excavation, we discovered lower down another small cup most rudely formed, but resembling some others in our museum, and which seemed to have been protected by a wall of burned bones placed round it as a safeguard. Amongst the bones was a very delicate pointed pin of metal, bearing

---

* Being satisfied that by this first operation, we had not found the interment, I made, at a subsequent period, a second section, but was equally unsuccessful.

P. Crocker del.

J.ª Basire Sc.

Published for W. Miller, Albemarle Street, London, Jan.ʸ 1. 1812.

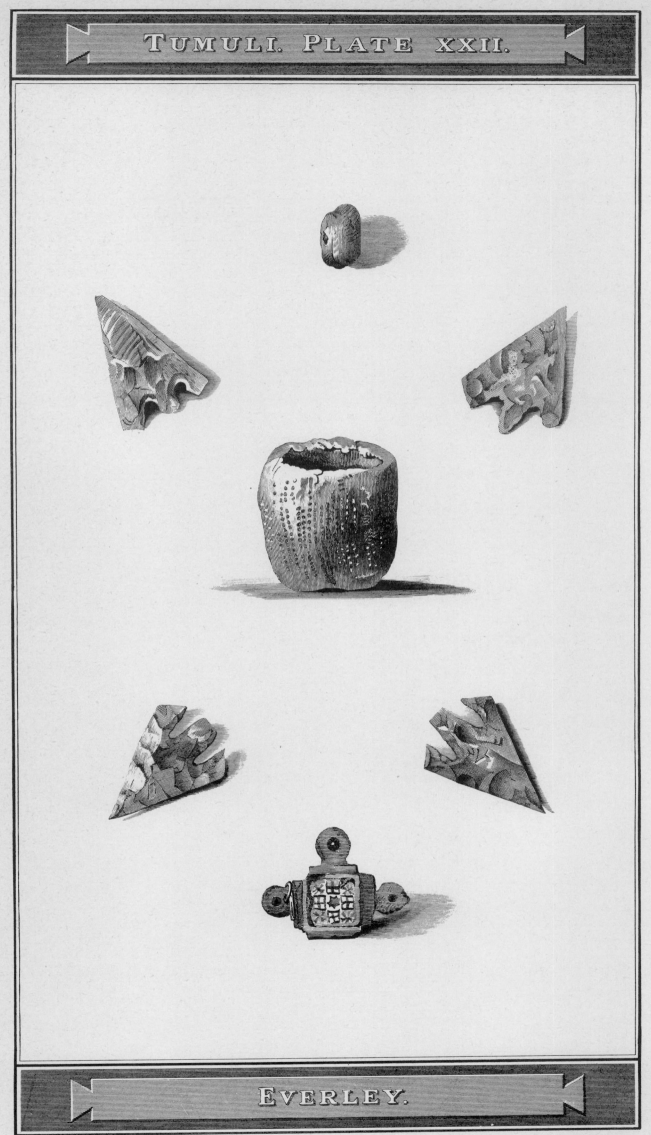

P. Crocker del.

J.º Basire Sc.

Published for W. Miller, Albemarle Street, London, Jan.ʸ 1. 1812.

some slight indications of having been gilt.   This interment appearing not to be in the centre of the mound, and observing a depression in the north-west side of it, we were induced to make another section, by which we discovered a large irregular cist, but no charred wood, or signs of sepulture.

No. 5.   In this barrow we found a deep cist cut in the chalk, but no interment.   In No. 6 was a deposit of burned bones enclosed in wood, and placed in a wide cist.   In No. 7 we discovered a large sepulchral urn rudely baked, and containing an interment of burned bones.   No. 8 had a simple deposit of burned bones.   In No. 9 we perceived near the surface the fragments of a rude unornamented urn, with a small interment of burned bones ; and lower down a deep cist cut in the chalk, and empty ; but as there was a great deal of charred wood, and many evident signs of cremation in this barrow, it is very probable that other interments may remain undiscovered.   In No. 10 we found nothing, and No. 11, though a respectable barrow in point of size, presented to us only a vacant cist.   In No. 12 we were equally unsuccessful, as also in No. 13, a very large *tumulus,* in which we made a wide section to the depth of twelve feet, and the only thing worthy of remark was a *stratum* of black earth, 5 feet 9 inches from the surface, which pervaded the whole section.   No. 14 is a Druid barrow which had been opened before, as we found the ashes and bones of the original interment disturbed and jumbled together.   In No. 15 were the remains of a skull very much burned, and some trifling fragments of unornamented pottery ; and in No. 16 was a deposit of burned bones within a cist.

No. 17.   After so much labour, loss of time, and disappointment, fortune seemed desirous of favouring us in this particular barrow, which had a large cavity in it, and bore every appearance of a prior opening ; and indeed the shepherds of the plain had assured us that it had been investigated, and had produced a quantity of beads.   Having often experienced the fallacy of these vulgar reports, we were not deterred in making a trial, and we were highly recompensed for our perseverance by the discovery of one of the most interesting interments we had ever witnessed.   The first object that attracted our attention, was the skeleton of a small dog deposited in the soil three feet from the surface, and at the depth of 8 feet 10 inches we came to the bottom of the barrow, and discovered the following very perfect interment collected on a level floor. The body of the deceased had been burned, and the bones and ashes piled up in a small heap, which was surrounded by a circular wreath of horns of the red deer, within which, and amidst the ashes, were five beautiful arrow heads cut out of flint, and a small red pebble. Tumuli Plate XXII. Thus we most clearly

3 A

see the profession of the Briton here interred. In the flint arrow heads we recognize his fatal implements of destruction ; in the stag's horns we see the victims of his skill as a hunter ; and the bones of the dog deposited in the same grave, and above those of his master, commemorate his faithful attendant in the chase, and perhaps his unfortunate victim in death.*

Can the language either of history or poetry speak more forcibly to our feelings, than these mute and inanimate memorials of the British hunter ; and may not the following beautiful lines of Pope be applied with equal truth to the Briton as to the Indian ?—

" Lo the poor BRITON, whose untutor'd mind
" Sees God in clouds, and hears him in the wind ;
" His soul proud science never taught to stray
" Far as the solar walk, or milky way :
" Yet simple Nature to his hope hath giv'n,
" Behind the cloud-top't hill an humbler heav'n.
" To BE, contents his natural desire,
" He asks no angel's wing, no seraph's fire,
" But thinks, admitted to that equal sky,
" His faithful DOG shall bear him company."

No. 19. On opening this large circular barrow, and on finding several pieces of burned bones dispersed amidst the soil, we had reason to suppose that the interment had been disturbed either by foxes or some other vermin. In No. 20 we found, at the depth of 4 feet 9 inches from the surface, a cist excavated in the chalk three feet, at one edge of which was a sepulchral urn, eleven inches in height, and eight in diameter, deposited with its mouth upwards, and containing an interment of burned bones. This urn is elegant in its form, well turned, and in good proportion. In this *tumulus* as well as in several others, I deposited a coin, which was cast on purpose to hand down to future ages our antiquarian researches, and which is inscribed, OPENED BY WILLIAM CUNNINGTON, 1805. No. 21 is a large barrow, measuring 10½ feet from its *apex* to the floor, in which there was a cist excavated in the chalk, of

* We learn from Cæsar, that amongst our neighbours the Gauls, the same mode of interment prevailed, and that not only precious articles were deposited with the bodies, but animals and even slaves sacrificed to the *manes* of the deceased: *Omnia, quæ vivis cordi fuisse arbitrantur in ignem inferunt, etiam animalia.*" The excellence of the British dogs, and their sagacity in hunting, seems to have been known in very early days, for Strabo notices them as *canes ad venandum aptissimi.* The other elegant little ornament of enamel set in brass, [engraved in PLATE XXII.] which I picked up near this barrow, bespeaks a more modern and refined æra.

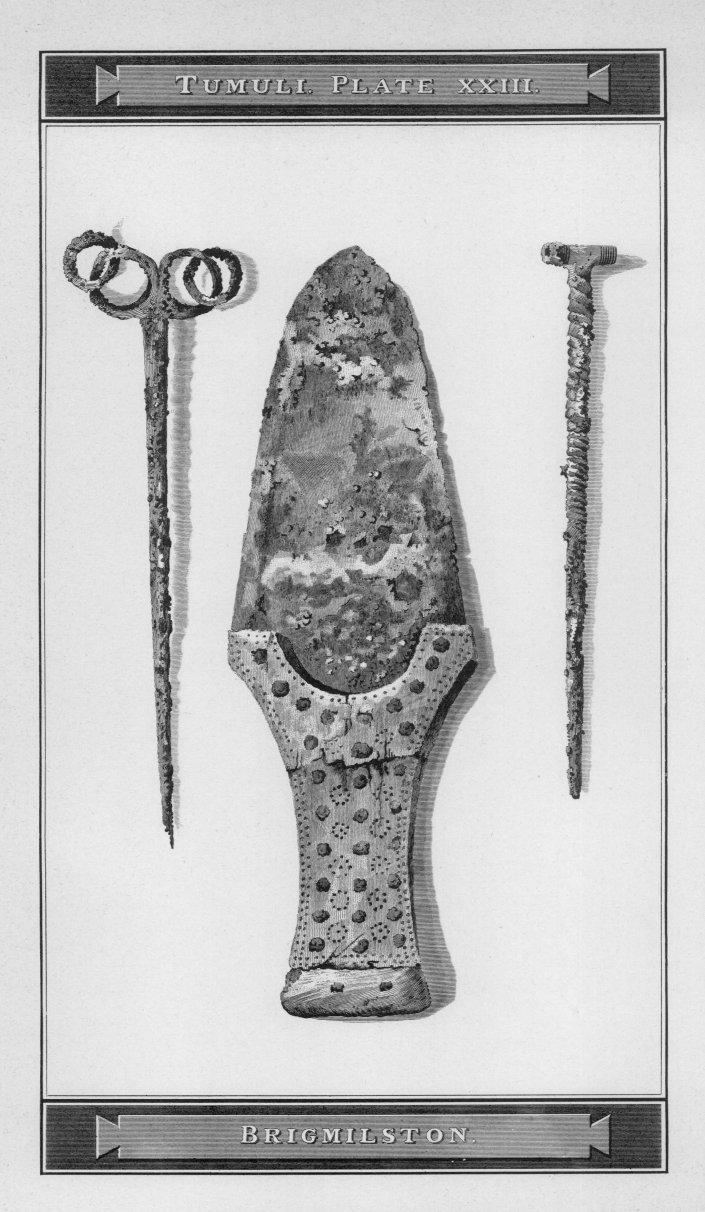

Publifhed for W. Miller Albemarle Street London Jan.ʸ 1. 1812.

BRIGMILSTON.

6½ feet in length, 5 feet in width, and 3½ in depth ; but we were once more disappointed in finding it empty : some small pieces of charcoal were mixed with the soil, but no other symptoms whatever of interment were discernible. The elevation of No. 22 is so slight and irregular, that doubts may be entertained if it was raised for sepulchral purposes, for on opening it, we could find no *indicia* of sepulture ; and the same remarks may be applied to the next barrow, No. 23.

No. 24 is a very large barrow, 97 feet 16 inches in diameter, and 11 feet 4 inches in depth from the summit to the floor, on which we found a very perfect interment of bones minutely burned, and enclosed in wood, which we traced very satisfactorily for the extent of six feet in length, and more than three in breadth. Within this wooden chest, or perhaps the more simple trunk of a tree, were the fragments of a beautiful little cup. The bones being tinged with green, we were led to suppose that we should find some articles of brass, and we were not disappointed in our expectations, for we shortly took out a spear head with three rivets, similar in form to those we had found on former occasions ; and from the mouldering remains of wood, adhering to it, we clearly perceived that it had been carefully protected by a scabbard. Close to this spear head lay another singular instrument of brass, which was also secured in a sheath of wood lined with cloth, the web of which still could be distinguished. Its figure and size are delineated in TUMULI PLATE XXIII ; but I cannot form a conjecture respecting its original use. By the manifest care which in many instances we see adopted for the preservation of these brazen articles, we may be induced to suppose that they were articles of ornament rather than of utility ; and daily experience convinces me, that those implements we originally supposed to be spear heads, may more properly be denominated daggers, or knives, worn by the side, or in a girdle, and not affixed to long shafts like the more modern lance. In some subsequent engravings I shall endeavour to prove this hypothesis, by submitting to you two specimens of the handles belonging to these daggers. This barrow is surrounded with a ditch, enclosing a smaller mound, which contained a simple but large interment of burned bones, perhaps of the slave or dependent of the chieftain who was buried in the larger one, as in both instances the same system of interment was adopted.

No. 25. This *tumulus*, from its superior size, might justly be denominated the KING BARROW. It is finely fossed round, and measures from its summit to the floor, thirteen feet ; yet though we made a very large section in it, and undermined it on every side, we could discover no symptom whatever of burial; and in the next barrow, No. 26, though we found abundant signs of cremation, we were equally disappointed in not discovering the interment.

Before I quit this group of *tumuli*, I cannot help remarking the singularity of having found so many empty cists: a singularity which has scarcely ever occurred during our researches in other parts of the county. Can we suppose that the Britons entertained the same ideas as the Greeks and Romans, who erected to the memory of those whose bodies could not be found, a *tumulus honorarius* or *cenotaphium*, from the superstitious notion that the soul could not rest unless deposited in a tomb?*

The whole valley to the east of these barrows, as well as the higher ground behind them, afford manifest *indicia* of a remote British population.

ITER II.   The object of this morning's ride was to examine the north-east corner of our county, and to endeavour to trace out the course of numerous banks and ditches which abound in that district, and which I venture to assert have an intimate connection with the ancient settlements of the Britons.   Following the turnpike road, which leads from Everley to Andover, I diverge on the left to a common bearing the name of Wick Down, and situated between the borough town of Ludgershall on the right, and the village of Collingbourn Ducis on the left, where I find the unmutilated remains of a bank and ditch running irregularly from east to west across the down, but they are soon lost in the arable lands on each side.+ On the west they seem to point towards Windmill-Hill, on which there is also a similar bank; but in tracing these ancient remains we have not the same unerring clue to lead us as in the Roman roads, whose course, except where prevented by the difficulties of nature, was always straight; whereas these British banks and ditches are most capricious and deviating in their windings, continually turning off in sharp angles from their supposed destination, and scarcely ever proceeding in a direct line.   In their course eastward, this bank and ditch point towards Collingbourn woods, a very extensive tract of thick coppice, belonging to the Earl of Ailesbury, whose woodman, residing at the Lodge, told me that a bank and ditch were visible in

---

* *Cenotaphium erat tumulus sine corpore. Fiebat religionis causâ, quod veteres existimarunt, animas non posse priùs quiescere, quam sepulcro essent conditæ.*

+ The down adjoining this bank and ditch bears a very verdant appearance, and has several irregularities of ground denoting apparently the existence of a British village upon it in former times; but though in digging into some of the excavations, I found some few fragments of rude British pottery, I cannot pronounce this spot to have been decidedly a British settlement.

two parts of Oxdown Copse ; which is situated between the Lodge and Crawl-bush, and formed, I make no doubt, a continuation of those before mentioned on Wick Down. About 320 yards north of Collingbourn Lodge, a large bank and ditch are to be seen in the middle of the copse wood, corres-ponding in character with those we have lately noticed ; these shortly after-wards issue from the wood, in a very bold form, and traverse a piece of common called CHUTE DOWN, at the extremity of which are some outworks attached apparently to the bank, but I doubt if they are of equal antiquity. The bank and ditch descend into the vale, and their traces are lost for a short distance ; but I was informed by some inhabitants of the neighbour-hood, that they continued along the ridge to Gammon's barn, where they are again very visible, and continue so on the left side of the road leading to Scots Poor, where there is a little public-house placed on a spot highly interest-ing to the antiquary ; for in the front of its door, the noble Roman road leading from VENTA BELGARUM, or WINCHESTER, to the station of CUNETIO, on the river Kennet, near Marlborough, meets this ditch, which on the Wiltshire map is erroneously styled WANDS DITCH. The Roman road, having been obliged to quit its usual straight line at the extremity of Chute Park, on account of a deep valley, after passing Scots Poor, hastens to regain it, whilst our bank and ditch con-tinue their devious course eastward behind the public-house. At the distance of about a mile, I observed another bank and ditch diverging more towards the east, and upon enquiry I learned that, after traversing a considerable tract of arable land, they quitted the county of Wilts near Henley. The other bank proceeds north-west, and crosses the Roman road a little to the east of Titcomb great barrow. But I must leave this line for the present, in order to follow the traces of another bank and ditch which take a more northerly direction, and appear first in the arable lands on the opposite side of the vale in which the little village of Titcomb is situated ; they afterwards become very visible on the edge of the down, bearing towards the point of a hill distinguished by a clump of trees planted on a long barrow, beneath which is a small circular barrow ditched round ; and the constructors of the bank and ditch have evidently made use of one of the *valla* of the barrow to form that of their bank. Crossing the corner of Botley Coppice, they continue their track over Shalbourn Down, but gradually diminish in size, and separate into two branches like the streams of a river, then making an acute angle, they descend from the hill, and traverse the arable lands in the vale to the Hungerford road. I had pur-posed extending this morning's ride to the farthest extremity of our county at

3 B

Buttermere Corner, but having already found so much to attract my attention, and having other more important objects in view on my return to Everley, I abandoned the project; and from the greater part of this district being in tillage, I am inclined to think that the antiquary would find but little worthy of his notice in it.

Returning from Shalbourn Down, I deviated on the left to Fosbury farm, a name derived from a strong earth work in its immediate vicinity called HAYDON HILL CASTLE, a corruption probably from HIGH DOWN,* to which its situation most aptly applies. The approach to it from the west is very striking, over a narrow ridge of land which leads directly to an opening in the ramparts, and which at first sight appears to have been the original entrance into the area of the camp; but on closely examining a second opening in the ramparts a little further to the right, but on the same ridge, I am inclined to think the latter was the true entrance, as the *valla* on each side are more finished and rounded off than in the former. This work is single ditched, and the outline of its ramparts is very irregular: the broadest and most perfect entrance is on the east side, near which is a large pond, that never fails in water; there is also another near the west entrance possessing the same useful quality. A large wood encroaches upon the *vallum* and a part of the area on the north-east side. The interior of the camp commands a very pleasing view, though not so extensive as Chidbury Hill.

To vary, and give a greater interest to our ride back to Scots Poor, we descended the hill from the eastern entrance, and crossing the vale, joined a road which divides the counties of Hampshire and Wiltshire. By the side of the hill under which we rode, I observed an irregular earthen work, and a barrow within it, and soon afterwards came to Upper Conholt, near which is Chute Park, the seat of the Medows family. The deer park, detached from the mansion house, occupies a lofty ridge, commanding a very rich and extensive view over Hampshire, and claims the antiquary's notice, from having a very bold and perfect specimen of the Roman road before mentioned within its precincts; and which, at the very extremity of the paling, begins to make that very long and singular curve which is noticed on the map of this station, and conducts us back over an elevated terrace to our little *taberna* at Scots Poor.

We must now return to that branch of the bank and ditch, which in our progress eastward, we quitted near Titcomb barrow, and which continue their

---

* From some manuscript papers of a celebrated antiquary, Smart Lethieullier, Esq. which have lately fallen into my hands, I find this camp distinguished by the title of KNOLL DITCHES.

HAYDON HILL CAMP.

Pond

Pond

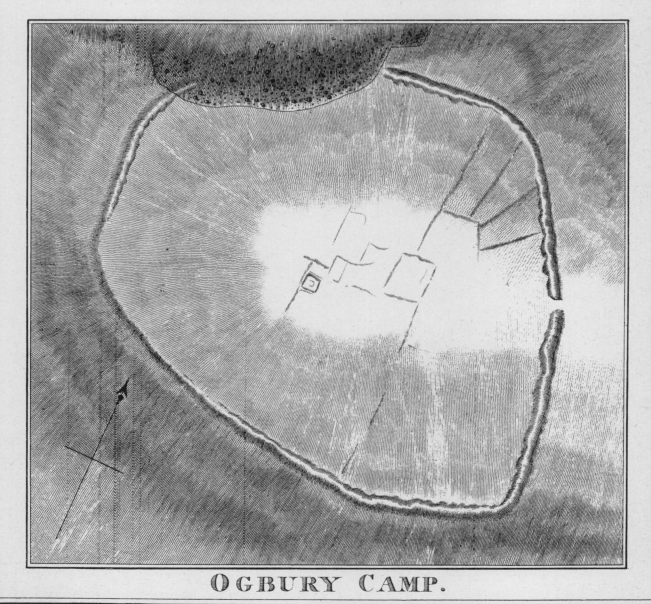

OGBURY CAMP.

P. Crocker del.

J. Basire Sc.

Published for W. Miller, Albemarle Street, London, Jan.ʸ 1 1812.

course along the down for some distance, and are then lost on the declivity of the hill.   A little on the west side of Titcomb barrow, I observed two different banks and ditches diverge from those we were following, and run in a parallel line, and south-west direction, across the arable lands towards Scots Poor.   These strongly excited my curiosity, for they differed materially in their construction, from those I have hitherto noticed.*   On pursuing their separate lines, I found they met on a heath a little to the north of Scots Poor, where the verdure of the turf, the cavities in the soil, and the general appearance of the country, gave me the strongest hopes of discovering a British village: the spade and pickaxe, those unerring *indagatores*, were employed, but neither ashes, charcoal, pottery, or any other marks of ancient population could be discovered.

On this spot the triple ramparts cease, and continue, as before, single, and much mutilated by a modern hedge placed on the old bank.   They steer their course towards Heath Barn; then traversing a little copse, are again visible in the arable lands, pointing to Collingbourn woods.   In my way home to Everley through Collingbourn Kingston I observed, on the declivity of a point of down, a group of four barrows, two of which, of the Druid form, exhibit a peculiarity which I have never before remarked, with respect to their *valla*, which intersect each other at their extremities like the figure 8.   In our road homewards, we came to another fine ridge of down called Fair Mile, on which are a few *tumuli*, and an irregular circle with a slight *vallum* adjoining the track-way, and an entrance towards the east, from which it measures in diameter about 320 feet; and there appears to have been a circular excavation, like a pond barrow, near the *vallum* on the opposite side.   The south side of the work is perfect, the north side defaced.

Iter III.   In our ride this morning, we followed the direction of the road leading from Everley to Marlborough, over a tract of heath and unenclosed land, on which are some scattered barrows, and some faint traces of banks and ditches.   A little on the right of the road is a round hill named Godsbury, whose summit has been crowned with a clump of trees by Lord Ailesbury.   It exhibits faint traces of a circular earthen work, from which circumstance it probably

* The generality of banks and ditches in this neighbourhood, present an outline of two banks nearly of an equal height, with an intermediate broad and flat ditch between them: whereas those I am now speaking of, present a triple row of *valla*, the one in the centre being the most distinguished for height.

gained the latter part of its name; for I have almost invariably found some earthen work, on or near those places bearing the termination of *bury*. Passing near some barrows in the vale beneath, we ascended a beautiful hill, whose superior verdure led us to suppose that it had formerly been inhabited by the Britons, and pastured by their herds; an ancient bank and ditch soon corroborated these our conjectures, and conducted us into a British village most delightfully situated near the summit of the hill, which has also been decorated by the same noble owner with a plantation of trees; but in so doing, the outline of a most elegant Druid barrow has been disfigured, but not so much so, as to occasion the doubt of a sepulchral memorial having once existed on this spot. The excavations of the British village, surrounded by an *agger* of earth, are very visible on the northern declivity of the hill; and I make no doubt but the spade would discover *indicia* of an extensive population on every part of this hill, which I cannot possibly leave without extolling the very beautiful and extensive view, which, on ascending it after a long and uniform tract of unadorned down, so unexpectedly presents itself, over the rich and highly cultivated vale which separates the chalk hills of our county, and naturally divides it into two distinct districts.

Quitting with regret this delicious eminence, and passing near some banks that appear to have been connected with the British village, we traversed a vale of verdant down, and ascended towards Milton farm, near which is a group of five barrows. Further on towards the west is a long barrow, vulgarly styled, " the Giant's Grave," and all around it we recognize the undoubted vestiges of a very extensive British town.

From hence I took a southern course towards a wild tract of heath and furze, where I found a group of eight barrows, and to the south of them a very perfect oblong earthen work, measuring 200 feet in length, and 150 in width, and placed on sloping ground. The *vallum* is tolerably perfect on three sides; but as I could discover no satisfactory entrance on either of them, I conclude it was on the south side, where the ramparts have been destroyed. The numerous marks of enclosures on each side of the little valley in which this work is situated, added to the extreme blackness of the soil cast up by the moles, induced me to search for a British village, which I very soon found in the immediate vicinity of the earthen work. The spade confirmed my suspicions, by discovering abundance of pottery, but it was chiefly of that superior species made by the Britons after the accession of the Romans; which, together with the broad iron headed nails and the sheltered situation, indicated this not to have been one of the very early British settlements, which were generally placed on high and more exposed eminences.

The extreme rudeness and singularity of some of the eight barrows composing the group before mentioned, tempted me to open some of them, particularly those two, which are engraved as specimens in my plates of TUMULI. No. 8. is remarkable for having a more pointed *apex* than any other barrow I remember to have seen, on which account I have named it the CONE BARROW. About three or four feet from the surface we discovered a more than usual quantity of burned bones, accompanied by a very small lance-head of brass. The primary interment of burned bones was deposited in a deep cist cut in the chalk.

No. 12 is a low long barrow, surrounded, contrary to usual custom, by a circular ditch. Its surface seemed to present three sepulchral mounds raised from east to west, and to indicate three different interments; but in the eastern mound alone we were successful in finding the deposit of burned bones with two jet beads, a small pin of brass, and the fragments of a very rude little cup. At a short distance from the interment were two circular *cineraria* full of burned ashes. We opened the two smallest of the bowl-shaped barrows; in one of which we missed the interment, and in the other found the deposit of a skeleton, with the legs gathered up, and the head laid towards the south-west. These barrows, owing to the clammy nature of the soil, occasioned much trouble in opening, and deterred me from exploring the remainder of the group.

From hence, taking a western course, and crossing the trackway leading from Everley to Pewsey, I discovered two very ancient and curious British circles, connected with each other by a hollow way. The first is the largest and most perfect, but I cannot speak with certainty about the entrance to it, as a passage from east to west has been made through it by waggons. The entrance to the second or most westerly circle evidently pointed towards the north. The *agger* to each of these works is slight, and the ditch on the outside. The blackness of the soil in these parts indicates ancient residence, and on digging within the area of the last mentioned circle, I found a great deal of pottery and animal bones.

I continued my ride along the edge of the down, enjoying a delicious view of the rich vale immediately beneath, and the distant range of North Wiltshire hills. Having crossed one valley, and then ascended a fine down pointing towards Upavon, I perceived some faint traces of ditches, and a small square work with a very slight *vallum*, and an entrance towards the south-east. The turf is fine, but I perceived no marks of enclosures, which are the never-failing marks of British population. Crossing the great road which leads from Everley to Upavon, I continued my ride partly over down, and partly over arable lands to the remains of a circular earthen work, vulgarly called Chisenbury Trendle.* Its area contains about five acres, its circumference is 594 yards, and the depth of its rampart is 16 feet. There are vestiges still remaining of an outwork to the south, on which side I imagine was the entrance. In form and situation this work bears strongly the marks of one of those circles appropriated in ancient times either to religious or judicial purposes. On the same ridge of hill, and at a short distance to the west, are the remains of another work forming the segment of a circle, and presenting a bolder rampart than the former. In the neighbourhood of this latter work we picked up some rude British pottery, and I was informed by a farmer that the soil in the neighbourhood of these works was remarkably fertile. At the extremity of the same line of hill, and in the parish of Chisenbury, we find a continuation of earthen antiquities, and still more considerable and unaccountable than the last. They consist of a very bold entrenchment, carried across the valley in which the mansion-house and spacious farm-offices of the Grove family are built. The avenue leading to the house intersects the ramparts. The space between them is nine paces, and is planted with a double row of trees.

Returning towards Everley in an eastern direction, the eye may distinguish some ramparts upon the horizon of the opposite hill. Here is a small but perfect square earthen work, with an entrance to the south : the circuit of the ditch is 330 yards, and the depth of the *vallum* 40 feet. It is distinguished by the name of Lidbury. A bank and ditch, the almost constant attendants on our British villages, conduct us from it into an adjacent valley, on the south-east declivities of which we once more recognize all the *indicia* of an extensive British settlement, situated not as the generality are, on a high and commanding point of land, but in a retired and tranquil valley. The whole surrounding country clearly demonstrates, by numerous banks and enclosures, a very remote and extended cultivation. The banks and ditches are so confounded with the lynchets, that it becomes a difficult matter to separate them. We traced one ditch up the hill, where it branches off towards the west, and is soon lost: it forms an angle round a large and fine bell-shaped barrow, then ascends the hills towards

* We find many circular earthen works, bearing the name of *trendle*, which is derived from the Saxon word *trendel*, signifying a globe, sphere, or circle.

the Twin Barrows, near which we find another bank and ditch steering westward towards the vale of the river Avon, and which is visible for some distance across the down and fields.

These Twin Barrows which are engraved as specimens No. 7, are situated near the track-way on Long-street down, and attract the eye from the regularity of their form, the resemblance they bear to each other, and the peculiarity of their being enclosed within the same ditch. One of those was opened by Mr. Cunnington in the year 1806, and produced only an interment of burned bones, and a bone pin.

In August 1811, I opened its companion, situated the nearest to the west. My labourers made a very large section, and explored the barrow most completely, yet found no sepulchral deposit. It was attended, however, with some peculiarities worthy of remark. On approaching the floor, we found an immense *stratum* of burned wood ashes, rising in some parts nearest the centre to the height of three feet; they must have amounted to a cart load; with them were found, promiscuously, bones of animals, a great quantity of chipped flints prepared for arrows or lances, and two small pieces of bone. Our researches in these two barrows would seem to imply that the first was honoured with the sepulchral deposit, and the other only with the ashes of the funeral pile.

Returning from these two barrows to my head-quarters at Everley, I meet with another very extensive British village on Comb Hill, a little to the north of Beeches farm. It seems to have been connected with the one before mentioned near Lidbury, by double and single ditches, or covered ways; and we may perceive by our map that these ditches are continued on the opposite hill towards another British village, before described. *Tumuli*, though few in number, are occasionally seen dispersed over these fine downs; and at a short distance from the track-way leading to Everley, is an imperfect circular earthen work, bearing marks of great inequalities within its area; but on digging into it, I did not discover any pottery.

Iter IV. Quitting Everley, and passing through a valley with Comb Hill and its British town on the right, and numerous old enclosures on the opposite hill to the left, the first mark of antiquity that attracted my notice, was an ancient bank and ditch in the corn fields to the right, after having passed a tenement called Beeches farm, and distinguished by a plantation of trees around it. This bank is very visible where it ascends the hill, but less so on traversing some lands that have been ploughed : its line, however, along the side of the hill, and nearly parallel with the valley, is very visible. Following its course, I observed the remains of an imperfect earthen work to the right, and the slight traces of another ditch descending the hill and uniting itself with the one I had followed. A little further on is a perfect, but slight square work with an entrance towards the north, near which the bank and ditch alter their course, and form- ing an acute angle, ascend the hill over a tract of rich down towards a clump of trees on its summit, which they leave to the left, and are lost, when pointing towards the vale of Avon. On the above down I perceived, a little on the east side of the aforesaid clump of trees, the appearance of a slight earthen work, and from the apparent richness of the soil, and the lynchets in the neighbourhood, was tempted to try the spade within the area of the earthen *agger ;* and the result of these researches was, the discovery of another British settlement.

Continuing my ride southerly towards Amesbury, I traversed a high and beautiful piece of verdant down, situated in the parish of Brigmilston, and noticed in the large Wiltshire map by the name of SILK HILL. Its summit is crowned with numerous barrows of various forms ; the singularity of some of which excited my curiosity and induced me to open them. Two of them having been selected, and engraved amongst the specimens of barrows, it was necessary that I should become acquainted with their interior as well as with their exterior.

The first researches were made in the loftiest and most conspicuous *tumulus* on the hill ; on making our section in it, we discovered the interment of a skeleton, with an iron lance placed near its head ; the whole range of teeth was perfect, but the breast bone had a perforation through it of the size of a bullet, but evidently natural, and not caused by any accident. This was an interment of a later date, and of a different nature from the primary one, which was found on the floor of the barrow, consisting of a deposit of burned bones, together with a small spear-head of brass, protected by a scabbard, to which a great deal of the wood (apparently willow) adhered ; also two whet- stones perforated, of different species, and an article of twisted brass, in the form of a crutch, ribbed and perforated at the handle, which is engraved of the full size in TUMULI PLATE XXIII.

The next barrow we attempted was one, little inferior in size and beauty to the former ; but though our section was very large from the summit to the floor, yet our researches were not crowned with the wished for success.

My attention was next directed to a very singular *tumulus*, which is figured No. XI. in my plates of barrows: it is surrounded by a beautifully formed *vallum*, and the area within it is quite flat, without the least appearance of any sepulchral mound. On adopting our usual maxim of *in medio tutissimus*, we attacked its centre, but did not succeed, for the interment of burned bones was deposited at some distance from the middle of the barrow.

Opposite to this *tumulus* is a small one with a circular excavation at top, resembling one of the pond barrows, or appearing as if the protuberant part of the sepulchral mound had been cut off and removed. The first article we met with was a small sepulchral urn, standing upright, and filled with black ashes; it measured a little above five inches in height, and four in diameter; the ornaments were rude, of the Vandyke pattern, and made out by distinct dots. In its form it resembles the sepulchral urn, with a projecting rim, and is the smallest of that shape we have yet discovered. I found, besides, the fragment of a bone article, like a whetstone, some chipped flints prepared for arrow heads, a long piece of flint, and a *pyrites*, both evidently smoothed by usage.

But the most remarkable of all these mounds, in point of construction, is the one figured No. X. in my plates of barrows. The *vallum* that encompasses it is considerably higher than in any other, and the whole appearance different from any I have before witnessed. I almost doubt if it was raised for sepulchral purposes, for we made a very large section in its centre, and discovered only a few animal bones of deer, &c. and no symptoms whatever of cremation.

From this fine commanding hill, I descend into the vale leading towards Amesbury, and nearly opposite to the X. mile-stone from Salisbury observe suspicious ground on the western side of a little watery valley, commencing here, and joining that of the Avon, at Bulford. The spade corroborated my suspicions, and added another British settlement to the numerous list contained within this Station. No tract of country abounds more in barrows than the one through which we are now travelling; many of them are of a large size, and disposed in majestic groups.*

I cannot quit this interesting Station without briefly retracing the numerous

* In one of these, but I cannot specify which, Mr. Cunnington discovered the curious dagger which is engraved of the full size, in TUMULI PLATE XXIII., and is one of the examples I promised to adduce in support of my conjecture, that these articles of brass were probably worn by the Britons in their girdles, as ornaments of dress.

3 D

vestiges of British antiquity, with which it abounds. In our progress from the adjoining Station of Amesbury northward, we see the same abundant continuation of sepulchral mounds, as in the immediate neighbourhood of STONEHENGE. The first British settlement is situated in the little vale adjoining Bulford Field ; the second on Haxton Down: the third on Comb Hill ; the fourth at Lidbury ; the fifth on Pewsey Heath ; the sixth on Milton Hill ; the seventh on Easton Hill ; the eighth between Everley and Chidbury Hill ; and the ninth on West-down Hill. Many others have doubtless been destroyed by the plough, especially on the western side of this Station, bordering the river Avon, where the land is under tillage: and although we have not been able to determine the site of any British settlements on the north-east side of this Station, yet the numerous banks and ditches which exist there, lead us to conclude, that this district also was well known to the Britons.

In no part of our county have we a greater assemblage of this latter species of antiquities, which are evidently connected with the Britons and their villages ; for on referring to our map, you will perceive two lines of banks and ditches running nearly parallel from south to north, and uniting their branches at the British settlement on West-down Hill and tending afterwards to the strong fortress on Chidbury Hill. On the north side of this camp, you will also see a connection, by means of ditches, between two other British villages, which is also continued to a third at Lidbury. In short, whether they are considered as boundaries of territory, or covered ways of communication, they are evidently the works of the Britons, and therefore deserving of the antiquary's notice. I can entertain no doubt, that some of these were lines of boundary and defence ; for their mode of construction warrants such a supposition ; whilst, for the same reason, I cannot but consider others as covered ways or roads of communication from one British village to another. Of this latter species chiefly, are those dispersed about this Station, and which are accurately laid down upon our map, and where my readers will perceive the respective connection they bear to the British villages. One circumstance cannot escape the notice of the antiquary, and which favours in the strongest manner this my favourite hypothesis as relating to covered ways, viz. the communication which these banks and ditches have with the fortress on Chidbury Hill, to which, you will observe, they lead from different parts of the country. This, therefore, seems to have been the strong-hold to which, in times of danger, the natives resorted for safety, whither they retired with their wives, their families, and their herds ; and in this instance, I think, we

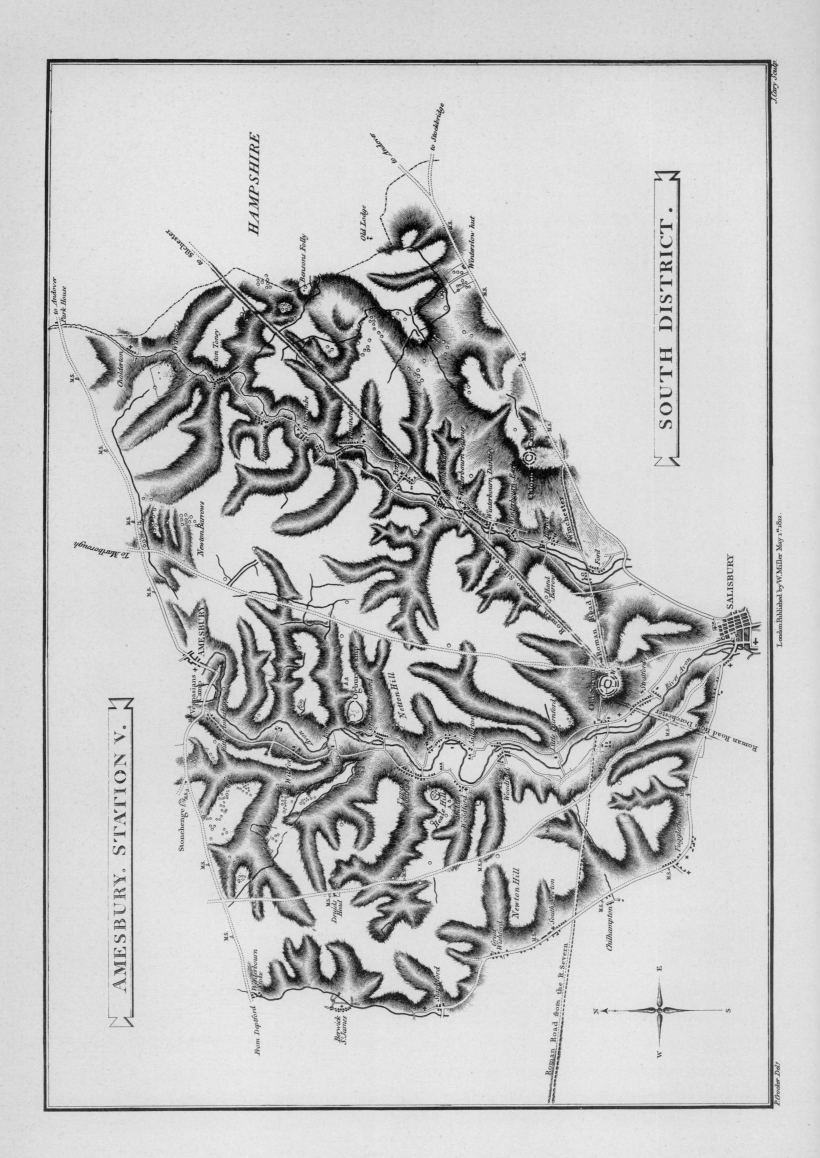

AMESBURY. STATION V.

SOUTH DISTRICT.

HAMPSHIRE

J.Cary Sculp.

London.Published by W.Miller May 1st 1812.

P.Crocker Delt.

N
W   E
S

must by conviction be obliged to abandon the idea, that these banks and ditches were thrown up solely for the purpose of forming boundary lines either of districts or of property.

STATION V. AMESBURY.

SOUTH DISTRICT.

In my account of Stonehenge, I took occasion to notice the very improbable idea, that the British King Ambrosius had imparted his name to the adjoining town of Amesbury; and we must now endeavour to trace its derivation to a more remote, more probable, and more dignified origin. There can be but one opinion respecting the high antiquity of the temple of Stonehenge, and the numerous sepulchral memorials around it, [some of which I have proved, in more than one instance, to have been raised since the construction of the building,] seem to attest the high veneration in which it was held by the Britons; thither they resorted as to the Great Sanctuary of the Dominion, and there they seemed desirous that their ashes should be deposited. In short, Stonehenge was to the Britons, what Mecca is now to the Turks.

I need not, by torturing etymology, endeavour to seek for an appropriate derivation for the word Amesbury or Ambresbury, as it has been frequently denominated; for in Ambres-bury, we recognize the town of the Ambres. Mr. Camden, in his description of Cornwall, tells us that near Pensans there was a noted stone called *Maen Amber*, which, though of vast bigness, you might move with your little finger; notwithstanding which, a great number of men could not remove it out of the place. It was, however, thrown down during the civil wars by the Governor of Pendennis. The Cornish historian, Mr. Norden, supposes these stones were so set, and subtilly combined, not by art, but by nature, and by referring to the drawing he has given of it, I am inclined to be of the same opinion.

Maen Amber signifies *Lapis Ambrosius*, or *Petra Ambrosia*, derived from the British word *maen*, a stone, and $AMBPO\Sigma IO\Sigma$, divine or holy. Dr. Stukeley, in his description of STONEHENGE, at page 50, has engraved one of the coins belonging to the city of Tyre, on which are represented two large upright stones placed before an altar, with the inscription of AMBPOCIE PETRE. I find also another coin in Vaillant, with a similar inscription. From these authorities, I think we may reasonably infer, that the modern name of Amesbury or Ambresbury, derives its origin from the *maen ambres*, or *petræ ambrosiæ*, and not from the British Emperor Aurelius Ambrosius.

ITER I. Let us now commence our perambulation of the southern district of this station, which is separated from the northern by the turnpike road leading from Wily through Amesbury to London. Passing through Vespasian's Camp, I deviate on the left to the little hamlet of West Amesbury in search of some antiquities, thus recorded by Mr. Aubrey, in his *Monumenta Britannica:* " There is a place called the *King's Grave*, where is now the sheep penning of West Amesbury. Here doe appeare five small barrowes, at one corner of the Penning. At the ends of the graves there were stones, which the people of late (about 1640) have fetch't away : for stones, except flints, are exceedingly scarce in these partes. 'Tis said here there were some letters on these stones, but what they were I cannot learne." In another part of his manuscript, he says, " neare to the farm house of West Amesbury, is a great ditch, where have been found rowells of spurres and other thinges, and near to the Penning is Normanton ditch, but why so called no tradition. Within the same farm is a place called PITT POOLE, wherein a king upon his escape riding hastily downe the steepe shoot was drowned."

In vain I searched for all these matters, for the remembrance of them exists not even by tradition. I was enabled, however, to ascertain the position of West Amesbury Penning, which lies in a little vale between *tumuli* 134 and 137. The *King's Grave* was a large solitary barrow on the hill above the river, on which a clump of trees has been planted, and is called *King Barrow* by Dr. Stukeley. Though all traces of the name of PITT POOLE are lost, its situation is clearly pointed out by the *steepe shoot* above the river. I could find no vestiges whatever of any ditch answering Mr. Aubrey's description, on Normanton Farm.

I must now resume the account of our researches in the very numerous *tumuli*

P. Crocker del.

J.⁵ Bafire Sc.

Tumulus 133

Tumulus 132

Publifhed for W. Miller, Albemarle Street, London. Jan.ʸ 1. 1812.

with which this district abounds, No. 128, 129, 130. The two first had experienced a prior opening, but the cist of the latter, containing an interment of burned bones with a lance-head of brass, had escaped unnoticed. The third also had been partially opened; but some of the interments remained perfect, and were attended with some novel and singular circumstances. At the depth of about a foot and a half from the surface, we discovered a skeleton with a drinking cup, and lower down a deposit of burned bones. On the east side of the barrow lay the skeletons of two infants, one with its head towards the east, the other towards the west, each placed over the head of a cow, which from fragments of the horns appeared to have been of a small size. We afterwards found a cist nearly four feet deep in the chalk, which contained, as we conceived, the primary interment, viz, the skeleton of a man; but these relicks had been disturbed, and some brazen articles, with which the bones were tinged, had been removed. No. 131 had been opened by the neighbouring farmers. No. 132. In this barrow we found, in a deep cist, an unusually large quantity of burned bones, and with them two drinking cups, two incense cups, and two brass pins. One of the incense cups was preserved entire, and is engraved of the original size in TUMULI PLATE XXIV. The quantity of bones, and the duplicate articles would induce me to suppose that this mound was raised over the relicks of two persons. No. 133 is a very high barrow, but the plough has made considerable encroachments round its base. It contained within a deep cist, a pile of burned bones, and a very beautiful and perfect grape cup, which is engraved in the same plate with the aforementioned cup. No. 134, 135, 136, 137, bear marks of prior openings.

NORMANTON GROUP. We now come to a noble group of barrows running in a line from south-east to north-west, diversified in their forms, perfect in their symmetry, and rich in their contents. I had always looked upon these barrows with a longing eye, but circumstances prevented my being present at the opening of them. The superintendance of our researches was therefore committed to the penetrating eye and experienced judgment of Mr. Cunnington, who, during his campaign in 1808, was gratified with the presence of several learned and well-informed people on the scene of action. No. 138 is a Druid barrow, which had been opened before. No. 139, a mean barrow, composed entirely of vegetable earth, produced within a shallow cist a pile of burned bones, and with them two fine daggers of brass, a long pin of the same metal in the form of a crutch, a whetstone, and a small pipe of bone. This last article is now broken, but it was originally about seven or eight inches long, and more than a quarter

3 E

of an inch in diameter at the small, and half an inch at the large end; it is thin, and neatly polished, and has a perforation near the centre. The brass pin and whetstone are engraved in Tumuli Plate XXIV.

No. 140, 141, 142, 143, have been all explored by the neighbouring farmers, and their history is of course unknown. No. 144, a wide bowl-shaped barrow, composed entirely of vegetable earth, contained the remains of a skeleton, much decayed, and deposited within an oblong cist, with its head towards the north, and accompanied by a small lance-head of brass. No. 145 is also a bowl-shaped barrow, which appeared to have undergone a prior investigation, but in examining the cist, we discovered a piece of ivory resembling the handle of a cup, and a large black pebble shaped like a kidney. No. 146 appears to have been the barrow opened by Dr. Stukeley, and marked B in Tab. IX. of his work.

No. 147. One of these two barrows, enclosed within the same ditch, was opened by Thomas, Earl of Pembroke, in the year 1722, and is marked A in Tab. IX. of Stukeley; and described at page 44 of his Stonehenge. Although the noble Peer made an entire segment in it from centre to circumference, his researches proved unsuccessful as to the primary interment, but he found the deposit of a skeleton three feet under the surface, with its head placed in a northerly direction towards Stonehenge. Our experience having given us repeated proofs that the system of opening barrows was but imperfectly understood in former days, we determined to try our luck, and on reaching the floor soon found, owing to a *stratum* of chalk, a clue to the cist, which contained an interment of burned bones, and with it two articles of ivory in high preservation. The one resembles in shape a small lance-head, the other is like the handle of a cup. Each is engraved in Tumuli Plate XXIV. The latter is the third article of the sort we have discovered, yet can we form no idea to what use it was appropriated. In the smaller barrow Dr. Stukeley had cleared a part of the floor, but not finding any interment, he left two half-pence covered with stones; one of the reign of King William the Third, the other of King George the First, 1718. This last is in high preservation, though the period of 86 years has elapsed since it was deposited. On meeting with these tokens, our labourers left off work, thinking that the learned Doctor had been beforehand with us, but from the circumstance of not meeting with any fragments of bones, Mr. Cunnington desired them to continue their researches; when, on exploring the floor of the barrow, they soon perceived the well known line of chalk, which led them to a cist at the east end of the barrow, and to an interment of

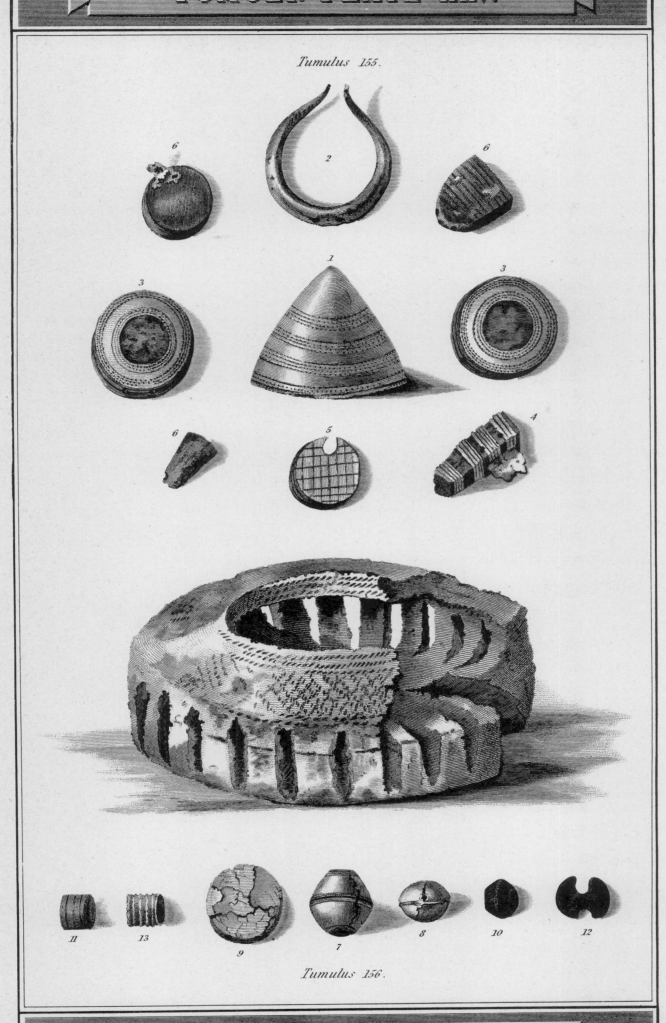

Tumulus 155.

Tumulus 156.

NORMANTON.

P. Crocker del.   J.ᵗ Basire Sc.

Published for W. Miller, Albemarle Street, London, Jan.ʸ 1, 1812.

burned bones, with which were deposited four amber beads, two of jet with convoluted stripes, and a little broken cup.

No. 148 was unproductive ; and No. 149, a Druid barrow, had experienced
a prior opening. In No. 150 we missed the interment. No. 151 is a small
long barrow ; and we found that No. 152, 153, and 154, had been opened
before.

No. 155 is a fine bell-shaped barrow, 92 feet in diameter, and 11 in elevation. On the floor we found a large quantity of burned bones, and with them
an earthen cup of a very singular and novel pattern, a cone of gold similar to
the one discovered in the Golden barrow at Upton Lovel, five other articles of
gold, and several curious ornaments of amber. The cup was unfortunately
mutilated on one side by the pressure of incumbent earth, but its size and pattern
will be sufficiently described by the annexed engraving, TUMULI PLATE XXV.
An enthusiastic antiquary, who was present at the opening of this barrow,
fancied that he could trace in this cup a design taken from the outward circle of
STONEHENGE. The elegant cone of gold, No 1, is ornamented at intervals with
four circular indentations, which are all dotted with a pointed instrument, in
the same manner as the lines on our British pottery, but none of the intervals
of these circular lines are filled up with the zigzag ornament, as in the gold
cone found at Upton. The base of the cone is covered with a plate, which is
also ornamented with indented circular lines, and is made to overlap the lower
edge of the cone, to which it is fastened : it is perforated at bottom in two
places for the purpose of suspension. The outward plate of thin, but pure,
gold, is supported by a cone of blackish wood, on which the indentations correspond exactly with those on the outward cone. The horn-like ornament,
No. 2, is made of brass, but covered with a thin plate of gold : two holes at the
broad part of it, seem to indicate that this also was an ornament of decoration,
and worn by suspension ; and from the position of the perforations in each of
these articles, we might suppose they were worn with their points downwards.
The two circular trinkets, No. 3, are extremely beautiful, and in high preservation ; they are composed of red amber set round with gold, and are also perforated for suspension : they bear a very strong resemblance to some articles
found by Dr. Stukeley in a barrow, north of STONEHENGE, and engraved in TAB.
XXXII. where he describes them as being of earth covered with gold. In
No. 4, we see another trinket of red amber, decorated with fluted stripes of
gold, and having the usual perforations : a thin bit of brass still adheres to it,
and which appears to have been fastened to the amber by two rivets. No. 5 is

a checquered plate of gold laid over a piece of polished bone. On first sight of this article we might be led to suppose that the hole on the top had been made for the purpose of suspension, but on a close examination of it, we evidently see that the points never joined ; and the holes for stringing are on the back part. Besides these various ornaments of gold, there were several articles of deep-coloured amber, and of a novel shape, No. 6. No barrow that we have yet opened has ever produced such a variety of singular and elegant articles, for except the cone of gold, all are novelties, both in pattern and design.

No. 156 is a fine bell-shaped barrow, 102 feet in base diameter, and 10 feet in elevation above the plain. It contained within a very shallow cist, the remains of a skeleton, whose head was placed towards the west, and a deposit of various elegant little trinkets ; the most remarkable of which are two gold beads, engraved of their original size in TUMULI PLATE XXV. No. 7, 8. The first is of an oblong form, large, and ornamented with circular rings ; the other is much less, and of a globular form ; they appear to have been formed by first making a wooden bead, and then covering it with two thin plates of gold, which were overlapped in the centre, and made fast by indentation ; for in none of these golden articles have we ever distinguished any marks of solder, or any other mode of fastening than by indentation. The large bead is perforated lengthways, the smaller one in two places on one side. Besides these beads of gold, there were several trinkets of jet, amber, &c. viz. a flat piece of amber, No. 9 ; two other pieces, the one plain, the other marked with transverse lines, both perforated ; also two round beads of amber ; a jet bead of a globular form, but much compressed, No. 10 ; another with convoluted stripes, No. 11 ; an article of jet, singular in its shape, No. 12 ; and some curious beads of stone, one of which, No. 13, seems to be the joint of a petrified *echinus*. Besides the above articles, the most remarkable of which are engraved in TUMULI PLATE XXV. we found another beautiful little grape cup, similar to those before described in TUMULI PLATES XI. and XXIV. in high preservation. There was also a drinking cup placed at the feet of the skeleton, which was unfortunately broken, but afterwards repaired. No. 157 had a prior opening.

No. 158. Though Dr. Stukeley has given an engraving of this *tumulus*, under the title of BUSH BARROW, it does not appear that he ever attempted to open it. It was formerly fenced round and planted with trees, and its exterior at present bears a very rough appearance from being covered with furze and heath. The first attempts made by Mr. Cunnington on this barrow proved unsuccessful, as also those of some farmers, who tried their skill in digging into it.

P.Crocker del.

J.º Bafire Sc.

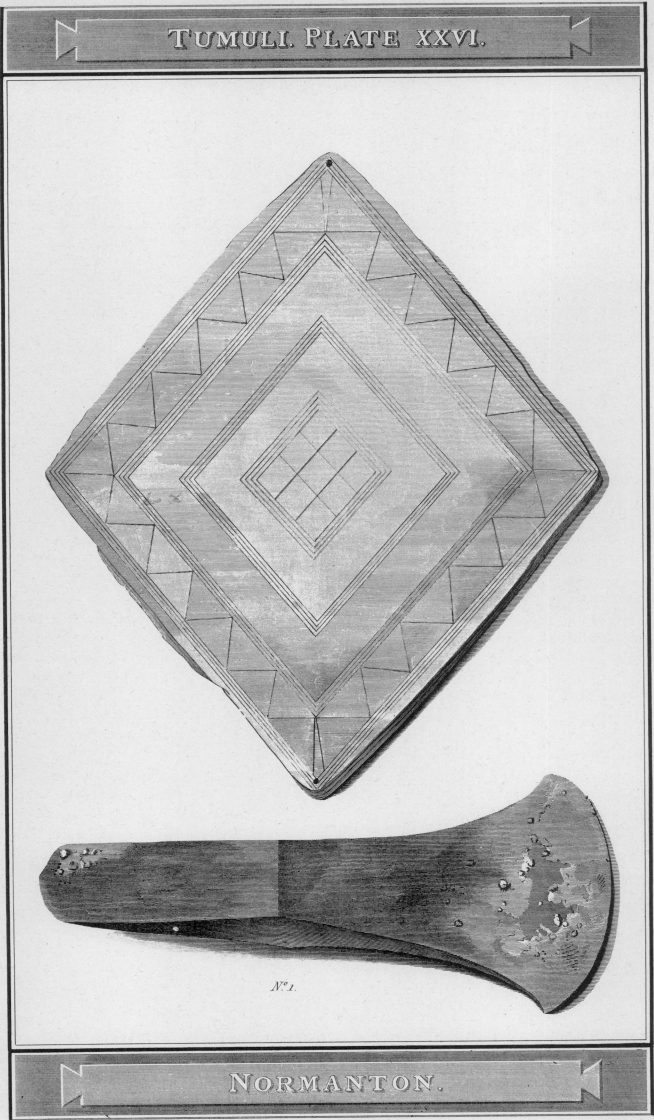

N.º 1.

NORMANTON.

Published for W. Miller, Albemarle Street, London, Jan.ʸ.1. 1812.

Our researches were renewed in September, 1808, and we were amply repaid for our perseverance and former disappointment. On reaching the floor of the barrow, we discovered the skeleton of a stout and tall man lying from south to north: the extreme length of his thigh bone was 20 inches. About 18 inches south of the head, we found several brass rivets intermixed with wood, and some thin bits of brass nearly decomposed. These articles covered a space of 12 inches or more; it is probable, therefore, that they were the mouldered remains of a shield. Near the shoulders lay the fine celt* Tumuli Plate XXVI. No. 1, the lower end of which owes its great preservation to having been originally inserted within a handle of wood. Near the right arm was a large dagger of brass, and a spear-head of the same metal, full thirteen inches long,

---

* The word CELT has been applied to instruments of a very different form as well as composition, and much has been written, engraved, and published concerning them. In the fifth volume of the *Archæologia*, we find a dissertation on them by Mr. Lort, accompanied by numerous engravings describing their different forms, some few of which resemble those that we have discovered; but one only is recorded as having been found in a Long barrow near Stonehenge by Dr. Stukeley, and not recorded as a certainty. Much conjecture and debate have been employed by various authors respecting the original use of this instrument. Mr. Thoresby, in a letter to the celebrated antiquary Thomas Hearne, supposes them to have been heads of spears, or walking staves of the civilized Britons; but this opinion is rejected by Hearne, who thinks they were chissels used by the Romans for cutting and polishing stones. A curious inscription at Pola, in Istria, ascertains that the word *celtis* denoted a chissel or graving tool, " *Neque hic atramentum, vel papyrus, aut membrana ulla adhuc, sed malleolo et celte literatus silex,* [Gruterus page 329]. Dr. Borlase also, in his Antiquities of Cornwall, page 281, has given an account of several brass celts found in that county, together with an engraving. He supposes them to have been offensive weapons, and to have been made and used by the Romanized Britons. Dr. Stukeley attaches a degree of religious authority to them, by supposing that they were used by the Druids for cutting the misletoe. These instruments differed in their constructions, and in point of antiquity, for I must give the priority of age to those discovered in our barrows, of which I am enabled to produce four specimens. The first engraved in Tumuli Plate XXI. is highly interesting, and shews the mode in which the brass instrument was inserted in the handle. The second, engraved in Plate XXVI. is of a much larger size, but also had its handle; as well as two others engraved in subsequent plates, which, though smaller, resemble the others in form. I am obliged, from conviction, and from the strong evidence afforded by this handle, to differ from the learned antiquaries who have delivered their opinions on this subject. I cannot, with Mr. Thoresby and Dr. Borlase, suppose them to have been spear-heads, or offensive weapons; neither can I agree with the laborious antiquary, Thomas Hearne, in supposing them edge-tools for cutting stones, for the metals of which they are formed are too soft for such a purpose; neither do we find the edges furrowed and scratched by hard usage; nor can my antiquarian zeal and enthusiasm persuade me to coincide, in this instance, with the Druidical system of Dr. Stukeley. They appear to me to have been instruments used for domestic, not for military, architectural, or religious purposes. These appear also to have been the *first* models, from which the pattern with sockets for the insertion of a handle was taken; for amongst the numerous specimens described by Mr. Lort in the *Archæologia*, not one of the latter pattern is mentioned as having been discovered in a barrow. As many similar instruments have been found in Gaul, and have been noticed by Montfaucon, and Caylus, I cannot attribute the sole manufacture of them to Britain, but rather suppose they were imported thither from the mother country on the continent; or perhaps the art of making them might have been introduced. One circumstance, I think, appears evident and conclusive; viz. that the earliest pattern, and which probably gave rise to the larger and more ornamented one, was that described

and the largest we have ever found, though not so neat in its pattern as some others of an inferior size which have been engraved in our work. These were accompanied by a curious article of gold, which I conceive had originally decorated the case of the dagger, TUMULI PLATE XXVII, No. 1. The handle of wood belonging to this instrument, No. 2, exceeds any thing we have yet seen, both in design and execution, and could not be surpassed (if indeed equalled) by the most able workman of modern times. By the annexed engraving, you will immediately recognize the British zigzag, or the modern Vandyke pattern, which was formed with a labour and exactness almost unaccountable, by thousands of gold rivets, smaller than the smallest pin. The head of the handle, though exhibiting no variety of pattern, was also formed by the same kind of studding. So very minute, indeed, were these pins, that our labourers had thrown out thousands of them with their shovel, and scattered them in every direction, before, by the necessary aid of a magnifying glass, we could discover what they were; but fortunately enough remained attached to the wood to enable us to develop the pattern. Beneath the fingers of the right hand lay a lance-head of brass, but so much corroded that it broke to pieces on moving. Immediately over the breast of the skeleton was a large plate of gold, TUMULI PLATE XXVI, in the form of a lozenge, and measuring 7 inches by 6. It was fixed to a thin piece of wood, over the edges of which the gold was lapped: it is perforated at top and bottom, for the purpose, probably, of fastening it to the dress as a breast-plate. The even surface of this noble ornament is relieved by indented lines, checques, and zigzags, following the shape of the outline, and forming lozenge within lozenge, diminishing gradually towards the centre. We next discovered, on the right side of the skeleton, a very curious perforated stone, some wrought articles of bone, many small rings of the same material, and another article of gold PLATE XXVII, No. 3, 4, 5. The stone is made out of a fossil mass of *tubularia*, and polished; rather of an egg form, or as a farmer who was present, observed, resembling the top of a large gimlet. It had a wooden handle, which was fixed into the perforation in the centre, and encircled by a neat ornament of brass, part of which still adheres to the stone. As this stone bears no marks of wear or attrition, I can hardly consider it to have been used as a domestic

in four instances as having been discovered amongst other sepulchral deposits in British *tumuli*. The celts of flint, engraved in TUMULI PLATES V. VI. were evidently used for chipping stone or other materials, of which I can adduce a curious proof, by the circumstances attending the discovery of one of these articles, which is now in my possession. Some workmen in cutting a canal, near Stockbridge, found several of these flint celts dispersed about the soil, and deposited near the rude trunk of a tree, which apparently was intended to have been fashioned by their means into a boat or canoe.

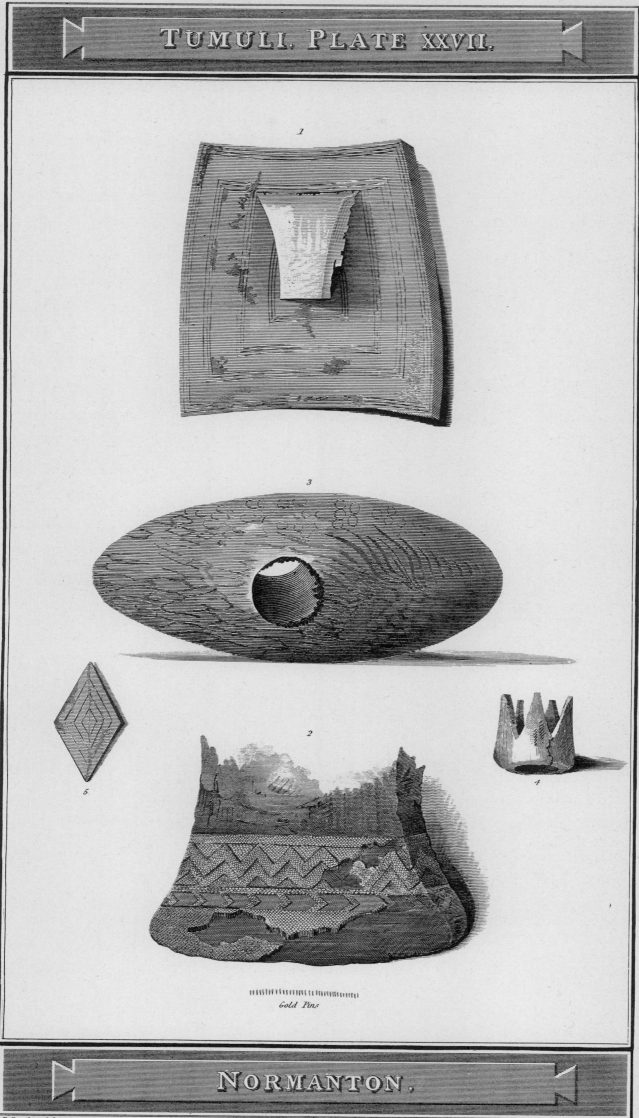

1

3

2

5

4

Gold Pins

NORMANTON.

P. Crocker del.

J⁺ Basire Sc.

Published for W.Miller, Albemarle Street, London, Jan.ʸ 1.1812.

implement, and from the circumstance of its being composed of a mass of sea-worms, or little serpents, I think we may not be too fanciful in considering it an article of consequence. We know, by history, that much importance was attached by the ancients to the serpent, and I have before had occasion to mention the veneration with which the *glain nadroeth* was esteemed by the Britons ; and my classical readers will recollect the fanciful story related by Pliny on this subject, who says, that the Druid's egg was formed by the scum of a vast multitude of serpents twisted and conjured up together. This stone, therefore, which contains a mass of *serpularia*, or little serpents, might have been held in great veneration by the Britons, and considered of sufficient importance to merit a place amongst the many rich and valuable relicks deposited in this *tumulus* with the body of the deceased.

No. 159 and 160 are both Druid barrows : the former had been opened by Lord Pembroke, or Dr. Stukeley: the latter was investigated by us in the year 1804, and produced within a small circular cist, an interment of burned bones, and with it a great variety of amber, jet and glass beads. In No. 161, which is a low barrow, elevated only two feet above the plain, we found a skeleton, with its head laid towards the south-east, and with it a drinking cup. Eighteen inches lower down was another, lying on its left side, with its head towards the east ; and beneath it, we discovered a cist of the depth nearly of six feet, cut in the chalky rock, and containing the primary interment, of a young man, with his head lying towards the north, and a drinking cup close to his right hand ; it had been neatly ornamented, but was broken by the pressure of the incumbent earth. No. 162, a fine Druid barrow, had been opened before ; and No. 163, contained an interment of burned bones, deposited in a shallow oval cist, with the fragments of a small cup, and a bone pin.

No. 164 may be considered as the most beautiful bell-shaped barrow in the plains of STONEHENGE. Its base diameter is 145 feet, and its elevation 14½ feet. It contained within a very shallow cist, the skeleton of a man with his head deposited towards the north-east upon a plank of elm wood : on the left side of the head was a fine dagger of brass, and a small lance-head of the same metal, the former of which had been guarded by a wooden case : at the feet of the skeleton was a richly ornamented drinking cup, which was unfortunately crushed to pieces. We also found some stag's horns at the head and feet of the skeleton. In making the section in this barrow, our labourers perceived three apertures in the soil at some considerable distance apart, which at first they considered as rabbit holes, but on working further, they found that they extended from the top of the barrow to the interment of a skeleton at the bottom: and in these apertures they frequently discovered large quantities of petrified oak wood. It is difficult to account for this singular circumstance, unless we suppose that, on the interment of this Briton, three pieces of oak timber had been placed either upon or near the body, which diverged in an angular direction towards the summit, and as in process of time the wood became nearly decomposed, the calcareous water, by draining through the apertures, might fossilize the decayed wood, and produce the above petrifaction.

No. 165 is a small oblong barrow, which was opened by a section at the broad end, where the interments in similar *tumuli* are usually found: but in this instance we were disappointed in not finding the sepulchral deposit.

No. 166 contained the remains of a skeleton, accompanied by a drinking cup, and stags' horns. No. 167 is a pond barrow. No. 168 produced an interment of burned bones; and No. 169 did not prove sepulchral. No. 170 is a long barrow, not opened; and No. 171 denotes a group of various *tumuli* of different sizes; the largest of which produced a rude urn, some jet beads, and a brass pin. In another, which had been opened before, we found the fragments of a large urn, and a piece of granite similar to one found in a barrow at Upton Lovel. Nearly all the smaller barrows in this group contained simple interments of burned bones. In No. 172 we at first discovered a circular cist, containing a vast quantity of black ashes, with a few fragments of burned bones; but the interment was placed on the floor, by the side of the cist. With the bones was found a large ring, and several beads of a dark olive brown colour, made from some bituminized substance. No. 173 is a long barrow. In making, as usual, our section at the broad end, where experience has taught us the sepulchral deposit was generally made, we discovered, at the depth of 18 inches from the surface, a skeleton, and on reaching the floor of the barrow, four other skeletons strangely huddled together; yet from the regular appearance of the *stratum* of chalk over them, we had no reason to think that the barrow had been opened before. The bones were in a high state of preservation, and one of the persons here interred seemed to have had no forehead, the sockets of his eyes appearing to have been on the top of his head, and the final termination of the *vertebræ* turned up so much, that we almost fancied we had found the remains of one of Lord Montboddo's animals. No. 174 had been opened before. No. 175 contained a simple deposit of burned bones; and in the small *tumulus* attached to it, and which had been investigated, we found fragments of another interment. In No. 176, a fine bell-shaped barrow, we found a

BARROWS ON WILSFORD DOWN.

BARROWS ON LAKE DOWN.

P. Crocker del.

Published for W. Miller, Albemarle Street, London, Jan.ʸ 1, 1812.

J⁰ Basire Sc.

skeleton lying on the floor with its head towards the north ; but the excessive severity of the weather prevented Mr. Cunnington from investigating this barrow as minutely as he could have wished.

No. 177 is only the base of a large circular barrow, the earth having been removed for agricultural purposes ; yet we were fortunate in finding the spot where the deposit of burned bones was made, and with them a fine spear-head of brass. No. 178 contained a simple interment of burned bones ; and No. 179, 180, had been opened by the neighbouring farmers. No. 181 is a group consisting of several mean barrows, which we did not think worthy of investigation, as several of them bore the marks of prior opening. No. 182 produced an interment of burned bones, deposited within a wooden box on the floor, and with them the head of a brass dagger, which had been secured by a sheath of wood lined with linen cloth, a small lance-head, a pair of ivory nippers, and an ivory pin. In No. 183 we found an interment of burned bones, and some stag's horns.

Pursuing from hence a southern direction, and crossing a little valley to the opposite hill, crowned with numerous *tumuli*, I observed a solitary barrow in the bottom, which we found to be composed entirely of flints ; and although we discovered the cist, yet we perceived no signs of any interment, or marks of a prior opening.

On ascending the hill, a compact and interesting group of various shaped barrows meets the eye ; and as they stand too close to each other to be numbered distinctly on our general map, I have engraved them on a separate plate, by which their forms will be much more clearly ascertained than by a reference to the large plan. Being situated on a piece of verdant down belonging to the adjoining parish of Wilsford, I have distinguished them by the title of the

WILSFORD GROUP.

No. 1 is a small circular barrow, which had been explored. No. 2 is a remarkably fine Druid barrow, which also had been opened, but not examined minutely, for on one side of the cist we found a neat lance-head of brass, and a pin of the same metal, intermixed with a part of the interment of burned bones. No. 3 is another barrow of the same species, which produced a similar interment by cremation, and a considerable quantity of glass, jet, and amber beads, together with a fine brass pin. In No. 4 we found only the *cinerarium*, containing the ashes, but missed the interment. No. 5, a flat bowl-shaped

3 G

barrow, produced on the floor a simple interment of burned bones, placed by the side of a circular cist, which contained another deposit of burned bones within a beautiful sepulchral urn, TUMULI PLATE XXVIII. No. 1. Close to this urn was another oval cist, containing a similar deposit, together with a spear-head of brass, which appeared to have been almost melted into a rude lump by the heat of the funeral pile. The discovery of three interments within so short a space, and so connected with each other, leads us to conjecture that this might have been a family sepulchre, and probably other interments may still remain undiscovered. No. 6, a Druid barrow, had been opened before. No. 7 is another of the same species, but has three sepulchral mounds within its area; in one of which we found the relicks of the skeleton of a youth, and fragments of a drinking cup; in the centre tump was a simple interment of burned bones, with a small brass pin; and the third seemed to have been opened before. No. 8 is a Druid barrow of the second class, which had also been examined.

No. 9 is a large and almost bowl-shaped barrow, eight feet in elevation. Within a cist two feet deep, we discovered a little pile of burned bones, and with them an ivory pin, a rude ring of bone, and the small brass celt, engraved in TUMULI PLATE XXVIII. No. 2. The cist was protected by a thick covering of flints, and immediately over it was the skeleton of a dog. No. 10 is a pond barrow. No. 11 and 12 adjoin each other, and are wide and low barrows. The former had been opened, and its scattered relicks seemed to indicate two interments having taken place within it, cremation, and the skeleton. The latter proved a singular, though not a productive barrow, and required a good deal of skill and perseverance in opening. From the small elevation of the mound above the natural soil we expected to meet with the interment in a few minutes; but we were obliged to dig ten feet below the level, when we discovered a skeleton, with its head laid towards the east. After digging to the depth of six feet, our labourers began to doubt if the chalk had ever been moved; but a stag's horn, and some charred wood, soon convinced them to the contrary, and encouraged them to proceed, until they finally discovered the object of their research. From the very extraordinary depth at which this body was deposited, we naturally expected to have found some of the rudest weapons of ancient times, but no arms, trinkets, or pottery accompanied this very original British interment. In No. 13, a large bowl-shaped barrow, we found the skeleton of a young and stout man deposited in a shallow cist, with the head towards the south-east, and near it a large and rude drinking cup, engraved in PLATE XXVIII. No. 3. No. 14, a Druid barrow, had experienced a prior investigation; and in No. 15

P. Crocker. del.

J.º Basire Sc.

Publifhed for W. Miller, Albemarle Street, London, Janʸ.1. 1812.

P.Crocker del.

J.ᵉ Basire Sc.

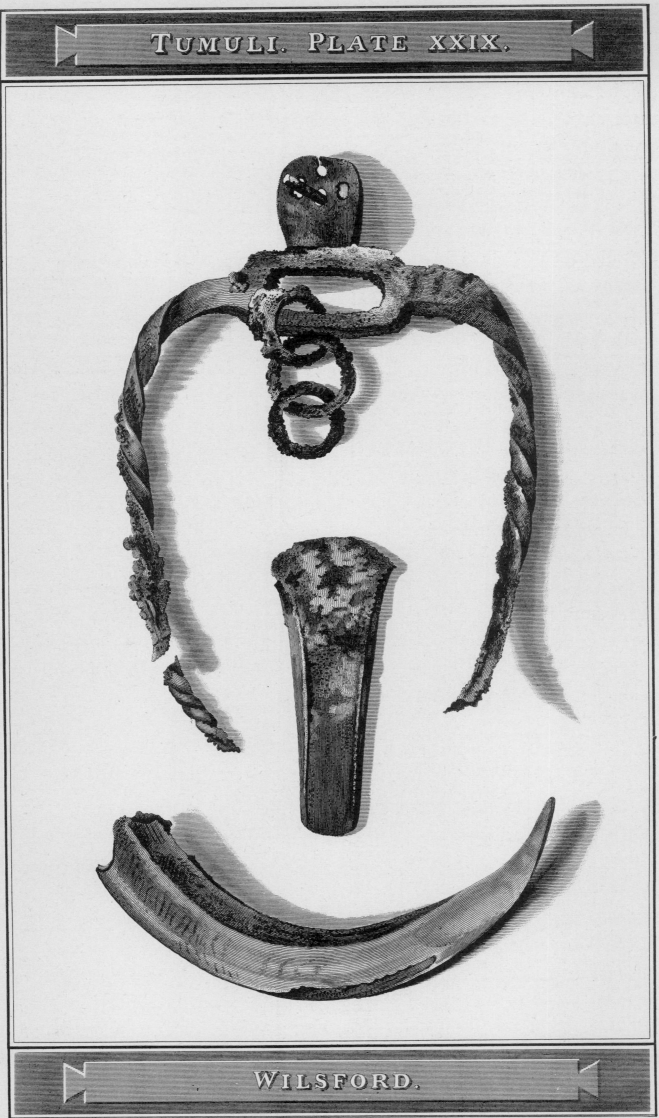

WILSFORD.

Published for W. Miller, Albemarle Street, London, Janⁿ 1. 1812.

we could find no interment. No. 16, a bowl-shaped barrow, produced, at a foot beneath the surface, an interment of burned bones, and some instruments made of stag's horns, some whetstones, an arrow-head of flint, another in an unfinished state, and a small spear-head. TUMULI PLATE XXVIII. No. 4, 5, 6. At a greater depth was the primary interment of a skeleton, with its head laid towards the north-west. No. 17 had been opened before.

No. 18. This large bell-shaped barrow, 121 feet in diameter, and 11 in elevation, may be considered as the monarch of this group, both as to its superior size, as well as contents. On the floor of the barrow we found the skeleton of a very tall and stout man, lying on his right side, with his head towards the south-east. At his feet were laid a massive hammer of a dark-coloured stone, a brass celt, a tube of bone, a handle to some instrument of the same, a whet-stone with a groove in the centre, and several other articles of bone, amongst which is the enormous tusk of a wild boar; but amongst these numerous relicks, the most curious article is one of twisted brass, whose ancient use, I leave to my learned brother antiquaries to ascertain. It is unlike any thing we have ever yet discovered, and was evidently fixed into a handle, as may be seen by the three holes, and one of the pins still remaining : the rings seem to have been annexed to it for the purpose of suspension. This article, together with the celt and boar's tusk form a very interesting engraving, and are all drawn of the same size as the originals in TUMULI PLATE XXIX. At a short distance to the west, on the same line of down, we meet with another fine group of barrows, which I have engraved on the same plate with the former group, and distinguished by the title of

LAKE GROUP.

No. 1 is a long barrow, situated at the south-west extremity of the group, and like many others of a similar form has not been opened, as they have in general proved so uniform in their modes of sepulture, and so very unproductive in articles of curiosity. The diminutive barrow, No. 2, produced, just under the surface, the very rude and perfect little cup engraved in TUMULI PLATE XXX. No.1, which is perforated at bottom like a cullender, and has holes on the sides for suspension. This article seems to corroborate the idea I started in my Introduction, that these small vases might, without any great impropriety, be called INCENSE CUPS, in which aromatic oils and perfumes, according to ancient usage, were burned and suspended over the funeral pile. This cup accompanied an interment of burned bones. No. 3 and 4 had been previously opened by other people. No. 5 was investigated by Mr. Cunnington, in 1805, who found in it an interment of burned bones, with 20 or 30 small black beads, which appear to have been composed of earth or wood, and to have passed the fire.

No. 6 is one of the finest barrows in this group, and is 13 feet 9 inches in elevation. On making our section, the workmen had the good fortune to dig close to the side of a large sepulchral urn which stood within one foot of the surface, without injuring it. It was rudely formed and baked, measured 15 inches in height, and 13 in width, and was placed with its mouth downwards over a large pile of burned bones, amongst which was a fine ivory bodkin, Plate XXX. No. 2. At a further depth of five feet were the remains of two skeletons; and at the bottom of the barrow, and total depth of 13 feet 9 inches, was an oblong cist, five feet deep, and seven feet long, cut in the chalk, containing the skeleton of a child, apparently not more than two or three years old, accompanied by a drinking cup.

The history of this *tumulus*, which our learned Doctor would, from its superior size and beautiful form, have styled a King Barrow, shews what little regard we ought to pay to system; for here, at the vast depth of nearly 14 feet, we find only the deposit of an infant, accompanied by a simple drinking cup: whilst in No. 21, a mean and insignificant barrow, we discover articles of the greatest beauty and importance. The motto of *fronti nulla fides* may be justly and strictly applied to barrows; and the antiquary who makes them his study, must neither be disappointed in finding only a simple interment in the largest barrow, and the finest urns and most precious trinkets in the smallest. Curiosity, however, is equally kept on the alert; and it matters little whether we gain our information by the operations of the spade on a large or a diminutive *tumulus*. No. 7 is a large bell-shaped barrow, composed entirely of vegetable earth. It contained, within a cist, a little pile of burned bones, with which had been deposited a very fine brass pin, a large stone bead which had been stained red, a bead of ivory, and a lance-head of brass, Plate XXX. No. 3, 4.

No. 8 is a very wide and flat barrow, elevated about six feet from the ground, and supposed to be the one from which the French Prophets,* about the year

* Dr. Stukeley says, that the country people call this group the *prophet's barrows*, " because the French " prophets, 30 years ago (A. D. 1710) set up a standard on the largest barrow, and preached to the enthu- " siastic multitude." Among the multitude of protestants who fled from France in consequence of the horrible persecutions which followed the revocation of the Edict of Nantz, were some enthusiasts, who pretended to the gift of prophecy, and other spiritual gifts. These enthusiasts travelled over various parts of the kingdom preaching to the people, and according to tradition, the summit of one of these barrows was chosen as a fit place for the prophet's oration.

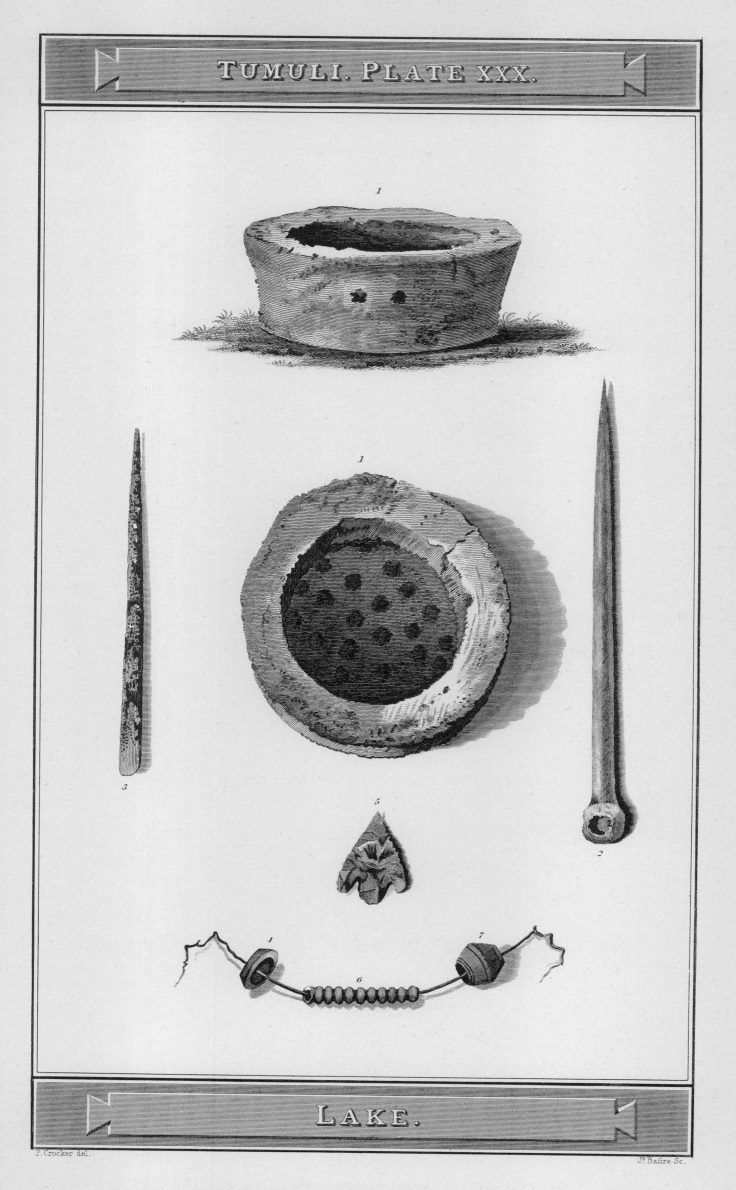

TUMULI. PLATE XXX.

LAKE.

P. Crocker del.

J.ᵒ Bafire Sc.

Published for W. Miller, Albemarle Street, London. Jan.ʸ 1.1812.

1710, delivered their doctrines, as its summit presents an even surface of 48 feet in diameter. To ensure success in a mound of such magnitude, we were obliged to make a very large section, in which, at the depth of two feet, we came to the top of a pile of marl, which encreased in size as we approached the floor. After considerable labour we found, on the north side of our section, the cist from whence this marl had been thrown out; it was eight feet and a half long, and above two feet wide, and contained a pile of burned human bones, which had been enclosed within a box of wood. Near the bones lay a fine spear-head, [PLATE XXVIII. No. 7.] and a whetstone. From the singular form and extraordinary size of this barrow, we expected to have made more important discoveries; and though most probably we found the primary deposit in the centre or place of honour, it is not at all unlikely that the sides of this large mound might produce other sepulchral deposits.

No. 9, a fine bell-shaped barrow, ten feet in elevation, produced only a simple interment of burned bones on the floor. In No. 10 we made two trials, but without success, having found nothing but the skeleton of a dog, and the head of a deer. No. 11 and 12 are two fine Druid barrows, which, from the little trouble attending the opening of them, had excited the curiosity of former antiquaries. No. 13 produced a simple interment of burned bones. In No. 14 and 15 we see a kind of double barrow, the smallest end of which had been opened before. The floor of the larger mound was strewed with an immense quantity of wood ashes, and in a small oblong cist we discovered an interment of burned bones, together with four glass pully-beads, one of stone,* two of amber, and a brass pin. This last *tumulus* is separated from the former group by a bank and ditch, which once formed an old enclosure, for from its situation, and slightness, I cannot consider it as an encampment. On the north side of it, but not within its area, are a few small barrows, scarcely elevated above the soil, which were more productive than their size seemed to promise. No. 21 had been opened before; but amongst the earth and scattered bones, we found some fragments of a fine drinking cup, some chipped flints, and one perfect arrow-head of flint.✝ No. 22 had also been partially opened, for amongst the unburned bones which had been moved, we found the remains of two neatly ornamented drinking cups; and on digging towards the south-east, we discovered the skeleton of a child, and over it a drinking cup.‡ No. 23 contained a simple interment of burned bones within a cist made in the form of a cone; and No. 24 produced a similar interment immediately under the turf, with fragments of a drinking cup.

* The bead of stone, and one of glass, are engraved in PLATE XXX. No. 6, 7.
✝ Engraved in PLATE XXX. No. 5.   ‡ Engraved in PLATE XXVIII. No. 8.

Two feet lower down, we discovered another deposit of burned bones immediately over the head of a skeleton ; and beneath this we found a second skeleton lying with its head towards the north-west, and several large pieces of stag's horns by its side.

In my description of this group of barrows, I made a deviation from the regular numerical course, and omitted those numbered 16, 17, 18, 19, 20. These claim a separate owner, under whose immediate inspection they were opened, and under whose fostering care the very singular and curious relicks which they produced, are cautiously preserved, at his venerable and picturesque old mansion-house in the adjoining village of Lake. These five *tumuli* were opened by the Rev. Edward Duke, in the year 1806 ; and I am happy to think that the zeal he shewed in his first antiquarian researches was so amply remunerated, as to induce him to resume them on some future occasion ; for few barrows ever proved so interesting as No. 19 and 20. A great similarity attended the three first of these *tumuli*, No.16, 17, 18, as they each contained an interment of burned bones, and each produced a small lance-head of brass ; but though No. 20 had also a lance-head, the uniformity was most pleasantly broken by the discovery of four curious little articles of bone, which were intermixed with the ashes and burned bones. They are a perfect novelty, and had their meaning and use in British times ; though in the more modern and enlightened period of the present day, we are at a loss to conjecture what that meaning and what that usage were. The obverse and reverse of each is faithfully delineated in Tumuli Plate XXXI. by which you will perceive that the superficies is flat on one side, and convex on the other ; they are made of bone, which appears to have been stained and polished by attrition ; and each side is marked with a different pattern and device, except in one instance, where both sides are left blank. We might be led to suppose by this circumstance that the custom of casting lots existed amongst the Britons, and that these articles were appropriated to that purpose ; or, perhaps, they might have been used like the ancient *talus* or *tessera*, for some kind of game. But in whatever light we view them, they must be considered as the greatest curiosities we have ever yet discovered ; and as forming a slight progressive step towards language and civilization.*

No. 21 is a wide and low *tumulus*, over which the plough has performed its agricultural rites for many years. The mode of interment was here varied, and the very rich and numerous trinkets discovered in this barrow, seem to

* The custom of casting lots prevailed in the earliest times amongst the nations of antiquity, and a late ingenious traveller, Mr. Barrow, informs us that it is still continued in China.

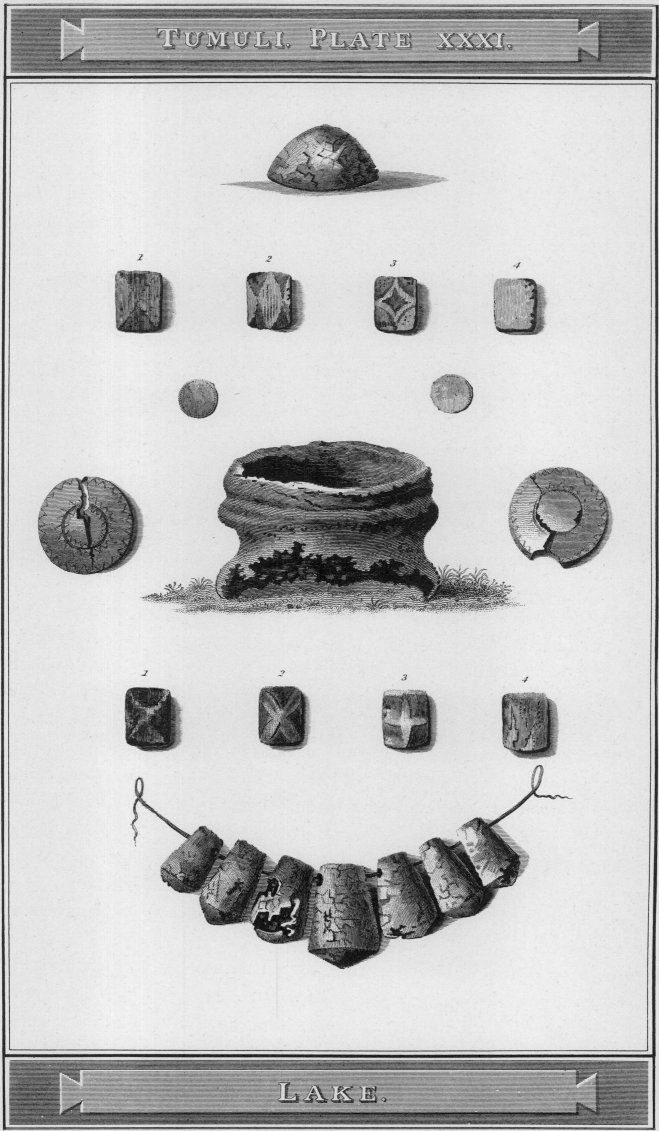

P. Crocker del.

J.º Basire Sc.

Published for W. Miller, Albemarle Street, London, Jan.ʸ 1. 1812.

announce the skeleton to have been that of some very distinguished British female. The most remarkable of these, and unique in size, though not in pattern, was an ornament of amber, similar to that before engraved in TUMULI PLATE III. but far exceeding it in all its proportions, being ten inches in height and above three in breadth ; it is formed of eight instead of six distinct tablets, and by being strung together, formed one ornament, as may be distinctly seen by the perforations at top and bottom. Besides the above were numerous beads of amber of much larger proportions than usual, and varying in their patterns, four articles of gold perforated, perhaps for ear-rings, and two small earthen cups, the one about seven or eight inches deep, the other little above an inch. The largest of the beads, the gold ornaments, and the fragment of the smallest cup are engraved of their full size in TUMULI PLATE XXXI.

Immediately on the back, or west side of this group of barrows, is an ancient bank and ditch, which in their northerly course may be traced to the junction of the Devizes and Deptford roads, where they are lost in the arable lands, when pointing towards the two British villages before described on Winterbourn Stoke down. You will also perceive by the map of this Station, that on the south side of the Wilsford group of barrows, two lines of bank and ditch run parallel with each other for a considerable distance, and ascending the hill, lead directly into another British village, where, on digging, we found the usual *indicia* of ancient population. In the intermediate space between these banks, are several barrows belonging to Mr. Duke, which were opened by him in the year 1806 ; but as their contents did not afford any particular novelty, and as I have already spoken so much at large on this subject, I shall not enter into the detail of his researches : it would, however, be an injustice not to mention the very fine and perfect sepulchral urn which one of these *tumuli* produced, and which constitutes the principal ornament of Mr. Duke's Museum at Lake. On the west side of this bank, sepulchral memorials are very thinly scattered over the plain : but the numerous marks of old enclosures, and the rich appearance of the turf, flattered me with the hopes of discovering some British village. I was not, however, successful in my researches, though the spade was made use of in the most likely places; yet from the general appearance of the down, I have strong reason to suppose that one existed in this neighbourhood.

At a short distance from the turnpike road, and nearly opposite to a solitary public house, dignified with the sign of the DRUID'S HEAD, there is a cluster of barrows, so diminutive in size, that their elevation above the soil scarcely exceeds a foot. A leisure hour enabled me to ascertain the mode of interment that had been adopted, which was cremation. Four of the barrows contained sepulchral urns of the rudest texture, and the fifth a simple interment of burned bones. The greater part of the ground on the western side of the turnpike as far as the river Wily, is in tillage ; chance, therefore, and a constant residence on the spot, can alone discover any settlement of the Britons in those parts ; but a little to the south-west of the DRUID's HEAD, on the declivity of a hill, is a large square enclosure surrounded by an earthen *agger* ; and still further to the south, we meet with an ancient bank and ditch, which abut against the turnpike road and trackway leading to some earthen works above Heale, which I shall describe hereafter. Following the great road to Salisbury, we may observe a barrow on its side, which owing to the high ground on which it stands. becomes rather a conspicuous object. It is called Newton barrow, and must have been of much larger dimensions before it was ploughed over. We opened it in July, 1805, but found that some antiquary, probably the Earl of Pembroke, or our good friend the Doctor, had been before hand with us. Our researches, however, were not totally fruitless or unproductive of novelty, as we found one amber bead, and a great many articles made of the teeth of some animal, and perforated, probably for the purpose of a rude necklace ; the bones also that were dispersed about a deep cist cut in the chalk, were strongly tinged with verditer, a proof that articles of brass were once deposited within this barrow, whose history, we regret, was not recorded by those who investigated it. We afterwards opened two small flat barrows on the apex of the adjoining hill, but found that they also had been explored.

Following the turnpike road that leads to Salisbury, we meet with an ancient bank and ditch, which in a former part of my work [page 110] I noticed as coming from the ridge of Groveley wood, crossing the road from Deptford to Wilton near the village of Chilhampton and the vale of Wily, and from thence pursuing its course across the Devizes road towards the vale of Avon. From the inequality of the ground where this bank seems to terminate, and from the commanding situation of the hill, I entertained a strong suspicion that a British village once existed on this spot, which was corroborated on a subsequent examination of the ground, by picking up the fragment of a well-turned vessel, and some other detached pieces of pottery ; but all these probabilities ceased when I investigated it with the spade, for the fragments were too few in number, and too thinly scattered about the soil to warrant the supposition of a British settlement having existed on this eminence ; but the most likely ground on its summit being in corn, could not be properly examined. On directing my eye across the vale of Avon, I observed on the down near Little Durnford, a bank and ditch ascending the side of the hill, and which, from their direction, might have formed a continuation with those upon this eminence.

As nothing interesting occurs in the interval between this spot and Salisbury, I shall return along the vale towards my head quarters at Amesbury. On a rough piece of heathy land to the west of Middle Woodford, I observed a little square earthen work with a slight *vallum*, and an entrance towards the east; some faint remains of a bank and ditch are still perceptible near the entrance to this work, from whence they descend into a vale, and are lost; but they seem to point towards a conspicuous eminence called Heale Hill, on the southern declivities of which our spade discovered the *indicia* of British population.* A few barrows are seen dispersed over this tract of heathy land, and on the brow of the hill, projecting towards the vale, are the traces of a very ancient British work: the area comprehends about five acres: the *vallum* of the ramparts is slight, and the form represents an irregular circle: from these circumstances I am inclined to think this was a religious or judicial circle, not a military work; its elevated situation, commanding a most delicious view of the rich vale of Avon, fully answers to the positions usually selected by the Britons for such purposes.

A pleasant ride through the vale, near the picturesque old mansion-house at Lake, conducted me back to Amesbury.

ITER II. In this Iter I shall examine that tract of country bounded by the river Avon on the west, and extending to the limits of our county on the east, a district still abounding in *tumuli*, and other evident marks of a remote and extensive British population.

Quitting Amesbury, and following the turnpike road which leads from thence to Andover, we perceive the hills on each side thickly strewed with barrows of large dimensions; and a little on this side the 76th mile-stone, we find a Druid barrow on the left, intersected by the turnpike road, and at a short distance to the right, a large bank and ditch running nearly in a parallel line with the road, and ascending the hill with it. It is very perfect on this spot, and may be traced along the vale in its course westward down to a barn, and through

---

* The lynchets are very decidedly marked on the declivity of this hill, and, contrary to the custom of modern cultivation, run from top to bottom, and not along the sides of the hill. One of these lynchets differs from the rest, and apparently forms an elevated terrace of approach to the British village.

one large arable field beyond it. In its eastern progress, it continues along side of the turnpike road as far as milestone LXXV. when it makes a bend to the right, and is lost at the commencement of the demesne lands of Sir Charles Malet, at Wilbury. At the 74th milestone an ancient bank and ditch join the turnpike from Beacon Hill; and at Park House another does the same; the course of each of which has been already described in the Everley Station. These banks and ditches are still more numerous on the other side of Park House, and are very visible from the road; but I shall not trespass on the antiquities of Hampshire, having sufficient game to pursue within my own county. I shall only observe, that on pursuing one that came from Quarley Camp on the right of the road, I was led directly into a British village upon an eminence to the left.

Following the boundary line of the two counties, and passing through the grounds of my friend Sir Charles Malet, and the little sequestered village of Newton Toney, I again find myself on turf, and soon rencounter the well known banks and barrows. Without much fanciful conjecture, we may suppose that one of these ditches formed a continuation of that before mentioned, as they correspond in their respective bearings. The first bank and ditch that occurred, crosses the Roman road, and after continuing for some time over down, ascends the hill in two branches towards a place called Old Lodge; and there takes leave of Wiltshire. The line of the second bank and ditch proves more interesting. It continues its devious course for a considerable distance over hill and dale, leaving on the right a fine group of barrows, several of which were opened by Mr. Cunnington in the year 1807, at the request of Sir Charles Malet.* On ascending the next summit, and carrying the eye

* The following minutes were sent to me by Mr. Cunnington, respecting his researches on these barrows. " August 6, 1807. About a mile and a half south of Wilbury House, in a shallow vale, immediately under the hills to the south-east, is a group of five barrows; three bowl-shaped, and two of the Druid form: they stand nearly in a straight line, and owing to the ground being in tillage, have been repeatedly ploughed over, therefore much reduced in height. No. 1 is a bowl-shaped barrow, 74 feet in its base diameter, and 3 feet 9 inches in elevation. It contained within an oblong cist, an interment of burned bones, over which was a brass pin. In making the sections, our men found at the depth of two feet the skeleton of a dog, which had been deposited immediately over the cist. No. 2, a bowl-shaped barrow, 69 feet in diameter, and 4 feet in elevation, produced a little pile of burned bones, unaccompanied by any arms or trinkets. No. 3, a fine Druid barrow, of the second class, contained a deposit of burned bones; but Mr. Cunnington thinks he may have missed the primary interment, or it may have been disturbed by a prior opening. No. 4 and 5 had both been examined before.

" From hence we proceeded to a group of eight barrows on Idmiston Downs, two of which are bell-shaped, four bowl-shaped, and two Druid; all situated on a piece of fine maiden down. One of the bell-shaped barrows produced a simple interment of burned bones; and in the other, the sepulchral deposit was not discovered.

CLEARBURY CAMP.

CHLORUS's CAMP.

CHISELBURY RING.

WINKELBURY CAMP.

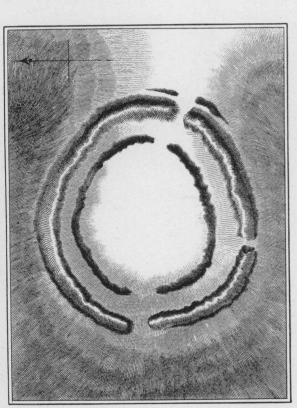
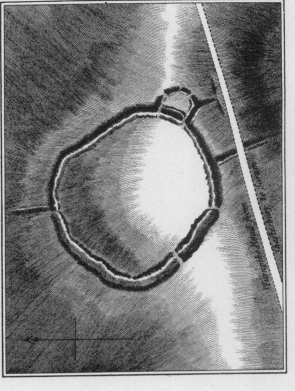

P. Crocker del.

Jᵃ Baſire Sc.

Publiſhed for W. Miller, Albemarle Street, London, Janᵞ 1, 1812.

forward in a southern direction, we perceive a singular coincidence of these banks and ditches ; the one we had been following, continued its course straight forward, and at a short distance further to the west, we see another running in a parallel direction: these are united on the top of the hill by a transverse ditch, and again at bottom by a similar *agger;* thus forming an oblong enclosure, at the lower end of which are the two largest barrows I have seen on our plains, besides many others of smaller dimensions, in the fields behind the public house on the London road, called Winterslow Hut. From the lower end of this enclosure the line of bank is continued, and pursues an easterly course into Hampshire. On returning to the down where I first noticed the branching off of these banks and ditches, I met with two others, the one pointing towards Idmiston in the vale, the other towards an earthen work on a hill, vulgarly called

Chlorus's Camp, but in Mr. Aubrey's *Monumenta Britannica*, as well as in Mr. Camden's *Britannia*, it is noticed under the title of Fripsbury. What the origin of the latter name is, I am at a loss to conjecture. The former may be derived from the British General Constantius Chlorus, to whom, perhaps, the construction of this camp may be attributed. In Kennet's *Parochial Antiquities*, I find this earthen work alluded to, and some history given of its supposed founder. " After the death of Carausius, in the year 297, the Emperors Dioclesian and Maximian succeeded to the government of the empire, and in order to withstand the rebellions that broke out in divers parts of it, elected Galerius Maximus and Constantius Chlorus as their generals. The latter having defeated the usurper Allectus, got a good footing in Britain, and a good governor he was, and was come forwards upon the downs as far as New Sarum,* where, upon the side of the downs he built a fortification, the rampers

" The fine Druid barrow contained within its area, which measured 194 feet in diameter, two raised mounds, in one of which, immediately under the turf, were discovered three large urns, placed within a few inches of each other; they were inverted, and covered the burned bones of three Britons. From being placed so near the surface, two of the urns were broken, but the third is preserved entire in our Museum at Heytesbury. They were all of rude pottery, and without any ornament. Beneath these three urns, in a shallow cist, were the burned bones of another Briton, piled up in a little heap. In the other tump, within the same barrow, was another interment of burned bones, accompanied by the following articles, viz. a small cup similar in size to the very diminutive one discovered at Everley, and engraved in Tumuli Plate XXII. but without ornament; a brass pin, and a considerable quantity of amber beads." In one of the bowl-shaped barrows Mr. Cunnington failed in finding the interment, and the others he did not open.

* For *New*, we must read *Old* Sarum, as the former dates its origin only from the year 1220, and this transaction must have taken place soon after the accession of Dioclesian and Maximian to the empire in the year 304.

whereof still appear very apparently, and is called CHLOREN, after the name
that the Britons gave him, by reason of his long train carried up after him; it
standeth in Wiltshire, upon the north corner of CHLORENDON Park, now called
CLARENDON, which taketh his name thereof; a park of that largeness and bigness
that it exceedeth any park in the kingdom; it hath a church covered over with
ivy in the north part thereof next CHLOREN, which thereupon is now called Ivy
Church: and if we give credit to a late poet, the park had twenty groves in it,
each of them of a mile compass, and without any sophistication, it had a house
of kings within, but long since dilapidated; it doth now belong to the Right
Honourable William Earl of Pembroke, Lord Chamberlain to his Majestie, whose
heart is as large and liberal as the park is wide. This CONSTANTIUS embraced
the Christian faith, and married Helena, daughter to King Coyl that built Colchester, by whom he had Constantine the Great, that removed the empire to
the east, and built Constantinople."

The situation of this camp is delightful, and the prospect from it pleasing and
extensive. Its form is circular, and the area comprehends nearly fifteen acres;
the circuit of the ditch is four furlong 198 yards, and the height of the *vallum* 46
feet; the principal entrance lies towards the east, where there are some slight
traces of an outwork; it had an exit on the opposite side towards the west. One
peculiarity attends this earthen work, and which must immediately arrest the
attention of every eye accustomed to view the ancient specimens of castrametation.
I allude to a deep and irregular ditch within the area of the camp, which forms
a circle within a circle, and appears to have been excavated for the purpose of
procuring materials to raise the *vallum* of the outward ramparts; for it is evident
at first sight, that a large supply of soil has been brought there for that purpose.
Dr. Stukeley, in his *Itinerarium Curiosum*, has given a rude sketch of this camp,
and at page 138 has noticed also this ditch within the area of the camp, which he
supposes was once " a lesser camp, but enlarged by CHLORUS, by removing the
earth of the inner *vallum* to the outward, or new circumvallation;" but I am
rather inclined to think, that there originally was no inner camp, but that the
ditch was merely excavated for materials to raise the ramparts of the camp.

From this camp, I descend into the vale of the Winterbourns, which is
thickly strewed with villages: the adjacent lands are all in a state of cultivation,
and afford no food for the antiquary. Crossing the Roman road, whose line is
but faintly to be distinguished, I direct my course to the adjoining vale of
the river Avon, on the eastern banks of which is a spacious earthen enclosure,
bearing every mark of remote British antiquity, and known by the name of

Ogbury Camp. On this hill we recognize the very early and simple handiwork of the Britons, unaltered by their successors and conquerors, the Romans and Saxons. Here we see a large tract of 62 acres enclosed within a single rampart, and without any fosse to strengthen it against the attacks of an enemy; and we see within the area the evident marks of enclosures, and only one entrance towards the east. On the northern side the ramparts followed the windings of the hill, and are interrupted by the plantations belonging to Lord Malmesbury's demesne at Great Durnford,* in which parish this earthen work is situated. The area contains 62 acres and a quarter: the circuit of the outward ditch is one mile, one furlong, and fifty-five yards, and the depth of the *vallum* is 33 feet. On the south-east and west sides, the ramparts are very much mutilated, and in some places nearly levelled. I cannot consider Ogbury as a camp, or work of defence against an invading enemy, but rather as an asylum or place of refuge, whither the Britons, in times of danger, retired with their families and herds of cattle. Such I am glad to find it was considered by the learned Stukeley, who, in his *Itinerarium Curiosum,* page 138, thus notices it. " On the east side of the river Avon, by Great Durnford, is a very large camp, covering the whole top of a hill, of no determinate figure, as humouring the height it stands on: it is made entirely without any ditch, the earth being heaped up very steep in the nature of a parapet, when dug away level at the bottom. I doubt not but this was a camp of the Britons, and perhaps an *oppidum,* where they retired at night from the pasturage upon the river, with their cattle; within it are many little banks carried straight, and meeting one another at right angles, square, oblong parallels, and some oblique, as the meres and divisions between ploughed lands; yet it seems never to have been ploughed; and there is likewise a small squarish work intrenched, no bigger than a large tent; these to me seem the distinctions and divisions for the several quarters and lodgments of the people within; for I have, upon the downs in Dorsetshire,

---

* The parish church of this little village deserves the antiquary's notice. The north and south doorways present curious examples of Saxon decoration, and the font is richly ornamented with sculpture in the same style.

This church also retains another relick of ancient usage, though not of so remote a date. John Jewel, consecrated Bishop of Salisbury in the year 1560, published, in the year 1562, an *Apology for the Church of England,* to which Harding published a *Confutation* in the following year. This was answered by Bishop Jewel, in 1564, in a book, entitled *A Defense of the Apologie of the Church of Englande.* This work was held in such estimation both abroad and at home, that an order was issued by Queen Elizabeth, King James, and King Charles the First, and by four successive Archbishops, that it should be read and chained up in all parish churches throughout England and Wales. One of these books, in a wooden binding, and chained to a reading desk, still exists in the parish church of Great Durnford.

often remarked the like of too small a compass to be ploughed fields. This camp has an aspect very old; the prominent partof the rampart in many places quite consumed by time, though the steep remains perfect; one being the natural earth, the other factitious. I know not whether we ought to derive the name of it from the British OG, signifying the hurdles and pens they fence their cattle in with, which perhaps stood upon those meres, or little banks, to distinguish every man's property."

I am again happy to do justice to the accuracy of the learned Doctor's description as to the general appearance of OGBURY CAMP, but I cannot attribute the same consequence, or antiquity which he does, to the little square work, which he describes " as no bigger than a tent," for I dug into it, and found no ashes, no bones, no pottery: and I can consider it only as a slight embankment to protect some trees which might have been planted on this very conspicuous eminence in former years. I dug also in several parts within the area of the enclosure, but found no one symptom of ancient residence: but that it was connected with some British establishment in this neighbourhood, I can have no doubt: and I was fortunate during my researches in these parts to discover and investigate that settlement of the Britons, which existed on some high ground adjoining the camp, and whose site is marked on the map annexed to this Station. The extraordinary verdure of the turf induced me to try the efforts of the spade and pick-axe, for the plough had at some very distant period nearly levelled the excavations so usually concomitant with British villages; and I was not deceived by these outward appearances; for we immediately, under a rich and black soil, dug up numerous bones of animals, with fragments of the rudest British pottery.

Pursuing my track from OGBURY CAMP towards Amesbury, I find continued marks of old enclosures, and a variety of banks and ditches, with a few scattered *tumuli:* the disposition of which will be clearly seen on our map. I must not, however, omit to notice two very singular banks and ditches, which run together in a parallel line over the down for the distance of 1716 feet; the breadth between them is 97 feet. At first sight, I thought they might have led us to the discovery of another CURSUS, but their short continuance puts a decided *veto* on such a conjecture. Their situation is marked on the map of this Station, in a line from the 7th mile-stone from Salisbury, to the village of Idmiston. In this same line, I was induced by the fine verdure, and divisions of land on Turpet Hill, to try the spade, and I have reason to think there was a British settlement in this neighbourhood, though I was not successful in discovering the exact site.

The remaining part of the district included within this Station, and hitherto undescribed, is not either of sufficient extent or importance to constitute a separate Iter; for although OLD SARUM is included within its limits, and ought therefore to be described in the account of this Station, I cannot with propriety separate it from the next Station, which derives its name from it, and to which I am now conducting my readers.

The road from Amesbury to Salisbury passes over a tract of open and heathy down, and on approaching the vale of Avon, has several sinuosities, and ridges of verdant down intermixed with corn fields. A few *tumuli* are dispersed about the hills. On Netton Down are two, one of which, composed of a stiff clay, Mr. Duke opened, but he found only a few bits of charcoal, and no sepulchral deposit. He was deterred from opening the other barrow by the stump of a very large yew tree standing on it, which he considered as a boundary mark.

Following the same ridge of down, which presents a most pleasing view of the vale of the River Avon, we approach the village of Little Durnford; then crossing a narrow valley, we ascend another verdant down, on which are a bank and ditch, and several diminutive barrows. One group, consisting of seven, was opened by the Rev. Mr. Duke, in the summer of 1811; and he has obligingly favoured me with the result of his researches. The four largest produced funereal deposits: one contained a simple interment of burned bones within a deep cist; two others produced large and rude urns which were secured by flints at top, but not sufficiently to prevent their being broken; and in the fourth was found another urn in a perfect state, containing, like the three former, a deposit of burned bones: near it were the fragments of two small rude and unbaked cups; and amongst them was the cover or lid of one of them, richly ornamented with indentations, and zigzags, according to the usual pattern made use of by the Britons. This may be considered a very interesting discovery, and is the first instance we have yet seen of a cover to a cup or vase. In the three smaller barrows of this group, nothing was found, so that probably they were not sepulchral. Before I quit this hill, let me notice the very advantageous point of view in which the proud fortress of OLD SARUM, and the more elegant spires and turrets of NEW SARUM, present themselves from this spot, and likewise a passage which I have lately met with in the manuscripts of Mr. Letheuillier, alluding most probably to this very piece of down. He therein notices two barrows " situated on a ridge of hill sloping down to the meadows through which the Avon runs, and where the parish of Durnford stands, from the east side of one of which, in the year 1731, a sepulchral urn was taken filled with ashes; and in the following year a second urn was dug up on another part of the same barrow. In the other *tumulus* the bones of a skeleton were discovered in the year 1732, and with them the head of a spear."

In the *Gentleman's Magazine*, for the year 1754, p. 188, I find an account of some discoveries on Little Durnford downs, which evidently allude to the barrows before mentioned by Mr. Letheuillier; but the contents of the two are confounded, as will be seen by the following extract. " As some labourers were levelling a small barrow on Little Durnford downs, near Salisbury, they found a human skeleton lying on the left side in a sloping posture. It was covered with large flint stones, not above two feet below the surface of the earth; the jaws and teeth were perfectly sound. About twenty years ago [A. D. 1734], two small urns of ordinary clay, and rude workmanship, were taken out of the same barrow, about three feet on the left side of the above skeleton; and not above two yards distant was found a human trunk with a dart in it, which urns and dart are in the possession of a member of the Royal Society, who was at little Durnford when they were dug up.

" The antiquaries are desired to account for the bodies of some, and ashes of others, being buried together in one and the same *tumulus*."

For a solution to this question, I beg leave to refer the antiquary to my Introduction to this Work, where, at page 24, I have described the various modes of sepulture adopted by the Britons, and endeavoured to distinguish the early from the later funereal rites. The customs of burying the body entire, and of burning it, were distinct; but I have reason to think that each custom prevailed at one and the same time; though, in general, when two interments are found in the same barrow, the deepest, and of course the primary one, displayed the deposit of a skeleton. No credit must be given to the assertion of the dart being fixed *in* the body, for no such circumstance has ever occurred, nor is it mentioned by Mr. Letheuillier in his manuscript account of these two barrows.

STATION VII. SALISBURY.

AMONGST the ancient cities of our realm, there are few whose vicissitudes of fortune have been more various, or whose history has been more perspicuously recorded, than that of OLD SARUM. The dry and elevated hill on which it formerly stood, was successively occupied by Britons, Romans, Saxons, and English, and during the empire of the Romans in Britain, was distinguished by the Latin appellation of SORBIODUNUM, and in the succeeding æra of the Saxons by that of SEARBYRIG, SEAROBYRIG, SEAREBERI, and SAERESBYRI, which in more modern times has been changed into SALISBURY. Each of these names may be traced most satisfactorily to their primeval root: for in the Roman title of SORBIODUNUM, we recognize the Celtic words *Sorbio*, dry, and *dun*, a city or fortress ; and in the more modern appellation of SEARBYRIG, we recognize the Saxon words *Sear*, dry, and *byrig*, a town ; so that both the Roman and Saxon titles applied equally to the dry quality of the soil on which the city of OLD SARUM was built ; and although the Saxons changed the word *Sorbio* to *Sear*, and *dunum* to *byrig*, they still preserved in their language the original signification of the *dry city*.

The name of SORBIODUNUM, and the numerous raised causeways issuing from it in various directions (of which I shall hereafter give a minute detail) most clearly attest the occupation of the Romans, though in the bold ramparts still remaining of the old city, we cannot trace any vestiges of that form of castrametation which was usually adopted by them. This strong post was probably wrested from the Britons during the reign of the Emperor Claudius, when his general, Vespasian, is said to have taken twenty British towns, and to have subdued two powerful nations, one of which is supposed to have been

3 L

the Belgæ, who inhabited the western counties of Hampshire, Wiltshire, and Somersetshire.

The Saxon Chronicle affords us many interesting particulars respecting the early history of OLD SARUM; the first of which records a battle fought between Kenric the Saxon and the Britons, in the year 552, at a place called SEAROBYRIG, which terminated in the flight of the latter. *Anno* DLII. " *Hoc anno, Cynricus depugnabat contra Britannos in loco qui dicitur* SEAROBYRIG, *et Britannos in fugam dedit.*"

We are also informed by some ancient manuscripts in the Bodleian and Cotton Libraries, that the illustrious ALFRED, King of the West Saxons, ordered Leofric, Earl of Wiltshire, to repair the fortifications of OLD SARUM. " I ALFRED, King and Monarch of the English, have ordered Leofric of Wiltunshire, not only to preserve the Castle of SARUM, but to make another ditch to be defended by palisadoes: and all who live about the said castle, as well as my other subjects, are immediately to apply to this work."

In the year 960, King Edgar convoked a parliament at Salisbury, which was attended by all the nobles of his realm, in order to devise means of protection for the kingdom of Northumberland, against the invasion of the Danes: " *Rex parliamentum suum apud Sarisberiam convocavit, ubi cunctis regni proceribus congregatis, de custodiâ terræ Northumbriæ, qualiter contrà ingressum Danorum melius posset custodiri, tractaverunt.*" [Bromton Chronicon, p. 866.]

In the year 1003, Sweyn, King of Denmark, availing himself of the unsettled situation of the Angles, conducted his army to Wilton, and having burned and pillaged it, proceeded to OLD SARUM, when that city experienced the same unlucky fate. " Anno 1003, *Suenus autem, videns Anglorum inconstantiam, ad civitatem Wiltoniam suum duxit exercitum, eamque devastavit et incendit; simili quoque modo Serasbyriam consumpsit, et postea suas naves repitiit.*" [Simon Dunelmensis apud X. Scriptores.]

We again learn by the Saxon Chronicle, that King William the Conqueror, after having held his court at Winchester, proceeded to OLD SARUM, where all the nobles, land-holders, &c. met him, and taking the oath of allegiance, acknowledged themselves as his vassals. *Anno.* MLXXXV. " *Hoc anno, Rex, indutâ coronâ, tenuit suam curiam in Winceaster ad Pascha. Postea sic itinera disposuit ut pervenerit in festo Primitiarum ad* SEAREBYRIG, *ubi ei obviam venerunt ejus proceres, et omnes prædia tenentes, &c., omnesque se illi subdidere, ejusque facti sunt vassalli, ac ei fidelitatis juramenta præstiterunt.*"

In the succeeding reign of William Rufus, a council was held at OLD SARUM, at which William, Earl of Ew was impeached of high treason, for having conspired with Robert Mowbray, Earl of Northumberland, against the King's life, and having, according to the usage of those times,* appealed to a trial by duel, and having been defeated, he was punished, by order of the King, with the loss of his eyes ; and William de Aldri, a relation of the King, who was an accomplice in the conspiracy, was ordered to be hanged. Anno. 1096. " *Octavis Epiphaniæ apud* SEARSBERIAM *celebrato concilio,* WILLIELMI DE OWE *in duellio victi oculos eruere, et testiculos abscidere, et dapiferum illius* WILLIELMUM DE ALDRI, *filium amitæ illius traditionis conscium, jussit Rex suspendi.*" [Simeon Dunelmensis, p. 222.]

A. D. 1106. OLD SARUM was honoured in this year with the presence of King Henry the First. Anno. MCVI. "*Ad Pascha Rex* [*Henricus*] *fuit apud Bathan, et ad Pentecosten apud* SEARBYRIG, *propterea quod nollet absens ab Anglia apud transmarinos curiam tenere.*" [Chronicon Saxonicum.]

In the year 1116, King Henry the First assembled the nobles and barons of his realm at OLD SARUM, where, in the presence of their monarch, they swore allegiance, and did homage to his son William. Anno MCXVI. " *Conventio optimatum et baronum totius Angliæ apud* SEALESRIRIAM 14 *calend. Aprilis facta est, qui præsentiâ Regis Henrici homagium filio suo Gulielmo fecerunt, et fidelitatem ei juraverunt.*" [Florent. Wigornensis, p. 657—Bromton, p. 1006.]

Some disturbances which took place, during the reign of King Stephen, between the military and the ecclesiastics, who dwelt together within the fortified ramparts of OLD SARUM, suggested the idea of separating the ecclesiastical from the military establishment, though some authors assert, that the removal was thought of, on account of the dry situation of the old city, and want of water. To these united causes, " *ob insolentiam militis, et ob penuriam aquæ,*" the present city of NEW SARUM owes its removal from a bleak and dry eminence, to the well watered valley of the Avon. In the year 1217, and at the commencement of the reign of King Henry the Third, Richard Poore being at that time Bishop of the see, application was made to Pope Honorius for leave to translate the church to some more convenient situation. In the following year, 1218, a convocation was held, and measures taken for raising money to defray the expenses of a new church. In 1219, a wooden chapel was erected and consecrated ; and in 1220, the foundation stone of the new

---

* The custom of an accused person's claiming the privilege of *duel*, as a proof of his innocence, was of high antiquity in our country, and was introduced soon after the Norman Conquest; we find also by the following quotation from a Danish writer, *Saxo Grammaticus,* that the same usage was adopted amongst his countrymen, " *Controversia ferro decerni sanxit* (Rex) *speciosiùs viribus quam verbis confligendum existimans.*"

cathedral was laid. In 1225 the building was so far advanced as to admit of the performance of divine service within it, at which time the Bishop consecrated three altars, and appointed mass to be sung every day. The charter, granted in the eleventh year of King Henry the Third to the church and city of New Saresbury, proved a death warrant to the city and castle of Old Sarum, of which one solitary house only now remains to testify the ancient occupation of this spot.

But however fallen are the walls of this once celebrated city, the remains of its proud ramparts, and its exalted situation, still continue to attract the attention of the antiquary, the stranger, and the neighbouring inhabitants. On comparing the plan of Old Sarum, with the camps already engraved, you will at first sight perceive, that the depth of its ramparts is far greater than any I have yet described ; they exceed one hundred feet, whilst those of the fine camps at Yarnbury and Amesbury scarcely exceed fifty. The form of this work inclines to the circle ; the area contains 27 acres and a half, and the circumference of the outward ditch is 7 furlongs 26 yards. Within the area is a circular earthen work, rising to a greater height than the outward one, and probably was the citadel : the *valla* of the outward and inner work are nearly of an equal height, those of the former being 106 feet, and those of the latter 100 feet. The area between the outward and inner work is in three places subdivided by earthen banks ; a few fragments of ancient walls remain, and the spot is pointed out where the old church was supposed to have stood, near the western portal. There were two entrances to this city : the principal one, guarded by a horn-work, towards the east, and a smaller one, towards the west.

Three well known Roman roads issued from the eastern port, and directed their respective courses to Venta Belgarum, or Winchester ; to Calleva, or Silchester ; and to Durnovaria, or Dorchester ; I think there must have been a fourth towards the sea coast of Hampshire, and a fifth towards the Roman station of Cunetio near Marlborough. Another Roman road issued from the western portal, and pursued its course through Groveley and Ridge woods, and over the Mendip hills, towards the river Severn ; a description of all of which is reserved for a future publication, in which I shall treat of the Roman æra in Wiltshire.

Iter I. From Old Sarum, I proceed along the track of the Roman road to the village of Ford, where it traverses the little brook that runs through the valley of the Winterbourns, and continue on the same causeway till I

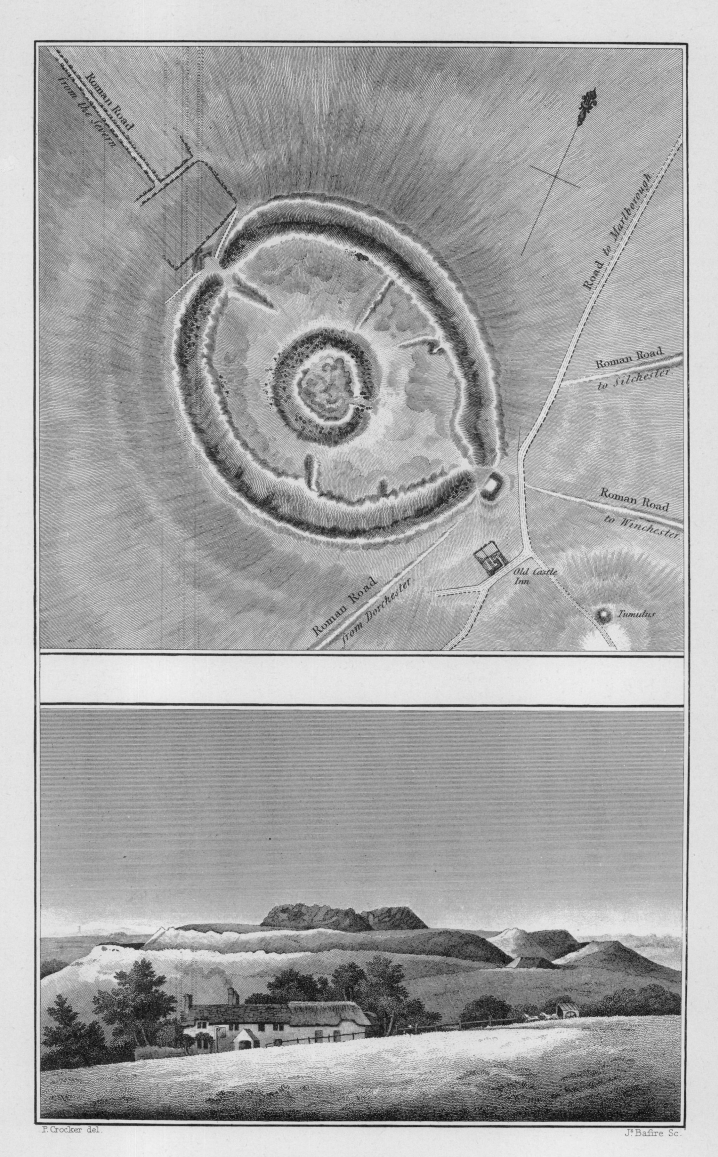

Roman Road from the Severn

Road to Marlborough

Roman Road to Silchester

Roman Road to Winchester

Roman Road from Dorchester

Old Castle Inn

Tumulus

P. Crocker del.

J.ᵃ Basire Sc.

OLD SARUM.

Published for W. Miller, Albemarle Street, London, Jan.ʸ 1. 1812.

ascend a hill a little beyond CHLORUS's CAMP, when meeting a broad bank and ditch, I turn off to the right, in order to develop its course. This earthen work is very broad and bold, and possesses some novel peculiarities, with regard to two semicircular works projecting from the straight line of bank and ditch, the one curving towards the east, the other towards the west, but not facing each other. This bank and ditch lead us (as in many other instances) directly into a British village, where the moles have thrown up great quantities of Romanized British pottery; and in digging both on this spot, and within one of the semicircular works, we found flat paving stones, with which the floors of the ancient huts were probably pitched. From hence, leaving the downy country, I passed through the villages of Pitton and Farleigh. Here the face of the country, and the nature of the soil, are completely changed; gravel succeeds to chalk, and woody districts of great extent succeed to sheep walks and open pastures. On my right was the extensive demesne of CLARENDON, which having been honoured with the residence of our English Sovereigns, ought not to be passed over unnoticed, although the more ancient history of our county is the principal object of my present enquiry. CAMDEN says, " that in the park at Clarendon are the footsteps of two royal palaces, KING MANOUR and QUEEN MANOUR," but he does not inform us who were the original constructors of these palaces. I feel indebted to my friend Mr. Wyndham, the worthy member of our county, for the following interesting particulars respecting this demesne.

" CLARENDON PARK was originally a forest, and the adjoining parishes of Laverstock and Milford are described in Domesday book as having part of their lands in the King's Forest. There is no account existing of the æra in which the old palace was erected; but the remaining walls or masses of flint, with their strong cement, indicate a very high antiquity, as remote, perhaps, as the time of the Saxons. It is, however, certain, that in the year 1164, and in the reign of King Henry the Second, the palace must have been of considerable magnitude and consequence, for history informs us that in the above year, the famous CONSTITUTIONS OF CLARENDON were, after three days debate, solemnly enacted in it, and that the King honoured the council with his presence, at which were assembled the two archbishops, 12 bishops, and 37 barons, all named in the CONSTITUTIONS, *cum multis aliis proceribus et nobilibus regni, tam laicis quam clericis.*

" In the following reign of Richard the First, it is clear, that the King, occasionally at least, resided in this palace, for we see in the Pipe Rolls of that Monarch, that 34 shillings and fourpence were charged for the carriage of the

3 M

king's wine from Clarendon to Woodstock. It is also to be supposed that his successor John did not totally neglect Clarendon amongst his numerous other hunting seats, as the present ruins are still vulgarly denominated KING JOHN's PALACE.

" But in the time of Henry the Third, the son of King John, this palace seemed to have attained its highest splendour, for in the Pipe Rolls of the 30th of Henry III. we find that the sum of £526. 16s. 5d. was paid to one Nicholas for sundry work done for the King and Queen at Clarendon, such as, for making a *marcelsia* with two closets, and two private chambers ; for removing the doors of the old hall into the porch, and for converting the said hall into a room with a chimney and windows ; for another private chamber, for building a large square kitchen, and for other works.* And again, in the 39th of the said king, for making in the New Forest 30,000 shingles, and for carrying them to Clarendon to roof the King's palace, £6. and 1 marc, and for the same number and carriage in another article £11. 10s.

" It appears also that King Henry the Third attended the dedication of the cathedral in New Sarum with his court from Clarendon in the year 1258. The royal chapel was also served by the canons of Ivy church, who received at one time from the King the sum of £35. 0s. 7d. for their attendance. This priory of Ivy church was founded by Henry the Second for four canons, and was situated at the south-west angle of the forest, for the purpose, probably, of ministering to the neighbouring palace. Many lands, even within the forest, were appropriated to this foundation.

" I have seen no account of Clarendon during the reign of Edward the First, but in the succeeding reign of Edward the Second, it appears to have been first called the park, instead of the forest of Clarendon, which name has been continued to the present times. It is said that a parliament was summoned to meet here by Edward the Second in the year 1317, but perhaps, the violent dissensions that prevailed at that time between the King and his barons, prevented its assembling.

" As we find nothing more relating to the palace of Clarendon from the time of Edward the Second, we may reasonably conclude that the buildings soon afterwards began to be neglected, and became ruinous. Many instances, how-

---

* " *Et in unâ marcelsiâ ad opus Regis et Reginæ apud Clarendon, cum duobus inclusoriis, et duabus cameris privatis; hostio veteris aulæ amovendo in porticu, et de eadem aulâ camera facienda cum camino et fenestris et camera privata, et quadam magna coquina quadrata, et aliis operationibus, contenti, in brevis, incepti per eundem Nicolaum, et non perfectis.*"

ever, occur, where this fine park has been subsequently granted by our kings for a term, to peers and other great men of the realm ; as we know that it was so granted by King Edward the Sixth, in the year 1552, to Sir William Herbert, who was created Earl of Pembroke in the preceding year by the same King, for the term of his own life and of his son's, which term ended on the death of the second Earl, in the year 1601.

" In the year 1574, Queen Elizabeth visited Wilton during her progresses, and during her residence there, took the diversion of hunting at Clarendon Park, where the Earl of Pembroke, as keeper, had prepared a sumptuous banquet for her Majesty, under a tent screened with boughs and tapestry ; but the rains were so violent as to oblige both her and her noble host to retire within the lodge, and therein to partake of the entertainment, from which circumstance we may conclude that the palace was then in a state of decay, as no notice is taken of it.

" This event is more minutely recorded in an account of the Queen's entertainment at Wilton, extracted from an unpublished manuscript of Sir Rice Merricke's *Antiquities of Glamorganshire*, written in the year 1578 ; and published in the first volume of Mr. Nichols's *Progresses of Queen Elizabeth*. ' On the Saturday [September, 1574] her Highnesse had appoynted to hunt in Claryngdon Park, where the said [Earl of Pembroke] had prepared a very fair and pleasant banquett - - - - - - - - - - - - leaves for her to dyne in ; but that day happened soe great raine, that although it was fenced with arras, yet it could not defend the wett, by meanes whereof the Queen dyned within the lodge, and the Lords dyned in the banquett house ; and after dinner the rayne ceased for a while, during which tyme many deare coursed with greyhounds, were overturned : soe, as the tyme served, great pleasure was shewed.'

" Other keepers were probably appointed by the Crown after the decease of the Earls of Pembroke, between the years 1601 and 1665, when the park of Clarendon, with many other large possessions, were granted in fee to George Monk, Duke of Albemarle, to all which, his son Christopher, Duke of Albemarle, succeeded, who dying Governor of Jamaica in 1688, without children, bequeathed it to his cousin, Granville, Earl of Bath, from whom, or from whose heirs, it was purchased by Benjamin Bathurst, in the year 1713, and whose family still continue to hold it in possession.

" The present vestiges of ruins occupy a space of about six acres : they consist of large masses of flint strongly cemented together, scattered about in the most irregular manner, rising in some spots to a considerable elevation, and in others fallen into deep cavities; but the whole is so thickly covered with thorns and briars, that few are discernible to the eye without a minute inspection; consequently no plan of the original building can be even surmized. One lofty blank wall of flint only remains upright, and towers above the rest of the ruins, which, from the breadth and slope of the wall, appears to have been the end of some great room, like the hall of a college, the height of which was terminated by the roof. The only remains of an arch that I could discover, were over a deep and wide excavation of some length, and intended perhaps for a cellar. It is not perfect, but the springs of a part of the wall are still apparent, which are formed with a single stone below, and then covered with cemented flints. A high ditched bank, which was formerly walled, surrounds the ruins, and encloses an oblong square of about 60 or 70 acres. This was, I suppose, the home-park of the forest; the palace stood at the south-east corner of this great enclosure. By the original grant from King Charles the Second to the Duke of Albemarle, the park is estimated at 4300 acres, and its value a £1000. a year. It appears that more than a third part of this demesne is at present wood-land."

Iter II. In this second ride, I pursue the Southampton road for nearly three miles; then leaving Longford Castle, the seat of the Earl of Radnor, on the right, and the village of Alderbury to the left, continue my track along the vale towards Standlynch, the seat of the Dawkins family. The only remnant of antiquity which I could perceive in this district, was a mutilated earthen work of a squarish form, on some elevated ground to the left of the road. At Standlynch I quitted the road leading through the vale to Downton and Fordingbridge, and ascended the high land behind the demesne of Standlynch, and although I gained no antiquarian lore, yet my sight was highly gratified with an extensive view, and my horse trod upon soft and verdant turf, until I came to Packam Common, where the country begins to assume the more dreary aspect of a large extent of uncultivated heath lands; but the more distant prospect to the left, or east, is varied by a spacious tract of cultivated enclosures and woodland. This district is distinguished by the name of the Earldoms, which, by a terrier of the Pembroke family, I find was granted in the patent of Ramsbury to William Earl of Pembroke, and the heirs male of his body, 7th May, 6 Edward VI. These woods also did anciently belong to the Duke of Somerset before his attainder; but being then forfeited, were granted out from the Crown as above. The Earldoms are situated in the forest

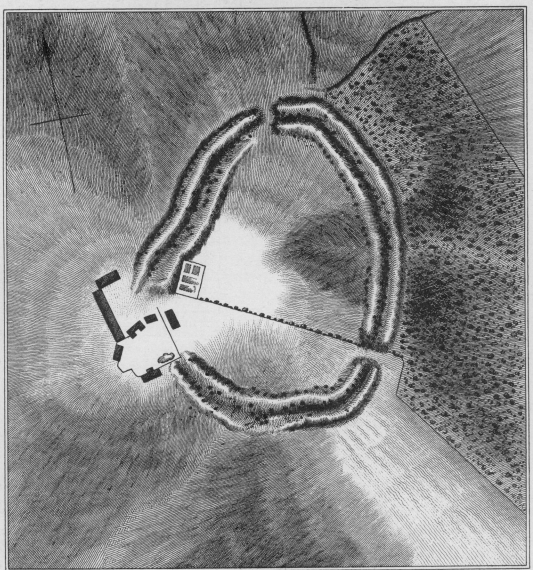

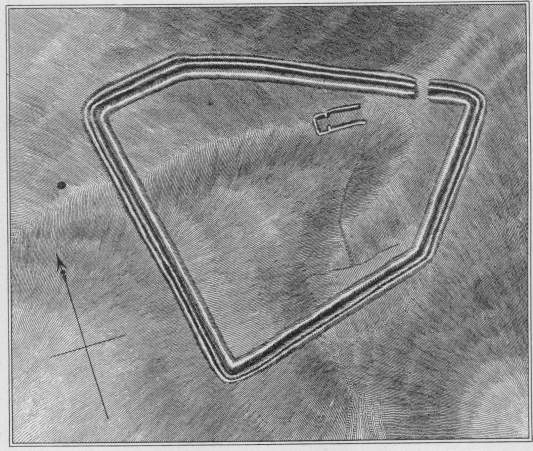

SOLDIERS RING.

P. Crocker del.

J.ᵃ Basire Sc.

Publifhed for W. Miller, Albemarle Street, London, Janᵞ 1. 1812.

of Milchett, and in the parishes of Whiteparish, Landford, and Plaitford. Continuing my ride over a most dreary and extensive tract of heath, and leaving the well-wooded seat of the May family on the right, I proceed to the town of Fordingbridge, on the banks of the river Avon, and there take up my quarters for the night.

Leaving Fordingbridge, I re-enter Wiltshire at Whichbury, and again find myself interested by a continuation of British antiquities. The first is a strong camp, situated on high ground, and occupied by the buildings and enclosures of Whichbury farm. It is single-ditched, and much obscured by copse wood, particularly on the eastern side. The area within the ramparts contains fifteen acres and a half, the circumference of the ditch is 1210 yards, and the height of the *vallum* is thirty-nine feet. There are three openings into the camp, two of which bear the appearance of ancient entrances ; these are situated on the north and south-east sides of the earthen work.

Pursuing my course in a northward direction, I observe an ancient bank and ditch issuing from the camp, and steering north towards an eminence called Gallows Hill ; and a similar bank and ditch is seen still more to the east, coming from the fortress, and pointing towards a Long barrow on Wick Down, where there is one of those relicks of antiquity called a maze. It has the appearance of a low barrow surrounded by circles within circles. I have been informed by a friend well versed in antiquities, that these mazes are to be found in various parts of our island.

Gallows Hill is distinguished by a clump of trees, and a few low barrows ; and the bank before mentioned, which has its *vallum* elevated towards the east, having traversed the point of the aforesaid hill, continues a northern course towards Charlton Down, where it divides into two branches a little to the south of a group of five barrows : one branch continues the same northern course, leaving an earthen work called Clearbury Ring to the right, and is lost amongst the arable lands.

Clearbury Ring is a mean earthen work when compared to the very fine specimens which our county has afforded, but it stands pre-eminent in point of extensive prospect, and is seen at a very considerable distance. Its form presents an oblong square, and it has one narrow entrance towards the south-west : the area is encumbered with heath, and planted with trees, to which it owes its very distinguished appearance from distant parts ; it contains within the ramparts 5¼ acres, the circuit of the ditch is 3 furlong 55 yards, and the depth of the *vallum* is 43 feet. I think it probable that this camp was occupied, or

3 N

perhaps constructed by the West Saxon Kings Cerdic and Cynric, who fought with the Britons in this neighbourhood at Charford in the year 519, and the latter of whom afterwards, in the year 552, defeated the same people at Salisbury.

From CLEARBURY CAMP, I returned to the spot where, as I before observed, the banks and ditches separated into two branches, and followed them over down, furze, and arable lands for many miles, looking around me most anxiously for the well-known *indicia* of British settlements; but although throughout the whole of this extensive line, I observed occasional groups of barrows, yet I could not perceive the slightest indication of any British village. In my progress westward, I passed through a tract of rough ground remarkable for the great quantity of yew trees dispersed over it. The course of this bank and ditch is, I think, more irregular and winding than any I have yet followed; and the *vallum* still continues on the right hand side. It is vulgarly called GRYM'S DITCH, which I imagine is a corruption from the Celtic and British word *grym*, signifying great, powerful, &c. *grim* also, in Saxon, has the same signification as is applied to it in the English language: and in other parts of England we meet with similar appellations; one of these earthen works bearing the name of the DEVIL'S DYKE. Having traversed the turnpike road leading from Salisbury to Blandford between the sixth and seventh mile-stone, this ditch pursues its course towards Vernditch Chace, and crosses the Roman road nearly in a line with the eighth mile-stone. It is to be observed that when the large map of Wiltshire was planned, the limits of this forest extended much further towards the east than they do at present, which will be seen by a comparison of that Map with the one appropriated to this Station. During the latter part of its course, it will be observed also, that the ancient bank forms the modern boundary of Vernditch Chace.

After a long and circuitous ride, I was obliged to abandon the pursuit of GRYM'S DITCH, and to seek out for quarters in the neighbourhood: to these I was conducted by following the bold and well preserved causeway of the Roman road to Woodyates Inn, which stands immediately upon it, and from whence I shall continue my rides through the remaining part of this Station.

ITER III. In following the Roman road from Vernditch Chace to Woodyates Inn, our attention is arrested by the circumstance of the junction of the said road, with an immense bank and ditch, called BOKERLEY. The question in this instance, as well as in the similar one at SCOTS POOR (page 187) viz. which was made first, the bank, or the road, may excite much controversy amongst antiquaries, but if I were allowed to give my opinion, I should say, that the banks and ditches existed before the formation of the causeway: for on the spot where I left off tracing GRYM's DITCH, I plainly saw a continuation of the bank on the west side of the causeway: and the same appearance exists at BOKERLEY DITCH; but the strongest circumstance in favour of this hypothesis is, that the Roman road which in its course westward from OLD SARUM had invariably pursued a straight line, except where prevented by intervening hills, on meeting this bank and ditch, makes a considerable angle towards BADBURY CAMP. It therefore appears probable that the Roman engineers, finding that they had deviated from the true and direct line, availed themselves of this large bank, and took an opportunity of correcting their error on this precise spot.

Following this bank and ditch in a south-east direction, I observed on the northern side of it one of those slight and irregular earthen works which are so common upon our downs, having an entrance towards the south-east: a little further I perceived a bank and ditch issuing from BOKERLEY, and apparently belonging to another marked down on our map, which points towards Vernditch Chace, and the Roman road. Just beyond it are two barrows, and further on near the summit of the hill are two more, which we opened in the year 1805. The one nearest the ditch contained an interment of burned bones and ashes, deposited within a large sepulchral urn of rude pottery, placed with its mouth upwards: it was protected by an immense heap of flints thrown indiscriminately over it. In the adjoining barrow we also found a similar interment within a sepulchral urn, placed with its mouth upwards, and nearly of the same dimensions as the former, but superior in point of shape. Some remains of the linen cloth, which probably covered the interment and mouth of the urn, were plainly distinguishable.

On the summit of the hill there is another barrow, and some excavations; which I was prevented from investigating. Here BOKERLEY DITCH separates into two branches; the largest and original work directs its course southerly, and is lost on Pentridge in some rough ground. The other line points due east, and leads directly into a British village upon a piece of down opposite to the village of Tippet. A little to the west of this village, we clearly see that the bank and ditch have deviated their course in order to avoid a Long barrow, a circumstance which has before occurred, and proves the high antiquity of the sepulchral mound. Adjoining the British village is a low *tumulus*, and the site of another that has been levelled. Of this latter I find the following account in the *Monumenta Britannica* by Mr. Aubrey. "In a barrow above Tippit, in the parish of Martin, by digging for a foundation for a windmill post A. D. 1650, an urne was found with small pieces of burned bones in it, and a spear's head, and the tusk of a boare with a hole made in it as if to put a string in it. I had it, but gave it to the Royal Society." Mr. Aubrey also thus notices the excavations, which are the marks of a British village. " About this Tippit, and other parts here about are pitts of great antiquity. I could never learn why they were made." The bank and ditch having crossed the valley, leave Allenford barn to the right, and ascend Windmill hill, on which there is a group of five barrows, and some others detached. Here the bank and ditch are soon lost. Northward from this eminence is Knowl Hill, on which are some very large Long barrows.

Recrossing the vale a little more to the eastward, I found a most curious earthen work, on the declivity of a vale of rich turf leading to Damerham. It is known by the vulgar name of SOLDIER'S RING. This work is very novel and singular both in its form and construction, and unlike any earthen work we have yet found. Its form presents an irregular pentangle: the western side is straight, and the eastern end terminates in a point: close to this angle is the only entrance into the work, and near it, within the rampart, is a little oblong work, open towards the east.

The inside of the area contains twenty-seven acres and a half; and the circumference of the work on the middle rampart is 1540 yards, the greatest depth of the *vallum* is eight feet. The construction of the *agger* differs from any I have seen, and from its weakness cannot have been raised for the purpose of defence: it is finished with a more than usual degree of regularity, and presents a section of one low rampart between two of a greater height: this work occupies the declivity of a hill at the head of two slight vallies.

From hence I continued my ride over a fine down, and crossed a ditch, which appears to issue from the British village before described. In my return to Woodyates Inn, I followed the western side of BOKERLEY DITCH, and in my way observed several barrows. Two of these are nearly opposite to those last described, and were opened by us at the same time. The largest contained two skeletons, and several instruments of iron, viz. a lance-head, two knives, and an article of bone. TUMULI PLATE XXXI. No. 1, 2. In the other barrow we found a large sepulchral urn of rude half-baked pottery, and simply ornamented, with its mouth placed upwards, and within it an interment of burned bones. The top of the urn seems to have been covered by two flat pieces of rude unworked flint. Having observed a cavity amongst the flints, and finding the ground soft,

P. Crocker del.

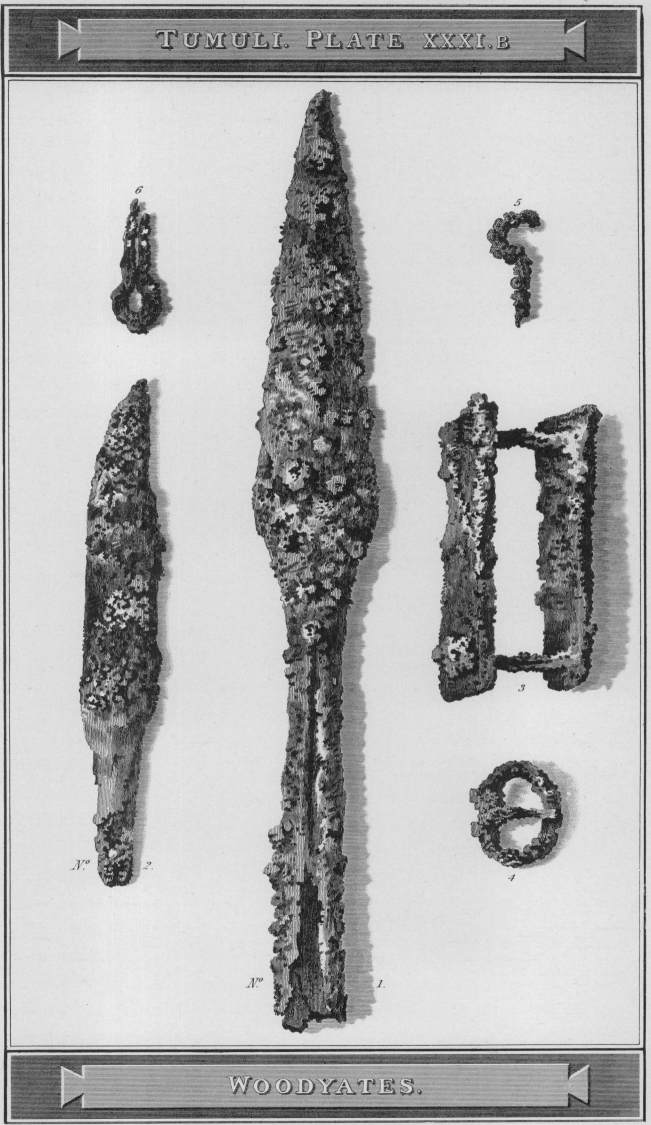

6

5

N.º 2.

N.º 1.

3

4

J.ª Basire Sc.

Publifhed for W. Miller, Albemarle Street, London, Janʸ 1.1812.

P. Crocker del.

J.ᵃ Basire Sc

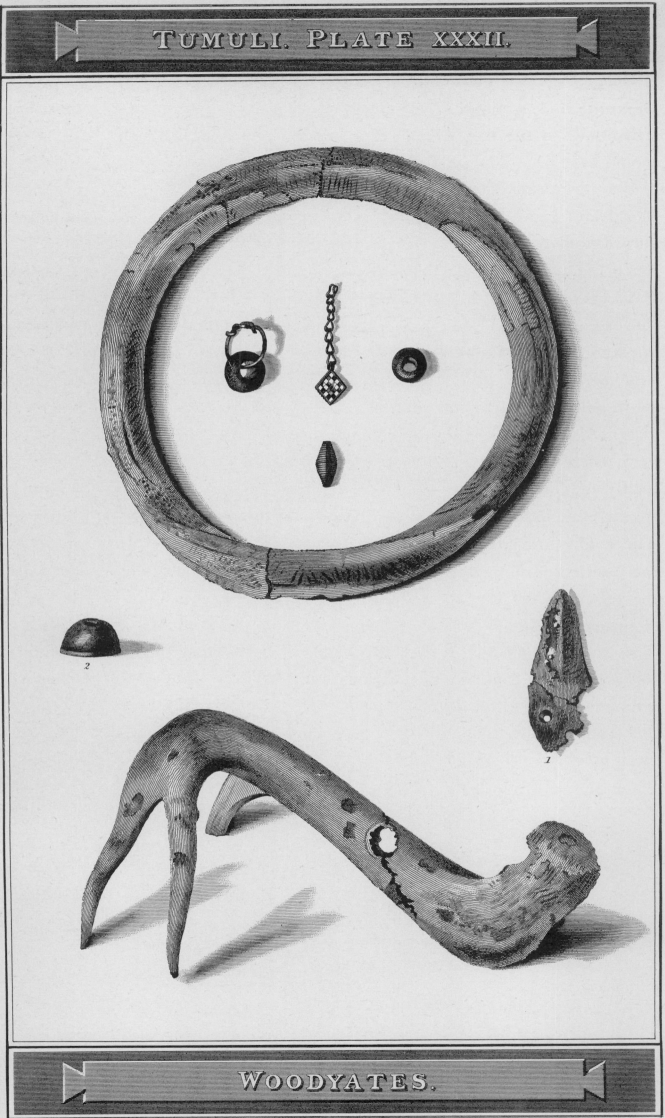

WOODYATES.

Publiſhed for W. Miller, Albemarle Street, London, Janʸ 1.1812.

we dug further towards the south, and discovered a large cist, three feet deep; on the floor of which was a smaller urn of that species which I have denominated DRINKING CUPS, coloured red, slightly glazed, and of infinitely better workmanship than the larger sepulchral urn. It is rather singular that this cup should have been deposited without its usual attendant, the skeleton.

We opened also another barrow on the same side of the ditch, but nearer to Woodyates Inn, which contained many new and curious articles. On making our section, we found the *tumulus* surrounded with large sarsen stones, and perceived several articles of iron intermixed with the chalk, TUMULI PLATE XXXI. No. 3, 4, 5, 6, and a circular *armilla* or bracelet of ivory, engraved of the original size in TUMULI PLATE XXXII. Beneath them was a skeleton, apparently of a female, extended at full length; every tooth was perfect, and near the head were two beads of blue glass, one of jet, and a beautiful ornament set in gold, enamelled and checquered like a chess-board. Through one of the glass beads was a wire hoop of gold, and through the other an elegant gold chain very nicely worked. These were the ear-rings of the British female: but I am totally at a loss to determine to what use the iron articles [No. 3], two more of which were found deposited near the head of the skeleton, were appropriated. The nature and workmanship of the trinkets found in this barrow, as well as the position of the body, prove this interment to have been more modern than the generality of those we have investigated, and perhaps that of a Belgic or Romanized Briton. These ornaments are engraved of their natural size in TUMULI PLATE XXXII. within the circle of the *armilla*. Nearly opposite to this barrow, the bank and ditch assume a different character: and the ramparts, which had been hitherto very bold and lofty, suddenly sink in height, continue low and weak for some distance, and afterwards reassume on each side their usual height.

STATION VIII. FOVANT.

We now enter the district allotted to this Station, but must rest some time longer at Woodyates, and trespass, as antiquaries, upon the limits of the adjoining County of Dorset. When I first visited this district in pursuit of the Roman road which led from SORBIODUNUM, or OLD SARUM, to DURNOVARIA, or DORCHESTER, I was so forcibly struck with the magnificent appearance of the causeway, and with the numerous vestiges of British antiquities in its immediate neighbourhood, that I was induced to repeat my visit, and to investigate the barrows and country more minutely. My researches proved successful and highly interesting, as they led to the discovery of the Roman Station of VINDOGLADIA.

The present turnpike road beyond Woodyates Inn, rests upon the substantial bed of the ancient causeway. On quitting the lane, and entering the down, the modern road to Blandford bears away to the right, whilst the Roman road pursues a direct line over the downs, and presents a very bold and perfect ridge. In the angle formed by the old and modern roads, is a fine group of barrows, which so far excited my curiosity as to induce me to open them.

No. 1 is so close to the Blandford road, that a part of it has been cut away. At the depth of two feet four inches we discovered a female skeleton lying in a direction from north-east to south-west, and with the limbs extended at full length. Round the neck were found a great many very small glass beads, two long pully beads of glass, with about twelve other beads rudely formed of amber ; there were besides two rings, one of which appeared to have been made from a metal like tin, the other was of brass. Near the ear or left shoulder was a circular clasp of brass, with a rim five-eighths of an inch in diameter, projecting

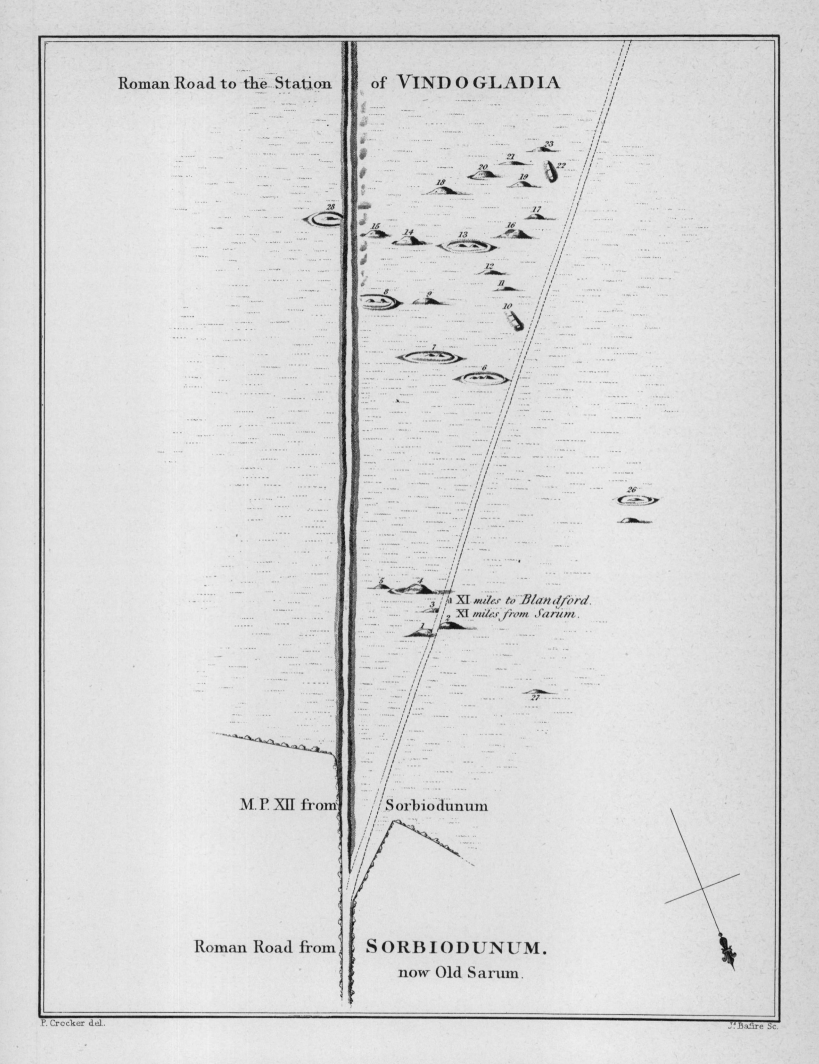

Roman Road to the Station   of VINDOGLADIA

XI *miles to Blandford.*
XI *miles from Sarum.*

M. P. XII from   Sorbiodunum

Roman Road from   SORBIODUNUM.
now Old Sarum.

P. Crocker del.

J.ᵉ Bafire Sc.

GROUP OF BARROWS NEAR WOODYATES.

Published for W. Miller, Albemarle Street, London, Jan.ʸ 1. 1812.

Published for W. Miller, Albemarle Street, London, Jan.ʸ 1.1812.

from it, and stamped or cut within with the rude figure of a human face ;* Tumuli Plate XXXIII. No.1. The whole interior of this little ornament is strongly gilt; the tongue of the clasp is of iron, and has some filaments of linen cloth adhering to it.   On the left side of the skeleton were some broken pieces of a thin iron ring, also a small ring of the same metal about an inch and a quarter in diameter ; and several other bits of iron were dispersed about, but too much corroded to ascertain for what purpose they were originally used.   This interment was probably of the same æra as that lately described near Bokerley Ditch. Beneath this skeleton, and at the depth of nearly ten feet in the native chalk, lay another body in the same direction as the former, which appeared to be that of a tall and stout man ; the bones and teeth were in high preservation, and the legs were gathered up according to the most ancient and primitive custom.   No. 2. This barrow has also been mutilated by the turnpike road.   Four feet beneath the surface, was the skeleton of a very young person, lying north and south. At the depth of five feet we found an interment of burned bones, accompanied by some beads of bone shaped like a lozenge, and a very perfect bone pin ; and at the depth of nine feet was the skeleton of an adult, deposited in the same direction as the first.   No. 3.   A part of this barrow also has been cut away by the road, which made us doubtful as to the success of our researches. The *apex* of the barrow was covered with flints and other stones, to which we may owe the preservation of a very fine sepulchral urn, measuring sixteen inches in height, and eleven in diameter, and which forms the principal decoration to the Frontispiece of my History. It was placed with its mouth upwards, and covered a very perfect interment of burned bones. The elevation of this barrow was not two feet. No. 4. This large bell-shaped barrow contained near the surface some fragments of a large ornamented urn ; and at the depth of ten feet and a half we discovered two skeletons lying in a direction from north to south, and near them a small vase of a novel and singular shape, having four feet to support it.   It measures four inches and five eighths at the mouth, and three inches and five eighths in height, and is engraved in Tumuli Plate XXXIII. No. 2. With it were found a black bead, and a spear-head of brass. At the further depth of twelve feet four inches from the surface, was another large skeleton lying north and south. The last barrow of this group, No. 5, contained a simple interment of burned bones within a cist at the depth of two feet from the surface. In No. 1, 2, and 4, we deposited new Bolton half-pennies, and square pieces of

* This is the first instance, amongst our researches, that has occurred of any thing like the representation of human features.

lead, stamped, " opened 1804. W. C." and in one of them a Southampton half-penny, " W. Beavis."

The next barrow, No. 6 varies in shape from the preceding, and is one of the Druid kind, having an oblong, or rather triangular mound within its area, the broad end of which points towards the north-west. This had been opened before ; but it appeared from the fragments interspersed with the soil, that it had originally contained the interment of a skeleton at top, and a deposit of burned bones beneath ; at the small end, pointing south-east, we found a regular interment of burned bones within a circular cist. Suspecting that this barrow might possibly contain something more, we made a section in a ridge that seemed to connect the two mounds, and discovered a very large urn, measuring nineteen inches in height and eleven in diameter at the mouth, in which an interment of burned bones, accompanied by beads of amber and glass had been deposited. No. 7, a fine Druid barrow with two mounds within its area, was examined by Mr. Cunnington in the year 1803 ; one of the *tumuli* had been previously explored, and the other contained an interment of burned bones, with amber beads. No. 8 is another Druid barrow with two tumps within its circle, both of which appeared to have been opened : but on examining them we found ourselves repaid for our want of confidence in former explorators. This fine *tumulus* is surrounded by a circular *vallum*, and the area measures from the centre of the ditch 190 feet. At the depth of rather more than three feet we discovered a small cist containing the burned bones of one person, accompanied by about a hundred amber beads of great variety, and some flat pieces of amber, which belonged to an ornament similar to the one engraved in Tumuli Plate III. There were besides a small brass pin, and an arrow-head of the same metal. Plate XXXII. No. 1. The other mound, and that nearest to the Roman road, had, as well as the former fragments of pottery intermixed with the soil ; but we persevered in our researches, and at the depth of about four feet from the surface, discovered a cist containing burned bones, with several beads of glass, jet, and amber, and the fragment of a similar flat ornament of amber. This interment also had its little brass pin, and a most beautiful little cup, engraved of the original size in Tumuli Plate XXXIII. No. 3.

No. 9. In this fine bell-shaped barrow, at the depth of about eighteen inches under the surface, we found two skeletons lying north-east and south-west, and apparently placed one above the other. At the head of the uppermost was a Drinking Cup of soft pottery rudely ornamented, and the fragments of another cup of still ruder texture and workmanship. On the eastern side of the *tumulus*,

P. Crocker del.

J.ˢ Basire Sc.

Publiſhed for W. Miller, Albemarle Street, London, Jan.ʸ 1.1812.

and near the feet of the skeleton, was a large heap of burned bones piled up together without any cist.   Under the skeletons was a considerable quantity of flints, which led us to suppose that we had not discovered the primary inter-ment; we therefore continued our researches. Amongst the flints we perceived large pieces of stag's horns, and half a stone celt; and at the depth of eleven feet, after the very laborious removal of an immense collection of flints, we dis-covered a skeleton of large proportions lying north-east by south-west, on its left side, with both legs gathered up according to the most ancient and primitive usage.   Near its side was deposited a most beautiful brazen dagger, that had been gilt, and protected by a wooden scabbard, some part of which was still seen adhering to it, also a large and a small ornament of jet, perforated with two holes for suspension.   Near the thigh-bone of the skeleton was another ornament of jet, resembling a pully, four very perfect arrow-heads of flint, as well as some pieces of flint chipped and prepared for similar weapons, and a small brass pin.   A fine urn, probably the DRINKING CUP, lay broken at the feet of this British hero.   A selection of these articles is engraved in TUMULI PLATE XXXIV.

The opening of this barrow was attended by so many awful circumstances, and gave birth to so beautiful and truly descriptive a Poem, by my friend the Rev. William Lisle Bowles, who attended our operations, that it will ever be remembered both with horror and pleasure by those who were present. During the tremendous storm of thunder and lightning by which my friend and companion Mr. Fenton, my surveyor Mr. Philip Crocker, &c. &c. were sur-prized, our only place of refuge was the barrow, which had been excavated to a considerable depth; the lightning flashed upon our spades and iron instru-ments, and the large flints poured down upon us from the summit of the barrow so abundantly and so forcibly, that we were obliged to quit our hiding place, and abide the pelting of the pitiless storm upon the bleak and unsheltered down. Mr. Bowles took leave of us the same evening, and the next morning sent me the following beautiful and spirited poem, so truly descriptive of the awful scene we had lately witnessed.

" Let me, let me sleep again;"
Thus, methought, in feeble strain,
Plain'd from its disturbed bed
The spirit of the mighty dead.

" O'er my moulder'd ashes cold
   Many a century slow hath roll'd,
   Many a race hath disappear'd
   Since my giant form I rear'd ;
   Since my flinted arrow flew,
   Since my battle-horn I blew,
   Since my brazen dagger's pride
   Glitter'd on my warlike side,
   Which, transported o'er the wave,
   Kings of distant ocean gave.
   Ne'er hath glared the eye of day,
   My death-bed secrets to betray,
   Since, with mutter'd Celtic rhyme,
   The white-hair'd Druid bard sublime,
   Mid the stillness of the night,
   Wak'd the sad and solemn rite,
   The rite of Death, and o'er my bones
   Were piled the monumental stones."
   Passing near the hallow'd ground,
   The Roman gaz'd upon the mound,
   And murmur'd with a secret sigh,
' There in dust the mighty lie.'
   Ev'n while his heart with conquest glow'd,
   While the high-raised flinty road,
   Echoed to the prancing hoof,
   And golden eagles flamed aloof,
   And flashing to the orient light
   His banner'd legions glitter'd bright ;
   The victor of the world confess'd
   A dark awe shivering at his breast.
" Shall the sons of distant days,
   Unpunish'd, on my relicks gaze ?
   Hark ! HESUS rushes from on high,
   Vindictive thunder rocks the sky,
   See TARANIS descends to save
   His Heroe's violated grave,

And shakes beneath the lightning's glare,
The sulphur from his blazing hair.
Hence ! yet though my grave ye spoil,
Dark oblivion mocks your toil :
Deep the clouds of ages roll,
History drops her mould'ring scroll,
And never shall reveal the name
Of him, who scorns her transient fame."

———————

No. 10 bore the appearance of a low Long barrow. Our first section was made towards the north, where we found a cist with burned bones, and at the southern end was a similar interment, but no cist.   In the centre was another deposit of burned bones and an elegant little INCENSE CUP [PLATE XXXIII. No. 4.] No. 11. This small barrow contained a similar interment at the depth of about twelve inches from the surface.   No. 12 is a large flat barrow, in which we made two sections, but could discover no sepulchral signs whatever.   No. 13, a Druid barrow with two mounds within it, had been examined by others, but a fine amber bead had escaped their vigilance. [PLATE XXXII. No. 2.]   No. 14 is a bowl-shaped barrow of a very smooth and regular shape. On the east side of it was a deep cist neatly cut in the chalk, and containing a large quantity of charcoal and burned bones very minutely pulverized.   Not satisfied with this discovery, and perceiving an irregular *stratum* of charcoal and burning round the barrow, we were induced to make a further trial ; and we shortly found a small cist cut in the chalk, but without either bones or ashes.   Pursuing our investigation, we soon had the good fortune to come to an urn with its bottom inverted ; and over it was the jaw-bone of an animal, apparently a cow. The urn was rudely baked, but neatly formed : it covered a most complete interment of burned bones. We afterwards came to a third cist, containing only ashes. In No. 15 we found a skeleton lying east and west. No. 16 is the largest barrow in the whole group, and has baffled our attempts, although we made a section of twelve feet square, and dug to the depth of twelve feet six inches. On the floor of the barrow we perceived evident marks of cremation.

No. 17. Immediately under the turf, we discovered an interment of burned bones, and proceeding further, saw a prodigious quantity of ashes and charred wood, and were afterwards gratified with the sight of a very large sepulchral urn inverted within a cist cut in the native chalk. On taking it out, we observed several pieces of decayed linen, of a reddish brown colour, lying like cobwebs on the calcined bones. This urn is rather of an oval form, and is the largest we have ever found, except the STONEHENGE URN engraved in TUMULI PLATE XVI. No. 18 is a large circular bowl-shaped barrow, ditched round. At the depth of seven feet and a half, and on the floor, lay a skeleton with its head to the north-east, and its legs and thighs drawn up close together. The skull was pressed flat, and near it lay part of a deer's horn, perforated in the stem, [TUMULI PLATE XXXII.] where it is drawn of the original size. No. 19 contained, within a round cist cut in the chalk, the burned bones of one body, and two very small arrow-heads. No. 20 produced a sepulchral urn which was broken. On removing the fragments, we discovered an interment of burned bones, over which was a considerable quantity of decayed linen cloth, the filaments of which, at first sight, appeared like hair. This deposit was accompanied by a round pin and an arrow-head of bone, and a very perfect spear-head of brass, with a great part of the wooden handle adhering to it, by which we were enabled clearly to see the mode by which it had been fastened. No. 21 is a small low barrow, in which we found a little cist full of charcoal very finely burned, and on the outside of it, some fragments of coarse pottery, and burned bone, which indicated a prior opening. No. 22 is a Long barrow, very similar in form, as well as in its contents, to No. 10, for it contained three interments. That towards the north consisted of ashes and burned bones enclosed within a cist. That towards the south produced a similar deposit within a very large urn of coarse and thick pottery, together with a pair of bone tweezers. The central interment was also enclosed within a sepulchral urn of rude pottery, together with one amber bead. These diminutive Long barrows differ very materially from those of the larger sort, in which we have almost invariably found the interments deposited at the east and broadest end. No. 23 being a low and broad barrow, we found some difficulty in ascertaining its centre, and we failed in our first attempts upon it; but a second trial, and a larger excavation, led us to an interment of burned bones deposited within an inverted urn of very coarse unbaked pottery.

On the opposite side of the Blandford road, towards the north-west, there is a very large Long barrow, and a small barrow on each side of it, both of which we tried, but found that the interments had been disturbed by the intersection of a boundary ditch. The fragments of bones intermixed with the soil seem to indicate that skeletons were originally deposited in each of these barrows.

On the same side of the road, but nearer to Woodyates Inn, is another small *tumulus*, in which the interment had been disturbed. Still nearer to Woodyates, and in the same line, there is another small barrow, in which we found some burned bones, and some large headed nails within a very irregular cist. The down on which these detached barrows are situated, present those excavations and irregularities, by which we are guided to the discovery of the settlements of the Britons ; here we dug, and here we found the most satisfactory evidence of a remote British population.

Immediately adjoining the left, or east side of the Roman road, is a Druid barrow, on whose *vallum* and ditch the road has trespassed. It contained the deposit of a skeleton. Numerous barrows are dispersed in every direction over this fine down, some of which were opened by Mr. Cunnington, and thus described in his manuscript. " Near a clump of trees to the left of the Roman road are three barrows. The largest, a beautiful bell-shaped *tumulus*, contained within a circular cist cut in the native chalk, an interment of burned bones in a very large sepulchral urn, accompanied by several beads of amber, jet, horn, and brass, and a brass pin. Within it also was a beautiful little INCENSE CUP richly ornamented, and containing a considerable quantity of decomposed wood. The two other barrows produced simple interments of burned bones." On the right of the Roman road, but on a higher level, is another group of three barrows, one of which only Mr. Cunnington seems to have investigated, viz. that on the east side of the large circular barrow. At the depth of one foot and a half from the surface, he met with two skeletons, which from their position, he well knew were not the original tenants of the mound. He therefore, with his usual spirit of research, pursued his excavation, and at the depth of four feet and a half found a cist containing a sepulchral urn, equal in size to the STONEHENGE URN, and nearly of the same form. It contained, together with an interment of burned bones, a smaller urn, both of which were unfortunately broken to pieces. At the bottom of the large urn was some ornamental work in high relief, resembling a wheel, or star with six rays ; a peculiarity which has not occurred to us before. In a subsequent excursion, Mr. Cunnington opened the large barrow, which in form is a perfect cone, the base of which is 95 feet, the height nine feet four inches, and the slope 38 feet. At the extreme depth he found a circular cist, in which was deposited a very large urn, which was crushed to pieces. In the cist, and over the urn, was the largest quantity of ashes and charred wood he had ever seen.

3 Q

When I treat of the Roman æra in our county, I shall again conduct my readers to this district, and lay before them some of the most interesting discoveries we have ever had the good fortune to make.

ITER I.   I shall now proceed on my journey westward, but many interesting objects of antiquity will retard my progress towards the head-quarters allotted to this Station.   I shall, in the first place, resume my account of GRYMSDITCH, which we left at the spot where it is intersected by the Roman road ; from whence it pursues a winding course through Vernditch Chace for a considerable space, and is very plainly discernible : it then traverses some open ground, and enters the thick copse of Cranbourn Chace, and in the last place we saw it, the direction it took was south-west.   Something more must be also said about BOKERLEY DITCH, which, as I before observed, is intersected by the Roman road near the lane leading to Woodyates Inn.   This also enters Cranbourn Chace, and having crossed GRYMSDITCH, directs its course to the ridge-way on the north of Cranbourn Chace.   On the west side of it, before it enters the wood there is a fragment of a large bank and ditch in an arable field, which I cannot account for.   I have frequently had occasion to mention the numerous banks and ditches with which the unenclosed district of our county abounds, and I have ventured to hazard an opinion, that they were not all formed for the same purpose, but that some were designed for boundaries, and others only for lines of communication between the British villages.   I am inclined to think, that both GRYMSDITCH and BOKERLEY were intended for the former purpose, for they vary materially in their mode of construction from those I have lately described in the Everley Station, and have a decided *vallum* on one side ; whereas in those banks which I denominate covered ways, or lines of communication, the most discerning eye cannot distinguish on which side the *vallum* is the highest, so equally is the ground thrown up on each side.   In GRYMSDITCH I found the *vallum* on the east and north sides during its whole course ; whilst that of BOKERLEY was on the south side in its progress westward.   This latter is by far the boldest rampart I have yet met with in the southern district of our county ; but each have the same character of irregularity.   I am the more inclined to think that GRYMSDITCH was a boundary ditch, as during its whole course, I could not discover any British village on its borders ;* but it is not so with BOKERLEY, as one branch of it leads directly into a British village (as

* I find GRIMESDICA mentioned in a grant by King Edgar to the Abbey of Wilton.   *Monasticon.* vol. ii. page 863.

before mentioned) on a down near Tippet, and the main ditch passes through another very extensive British town on the northern side of Cranbourn Chace.

Before I proceed on my course westward, I must diverge in a contrary direction towards the vale in which the village of Broad Chalke is situated. From the British town just mentioned, I observed some faint remains of a ditch pointing east, and shortly afterwards discovered a British village in a very perfect state, and attended with all the usual earth-works, excavations, and irregularities.   Near it is a group of small barrows on a piece of rough ground now breaking up. Pursuing my road northwards towards Broad Chalke, I pass by a small barrow on high ground, which has been thus noticed by Mr. Aubrey in his *Monumenta Britannica*.   " On the southe downe of the farme of Broad Chalke, on the top of the plaine, is a little barrow (not very high) called by the name of GAWEN's BARROW.   This farme (of which I have a lease from the Earle of Pembroke) as also the manour, did belong to the Abbey of Wilton, and was graunted to that monastery by the name of CHEOLCAN,* by King Edgar A. D. DCCCLXXIV. *annoque regni* XV. as appears by the legier booke of the sayd Abbey in the hands of the Earle of Pembroke, with one page in Saxon, the other in Latin.   The Ladie Abbesse of Wilton kept the two downes here in her owne hands for the flocks of sheep, which is the greatest benefit of the farme; the corne does but little more than pay the corne rent.   The family of the Gawens is very ancient, for he was one of the Knights of the Round Table ; and Caxton in his Chronicle, mentions Gawen, King Arthur's nephew, slain in the fight against the traitor Mordred, at the landing at Sandwich : his body was carried into his owne countrey in Scotland to be enterred.   This Gawyn was sister's sonne to Arthur, the Great King of the Britains, a most famous man in warre, and in all manner of civilitys, as in the actes of the Brittaines we may read.   In the year 1082, in a province of Wales called Rose, was his sepulchre found, and his body affirmed by many to have been of the length of fourteen feet.✝

" This Sir Gawayne is thus mentioned in the *Squier's Tale*, by our poet Chaucer.

* I find in Dugdale's *Monasticon*, vol. ii. page 859, a grant of the district of Chalke, then called CEOLCUM, made in the year DCCCCEV. by King Edwy to the monastery of Wilton.   The former grant also of King Edgar may be seen in the *Monasticon*, page 865.   The district is there written CEOLCAN.

✝ The more received opinion respecting the interment of the illustrious Prince Arthur is that he was buried in the church-yard of Glastonbury in Somersetshire, where, in the reign of King Henry the Second, A. D. 1191 his body was discovered, together with an inscription. [*Lewis's Hist of Britain, page* 196.]

    " This straunge knight that come thus sodeinly,
        All armid save his hede full royally,
        Salued the King and Quene, and Lordis all,
        By order, as they sittin in the hall,
        With so hie reverence, and obeisaunce,
        As well in speche as in countenaunce,
        That GAWAYN with his old courtisye
        Though he came agen out of fairye
        He cou'de him not amende in with no word."

" The Gawens have had Norrington (in the parish of Alvadeston) in their possession fouer hundred yeares; and about 1665 it was sold to Sir Wadham Windham, one of the Justices of the King's Bench. " *Fors sua cuique loco est.*' They have some estate yet in the parish of Chalke, and at Hurcot, two miles north. But in the yeare 1648, this family, (old John Gawen, Esq.) had in Wiltshire, and Somersetshire £1800. per annum. But to return to the barrow, that must be raised before the Christian religion was thoroughly established. This family was too great to be farmers of this farme in the time of the Lady Abbesse, who kept it in her hands; so that perhaps this barrow takes its name from a GAWEN that might be before King Edgar. N.B. the last abbesse of Wilton was the Lady Gawen, I think, Anne.

" Sir GAWEN was a Knight of the Round Table, as is to be seen in the limbe about the Round Table in the Castle Hall at Winchester.* The coate of GAWAIN D'ORCANIE " *de pourpre a un aygle esployè d'or.*"

The same author in his manuscript takes notice of some works near the river at Broad Chalke, but their low situation proves them not to have been of high antiquity: he says: " At Broad Chalke (just by the farme) neer the river side, south of the church, between the farme and the vicars house, is a ground called BURY ORCHARD, containing five acres, three roods, four poles. It is (except on the west side, where the vicar's house stands) encompassed with a bank of great breadth, not now very high: it is square, and with great convenience for aquation, which, (as Livy saieth) the Romans did ever principally respect. The banks are as big as those at Norbury in Gloucestershire, but nobody has

---

* The chief curiosity in this ancient chapel, now termed the County Hall, is Arthur's Round Table, as it is called. This hangs up at the east end of it, consisting of stout oak plank; which, however, is perforated with many bullets, supposed to have been shot by Cromwell's soldiers. It is painted with the figure of that Prince, and the names of his 24 Knights, as they have been collected from the romances of the 14th and 15th centuries. *Milner's Winchester*, vol. ii. p. 182.

taken notice of it before, though obvious enough. The camp went up above the vicarage house to the brow of the hill westward, perhaps as much more at least." I have, during my perambulation, observed the remains of several earthen works in the vales immediately under the chalk hills, most of which, may be attributed to the Saxons.

Mr. Aubrey also thus notices two camps in the neighbourhood of Broad Chalke. " In the parish of West Kington (Knyghton) is a Roman camp called EBBEDOWNE; no graff, slight rampire, and no *vestigia* left of any ports. Over against it on the other hill, is a less Roman camp. These two, Mr. Robert Davenant, the Rector there, shewed me. Bishop Latimer was Rector there; and in the walke at the parsonage-house, is yet the oake, a little scrubbed oake, and hollow, where he did use to sitt, called ' *Latimer's Oake.*' "

When I examined the ground near Broad Chalke, I could not, by inquiry, ascertain the hill called EBBDOWN; but I observed a very small square work, similar to those we have so frequently found and noticed, and one *tumulus* near it. The hills in this neighbourhood are very bold in their outline, and indentations, and a deep valley takes its course from the Ridgeway to the vale in which Broad Chalke is situated. On the western side of this vale, I perceived the remains of another earthen enclosure, similar in its construction to the SOLDIER's RING near Damerham; and these two works may have been those alluded to by Mr. Aubrey. Let us now return to the Ridgeway, and the large British town before described, into which we are led by BOKERLEY DITCH. This settlement is very extensive, and presents all the decided marks of ancient habitation. Following the Ridgeway, I observed a slight bank and ditch, which guided me to another British village, not so extensive as the former, but situated on a bold point of hill, and commanding a beautiful view of the rich vale beneath. In my further progress on this British trackway, I traversed another bank and ditch coming out of the Chace, and descending into the vale on the right; and still further on, a third in the same direction. Two large *tumuli* adjoin the trackway, and there are four more on an eminence to the right distinguished by a clump of trees. On the next point of hill we again find ditches, barrows, and a very interesting earthen work, known by the name of

WINKELBURY CAMP. This earthen work is situated on a point of down projecting towards the village of Berwick St. John, and commanding a very extensive and beautiful view. It differs very materially from any camp that I have yet seen, especially in its entrance, which is very singular, as will be seen by a reference to the annexed plan. It is single ditched, and is accessible in three places towards the south ; the area, which is intersected by a ditch near the centre, contains twelve acres and a half ; the circumference of the work is 1056 yards, and the greatest depth of the ramparts is thirty-nine feet.

The generality of our Ridgeways, which were undoubtedly the trackways of the Britons, before the regular formation of roads was introduced by their conquerors, the Romans were carried over very high ground ; and this, like the one before-mentioned in the Heytesbury and Everley Stations, commands a very comprehensive and interesting view over Dorsetshire and a part of Hampshire, as far as the abrupt point of the Needles in the Isle of Wight ; the rich forest of Cranbourn occupies the foreground, and the view over our own county towards the north is beautifully varied. The prospect was so bewitching, the air so pure, and the turf so soft, that I could not resist the pleasure of pursuing the Ridge beyond the limits of Wiltshire. Passing the forest boundary, and leaving Rushmore Lodge, the residence of Lord Rivers, who is Ranger of the Chace, in a vale deeply embosomed in wood to the left, I continued my ride along the heights ; and although I partly knew the situation of Ashcomb (a seat belonging to the Arundel family,) yet my surprize was great on its first appearance. The situation of this demesne is very singular, being placed in a hollow like a punch-bowl, and surrounded on all sides by hanging woods, and verdant pastures ; the outward boundary is bleak down ; and I believe so singular a retreat cannot elsewhere be met with. Should any of my readers be induced to follow my steps, let me recommend to their attention the very beautiful view from a clump of trees on a high part of the hill beyond Ashcomb, which cannot be exceeded, if equalled, by any on our Wiltshire downs. This eminence is called Wingreen Hill, and was one of the points selected by Colonel Mudge in his *Trigonometrical Survey of England*. In his third volume, lately published, he states the height of this hill to be 941 feet. Still continuing my ride over the finest turf, and steering towards Shaftesbury, I meet with another very bold bank and ditch, having its *vallum* towards the south-west, and intersecting the hill, as if for a line of defence. A few barrows are dispersed over this tract, and I observed frequent traces of ancient banks and ditches, but they did not lead me to the discovery of any British settlement.

Iter II. From Shaftesbury, I return towards Salisbury over an elevated ridge of hill, running nearly parallel with the one I described in my last Iter, and over which the turnpike road between Salisbury and Shaftesbury formerly was carried. Ascending White-sheet Hill, I immediately recognize in banks, ditches, and barrows, the rude memorials of the Britons. The first bank and ditch worthy of notice is of great strength, and has its *vallum* towards the south-west. In its progress over the down southwards, it tends towards the vale between Berwick St. John, and Alvadeston, and perhaps (though now interrupted by tillage) may have originally formed a part of the same *agger* which is marked on the opposite Ridge-way towards the South. In its northern course, having descended a steep declivity, it is lost in the cultivated lands towards Wardour Castle. Pursuing the old track-way, I traversed two other banks and ditches, which lose themselves in the precipitous valleys on the right, and a little beyond the last of these, I perceived the *indicia* of a British village encompassed by a slight earthen *agger*, and in front of it the segment of an earthen circle. On digging into the excavations of this village, I found animal bones, and a great deal of pottery of the very rudest and coarsest texture, but none of that made by the Romanized Britons ; so that in all probability this was one of the primitive settlements of our *aborigines*. Continuing along the same track, the ridge is again intersected by an ancient bank and ditch, which are lost in the valleys on each side. On a projecting point of down to the north, called Boxbury Hill, are two barrows, and another earthen *agger*. We now come to a solitary house called Fovant Hut, which once proved an useful and comfortable *taberna* to the benighted traveller over these bleak and uninhabited heights. The same fine ridge of down continues, and leads us to an earthen work situated on the commanding brow of a hill facing the village of Compton Chamberlaine, and the seat of the Penruddocke family.

Chiselbury Camp forms an irregular circle, has a single *vallum* and ditch, with an outwork and entrance towards the south-east. The area within the ramparts contains ten acres and a half, the circumference of the work is three furlongs 154 yards, and the height of the *vallum* is twenty-seven feet : a great part of the camp is covered with heath and furze. Two ancient banks and ditches issue from the work, and descend into the vallies on the north and south sides of the Ridge. From the form and regularity of the work, I am inclined to think this camp to have been one of a modern date, perhaps of the same æra as those of Chlorus, and Clearbury, for we dug in several parts of the area, but discovered no bones or pottery, which are the never-failing *indicia* of ancient residence and population.

From hence I still continue my ride on the edge of the downs, and meet with an occasional barrow ; and a little to the east of the 8 mile-stone, I find a strong bank and ditch, which are lost in a deep vale to the south, whilst pointing

towards Broad Chalke. Another bank and ditch traverse a very narrow ridge
of the down near Compton Hut, and which a terrier of the *Terræ Pembrochianæ*,
in the possession of my friend Mr. P. Wyndham, mentions as being the boundary
between the down of Compton and Burcomb. On a very irregular neck of
down projecting towards the latter village, the barrows become more frequent,
from one of which, distinguished by a fir-tree, there is a most delightful
view, commanding in front the bold point on which the strong camp of Castle
Ditches is situated, and a long extended line of rich wood belonging to the
estates of Compton and Dinton, whilst the more distant horizon is broken by
the lofty turret of Fonthill Abbey, and the conspicuous eminence of Bradley
Knoll.

From the same terrier I find, that one of the barrows in this district bore
originally the name of OTT's BARROW, and another that of LYON's BARROW.

Immediately to the north of the barrow commanding so fine a prospect, are
two strong banks and ditches, which intersect the hill in a parallel line. There
are several lines of lynchets upon this down, but I could not discover any
British village on it.   From hence the trackway passes near a wood belonging
to Lord Pembroke, called the Hare Warren, where, amidst some furzy ground,
lately planted, I discovered three barrows, the largest of which has been dignified by Dr. Stukeley with the title of " The Tomb of King Carvilius." He
tells us that Carvilius was one of the four Kings who fought with Julius Cæsar,
and he gives the name of Carvilium, (Caer-wily, or the fortress on the river
Wily) to Wilton.* The old trackway having passed over the race-course,
and the Roman causeway which led from Old Sarum to Dorchester, crosses
the united streams of the Wily, the Avon, and the Nadder, at Harnham Bridge,
and conducts us to the modern capital of our county.

Nothing interesting occurs in the antiquarian line between Salisbury and
Fovant, the head quarters, though hitherto not visited, of this Station. At the
village of Barford, two roads separate ; the one leads to Hindon and the west of
England, the other to Shaftesbury, in lieu of the old and dreary road over
Salisbury Plain. The little village of Fovant is situated in a fertile vale, and
bounded towards the south by the ridge of hills we have lately traversed. From
hence I made an excursion to a very fine earthen work called

CASTLE DITCHES ; but probably its ancient name was SPELSBURY, as a village

---

* At the time when Carvilius reigned, I much doubt if this western district was known to the Romans ;
for we are informed by Cæsar himself, that this said King ruled in Kent. " *Dum hæc geruntur, Cassive-
launus ad Cantium, quibus regionibus* IV *Reges præerant, Cingetorix, Carvilius, &c. &c. nuncios mittat.*"

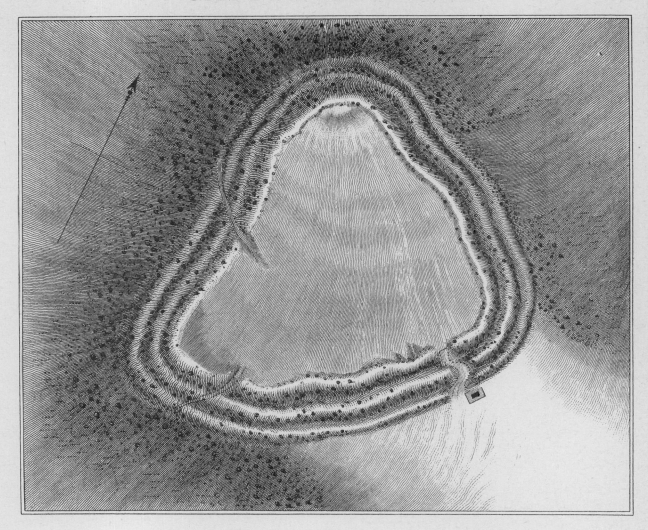

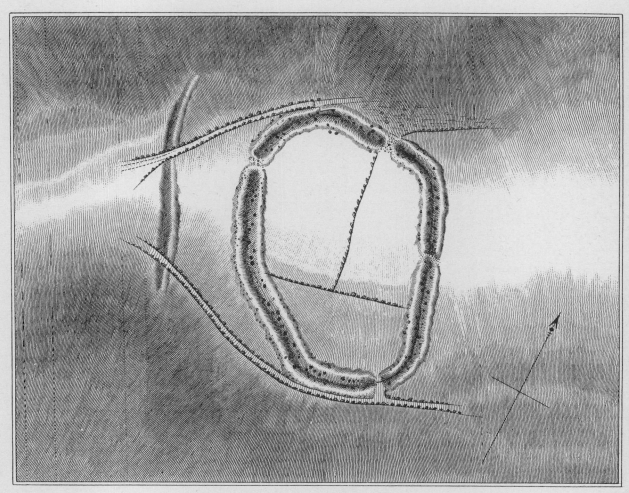

CASTLE RING.

P. Crocker del.

Jⁱ. Baſire Sc.

Publiſhed for W. Miller. Albemarle Street, London, Janʸ 1.1812.

immediately beneath it, still retains that appellation. It is so surrounded by corn fields and wood, that I perceived no signs of it until I found myself almost within the area of the camp. Its situation is very commanding, and many beautiful points of view are caught from its summit. This earthen work is strengthened by a triple row of ramparts, which are covered on three sides with wood. I can only speak with certainty respecting one entrance, which was towards the south-east; but there is a narrow adit on the opposite side. The area within the intrenchment, contains twenty-three acres and three quarters; the circuit of the outward *vallum* is seven furlongs, eighty-eight yards; and the height of the ramparts is about forty feet. The entire area of this camp is under tillage, and the greater part of the ramparts is so concealed by thick copse wood, that no adequate idea of their strength and boldness can possibly be formed.

The northern and western sides of this Station, which are bounded by the river Nadder, have been for many years in a state of successive cultivation. In vain therefore we may search for those antiquities which come peculiarly within the scope of our inquiry. From the name of Tisbury, I should have concluded there had been some earthen work or *bury* in its immediate neighbourhood, but I have never gained intelligence of any that is nearer to it than the strong camp of CASTLE DITCHES, which has been already described.

Amongst the manuscript papers of the late Mr. Cunnington, I find the following note. "In a field near Place Farm, in the parish of Tisbury, was a circular work with a *vallum* set round with stones, and a large stone placed erect in the centre. On removing this stone (which was twelve feet high, and four feet wide) by Lord Arundel's order, to the Old Castle at Wardour, a skeleton was found, at the depth of eighteen inches under the surface, deposited close to the central stone.

STATION IX. HINDON.

W<small>E</small> are now come to the ninth and last Station allotted to the History of the Southern District of Wiltshire, and as we proceed towards its termination, we find a considerable decrease of interest as well as of antiquities. The latter are confined to two earthen works and a few barrows dispersed very sparingly over the face of the country.   The local beauty, however, of the greater part of this district does in some degree compensate for the want of antiquarian matter ; for the vale extending from Mere to Shaftesbury and Knoyle, and from thence to Dinton, Compton, and Wilton, may be justly said to produce more beautiful specimens of varied landscape than any other part of the Southern district of our county.

The first of the above-mentioned earthen works bears the name of W<small>ICK</small> B<small>ALL</small> C<small>AMP</small>, and is situated on an eminence behind the house and beautiful demesne of William Wyndham, Esq. of Dinton, who has lately planted the hill on which this work is placed. This camp is single ditched, of an irregular oblong shape, and widest towards the eastern end. The works are the strongest and most perfect on the northern and western sides, but the thick wood which covers the greatest part of the intrenchments renders access to the works rather difficult. The area of the camp comprehends nine acres ; the circumference of the ditch is three furlongs, one hundred and seventy-six yards ; and the depth of the ramparts is thirty-three feet ; the entrance appears to have been at the north-west angle. This fortification was made (as in many other instances) conformable to the natural shape of the hill.

From Dinton, the great western road leads us through Chilmark, a village famous for its excellent stone quarries, to Bishop's Fonthill, and the borough town of Hindon.   On a piece of verdant down between that place and East Knoyle, there are a few mutilated barrows, and in an opposite direction towards Chicklade, our pioneer, John Parker, has lately discovered another settlement of the Britons, which is noted down in the map of this Station.   The elevated spot also, near which Mr. Beckford has placed his stately Abbey, bears, in its name of Cold Harbour, some marks of antiquity.

At a short distance to the south of Fonthill, is Pyt-house, the seat of John Benet, Esq. who obligingly pointed out to me some vestiges of antiquity in his neighbourhood.   The first was a small square earthen work, situated in a field to the right of a road leading in a southern direction to Shaftesbury, and which from the size and construction of its ramparts, I conclude was once the site of a moated castle or mansion of the Saxon æra, for its low situation evidently proves it not to have been British.   Having diverged to the left through the little village of Semley, in a direction towards Donhead, we noticed a small *tumulus* very much depressed by tillage, in an arable ground ; and continuing our ride in a southern direction, ascended an eminence which is distinguished by the name of TITTLE PATH HILL, a spot worthy of notice as commanding many beautiful and extensive prospects.   To me it was interesting in another point of view, for its summit is crowned with a fine earthen work commonly called

CASTLE RING. This camp is single ditched, and according to its present plan appears to have had four entrances ; those to the north and south sides, which bear the marks of the greatest originality, are still used as road-ways to the fields within the intrenchment ; the other two openings are so obscured by wood, as to be scarcely distinguishable.   According to the usual mode of cas-trametation, we find the approach to camps made on the lowest and most level ground ; as for instance, in that of CASTLE DITCHES, engraved on the same plate with the camp I am now describing : the same remark may also be made with respect to those of CHLORUS, CLEARBURY, WINKELBURY, and CHISELBURY, engraved on a preceding plate, in all of which the approach is from the most level ground.   This also might have been the case in the camp of CASTLE RING, for there are marks of two openings on the plain part of the hill, though those on the north and south sides appear most like entrances in their present state.   The intrenchment, which is divided by hedges into three separate fields, comprehends fifteen acres and a half ; the circuit of the ditch is four furlongs, and one hundred and thirty-two yards, and the depth of the *vallum* is forty feet. On the west side of this camp there are the vestiges of a strong bank and ditch, which were probably designed to guard it more effectually from any attack on that quarter.

From this fascinating eminence, I direct my steps towards the western extremity of our county, and the termination of my Iter. Passing through Sedghill, and near Mere Park, I come to one of my own farms, bearing the name of Barrow Street, and from thence proceed through a lane which leads in a direct line to another farm tenanted by Mr. White, in the parish of West Knoyle. On the right hand side of this road there is a very large barrow in a meadow, from which, probably, Barrow Street derived its name, as the road from that farm leads directly to this *tumulus*. In later times a windmill had been built upon it, and the field still bears the name of Windmill Ground. I have been so often disappointed in my researches on barrows raised in a moist soil, and in similar situations, that I have not been induced to open it. On the high ground above West Knoyle Church there is a small solitary *tumulus*, which produced only a vacant cist, without any signs of charcoal or cremation. Between Charnage or Chaddenwich farm and Mere, there is another large barrow situated in a field near the little hamlet of Burton, and intersected by a hollow way; and to the south of Mere, on Mappledore Hill, I observed many low barrows, which by a late enclosure of the waste lands in that parish have been nearly levelled. In cutting a ditch through one of these, the labourers discovered some vases of rude pottery.

CONCLUSION.

I have now brought to a termination my Ancient History of South Wiltshire, and it is my intention to prosecute the same researches throughout the Northern District of our County, where a spacious and unexplored field is left open for inquiry and investigation. In the work now submitted to the publick, I have related with accuracy, (and some of my readers may think with too tedious a minuteness) the detail of our subterraneous researches; I have wandered as little as possible into the regions of fancy and conjecture, and I have endeavoured throughout my whole progress, to adhere most scrupulously to my motto, and to

SPEAK FROM FACTS, NOT THEORY.

GENERAL INDEX.

STATIONS.

BRITISH SETTLEMENTS.

3 T

GENERAL INDEX.

INTRENCHED CAMPS AND EARTHEN WORKS.

EARTHEN CIRCLES.

GENERAL INDEX.

REMARKABLE BARROWS.

REMARKABLE PLACES, EVENTS, OBJECTS, &c. &c.

ANCIENT WILTSHIRE.

ORDER OF THE PLATES.

ORDER OF THE PLATES.

LONDON:

PRINTED FOR WILLIAM MILLER, ALBEMARLE STREET,

BY W. BULMER AND CO. CLEVELAND-ROW, ST. JAMES'S.

1812.

3 U

APPENDIX

A copy of each of these leaflets was inserted in each *Livraison* of Volume I
on publication for the convenience of purchasers of the work. This set of leaflets,
with the author's notes on the cost of the plates, now too faded with age for
satisfactory reproduction, was found in a copy of this volume in the
Library at Stourhead.

ANCIENT WILTSHIRE.

PART I.

ORDER OF THE PLATES.

This List is not intended to be bound up with the work, as a general index of all the plates will be given on the completion of it.

The Author regrets, that owing to some important discoveries which have been made since the work was printed, he is obliged to defer the delivery of the Maps annexed to each Station. As they will serve as guides to the different antiquities, he must revisit with his surveyor, an extensive tract of country, in order to render them correct. The large Map of Wiltshire lately revised and corrected by Mr. Faden, will be found a most useful appendage to this History, as it is planned upon a large scale, and when bound up, will match it in size.

The next *Livraison* will comprehend the station of Wily ; and the interesting district of Amesbury, and Stonehenge.

ON OPENING BARROWS.

As the curiosity of some of my readers may be so far excited by the perusal of this History, as to induce them to investigate the barrows in other parts of England, I beg leave to suggest to them a few hints, whic may facilitate their operations, and promote the probability of success. Make a section in the centre of the barrow, large or small, according to the size of the *tumulus;* if its elevation is so great, that the earth cannot be thrown up at once from the bottom, a level must be left half way, upon which the labourers working at the bottom will cast the soil ; and from thence it will be thrown up by others to the top. Be not deterred on finding interments before you come to the floor of the barrow, by which I mean the level of the adjoining plain ; for experience has proved these to have been *subsequent* deposits, and the *primary interment* will be found either on or under the natural level. Let due reverence be paid to the *manes* of the Britons ; and though you rob them of their instruments of war and decoration, let their bones and ashes be properly respected, and carefully reinterred.

P.S. I recommend the same method of description as that we have adopted ; and I shall be happy either to receive or give information on this subject, to any antiquary who may be tempted to prosecute these British researches in other parts of England.

RICHARD COLT HOARE.

Stourhead,
1 *May,* 1810.

ANCIENT WILTSHIRE.

PART II.

ORDER OF THE PLATES.

N.B.—You are desired to cancel page 95 of the last *livraison*, and to substitute the one now printed. Three of the Maps now delivered, belong to the first *livraison*, and are to be placed opposite to the respective Stations of Stourton, Warminster, and Heytesbury.

The next *livraison* will include the Station of Everley, and the Northern District of Amesbury.

During the ensuing summer, it is my intention to investigate the three remaining Stations of Salisbury, Fovant and Hendon ; and if the matter they supply, does not prove too abundant, I shall unite them with the two preceding Stations, and thus complete the Southern District of our County, which will form the First Volume of my intended Publication.

A Perspective View of STONEHENGE, in its present dilapidated state, will be given in the next *livraison*.

R. C. HOARE.

Stourhead, May 1, 1811.

ANCIENT WILTSHIRE.

PART III.

ORDER OF THE PLATES.